A Bridge to the Sky

A Bridge to the Sky

Science and Arts in the Age of ʻAbbas Ibn Firnas

GLAIRE D. ANDERSON

OXFORD
UNIVERSITY PRESS

OXFORD
UNIVERSITY PRESS

Oxford University Press is a department of the University of Oxford. It furthers the University's objective of excellence in research, scholarship, and education by publishing worldwide. Oxford is a registered trade mark of Oxford University Press in the UK and certain other countries.

Published in the United States of America by Oxford University Press
198 Madison Avenue, New York, NY 10016, United States of America.

Library of Congress Cataloging-in-Publication Data
Names: Anderson, Glaire D., author.
Title: A bridge to the sky : science and arts in the age of ʿAbbas Ibn Firnas /
Glaire D. Anderson.
Description: New York, NY : Oxford University Press, [2024] |
Includes bibliographical references and index. |
In English with selections in Arabic with English translations.
Identifiers: LCCN 2023023402 (print) | LCCN 2023023403 (ebook) |
ISBN 9780190913243 (hardback) | ISBN 9780190913267 (epub)
Subjects: LCSH: ʿAbbās Ibn Firnās, 810–887. |
Astronomers—Spain—Córdoba—Biography. |
Aeronautics—Spain—Córdoba—Biography. |
Muslim scientists—Spain—Córdoba—Biography. |
Scientists—Spain—Córdoba—Biography. |
Poets, Arab—Spain—Córdoba—Biography.
Classification: LCC Q143.A183 A84 2023 (print) |
LCC Q143.A183 (ebook) | DDC 509.2 [B]—dc23/eng/20231002
LC record available at https://lccn.loc.gov/2023023402
LC ebook record available at https://lccn.loc.gov/2023023403

DOI: 10.1093/oso/9780190913243.001.0001

To my parents, who taught me that
knowledge is a treasure that can't be lost,
and to Clay and Tommy, for sharing the journey

Contents

Acknowledgments ix
A Note on Dates and Terms xi
'Abbās Ibn Firnās and His Career: Selected Passages from Ibn Ḥayyān xiii
I. Overview of 'Abbās's Character and Career xiii
II. On 'Abbās's Background and Skills xvi
III. On the Aeronautics Experiment xviii
IV. On the Meteorological Chamber xxi
V. On Two Precision Instruments Made for 'Abd al-Raḥmān II and Muḥammad I xxiv
VI. His Poem on the Villa (*Munya*) al-Rusāfa xxvi

Introduction: Ibn Firnas and His Legacy 1
Arts and Intellect 7

1. The Sage of al-Andalus 14
Remembering a Ninth-Century Polymath 14
The Informants 20
A Portrait 22
His Intellectual World 28
Conclusion 33

2. Mind and Hand 35
Inventor, Designer, Maker 35
The Earliest Andalusi Instruments 41
Signatures, Makers, and Making 60
The Celestial Globe of Ibrahim ibn Sa'īd al-Sahli al-Wazzan 65

3. Visualizing Science at Home 79
Representing the Heavens at Home 80
Visualizing Ibn Firnas's Celestial Creation: A Painted Astronomical Vault? 83
Art, Science, and Medieval Diplomacy 87
Andalusi Automata: Al-Muradi's *Kitab al-Asrar Fi Nata'ij al-Afkar* 93
An International Taste for Automata 106
Science, the Occult, and Intellectual Culture 109
Architecture as Scientific Instrument: The Abbasid Nilometer 112
Conclusion 119

4. Where Eagles and Vultures Dare 122
Imagining Flight—Early Visual Sources 123
Comparing the Sources 125
The Earliest Source 129
Palace of Science: Al-Rusafa 131
Vultures 139
Imagining a Medieval "Flight" 144

5. Epilogue: Echoes 153

Notes 163
Bibliography 195
Index 211

Acknowledgments

This book was begun at the University of North Carolina at Chapel Hill and completed at the University of Edinburgh. I am grateful to both institutions for generous support that made this work possible, and to many colleagues and students at both institutions for their enthusiasm and support over many years.

The project had its genesis at the University of North Carolina (UNC) at Chapel Hill, in the *A Medieval "First in Flight"* project. I owe an incredible debt to my co-collaborators Jan Chambers and Laura Miller, Julie Kimbell, and our student research collaborators Jesse Hall, Sarah Molina, Kevin Simpson, Claire Drysdal, Aaron Scheets, and Joseph P. Smith. I would like to thank Senior Associate Dean Terry Rhodes and the UNC College of Arts and Sciences Interdisciplinary Initiatives Program for generous support that laid the groundwork for this book. Travel to archives and museums, and study in the History of Science and Technology graduate program at Duke University was made possible thanks to a Senior Faculty Research and Scholarly Leave for Academic Year 2016–17 from the Department of Art & Art History, and a Senior Faculty Research Leave from the College of Arts and Sciences.

At the University of Edinburgh the project was supported thanks to generous funding from the Edinburgh College of Art Research and Knowledge Exchange Committee. Travel to collections and the final work on the book was completed during a College of Arts, Humanities and Social Sciences Research Sabbatical, with support from the School of History of Art's New Funds in History of Art Research Fund. I am grateful to my wonderful colleagues in the School of History of Art; the Edinburgh College of Art; the Late Antique, Islamic and Byzantine Studies Centre; Islamic and Middle Eastern Studies; the Alwaleed Centre; the Women of Colour Senior Leadership Group; and to my students, especially Sarah Slingluff and Deniz Vural.

I owe thanks to many other colleagues for invitations to present the project, and for suggestions and conversations that informed the book at various stages, especially Sussan Babaie, Rafael Blanco, Moya Carey, Maribel Fierro, Julia Galliker, Alain George, Julie Harris, Azucena Hernández, Cecily Hilsdale, Renata Holod, Andrew Janiak, Michele Lamprakos, Sarah Lane Ritchie, Therese Martin, Marcus Milwright, Mary Pardo, Jennifer Pruitt, Hassan Rabbani, Ahmed Ragab, Juan Murillo Redondo, Dwight Reynolds, Mariam Rosser-Owen, Matt Saba, Julio Samsó, Antonio Vallejo Triano, and Lyneise Williams. Special thanks to Stuart and Irina Sears for their collaboration over many years on the translations and transcriptions of my Arabic sources.

It is a pleasure to acknowledge all those who helped with access to objects, archival materials, and the images that are central to this book: José Escudero Aranda of Madinat al-Zahra'; Sergio Vidal Álvarez of Museo Arqueológico Nacional (MAN), Madrid; Margaret Wilson of the National Museum of Scotland; I. Giovanna Rao of the Biblioteca Laurenziana; Giorgio Strano and Susanna Cimmino, of the Museo Galileo; Elisabetta Bandinelli of the Uffizi's Gabinetto dei Disegni e delle Stampe; and Joachim Meyer of the David Collection; J.J. Bauer of the Visual Resources Library at UNC; Felipa Díaz of MAN; Susanna Cimmino of the Museo Galileo; Marc Pelletreau, Samar Kassab, and Mounia Chekhab Abudaya of the Museum of Islamic Art, Doha; Tacye Phillipson and Margaret Wilson, National Museum, Scotland; Jennifer Jeffrey, AKG images; Eugenia Antonucci and Anna Rita Fantoni, Biblioteca Laurenziana; Kristina Münchow and Thoralf Hanstein of the Orientabteilung Staatsbibliothek zu Berlin; Óscar Torre and Jaime Olmedo Ramos, Real Academia de la Historia; Jennifer E. Berry, Freer Gallery of Art and Arthur M. Sackler Gallery; Rebecca Carpenter, Boston Museum of Fine Arts; Robyn S. Haggard, History of Science Museum, University of Oxford; Susi Piovanelli, Gallerie degli Uffizi; Matt Saba, MIT Aga Khan Program for Islamic Architecture (AKPIA); Melis Taner, Esra Müyesseroğlue, Directorate of National Palaces; Çiğdem Yürür and the staff of the İstanbul İslam Bilim ve Teknoloji Tarihi Müzesi; Iman R. Abdulfattah, Joachim Meyer, and Mette Korsholm of the David Collection; and Lee Macdonald of Oxford History of Science Museum (MHS).

I am especially grateful to Nasser Rabbat and Sarah Pirovitz Humphreville, who encouraged me to pursue the idea in its earliest stages; to Molly Mullin, for her keen eye and insights that improved the text; and to the press's anonymous readers, whose comments saved me from many errors and gave the book its final shape. Any mistakes that remain are my own. My sincere thanks to Chelsea Hogue at Oxford University Press for seeing the book through to publication.

Words are not enough to express my love and gratitude to my parents, my family, and friends for enthusiasm and support of every kind. To those of you who shared my journeys as I carried out the research for this book, I remember our travels together with so much joy.

Finally, to my son Tommy and my husband Clay, who have shared my journey from the start, and who are my constant source of inspiration, I dedicate this book to you with deepest love and gratitude.

A Note on Dates and Terms

In using terms that refer to the "caliphal" period, or the "caliphate," in general I am referring not strictly to the internal political dynamics of al-Andalus, but to the broader framework of medieval Islamic history and civilization—what Amira Bennison has called the "Age of the Great Caliphs" and the era that historians of Islamic art generally designate as roughly 650–1250 CE.

The caliphal period is bracketed at its inception by the establishment of the Umayyad dynasty of Syria circa 650 and encompasses the brief subsequent period that witnessed the coexistence of three major dynasties (and for a certain period between circa 936 and 1031, competing caliphates): the Abbasids, the Córdoban Umayyads, and the Fatimids. The end of the period is marked by the Mongol invasions and sack of Abbasid Baghdad in the mid-thirteenth century.

Ibn Firnās, who died in 887, was active in the Umayyad court during the period of the Andalusi emirate, which corresponds to the period from 711 and the conquest of the Iberian Peninsula by the Umayyads of Syria to the declaration of the Córdoban caliphate in the year 929, some four decades following Ibn Firnās's death.

I have used the broader designation of "caliphal" to underscore that al-Andalus and Ibn Firnās, his contemporaries, and other intellectuals I discuss in the book were inextricably part of, informed, and were informed by broader international historical, social, and intellectual currents beyond the borders of al-Andalus.

ʿAbbās Ibn Firnās and His Career: Selected Passages from Ibn Ḥayyān

I. Overview of ʿAbbās's Character and Career

[130v[1]]

Mention of ʿAbbās b. Firnās, his noteworthy travels, & admirable deeds*

He says:

In the time of the emir al-Ḥakam appeared ʿAbbās b. Firnās, the wise man (ḥakīmu) of al-Andalus who superseded all others in the number of skills and arts (al-adawāti wa-l-funūni). His complete name is Abū al-Qāsim ʿAbbās b. Firnās b. Wardās, client of the Umayyads, of Berber lineage, originally from the province (*kūra*) of Takurunna, but having moved to Córdoba. He was learned (ʿāliman), refined (mufanninan), an able philosopher (faylasūfan ḥādhiqan), brilliant poet (shāʿiran mufalliqan), inspired and truthful astrologer (munajjiman maṭbūʿan muwaffaqan), sensible and penetrating in his excellent thoughts, full of inventiveness (ḥasana al-ikhtirāʿi) and of the capacity for innovation (kathīra al-ibdāʿi). He was the first to develop in al-Andalus the manufacture of glass from stones (ṣināʿata al-zujāji min al-hajārati), tracing his steps with knowledge, as I was told by a companion of the *faqīh* Ibn Lubāba, he was also the first to explain here the contents of the book on metrics of al-Khalīl [b. Aḥmad], the first here to explain music and to discover intricate issues, fabricating (ṣanʿa) with neither plan (ʿalā ghayri rasmin) nor model (wa-lā mithālin) the instrument known as clepsydra (*minqānah*) to tell the time, and the first of those to unravel and understand prosody or poetic meter, on which he composed a good book which reached the height of excellence.

The *faqīh* Muḥammad b. ʿUmar b. Lubāba says:

A certain merchant brought the book *Al-mithāl min al-ʿarūd (Model of Meter)* of al-Khalīl b. Aḥmad, which was placed in the hands of the emir ʿAbd al-Raḥmān

* Translations and transcriptions by Stuart Sears, except translations of III/Critical Edition and VI, Stuart Sears and Manal Alfaouri; transcriptions III/Madrid Mss, Stuart Sears and Mamoun Sakkal. The author and translators wish to thank Julio Samsó, Dwight Reynolds, Camilo Gomez-Rivas, Rodrigo Alem, and the anonymous reviewer for generous comments and suggestions to improve the translations.

b. al-Ḥakam, without its being clarified or understood, [by him] or by his companions. The eunuch Abū al-Faraj, one of the principal servants, told me that the book was brought to the palace, as entertainment for the slaves, up to the point that they said to one another: "God give you the judgment like that which filled the book with *mafāʿil and mafāʿil*."

وذكر عباس بن فرناس
ونوادر أخباره، وعجائب أموره

قال:

وفي عصر الأمير الحكم، نجم عباس بن فرناس [209]، حكيم الأندلس الزائد على جماعة علمائهم بكثرة الأدوات والفنون. وهو أبو القاسم عباس بن فرناس ابن ورداس، يتولى بني أمية، وينتسب في البرابر، وأصله من كورة تاكرنا، انتقل إلى قرطبة. كان عالمًا مُفَنِّنًا فيلسوفًا حاذقًا، وشاعرًا مفلقًا، ومُنَجِّمًا مطبوعًا موفقًا، صحيح الخاطر، ثاقب الذهن، جيد الفكر، حسن الاختراع، كثير الإبداع. هو أول من استنبط بالأندلس صناعة الزجاج من الحجارة، ودبرها بالحكمة. حدثني بذلك بعض أصحاب ابن لبابة الفقيه، وهو أول من فك بها كتاب العروض للخليل، وأول من فكّ فيه الموسيقى، وكشف غوامض الأشياء، وصنع الآلة المعروفة بالمنقانة، لتعرف الأوقات على غير رسم ولا مثال، وأول من فك منهم العروض، ميزان الشعر وفهمها، فله فيها كتاب حسن بلغ فيه من التجويد الغاية.

فذكر الفقيه محمد بن عمر بن لبابة قال:

أدخل بعض التجار كتاب المثال من العروض للخليل بن أحمد، فصار إلى الأمير عبد الرحمن بن الحكم، ولم يَبِنْ عليه ولا على أصحابه ولا فهموه. فأخبرني أبو الفرج الخصي – وكان من خيار خدمهم – قال: صار ذلك الكتاب مطَّرَحًا داخل القصر يتلهَّى به الجواري، حتى إن بعضهن ليقول لبعض: صيَّر الله عقلك كعقل هذا الذي ملأ كتابه من مفاعيل مفاعيل!

II. On ʿAbbās's Background and Skills

[131v]
The vizier ʿAbd al-Ḥamīd b. Basīl said:

> ʿAbbās b. Firnās devised during all his life subtle inventions (ibdāʿātin laṭifatan) and marvelous innovations (ikhtirāʿātin ʿajībatan) in more than one art (ṣināʿatin), in jest and in seriousness; he also played the *ʿūd* and composed beautiful melodies. At the same time, he dominated poetry and developed well in its paths, being a person of many merits and enormous advantage, splendid qualities and well-known anecdotes. His life was prolonged, until his death in the year 274 h. Having served with three rulers, between him and his grandfather al-Ḥakam, to all of whom he dedicated select panegyrics, and with all of them excellent anecdotes.

I read the following words of the poet ʿUbāda, handwritten by the poet himself:

> It has been said that Ibn Firnās was *mulad* [*muwallad*], and at other times, that rather he was Berber. He was born in Cordoba, he lived in its western suburb, and he excelled in all the sciences, ancient and modern (al-ʿulūmi al-qadīmati wa-l-muḥdathati). He dominated Arabic and was adept at making good poetry, excelling as well in philosophy, astronomy, and astrology; he also knew enchantments, occult powers and magic (ṣāḥiba nayranjātin wa-alṭāfin wa-asḥārin); about this stories and anecdotes are told . . . [2]

وذكر عبد الحميد بن بسيل الوزير [213] قال:

أبدع عباس بن فرناس طول أمده إبداعات لطيفة، واختراعات عجيبة، في غير ما صناعة من جد وهزل، إلى أن ضرب بالعود، وصاغ الألحان الحسنة، وكان مع ذلك مجيدًا للشعر، حسن التصرف في طريقه، كثير المحاسن، جم الفوائد، ذا خصال رائقة، وأجبار سائرة، واستأخر أمده إلى أن هلك في أيام الأمير محمد بن عبد الرحمن بن الحكم، سنة أربع وسبعين ومائتين، قد والى صحبة الملوك الثلاثة، ما بينه وبين جَدِّه الحكم، ومدحهم أجمعين بمدائح مختارة. وجرت له معهم أخبار حسنة.

وقرأت بخط عبادة الشاعر قال:

قيل في ابن فرناس: إنه من المولدة، وقيل بل من البرابر، نشأ بقرطبة، وسكن منها في الربض الغربي. ونَبُلَ في جميع العلوم القديمة والمحدثة، أحكم لسان العرب، وحذق صنعة الشعر الحسن، وفاق في علم الفلسفة والنجوم والهيئة، فصار صاحب نيرنجات وألطاف وأسحار، تحمل عنه في ذلك أنباء وأخبار.

III. On the Aeronautics Experiment

Ibn Ḥayyān's Account (Madrid Manuscript)
[131r][3]
He [Muḥammad b. 'Umar b. Lubāba] says:

> ['Abbās] was so full of ingenuity (ṣāḥiba nayranjātin), creativity, originality, invention (kathira al-ibdā'i / al-ikhtirā'i wa-l-tawwaludi wa-l-istinbāṭi) and resourcefulness (wāsi'a al-ḥiyali) that he was attributed with the knowledge of magic and alchemy (al-siḥra wa-'amala al-kīmiyā'), and was often challenged on religious grounds. Some sheikhs said that he [once] managed to launch himself into flight. He clothed himself in feathers [fastened to *light colored*] silk and spread for himself (*madda*) two wings of calculated structure (jinaḥayni 'alā wazni taqdīrin qaddarahu), with which he was able to rise in the air (istaṭāra fī al-jawwi). He flew (ṭāra) from the vicinity of Rusāfa, moved through the air and then circled until he landed in a place far away from where he departed. But this landing went poorly when he hurt his tailbone. He had not managed the landing very well. He did not take into account that a bird, when landing, does so on its tailhead, which he [*neglected*]. He was more frightening than [*the clamor*] of the scattered places of Saharan nomads who [*ruminated*] at length over what they had witnessed, without knowing what it was all about. For this reason, the poet Mu'min b. Sa'īd, his equal in some of what transpired between them, said:
>
> He soars above the phoenix in flight
> When he covers his body in [*vulture/eagle*] feathers

Critical Edition

He said:[4] 'Abbās was a master of white magic (*wa kāna 'Abbās sāhib nairanjāt)*; he was full of ingenuity (*ibdā'i*) and creativity (*ikhtirā'i*) and the capacity for invention (*al-tawwludi)*, and the capacity to observe and to derive rules and principles from his observations (*instinbāt)*. He was resourceful, up to the point that he was attributed with [knowledge of] magic (*al-sihra*) and alchemy and frequently his religious beliefs were challenged. Some sheikhs mentioned that he managed to fly; he clothed himself with feathers on pieces of silk (*saraqi al-ḥarīri*)[5] and spread for himself two wings whose structure [and] estimate he calculated (*wa madda li nafsihi janāhayni 'alā wazni taqdīrin qaddarahu*); he was able to rise up and fly (*fatahayya' lahu 'an istatāra*) in the air; he flew from the vicinity of Rusāfa, and he moved through the air and circled until he fell, far away from the place where he departed; his landing was poor when he hurt the root of his tail, since he did not manage his landing very well. He did not take into account that birds usually land on the root of the tail; he had forgotten that. He frightened those who witnessed his flight (*matāriḥa*), from among the people of the desert (*min ahli al-ṣaḥrā')*.[6]

They talked a lot about what they witnessed from him and they didn't know what he was doing. And so Muʾmin b. Saʿīd, the poet who was his rival in some of what happened between them, said about him:

He soars above the phoenix in her flight
When he covers his body with the feathers of the vulture/eagle (*qashʿami*)

كثير الابداع والاختراع والتوّلد والاستنباط وَاسع الحيل حتى أَن نسب اليه السحر وعمل الكيما وكثر عليه بالطعنان في دينه وذكر بعض المشيخه انه احتال في تطيير جثمانه فكسا نفسه الريش على [سدف] الحرير ومد لنفسه جناحين على وزن تقدير قدره فتهياً له ان استطار في الجو فطار من ناحية الرصافه واستقل في الهوا فحلق فيه حتى وقع في مكان مطاره على مسافة بعيده وساءَ على ذلك موقعه لما تاذى في [عجب] ذنبه اذ لم يحسن الاحتيال في وقوعه ولم يقدر ان الطاير انما يقعُ على زمكائه [فلمى] عن ذلك وقد كان [أفزع] [من دن] مطارح من أهل [الصحراء] بكثر [نخرتهم] عما عاينوا منه ولا يعلمون شانه ولذلك قال فيه [مؤمن] ابن سعيد الشاعر قرنُه في بعض ما جرى بينهما

يطم على العنقاءِ في طيرانها اذا ما كسى جثمانه ريش [قشجم]

وذكر محمد بن يحيى بن عبد العزيز قال لما صنع عباس بن فرناس في بيته هيئَة السما التى ركبها على منهاج الحكمة ومثل فيها افلاكها واقام فيها ءَالات تخيل الى الناظر فيها انها نجوم وَغيوم وبروق ورعود فاراهَا كثيرا من عيون الناس مفتخرا عليهم بحكمته شاع ذكرها في الناس وحديثهم عنها [فمما] ذلك قوله مومن بن سعيد الشاعر وعارض ذاكريه بالذم لفغله والطعنان في دينه وقال في ذلك اشعارا كثيره شاب فيها السخرية بالافحاش منها قوله

قعدت تحت سما لابن فرناس فخلت ان رحا دَارت على راس
[مما انوكِ سواها وحيفها] حية ذات انياب واضراسِ
لها نجوم تنبى أن خالقها اذا نظرت [اِليها] أحمق الناس
يمسى ويصبح من شغل بصنعتها [نجتى هم] وتفكير ووسواس
كان الجديربان يرقى [اِليه، إليه] بها رَاقٍ [فيدحُر به] منها على الراس

قال فلما وردت على ابن فرناس قال لمن معه ليس كذا قال قد غير هذا البيت الأول على ابي مروان وحُرف انما قاله ابو مروان هاكذا

قعدت من فوق [عرد، عود] لابن فرناسِ فخلته ناتيا [شبرا] على راسِ

فلما قرووه [الا ها] كذا كما اقول لكم فهو الصحيح عنه قال وكتب عباس ابن فرناس الى [مؤمن بن] سعيد في شان[سمائه] هذه لاول ما اتخذها ابياتا يهازله بها أولها

دِن[لِسمائي] ياخلق خالقها واستشعر الخوف من صواعقها

فهاج [مؤمن] بشعره هذا واجابه عنه بابياتٍ اكثر منها افحش فيها [جزأ] مِنهَا

IV. On the Meteorological Chamber

[131r]

Muḥammad b. Yaḥyā b. ʿAbd al-ʿAzīz related:

As ʿAbbās b. Firnās had manufactured a reproduction of the heavens (hay'ata al-samā'i) in his house, which he assembled in scientific fashion (rakkabahā ʿalā minhāji al-ḥikmati), representing the stars and setting up mechanisms that appeared (wa-aqāma fīhā ālātin tukhayyilu) to its viewer as though they were stars, clouds, thunder and lightning, he showed it often to the notables among the people, boasting of his wisdom. News and talk of it spread. [*Regarding this talk]*, the poet Mu'min b. Saʿīd opposed those who spoke of him by criticizing his actions and challenging him on religious grounds. He recited many verses on this [subject] in which mockery degenerated into obscenity. Among these was his remark [*basīṭ*]:[7]

[131v]

I sat under a firmament (samā'in) of Ibn Firnās,
And fancied that a windmill revolved (raḥan dārat) around my head:
It is the heavens fabricated (sawwāhā) by a silly fellow, encircled
By a serpent with fangs and teeth;
It has stars that will tell you that its creator,
if you looked at [this firmament], is the biggest fool.
Come morning and afternoon he works (min shughlin) on his creation
Secretly preoccupied, [with the] reflection and suggestion of Satan:
He deserves someone to raise him to the top [of the building/structure]
And then make him jump head-first

When this reached Ibn Firnās, he told those around him:

[The poem] is not like that. He said, [Mu'min b. Saʿīd] changed and altered the first verse of [the poem of] Abū Marwān, who actually said as follows: I sat on the stiff penis of Ibn Firnās, and fancied that it jutted out [*the span of a hand*] above [my] head. Transmit it like that, which is the correct one.

He said [the same source, i.e. Muḥammad b. Yaḥyā b. ʿAbd al-ʿAzīz]:

ʿAbbās b. Firnās wrote to Mu'min b. Saʿīd regarding [this reproduction of the heavens/firmament], and as soon as he learned of [the latter's poetry], [he replied] with some verses mocking him. They begin:

Come near [*my firmament*], O, creature of its creator!
And experience the fear of its lightning.

Mu'min grew upset at this poetry, and responded with more verses containing more obscenity, a portion of which are:

> The firmament of the ingenious 'Abbās Abū al-Qāsim (samā'u 'Abbāsin
>   al-aryabi Abī al-Qāsimi)
> Suffice as splendid beauty
> The farts from his backside are his thunder,
> I would like to know what is the brightness of his lightning.
> I ran my view along its west,
> And my gaze wandered its east:
> An old senile in his madness you see
> Whose height is less than Saturn
> And, to which I achieved with my thoughts,
> I felt like spitting on the back of its creator.[8]

وذكر محمد بن يحيى عبد العزيز قال [211]:

لما صنع عباس بن فرناس في بيته هيئة السماء، التي ركبها على منهاج الحكمة، ومَثَّل فيها أفلاكها، وأقام فيها آلات تُخَيِّل إلى الناظر فيها أنها نجوم وغيوم وبروق ورعود، فأراها كثيرًا من عيون الناس مفتخرًا عليهم بحكمة شاع ذكرها في الناس وحديثهم عنها، فساء ذلك قرنه مؤمن بن سعيد الشاعر، عارض ذاكريه بالذم لفعله والطعان في دينه، وقال في ذلك أشعارًا كثيرة شاب فيها السخرية بالإفحاش منها قوله: [البسيط]

قَعَدْتُ تحت سماءٍ لابنِ فرناسِ — فخِلْتُ أن رَحىً دارت على راسي
سماءُ أنْوكَ سوَّاها وحفَّفها — بِحَيَّةٍ ذاتِ أنيابٍ وأضراسِ
لها نجوم تُنَبِّي أن خالِقها — إذا نظرتَ إليها أحمقُ الناسِ
يُمْسِي ويُصْبحُ من شُغْلٍ بصَنْعَتِها — نَجِيَّ هَمٍّ وتفكيرٍ ووَسْواسِ
كانَ الجديرَ بأنْ يَرْقَى إليه بها — راقٍ فَيَدْحُو بِه منها على الرَّاس

قال:
فلما وردت على ابن فرناس قال لمن معه: ليس كذا قال، قد غُيِّر هذا البيت الأول على أبي مروان وحُرِّف. إنما قاله أبو مروان هكذا:

قَعَدْتُ من فوقِ عَرْدٍ لابنِ فرناسِ — فخلته ناتِئًا شِبرًا على راسي

فلا ترووه إلا هكذا، فهو الصحيح عنه.

قال:
وكتب عباس بن فرناس إلى مؤمن بن سعيد في شأن سمائه هذه لأولِ ما اتخذها أبياتًا يُهازِله بها أولها: [المنسرح]

دِنْ لسمائي يا خَلقَ خالِقِها — واسْتَشْعِرِ الخوفَ من صواعقها

فهاج مؤمن لسخره هذا وأجابه عنه بأبيات أكثر منها أفحش فيها جداً منها [212]:

/ سماءُ عباسِ الأريب أبي ال — قاسم ناهيكَ حُسْنُ رائِقِها
أمَّا ضُراط اسْتِهِ فراعِدُها — فليتَ شعرِي ما لَمْعُ بارِقِها
أَجَلْتُ عَيْنَيَّ في مغارِبها — فحار طرفي وفي مشارقها
هِمٌّ له في جُنونِهِ هِمَمٌ — يقصر كِيوانُ عن شواهَقِها
لقد تمنَّيْتُ حين دَوَّمها — فِكْرِيَ بالبَصْقِ في اسْتِ خالقِها

V. On Two Precision Instruments Made For ʿAbd al-Raḥmān II and Muḥammad I

[131v]
I read the following words of the poet ʿUbāda, handwritten by the poet himself: ". . . He was the one who made in al-Andalus the clepsydra (alladhī ʿamila bi-l-Andalūsi al-minqānata) for knowing the hour, which he sent to the emir Muḥammad, grandson of the emir al-Ḥakam, engraving on it (wa-naqasha fīhā) some verses of his that said (*tawīl*)":

> I am the best instrument (khayru adāti) for religion,
> When you (pl.) don't know the moment of each prayer,
> When one can not see for oneself the sun in the day, nor
> the stars in nights of deep darkness;
> For the blessing of Muḥammad, imam of the Muslims,
> With me the moments of prayer are clear.

Before that ʿAbbās had also made an armillary sphere (wa-ʿamila ʿAbbāssun ayḍan min qablu, dhāta al-ḥalaqi . . .) for the emir ʿAbd al-Rahmān b. al-Ḥakam, which he sent, inscribing upon it (wa-kataba maʿahā) [*kāmil*]:

> Complete is the instrument (min ālatin) that was commissioned of me
> That great philosophers could not achieve, save for me;
> If Ptolemy had been successful in doing so,
> I wouldn't be occupying myself with the tables of the *Qānūn*[9]
> And if the sun was seen on its horizon,
> It would be sending its measured light,
> And the lunar mansions (manāzilu al-qamari), hidden to all eyes with the
> horoscope of each moment (dūna al-ʿuyūni li-kulli ṭāliʿ ḥīni) ,
> They would see during the day, the same as they appear
> In the night, in its deep darkness[10]

وقرأت بخط عبادة الشاعر قال:

... وهو الذي عمل بالأندلس المنقانة لمعرفة الأوقات، ورفعها إلى الأمير محمد حفيد الأمير الحكم، ونقش فيها أبياتًا من قوله [214]: [الطويل]

ألا إنَّني للدينِ خيرُ أداةِ إذا غابَ عنكم وَقْتُ كُلِّ صلاةِ
ولم تُرَ شمسٌ بالنهارِ ولم تَبِنْ كواكبُ ليلٍ حالكِ الظلماتِ
بِيُمْنِ إمامِ المسلمين محمدٍ تجلَّت بِيَ الأوقاتُ للصَّلواتِ

وعمل عباس أيضاً من قبلُ، ذاتَ الحَلَق، للأمير عبد الرحمن بن الحكم، ورفعها إليه بها، وكتب معها [215]: [الكامل]

قد تَمَّ ما حَمَّلْتَنِي من آلةٍ أعيا الفلاسِفَةَ الجهابِذَ دُوني
لو كان بَطْلَيموسُ أُلْهِمَ صُنْعَهُ لم يشتغِلْ بجَداولِ القانونِ
فإذا رأتْهُ الشمسُ في آفاقِها بَعَثَتْ إليهِ بنُورِها المَوْزُونِ
ومنازِلُ القَمَرِ التي حُجِبَتْ مَعًا دونَ العيونِ لكُلِّ طالعِ حِينِ
فَيَرَوْنَ فيها بالنهارِ كما بَدَتْ بالليلِ في ظُلُماتِهِنَّ الجُونِ

VI. His Poem on the Villa (*Munya*) al-Rusāfa

[p. 227][11]
He [the emir Muḥammad] summoned the words of his poets in describing it [Rusāfa] in congratulating him in what of it was there for him.

Their master, the great orator ʿAbbās b. Firnās b. [Wa]rdā[s], his peerless poet, [p. 228] said concerning this what [all of them] agreed was the best of what has been said in its substance.

[How lovely is the palace of] Al-Rusāfa with its gold,
. . . and the magic
(*wa-l-siḥri*),

/ and its lofty heights, under which appears
the stars of the Pleiades (al-Thurayya) and al-Simākayni [Arcturus and Spica Virginis] and al-Ghafri [one of the stations of the moon],

[p. 229]
If the abundant gold reached its height, and then poured down, it wouldn't reach the ground for a month

It has white chambers (*lahā al-ghurafu al-bīḍu*) at whose light the morning sun laughs,
These chambers encompass the heights with their light, as if by the brilliance of bright faces

It is as though the palaces of the world after its [Rusāfa's] completion,
are just tiny specks [literally "bumps on a [camel's] hump"], that are more obscure than dust

And from it the eyes wander
Over birds, beasts, and flowers

I wonder at its brilliant, shaded courts in which coolness naps from the scorching heat,

Its echoes reveal its most subtle secrets, without concealment, for the most hidden of secrets in it is announced,

[p. 230]

As if the one who hides his words when conversing with them [the courts] in the lowest of voices is singing with an accompaniment

They [the courts] are like a dawn sleeper, dignified and glowing,
they cast light without exposure to the sun or moon

O, how excellent are its green plants around it,
And its white rivers which flow beneath it,

You could see the tall majestic trees spreading their branches,
swaying from the weight of their fruit,

It is as though a goldsmith had forged clusters of dates from fiery gold over their branches

They changed into three states
The molten vessel of [the two hands full of gold pieces] and in the jewels the radiant,

They began as pearls and then transformed into emerald,
Which turns back into gold after the plucking of dates

One may desire a drink from it that is more delicious than
The yearning of a yearner for a lover of grandeur

And from fragrances in the boughs/branches, it is as though,
The cheeks of virgins in their green veils,

You see redness in some

Women wearing anklets [. . .] white [alternatively, could refer to the white legs of a horse]

Motivations . . .

[p. 232]

Birds with henna-dyed heads chirp in it,
They have colored backs, bright necks, and green chests

To every female who doesn't dye her hair, who misplaced her dye
Whose flanks, abdomen and backs are embellished

If she starts with her tender singing,
[Her song] makes you forget the melody of the flute, even though she is not playing an instrument

[p. 233]

[And it also makes you forget] The type of slim-waisted maiden with a *qalami* way of singing, and a flute-like melody and tone

She who keeps two dirhams in her cheek,
Which do not leave no matter what she buys or sells

She wrapped herself in white silk,
And at that the water crow (*ghurāb al-māʾ*) lent her his shoes for recompense,

Every marvelous thing in it, the like of it was not seen,
Of birds, and large fish, and date and pigeons (*al-qumrī*),

The inheritance of fathers who became caliphs,
Princes of generous kings are radiant,

[p. 234]

God refused but to complete His construction (*yutimma binā'ahu*) . . .
. . . by which the object of gratitude was completed,

The namesake of the Chosen prophet and his intimate,
And the seal of what was recorded of the prophethood in remembrance

واستدعى أقوال شعرائه في وصفها وتهنئته بما حصل له منها.

فقال في ذلك فحلهم الخنذيذ عباس بن فرناس بن [ور]دا[س، شاع]ره البديع الذي اتفقوا [كلهم] على أنه أحسن ما قيل في معناه:

الرُّصَافَة من   والتِّبْرِ
وَالسِّحْرِ

/وأعْرافُهُ الشُّمُّ التي لاح دُونَها
نجومُ الثُّرَيَّا والسِّماكَيْنِ والغَفْرِ
إذا بَلَغَ النَّضْرُ المُكَثَّرُ فَرْعَها
وصَوَّبَ لم يَبْلُغْ إلى الأرْضِ في شَهْرِ
لها الغُرَفُ البِيضُ التي يَضْحَكُ الضُّحى
وتُلْحِقُها من نُورِها في سَنا الغُرِّ
كأنَّ قُصورَ الأَرْضِ بعد تَمامِهِ
نُتُوءُ الذُّرى أخْفى شُخوصاً مِنَ الذَّرِّ
وتَنْتَشِرُ الأبصارُ منها إلى مَدى التَّ
نَزُّهِ بالأَطْيارِ والوَحْشِ والزَّهْرِ
وأعْجَبُ من أفْيائِها الغُرَرُ الَّتي
يَقيلُ بِهِنَّ البَرْدُ في وَغْرَةِ الحَرِّ
يَنِمُّ بأخْفى سِرِّها غَيْرَ كاتِمٍ
صَداها فأخْفى السِّرِّ فيها من الجَهْرِ
كأنَّ الذي يُخْفي الحديثَ بنَجوِها
على أخْفَضِ الأصْوَاتِ يَشدوَ على وِتْرِ
نؤومُ الضُّحى ضافي العُلى سَجسَجُ السَّنا
تُضيءُ بلا شمسٍ عليها ولا بَدْرِ
ويا حبَّذا أنْباتُها الخُضْرُ حَوْلَها
وأنهارُها البيضُ التي تحتها تَجْري
تَرَى الباسِقاتِ النَّاشِراتِ فُرُوعَها
مَوَائِسَ فيها من مُزَاوَلَةِ الوَفْرِ
كأنَّ صَيَاغاً صاغَ فوق غُصُونِها
من الذَّهَبِ النَّارِي عَرَاجِينَ من تَمْرِ
تبدَّلْنَ حالاتٍ ثَلاثاً لَهُنَّ في
مَصُوغِ الحُلى شكلٌ وفي الجوهَرِ التَّضْرِ
نَشَتْ لُؤْلُؤاً ثم استحالَتْ زُمُرُّداً
يعود إلى العِقْيانِ بَعْدَ جَنى البُسْرِ
وقد يُشتَهَى منها شرابٌ ألَذُّ مِنْ
تَضَرُّعِ مُشتَاقٍ إلى عاشِقِ الكِبْرِ
ومِنْ أرجاتٍ في الغصونِ كأنَّها
خدودُ عَذَارى في مَقانِعِها الخُضرِ
تَرَى حُمْرَةً في بَعضِ
مُحَجَّلَةٍ غُرِّ

بَوَاعِثَ

/يُغرِّدُ فيها كُلُّ مُخْتَضِبِ الشَّوَى — مُوَشَّى الْقَرا قاني الطُّلى أخضرِ الصَّدْرِ

إلى كُلِّ سَلْتَاءٍ أضاعَتْ خِضابَها — مُدَبَّجَةِ الكشحَيْنِ والبَطْنِ والظَّهْرِ

إذا ما استَهَلَّتْ في شَجِيِّ غِنائِها — يُنَسِّيكَ تَرْجاعَ اليَرَاعِ بلا زَمْرِ

وما شِئْتَ من هَفْهافَةٍ قَلَمِيَّةٍ ال.. — ..غناءِ إلى نايِيَّةِ النَّغْمِ والنَّبْرِ

وحابِسةٍ في ذقْنِها دِرْهَمَيْنِ ما — يَزُولانِ فيما تَشْتَرِيهِ وما تَشري

قد اشْتَمَلَتْ في يَلْمَقٍ وأعارَها — [هناك] غُرابُ الماءِ خُفَّيْهِ للأجْرِ

وكُلِّ بديعٍ فيه لم يُرَ مِثْلُهُ — من الطَّيرِ والنِّينانِ والتمر والقُمْري

وِراثَةُ آباءٍ تَوَلَّوْا خَلائِفٍ — بَهاليلَ أمْلاكٍ خَضارِمَةٍ زُهْرِ

أبى اللهُ إلا أنْ يُتِمَّ بناءَهُ [ال..رَّ.. — ..فِيعَ] الذي تَمَّتْ بِهِ غايةُ الشُّكْرِ

سَمِيُّ النَّبِيِّ المصطفى وحَمِيمُهُ — وخَاتَمِ مسطورِ النُّبوَّةِ في الذِّكْرِ

Introduction

Ibn Firnas and His Legacy

The dream of flying has a long premodern history. Think of the myth of Daedalus, the ancient Greek inventor, or of Leonardo's sketches and studies of birds and flying devices.[1] Many would nevertheless be surprised to know that centuries before Leonardo depicted birds in flight and flying machines, intrepid medieval peoples around the globe carried out aeronautics experiments, including experiments in early human flight.[2] This book focuses on one of these individuals, ʿAbbas b. Firnas (d. 887). He is best known as an eminent scientist of early Islamic Iberia, and for conducting an aeronautics experiment that has been celebrated as a milestone in the history of human flight.[3] The memory of Ibn Firnas's significance in the realms of aviation and science might be gauged by his evocation on the very first page of the 2015 book *The Wright Brothers*, penned by no less an authority than Pulitzer prize–winning historian David McCullough. He wrote, "from ancient times and into the Middle Ages, man had dreamed of taking to the sky, of soaring into the blue like the birds. One savant in Spain in the year 875 is known to have covered himself with feathers in the attempt."[4] A curious and enduring image of Ibn Firnas to be sure, and one to which I will return in the pages that follow. The eminent contemporary British physicist, author, and broadcaster Jim al-Khalili likewise observed in his 2010 *Pathfinders: The Golden Age of Arabic Science* that Ibn Firnas was the only medieval scientist he had heard of, as a boy growing up in Iraq, and calls him the Leonardo da Vinci of Islamic Spain.[5]

The first and best-known polymath of the early Islamic West, Ibn Firnas was a courtier in Córdoba, in present-day southern Spain. It is in connection to the suburban villas and court culture of this medieval city, the subject of my first book, that the man and his flight first drew my attention. I mentioned his flight as an intriguing example of the range of court activities that medieval Arabic sources recount took place in the Umayyad suburban villas, or *munyas*.[6]

The capital of Islamic Iberia (known in Arabic as al-Andalus), Córdoba had been an important commercial center and a Roman provincial capital that produced some notable figures such as the poet Lucan and philosopher Seneca. It subsequently flourished in the early Middle Ages as the seat of the Umayyad dynasty (r. 756–1031).[7] This was an Iberian branch of the first major dynasty, or caliphate, that ruled the Islamic lands in the caliphal period (roughly 650–1250).[8] During

A Bridge to the Sky. Glaire D. Anderson, Oxford University Press. © Oxford University Press 2024.
DOI: 10.1093/oso/9780190913243.003.0001

Ibn Firnas's lifetime in the ninth century, Córdoba was emerging as one of the great metropolises of the medieval globe. By the year 1000, little more than a century after his death, Córdoba was arguably the major intellectual, cultural, political, and artistic center of the western Mediterranean.[9] Medieval authors often compared Córdoba to other famed medieval capitals such as Damascus, Baghdad, and Constantinople. While to today's audiences medieval Córdoba, a Western European city that was also a major capital of the medieval globe, may be less familiar than other great medieval European capitals of Christendom, Córdoba's impact on the cultural and political landscape of Iberia and Europe north of the Pyrenees is difficult to exaggerate.[10] If, by the tenth century, its fame as an intellectual center was without peer, this was in large part due to the Umayyad rulers, who cultivated an enduring reputation as patrons of the arts and sciences and whose court was a magnet for intellectuals from Iberia and beyond.

Although he lived in the ninth century, Ibn Firnas is still known today as an early scientist and aviator. Since the turn of the twentieth century, especially, his image and reputation as an early scientist have been continually invoked and reimagined.[11] He has even been commemorated by NASA, which in the 1970s named a crater on the moon in recognition of his reputation as a "humanitarian and technologist."[12] Historians of technology, science, and aviation continue to discuss and debate Ibn Firnas's significance. He has often appeared in popular and visual culture in Spain and in Muslim-majority contexts[13]: for instance, in Spain he has been memorialized on postage stamps and commemorated in a 2011 public monument and bridge in the city where he lived and worked. A conjectural model of the man and his flight device has been displayed since 2005 as consumer "edutainment" in Dubai's Ibn Battuta shopping mall. The conjectural model seemingly inspired the model that then figured prominently in the popular *1001 Inventions* traveling exhibition that debuted at the London Science Museum in 2010, and that subsequently was seen

Figure I.1. Córdoba and other cities mentioned in the text.
Leanne Kelman /L Wright Design.

by audiences at science museums around the globe. In the same year Ibn Firnas was even parodied in a Vodafone corporate marketing campaign, while in 2013 Rolls Royce invoked him in unveiling its "Ghost Firnas Motif" collection of bespoke luxury automobiles.

Few would suspect, however, that this polymath's aeronautics experiment and his career as a notable intellectual also illuminate connections between science, the arts, and design practices in early Islamic Spain. Yet the earliest and fullest account of Ibn Firnas's career in the Umayyad court reveals such connections. Preserved in the Córdoban court chronicle, a general history of al-Andalus written in the eleventh century by the Córdoban intellectual Ibn Hayyan (d. 1076), the account presents Ibn Firnas as one of the leading intellectuals of early Islamic Iberia and a pioneer in the design and construction of the court's fine scientific instruments. The chronicle tells us that he designed and made a water clock, an armillary sphere, and a wondrous object for visualizing astronomical and meteorological phenomena. The latter was installed in his own residence, where it became a spectacle that fascinated members of elite social and intellectual circles. The chronicle even preserves poetry that Ibn Firnas is said to have composed and inscribed on the objects he created, as well as his lengthy poem about the Umayyad royal villa of Rusafa, which the chronicle discusses alongside the scientific pursuits that took place there. The chronicle provides us with a rare portrait—or more accurately, perhaps, a rough preparatory sketch—of an early Islamic court intellectual, designer, and maker. It is this early and relatively substantial account of Ibn Firnas's career that is at the heart of this study of a medieval polymath at the intersection of science, arts, and court culture.

This book takes ʿAbbas Ibn Firnas's career in the Córdoban court, as recounted in one profoundly important medieval Arabic source, as a departure point to explore the social standing of scientist-intellectuals as designers and "makers" of visual culture, against a backdrop of early Islamic court culture and the intellectual advances that occurred during the formative centuries of what historians of science have conceptualized as the Islamic Scientific Revolution.[14] ʿAbbas Ibn Firnas's career underscores the actuality that he and other medieval intellectuals could also be designers and artisans in their own right. They designed at scales from the portable to the monumental—from fine objects, such as small precision instruments that could fit in the hand, to monumental objects that were integral to the material spatiality of architectural and urban spaces. Ibn Firnas's career illuminates a fundamental early Islamic connection between the realms of what today we mostly separate into categories of science on the one hand and art on the other, a false distinction, as Müller-Wiener has pointed out.[15] This issue lies at the heart of the contribution this book seeks to make by demonstrating how these fields intersected in the lives of members of the court. For ʿAbbas Ibn Firnas and other intellectuals of the caliphal period, art and intellect, science and visuality, were mutually informative. Moreover, the dialogue between science and craft that his career and the surviving works that I discuss in the pages that follow created a powerful way of understanding the world and a visual culture that spoke to a variety of interests

Figure I.2. A conjectural model of Ibn Firnas and a glider on display in the Ibn Battuta Mall, Dubai. Photo, Dick Doughty / Saudi Aramco World/SAWDIA.

Figure I.3. Ibn Firnas Bridge, Córdoba, Spain. Designed by José Luis Manzanares Japón (AYESA), completed 2011. Edmundo Sáez. © Creative Commons ShareAlike4.0 International.

and concerns, including those held by people outside Islamic lands. It tells us that we must re-evaluate premodern Islamic visual culture and scientific texts. Such a reassessment can enhance appreciation of the value of visual culture to intellectual work. To put it another way, Ibn Firnas and the instruments and manuscripts I discuss in this book suggest the inseparability in premodern Islamic contexts of craft and intellect, what Pamela Smith calls "making and knowing" and what Margaret Graves calls "the intellect of the hand," and indeed the primacy of making as process over textual instruction.[16]

In examining the material and textual evidence my aim is to use Ibn Firnas as a case study that illuminates the complex connections between an early intellectual's work as a scientific practitioner and the society that he lived in.[17] Arabic chronicles, biographies, and scientific treatises—especially works on mathematics and engineering—contain important information about intellectuals who engaged in what today we would consider the design professions, alongside both scientific and religious pursuits. If we expand our conception of the designer, artist, or architect to include early Islamic scientific and intellectual practices, figures such as ʿAbbas Ibn Firnas can clarify our understanding of the careers and social standing of other premodern artists, architects, and designers in early Islamic societies. For instance, we might consider in this vein Ibn Daniyal (d. 1310) of Cairo, who was a physician who practiced ophthalmology, but who was also a poet and playwright, known for composing some of the earliest Egyptian shadow plays that offer a glimpse into theater, performance, and visuality in medieval Islamic contexts.[18]

Aside from brief references, ʿAbbas Ibn Firnas and his career in the Umayyad court have not figured in the art history of al-Andalus.[19] Yet the tenth- and eleventh-century intellectuals of the Córdoban court praised him as a wise man, a philosopher, a poet, as an intellectual who had mastered the sciences ancient and modern, and—most importantly—as the first designer and maker of precision scientific instruments for the Córdoban Umayyad rulers. This book therefore explores ʿAbbas Ibn Firnas's career, focusing on his reputation as the first maker of fine precision instruments for the Córdoban Umayyad court. It examines the earliest and most substantive Arabic account of his career (both the Arabic passages and new English translations preface the main text) in tandem with early Islamic precision instruments and illustrated scientific manuscripts, which are valued today as works of both intellect and art. Together with the account of Ibn Firnas's career, we can use these materials to trace connections between medieval Islamic visual culture and the exact sciences, especially astronomy and engineering. The knowledge and skills that he brought to designing scientific instruments and objects would have informed his design for a flight device and the optimum conditions of time and place for the aeronautics experiment that he devised near the end of his long and prominent career.

Ibn Firnas's famous flight and his career as a court intellectual provide a point of departure from which to explore the intersection of arts and design, intellectual experimentation, and court culture in Córdoba and other contemporary courts. I argue for a symbiotic relationship between science and design fully evident in the early Islamic texts and in a variety of visual and material forms by the ninth century, when Ibn Firnas lived and carried out his work for the rulers of Córdoba, and where court spaces (notably residences, including royal *munyas*, or villas) served as stage and laboratory. As I hope to show in this book, design and making were an important part of intellectual and scientific processes during the early caliphal era. If we expand our conception of design and its allied spheres to include the work of astronomers, mathematicians, engineers, and other early intellectuals, figures such as ʿAbbas Ibn Firnas can be seen as "makers" of early Islamic visual culture. The account of Ibn Firnas's career that has come down to us in the Córdoban chronicle provides a window on Andalusi science and visual culture and the work of an early court intellectual who shaped that culture. We know so little about medieval Islamic designers and makers, but by employing an interdisciplinary approach that makes the most of a wide range of resources—textual, visual, material, and spatial—we can know more.

At the heart of this study is the dialogue between the intellectual, the visual, and the material in Iberia. Those who designed and crafted early Islamic arts rarely appear in medieval Islamic textual sources. The window the chronicle affords on Córdoban intellectual pursuits also offers a corrective view of the medieval world. The Islamic West has often been perceived as a passive recipient of Eastern trends, but in the chronicle we see that the Córdoban court was a place in which design and making were key aspects of scientific intellectual pursuits that had far-reaching influence. My aim is not to celebrate Ibn Firnas or even the Córdoba of his day, but to better understand his significance in the period and the categorical distinctions that have impeded that understanding.

Arts and Intellect

While today scholars tend to focus on our polymath's reputation as an early aviator, in the medieval period Ibn Firnas was renowned for the entire breadth of his skills and talents, especially in music and poetry. The intellectuals who had known him personally and those who lived shortly after him and who moved in Córdoba's court circles, and whose anecdotes the chronicler compiled, recalled Ibn Firnas as one of the towering intellectual figures of ninth-century al-Andalus and marveled at his mastery of both ancient and "modern" spheres of knowledge. The terms thath they used to refer to him include philosopher (*faylasufan*), astrologer (*munajjiman*), and the wise man (*al-hakimu*) of al-Andalus. Arabic-language biographers and littérateurs remarked on his superlative skills as a poet and musician, and they passed down lines of his poetry, generation after generation.[20] They celebrated his mastery of the "modern" Islamic areas of knowledge—especially Arabic grammar and prosody—as well as the "ancient" sciences that encompassed philosophy and the exact sciences. They tell us that Ibn Firnas introduced to the court new works on mathematics as well as poetry from the Islamic East, which suggests his participation in international intellectual networks.

Scholars have now firmly established that the exact sciences arose and flourished in response to the specific needs of the scientific movement early in the caliphal era, and they have firmly laid to rest the notion that there was a conflict or a divide between the rational or exact and the theological sciences in medieval Islamic societies.[21] The Islamic scientific revolution likely began during the Syrian Umayyad reign of the eighth century, and by the tenth century its currents had extended the practices of the rational, or exact, sciences to the scale of an international activity that was firmly ensconced in medieval Islamic institutions and supported in Islamic societies.[22] In his 2010 *Islam, Science, and the Challenge of History*, Ahmad Dallal sets out in broad strokes what he sees as a distinguishing feature of the early Islamic scientific revolution: "the tendency to correlate theoretical and practical knowledge and *to treat crafts as sciences*, thereby establishing a stable unity of theory and practice."[23] Dallal demonstrates by way of other early Islamic intellectuals how theoretical and practical knowledge intersected in the caliphal period across a number of scientific disciplines—astronomy, agronomy, mechanics, medicine, optics, and botany. He demonstrates that in each case scientific developments were rooted in exhaustive overviews and a synthesis of previous knowledge, combined with critical evaluation and transformation of that knowledge as practitioners applied new mathematical and other methods across fields, which itself resulted in the creation of entirely new scientific fields. His sources are the intellectual content of the treatises as well as the careers of the scholars themselves who were working within and across scientific, philosophical, and religious fields. Ibn Firnas's career in the Córdoban Umayyad court provides an additional illustrative case study of how intellectuals worked to achieve the unity of theory and practice that Dallal invokes as one of the signal contributions of the early Islamic scientific revolution. Besides sources such as the Córdoban chronicle, early philosophical and scientific treatises reveal this symbiotic relationship between craft and intellect.[24]

I have throughout this book called Ibn Firnas a scientist, even though the term is a nineteenth-century invention and thus anachronistic. In doing so, I have followed the example of modern scholars whose work has clarified the nature of the early and medieval Islamic contributions to the exact sciences.[25] In using "scientist" I am also referring to what Thomas Kuhn defined in his foundational book *The Structure of Scientific Revolutions* (1962) as someone who was concerned with understanding the world and extending the precision and scope with which it has been ordered.[26] This definition certainly applies to Ibn Firnas and the other Islamic intellectuals whose investigations, from at least the ninth century, forever changed mathematics, astronomy, geography, medicine, and other realms of scientific knowledge. Likewise, when I use the term "science" here I have Kuhn's definition in mind: facts, theories, and methods collected in current texts that include bodies of belief incompatible with those we hold today, but that were based upon past scientific achievements.[27] Sonja Brentjes and Robert Morrison have proposed a less loaded alternative—the Arabic term *'ilm* (pl. *'ulum*). As they note, *'ilm* was the term generally used in medieval Islamic societies to refer to exact sciences, such as mathematics and astronomy.[28] In comprehending Ibn Firnas's career and activities, the more expansive meanings encompassed by the term *'ilm* are perhaps more helpful to us than our contemporary notion of "science."

Chapter 1 attempts a character sketch of Ibn Firnas as recounted in the court chronicle's description of his career. Presented in the chronicle as the "Sage of al-Andalus," Ibn Firnas is intriguing as an early polymath who, in his own time and subsequent centuries, was viewed as an intellectual giant but also as someone who seems to have overstepped the boundaries of licit knowledge to venture into realms of sorcery and magic. It considers the informants whose words provide an unusually vivid portrait of this early Islamic intellectual. Attention to the identity and social status of the informants and the specific vocabulary they use to describe 'Abbas's activities and his place in the dynamic social setting of the court allows us to contextualize this medieval intellectual to an extent that is unusual, given how reticent the Arabic sources tend to be about figures other than religious scholars.[29]

Although reticent in comparison with accounts of later and better-documented times and places, the chronicle nonetheless allows us to catch a suggestive glimpse of the people and social currents to which the scientific objects and spaces of caliphal visual culture belonged. The possibility that scientists were also designers and makers of fine objects in the caliphal era is attested in the form of signed early precision scientific instruments and other types of objects and in surviving illustrated scientific treatises. It is attested as well in textual sources: annalistic literature like the court chronicle on which this study is based, as well as literary, philosophical, and other types of texts of the caliphal period. For example, the chronicle contextualizes Ibn Firnas's early rise within the court and the relationship between Ibn Firnas and his rival, providing an unusual perspective on the career trajectory of a designer-practitioner within a highly competitive circle of intellectuals. Competition, as George Saliba has argued, was a major factor driving the intellectual developments that we now think of as the Islamic scientific revolution.[30]

Chapter 2 discusses ʿAbbas Ibn Firnas as a designer and maker of the court's first early scientific instruments: an armillary sphere and a water clock made for the Córdoban Umayyad emirs. I examine the Arabic text in tandem with the earliest signed and dated instruments from al-Andalus and elsewhere, arguing that these exemplify the strong affinities between craft and intellect emphasized in the chronicle. In contrast to later premodern and early modern periods, when the evidence allows us to say more about the identities and careers of various artisans, we still know relatively little about those men (and, in some cases, women) who designed and crafted the early medieval objects and structures that we still admire today, nor do we know as much as we would like to about design and craft processes in the early Islamic contexts.[31] Two persistent tropes have inflected the way we understand design and designers in Islamic societies.[32] One holds that medieval Islamic society held a negative opinion of artistic practices, largely rooted in religious mores. The second holds that those who designed and crafted buildings and arts in the medieval Islamic lands were anonymous individuals operating at a remove from elite social and intellectual circles. The entwining of craft and intellect that I describe in the pages that follow challenges such assumptions. ʿAbbas Ibn Firnas and other medieval Islamic intellectuals were among the makers of early Islamic visual culture (though this does not mean that humbler, nonelite people did not or could not also shape that culture).

When we consider the Arabic texts alongside the earliest scientific objects, what emerges is a sense that, by the eleventh century, designing and making fine objects that unite art and science were not alien to an intellectual's work. In other words, it seems that there were times and places in the medieval Islamic past when making *was* thinking, and that this was acknowledged and appreciated by medieval authors of the historical sources. The setting of our polymath's life in Umayyad Córdoba, at least as remembered in al-Andalus's court chronicle, was one of those places and those times.[33] Thanks to Margaret Graves, who has established the centrality of craftsmanship to medieval Islamic intellectual culture, it seems clear now that Ibn Firnas was not an anomaly, nor was al-Andalus exceptional in producing such a figure.[34] We cannot say for sure whether the writings of Ibn Hayyan or his sources corresponded in any exact way to the realities of ninth-century Córdoba. However, by paying close attention to the way Ibn Hayyan and his sources chose to portray someone whom *they* clearly saw as a major intellectual and cultural figure in the Umayyad court, we can gain valuable perspective on the social significance of science and visual and material culture among the court intellectuals of al-Andalus, which historians today look back on as a high point in the history of those exact sciences of which Ibn Firnas was said to have been a master.[35] The account of his career may help to contextualize and nuance the way we understand the social standing and roles of intellectuals like Ibn Firnas in other times and places in the Islamic past, and the affinities between Islamic art, architecture, and the exact (and perhaps occult) sciences.[36]

Because this book is concerned with the identity and social standing of intellectuals engaged with the production of early Islamic art and visual culture, of particular interest is the relationship between designer, maker, and object (whether portable or at the scale of architecture) with an emphasis on the intellectual contexts that may have informed the process of design and making. Despite the progress that has been made in our field, this is still a daunting task, as the Arabic texts and surviving evidence, while suggestive, are also sparse, especially in comparison with the evidence available to scholars working on later times and places. While scholars of Leonardo, for instance, have volumes of his writings and numerous surviving sketches, paintings, and other works with which to work, those of us who carry out our investigations in the caliphal era have perhaps not been so fortunate in our evidence. There is some value in being pressed to make the best possible use of the material available, and in this case "material" is particularly literal.

Historians of Islamic art and historians of Islamic science and technology have long acknowledged the artistic importance of fine Islamic scientific instruments and illustrated manuscripts dealing with the exact sciences, and Michael Yonan has discussed the tensions between the practices of art history and material culture.[37] Objects of science have perhaps not generally been viewed as works of art in the broader discipline. Rather, objects of science have been relegated to the category of material culture. That attitude is changing, encouraged by preoccupations with interdisciplinarity, STEM, and the place of the humanities in today's academy. The 2020–2021 exhibition curated by Dr. Federica Gigante, "Precious and Rare: Islamic Metalwork from the Courtauld," for instance, exhibited some of the finest Islamic metalwork objects from the Courtauld's collection alongside the outstanding early Islamic instruments collection in Oxford's History of Science Museum, and one hopes that there will be further exhibitions that address long-standing intellectual taxonomies.[38] A central assertion underpinning this study is that the fine instruments and the diagrams and illustrations that appear in scientific manuscripts and treatises discussed in the following chapters were central to the visual and intellectual culture of al-Andalus and other premodern Islamic societies. Fine instruments and illustrated scientific treatises are as worthy of investigation in the history of Islamic art as canonical works that fit more easily into the traditional art historical frameworks, such as the Great Mosque of Córdoba or the celebrated Córdoban ivories. It might be useful here to remember that the field's traditional distinctions between the so-called high or fine arts of architecture, painting, and sculpture on the one hand and craft on the other do not necessarily apply in Islamic contexts.[39] As Graves has established, the medieval engagements between architecture and portable arts were close and complex, as craftsmen used objects as sites of engagement with architecture and painting, as well as poetry and other literary texts.[40] Moreover, as Marcus Milwright has pointed out, our contemporary notions of "art," "artist," and the distinction between "art" and "craft" are theoretical constructs that arose in later European contexts and did not pertain in medieval Islamic societies.[41]

In this book I use "visual culture" and "material culture" interchangeably. In speaking of "visual culture," I am referring to the social practices, contexts, and symbolic content of visual representations that could fall within the categories of art, architecture, and material culture.

By "material culture," I mean objects produced within a given culture, including technological as well as artistic artifacts. Material culture approaches are particularly useful in times and places for which scholars lack other types of evidence available for analysis.[42] By referring to "visual culture," I want to call attention to art history's formative Eurocentric hierarchies, which did not include objects of science within the disciplinary purview. It serves as a reminder that people in the medieval Islamic lands did not understand the objects they made, used, and viewed in accordance with art history's traditional values, hierarchies, and canons.[43]

Chapter 3 takes up the idea of elite residences as early Islamic spaces of scientific experiment and display, exploring a wondrous object that Ibn Firnas is said to have designed and constructed within a chamber of his own home. There has been some confusion about exactly what it was that Ibn Firnas created in his chamber. Fusing architectural space and scientific visualization, this creation astounded other intellectuals of the time by replicating lightning, thunder, and clouds. This meteorological chamber became a spectacle among intellectual circles and inspired a heated exchange between Ibn Firnas and a detractor, conducted in mocking, ribald poetry circulated within their circles and preserved in the chronicle. Moreover, the chronicle preserves contemporaneous poetry by other intellectuals that provides tantalizing glimpses of Firnas's creation. I argue that his creation is best understood as an early automaton, closely related to the better-known Eastern automata but also distinct from them. Moreover, the meteorological chamber offers an additional context for understanding the flight experiment that came later in his career. Ibn Firnas's replication of atmospheric phenomena suggests that the close observation and understanding of how such phenomena, especially patterns of weather and wind, may have informed the design, construction, and outcome of the aeronautics experiment.

Considering the Arabic texts along with early precision instruments reveals a role for court scientists or intellectuals as makers of medieval Islamic visual culture. We gain a fuller picture of the social significance of design and craft by investigating texts, objects, and spaces together, and bringing together these different categories of evidence highlights the limitations of relying on only one type of source. Indeed, it seems not only that elite social and intellectual status were commensurable in medieval Islamic societies, but also that in some cases elite social and intellectual status and technical, scientific, and craft knowledge and ability were united in one and the same person. These texts and surviving objects together thus help to fill a gap in our knowledge about the identities and personal circumstances of one fascinating (if small) subset of early Islamic makers.

Taken together, texts and scientific instruments and manuscripts complicate long-standing and persistent notions about medieval Islamic societies' ambivalent views of art and art making as reflected in early Arabic texts, including the Qur'an. While appreciation of the aesthetic qualities of objects and architecture is discernible, there were also negative attitudes toward the arts in early contexts, which arose in part from moral concerns of the early Muslim community toward luxury and figural representation.[44] Medieval authors convey a generally negative attitude toward those who produced works of visual and material culture as well, although this was an attitude that was prevalent in antiquity and not exclusive to Islamic society.[45]

By contrast, ʿAbbas Ibn Firnas and the makers of the instruments I will discuss in the pages that follow show that we can and should make a place within Islamic art history for scientists and other intellectuals who were deeply engaged in creating early Islamic visual culture. I have approached the topic in way that is sympathetic to studies that seek to broaden the understanding of medieval art making to include those who have long been all but absent in traditional narratives of art making. In arguing for the need to reassess the roles of women in the production of medieval art and architecture, Therese Martin has argued that the term "maker" allows us to move beyond restrictive later notions surrounding the anachronistic term "artist," which often has encouraged neglect of the multiple actors involved in making medieval art and architecture.[46] Martin's point applies, I believe, equally to premodern "scientists" as it does to medieval women, and I have therefore used the term in the pages that follow.

Chapter 4 analyzes the earliest account of the flight experiment, comparing it with the seventeenth-century account and its nineteenth-century translation. I argue that the chronicle provides the earliest and most important historical evidence for this medieval milestone in the history of human flight, and that it contains key details, missing from or unclear in the later versions, that may clarify the nature of the experiment. Aviation experiments comparable to the one Ibn Firnas carried out in Córdoba were not, to my knowledge, conducted elsewhere in the Islamic territories, in Byzantium, or Eurasia until centuries later. Nor do court intellectuals elsewhere seem to have been designing spaces of scientific visualization comparable to the meteorological chamber he is said to have created in his own residence.

I first mentioned Ibn Firnas and his aeronautics experiment in my first book, as a noteworthy example of the range of court activities that took place in the *munyas*, or villas of Umayyad Córdoba.[47] To my knowledge no one has yet fully considered the topographical landscape dimensions or the court settings as factors in Ibn Firnas's famed flight experiment. Chapter 4 therefore also explores the significance of Rusafa, the Córdoban royal *munya* that the Arabic accounts mention in relation to the experiment. I propose that the specific topographical and other natural features of the landscape in which Rusafa was situated may have initially inspired the experiment and contributed to its success. The villa and its landscape setting offer an architectural, material, and social context for Ibn Firnas's activities, which can be understood in terms of the spatialization, as well as the visualization, of science in a medieval Islamic court. Besides discussing makers, making, and precision instruments as works of visual culture, here I explore how architecture played a role in the practice of early science, considering the connection between elite residences and science in the Córdoban Umayyad court.[48] Space and place, along with social and religious contexts, combined to create the atmosphere in which the exact sciences and art flourished in close dialogue.

Throughout, I have tried to situate ʿAbbas Ibn Firnas in the broader intellectual and artistic currents of his time.[49] Expanding our focus beyond Córdoba reveals a key role that science and technology played in the visual, architectural, and urban expression of power, which emerges as a common theme in early Islamic courts and intellectual culture.[50] This provides a broader background and context for understanding later times and places that have fared better in terms of surviving visual and material evidence.

The caliphal union of science and art did not remain confined within the Islamic courts or even the empire's boundaries but spread beyond the Islamic lands, to be appropriated and adapted in other times and places. The epilogue briefly considers the reception of medieval Islamic scientific instruments in Renaissance Florence, proposing that, by the sixteenth century, designers, artists, and patrons in Italy were aware of medieval Islamic astrolabes and other works of science in part because of these objects' connections to what, by the thirteenth century, was an influential caliphal culture of craft and intellect. I propose that these early modern European encounters and experimentation with Islamic science and visual culture may have informed the artistic culture of the Italian Renaissance, and perhaps the European Scientific Revolution.

Ibn Firnas's career suggests that the Córdoban court did not simply receive new knowledge from Baghdad and the Islamic East: it was a vibrant center of intellectual innovation in its own right by the eleventh century. My study counters the long-standing center–periphery model that casts Córdoba in the role of passive recipient of innovations from the East. Ibn Firnas and the works of art and science that I discuss in this book show that innovation occurred early and continued to flourish in this Western "frontier" capital, and that these innovations resounded for many centuries after, and far beyond the boundaries of Iberia. Ibn Firnas shows us nothing less than a medieval Islamic culture of craft and intellect that was fully established by the Mongol invasions of the thirteenth century, and that may have shaped the arts of Renaissance and early modern Europe in ways we have not yet fully appreciated.

1

The Sage of al-Andalus

Who was ʿAbbas Ibn Firnas? Early Arabic accounts of his life and career portray him as one of the most famous intellectuals of ninth-century al-Andalus. These texts sketch a picture of a man who comes across as both larger than life and all too human. In this chapter I examine the accounts on which our knowledge of Ibn Firnas is based and try to help the reader understand how he has been remembered over the centuries. I address how and what we might learn from these, even when they are fragmented, written long after his death, or clearly not "objective." With a focus on the earliest accounts compiled in Ibn Hayyan's Córdoban history, and comparing one account with another, I consider what they say about this colorful character's background and identity, and his reputation as a polymath whose knowledge of both ancient sciences as well as "modern" ones valued by ninth-century learned elites in Islamic societies was viewed as second to none by those who knew him. I consider different perspectives and possible motivations for the accounts, including a certain nostalgia for a perceived Córdoban Umayyad "golden age" that had been destroyed. I show how what might be seen as a departure from truth telling can be nonetheless instructive about ʿAbbas Ibn Firnas and about the world in which he lived.

Remembering a Ninth-Century Polymath

The earliest and most substantive source for the career of Ibn Firnas is the section of the *Muqtabas* (or *al-Muqtabis*), which is the chronicle compiled by the eleventh-century Córdoban court historian Ibn Hayyan (d. 1076). The manuscript containing this section of the chronicle has been aptly described by Manuela Marín as the "Maltese Falcon" of Andalusi studies due to its rarity, its value as a historical document, and the story of its modern disappearance and subsequent rediscovery.[1]

The unique Arabic manuscript is an incomplete copy of the annals of the Córdoban emirs al-Hakam I and ʿAbd al-Rahman II, covering the period between 796 and 847.[2] Now preserved in the Real Academia de la Historia in Madrid, the manuscript first came to the attention of European scholars in the early twentieth century, when it was identified by the Arabist Evariste Lévi-Provencal (d. 1956) in the library of the Qarawiyyin Mosque in Fes in the 1930s.[3] Lévi-Provencal and his fellow Arabist Emilio García Gómez (d. 1995) published translations extracted from the manuscript in the 1950s and were working on a critical edition of the text,

A Bridge to the Sky. Glaire D. Anderson, Oxford University Press. © Oxford University Press 2024.
DOI: 10.1093/oso/9780190913243.003.0002

which never materialized. Following the death of these two scholars, the manuscript disappeared until Joaquín Vallvé Bermejo published it in facsimile in 1999.[4] This facsimile edition was followed by a critical Spanish translation by Federico Corriente in 2001 and a critical Arabic edition by Mahmud Makki in 2003.[5]

The manuscript is not securely dated, as its beginning and ending folios are missing (it begins at folio 88r and ends on 188v). Nevertheless, the Kufic calligraphy and its overall appearance are generally in keeping with other medieval manuscripts from the Islamic West.[6] While the question would benefit from further research, it is possible that the Madrid manuscript was created around the fourteenth century, as it resembles other fourteenth-century manuscripts from the Maghrib.[7]

Until the rediscovery of this manuscript, historians had to rely on abbreviated accounts of ʿAbbas Ibn Firnas, which were composed by later medieval and early modern authors. For example, in the twelfth century, the Andalusi scholar al-Dabbi (d. 599/1203) included an entry about Ibn Firnas in his biographical dictionary of Andalusi scholars.[8] Until the discovery and publication of Ibn Hayyan's lost volume of the Córdoban chronicle, historians relied on the abbreviated accounts that were compiled or composed in later centuries. The most influential biography of Ibn Firnas was penned in the seventeenth century by the Maghribi intellectual Ahmad ibn Muhammad al-Maqqari (d. ca. 1632), who wrote an important history of Islamic Spain based on earlier sources, many of which are now lost. The work was edited and published by the great nineteenth-century orientalist scholar Reinhart Dozy.[9] In a section devoted to the inhabitants of al-Andalus as intellectuals, al-Maqqari begins his account with ʿAbbas Ibn Firnas and emphasizes the polymath's elevated reputation as an intellectual known for significant contributions to more than one realm of inquiry, namely, poetry, design and manufacturing, and music. He writes:

> Among their accounts about intelligence and scientific deduction and discovery, writers mention that Abu al-Qasim ʿAbbas b. Firnas, the philosopher of Andalus, was the first in Andalus to discover how to manufacture glass from stones, the first there to introduce al-Khalil's [al-Khalil b. Ahmad al-Farahidi] book of prosody, and the first to introduce music. He made the device known as the *minqal* to tell time without plans and model.[10]

I will have more to say in the pages that follow about these intriguing and somewhat opaque references to Ibn Firnas's activities in the realms of glass manufacturing, music, and the time-keeping device. For now I'd like to call attention to the way al-Maqqari brings in al-Khalil b. Ahmad al-Farahidi, or al-Khalil for short. This notable figure flourished in the middle of the eighth century and is one of the most important early Arabic philologists, known for, among other things, his important work on poetic meter.[11] His treatise on this topic, the *Kitab al-ʿAruḍ*, is known through the work of later authors such as the Córdoban poet Ibn ʿAbd Rabbih

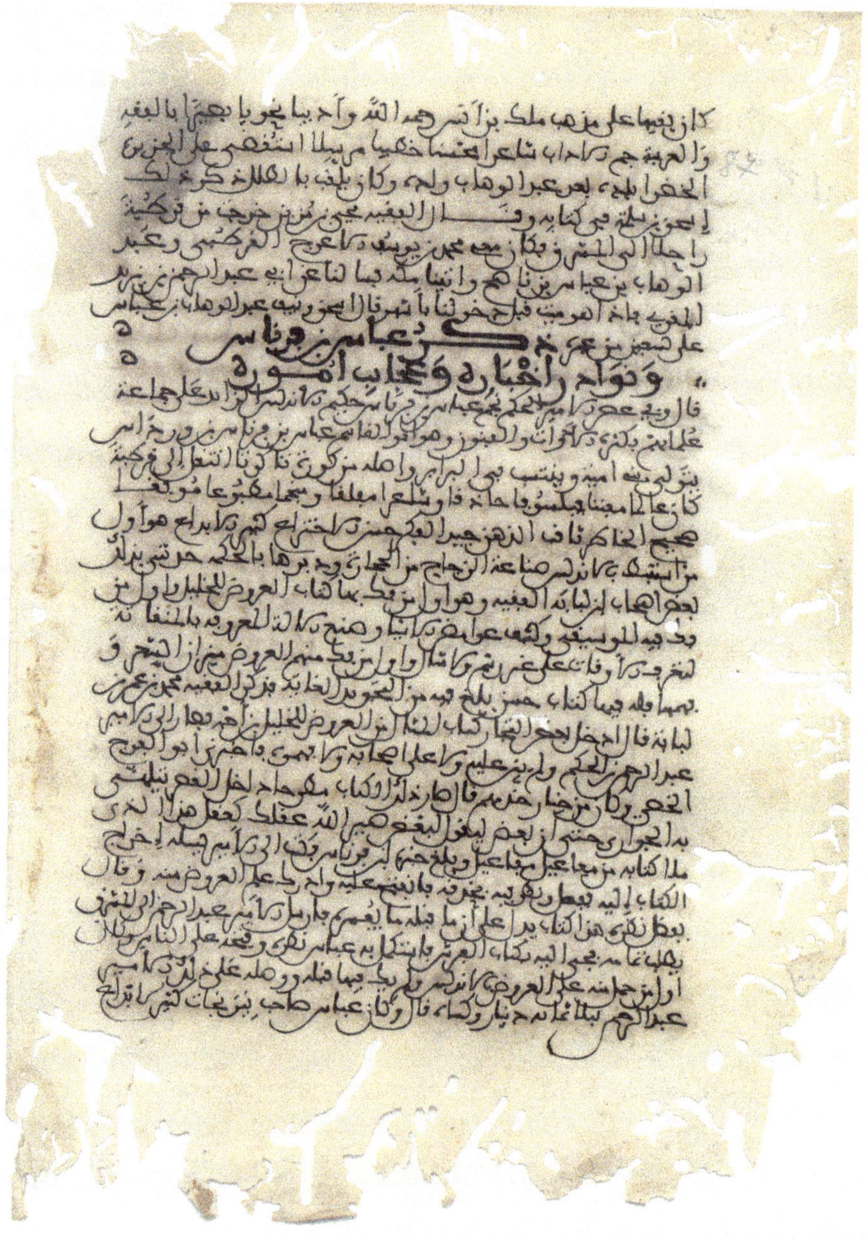

Figure 1.1. From the long-lost volume of Ibn Hayyan's Córdoban court chronicle, the oldest and most substantive historical source on Ibn Firnas's career. The section begins with the heading "Mention of 'Abbas b. Firnas, his noteworthy travels, & admirable deeds." Folio 130v, *Anales de los Emires de Córdoba Alhaquém I (180–206 H. / 796–822 J.C.) y Abderramán II (206–232 / 822–847)*. Photo, © Real Academia de la Historia.

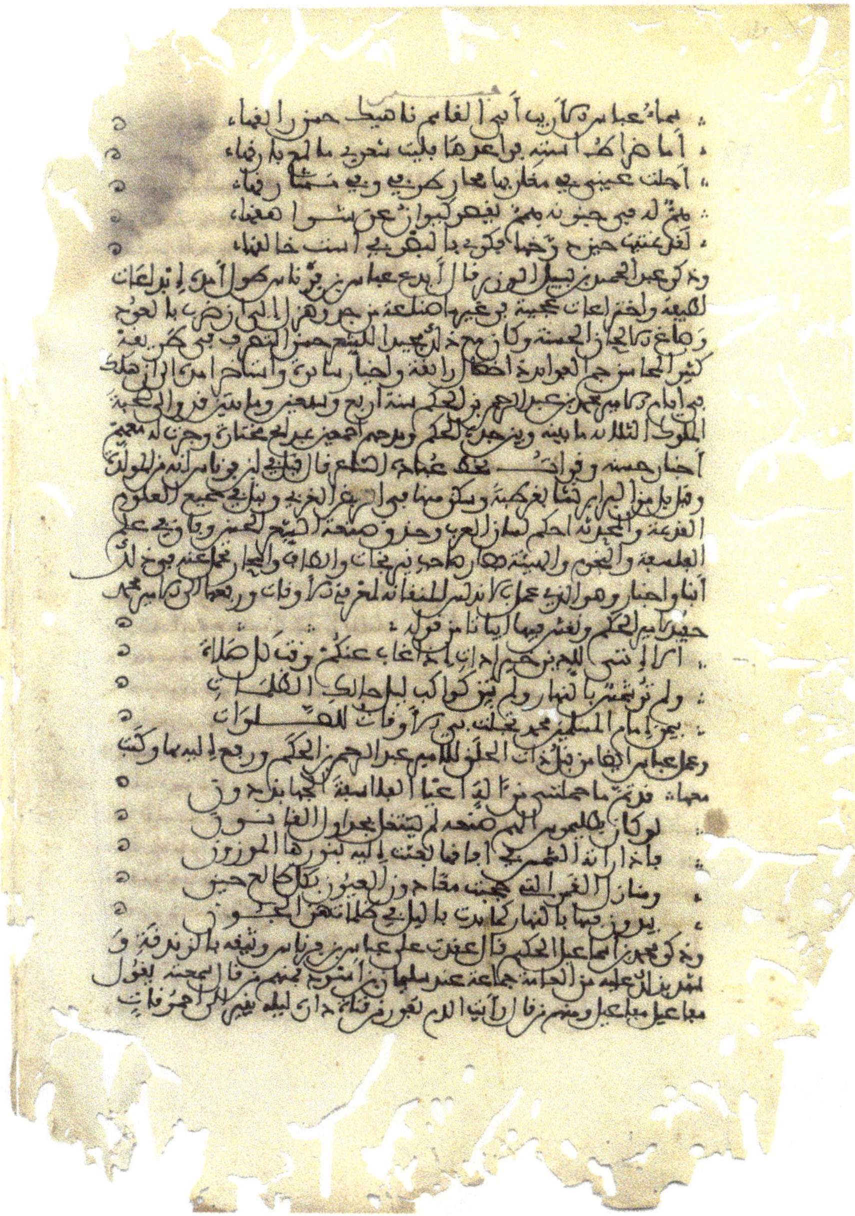

Figure 1.2. The passages on ʿAbbas Ibn Firnas's background and skills. Folio 131v, *Anales de los Emires de Córdoba Alhaquém I (180–206 H. / 796–822 J.C.) y Abderramán II (206–232 / 822–847)*. Photo, © Real Academia de la Historia.

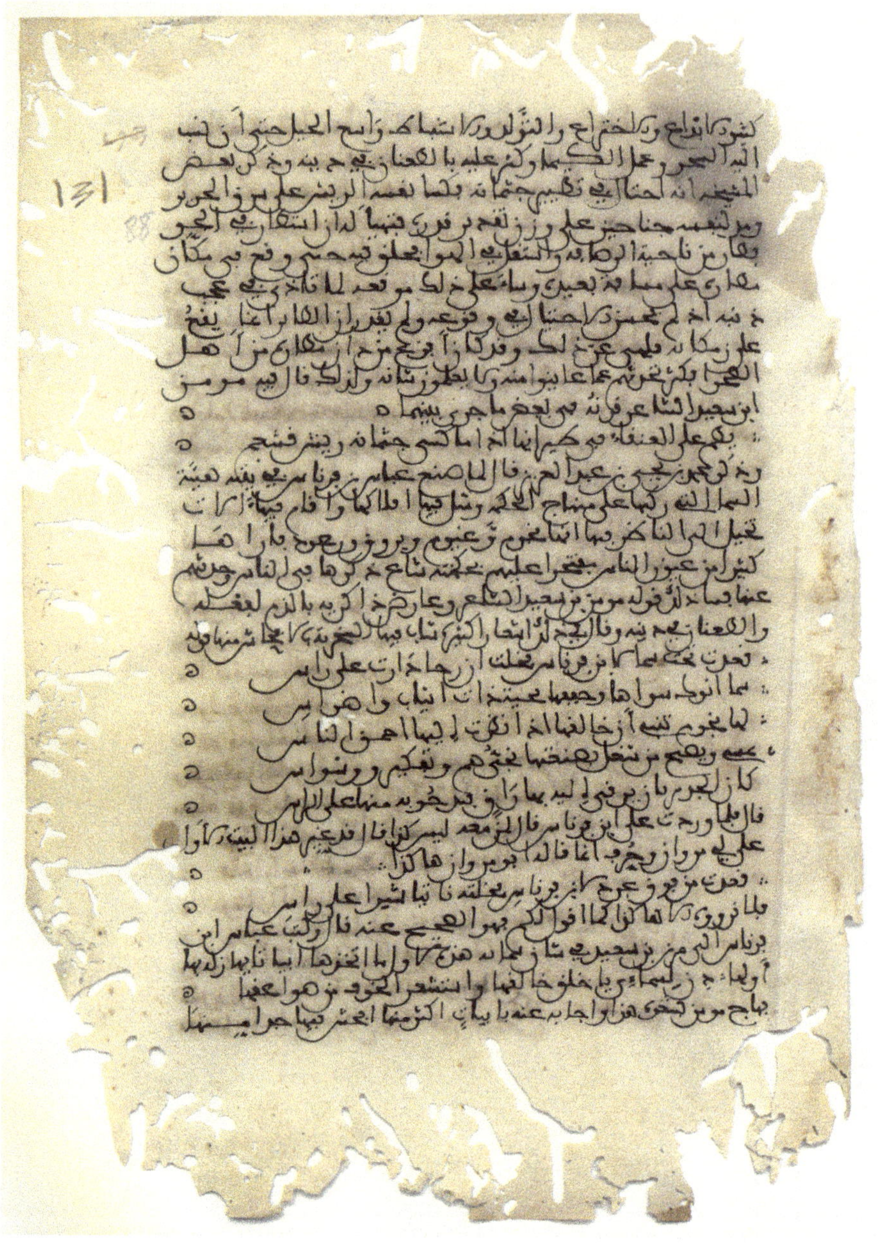

Figure 1.3. The folio with passages recounting Ibn Firnas's aeronautics experiment. It is the oldest historical document attesting to this medieval milestone in the history of human flight. Folio 131r, *Anales de los Emires de Córdoba Alhaquém I (180–206 H. / 796–822 J.C.) y Abderramán II (206–232 / 822–847)*. Photo, © Real Academia de la Historia.

(860–940), who includes a chapter on metrics in his famous *adab* compilation, the *ʿIḳd al-farid* (*The Unique Necklace*).[12] In alluding to this important Arabic literary figure, this passage contains one of the themes that is discernible in the medieval texts in relation to ʿAbbas Ibn Firnas, namely, his significance as an intellectual who transferred knowledge from the Eastern Islamic lands to al-Andalus.

At the height of the nineteenth-century Anglo-European fascination with Spain and a romanticized "Moorish" past,[13] the Spanish Arabist and diplomat Pascual de Gayangos prepared an abridged English version of al-Maqqari's text as part of his *History of the Mohammedan Dynasties in Spain*, which has remained popular and influential since its publication in 1840–43.[14] Gayangos's version has a distinctively nineteenth-century Victorian flavor in keeping with the tastes and conventions of his Anglophone audience, which makes his work distinct from the original history composed by al-Maqqari for his audience of seventeenth-century Islamic intellectuals.[15] This is Gayangos's version of al-Maqqari's passage:

> The aptitude of the Andalusians for all sorts of sciences will be likewise acknowledged by every reader conversant with their history and literature . . . we deem it in place to mention, in a few words, those illustrious men to whose labors, talents, or perspicuity, the sciences are indebted for their advance, and who are placed by their countrymen at the head of their respective faculties. Abu-l-ʾAbbas Kasim Ibn Firnas's [sic], the physician was the first who made glass out of clay, and who established fabrics of it in Andalus.[16]

Gayangos translated *al-hakim* as "the physician," which reflects the specifically medical association that the term came to hold in later Eastern Islamic contexts, but which did not pertain in early Islamic Iberia.[17] For Ibn Hayyan and Andalusi intellectuals, *hakim* was the word used to refer to intellectuals who were expert in the "modern" sciences of Arabic grammar and theology as well as the "sciences of the ancients," which, for early Islamic intellectuals, encompassed the natural sciences and philosophy.[18] Elsewhere in the chronicle, for example, Ibn Hayyan notes that the prominent Córdoban theologian, grammarian, and mathematician Muhammad Ibn Ismaʾil al-Nahwi (d. 943), tutor to the learned caliph al-Hakam II, was called "the sage (*al-hakim*) of Cordoba."

In any case, Gayangos goes on to say that ʿAbbas Ibn Firnas

> passes also as the first man who introduced into that country the famous treatise on prosody by Khalil, and who taught the science of music. He invented an instrument called *al-minkalah* [sic], by means of which time was marked in music without having recourse to notes or figures.[19]

Both Gayangos and al-Maqqari go on to briefly discuss other highlights from ʿAbbas Ibn Firnas's career, about which we will have more to say in the chapters that follow. What is important to note here is that the Córdoban polymath's reputation as a leading Andalusi intellectual, particularly known for technological innovation, as well as for his contributions to fields more commonly associated with early Islamic intellectuals such as grammar and poetry, persisted into the early modern era.

The Informants

Despite the clear emphasis al-Maqqari and Gayangos, in the seventeenth and nineteenth centuries, placed on 'Abbas Ibn Firnas as an intellectual of early Islamic al-Andalus, both treatments of him are brief. Writing in the eleventh century and drawing on tenth-century sources, Ibn Hayyan provides a much fuller portrait of Ibn Firnas in the section preserved in the Madrid manuscript. At least twelve full manuscript pages are devoted to 'Abbas Ibn Firnas, divided across the various volumes of the *Muqtabis*.[20] Indeed, the attention that the chronicler devotes to the polymath compares favorably with his treatment of Ziryab (d. 852), perhaps the most famous musician in the history of Islamic civilization, who was a contemporary of 'Abbas Ibn Firnas and, like him, a boon companion (*nadim*) of the emir and something of a celebrity in Córdoban court society.[21] Boon companions were an important feature of the courts and the institution known as the *majlis* (pl. *majalis*), gatherings that served as a major social and cultural institution of caliphal society.[22] The companions recruited to join these elite social circles were chosen by the host for their desirable social attributes, which encompassed wide-ranging intellectual horizons, refinement, and skill at music and poetic recitation.

Ibn Hayyan clearly identifies the sources on which he relied to compile his history of the Córdoban Umayyad dynasty. These sources are the works of earlier authors from which he quoted in compiling his chronicle. Often when he introduces direct quotations, he notes that he saw the author's words "written in his own hand, which suggests that he was working directly from manuscripts preserved in his own or other celebrated libraries of al-Andalus." It is worth emphasizing that Ibn Hayyan's sources came from the ranks of the learned class, scholars of the religious sciences (*'ulama)* as well as poets and others who operated within the court sphere. An open question, which is beyond the scope of my interests and that I leave to literary scholars to address, is the extent to which we can consider Ibn Firnas a creation of such poets. Two scholars on whose authority Ibn Hayyan transmits anecdotes about 'Abbas Ibn Firnas are the *faqih* Muhammad Ibn 'Umar Ibn Lubabah (d. 942) and the aforementioned "sage of Cordoba" Muhammad Ibn Isma'il al-Nahwhi, who had been a companion of 'Abbas Ibn Firnas before his later appointment as tutor to al-Hakam II.

The court sources include 'Abdalhamid Ibn Basil, who is identified as a vizier; Abu al-Faraj, identified as a prominent court eunuch; and the tenth-century Umayyad court historian 'Isa b. Ahmad al-Razi. In medieval Islamic courts, poets were expected to have a large stock of entertaining stories and anecdotes to share, so given Ibn Firnas's colorful personality it is not surprising that many of Ibn Hayyan's sources are identified as poets. These include the following: 'Ubada, Muhammad Ibn 'Abd al-Malik Ibn Ayman, 'Ubadah Ibn Ma' al-Sama, Muhammad Ibn 'Utbah al-Shaffaq, Ishaq Ibn Salama (on the authority of one Ahmad Ibn 'Abdallah al-Habibi), and Muhammad IbnYahya Ibn 'Abd al-'Aziz, as well as 'Abbas Ibn Firnas's rival, Mumin Ibn Sa'id, about whom I will say more later. While acknowledging the earlier authors on whom Ibn Hayyan drew in presenting his portrait of Ibn Firnas, we probably cannot assume that this is an objective account of our protagonist's life and times as related by these multiple voices. It may be, but as Hämeen-Anttila has observed about Arabic literary anecdotes of the eighth through the tenth centuries, a multilayered early Arabic account such as Ibn Hayyan's chronicle is "not necessarily polyphonic, . . . speaking in a variety of tongues" but most likely represents the final voice of the compiler, who has chosen and shaped the words of his predecessors.[23] I suspect that that is what is happening here—Ibn Hayyan has carefully chosen and shaped the words of his predecessors regarding Ibn Firnas.

A point that requires consideration is the issue of literary genres within which the Córdoban court chronicle should be understood. If we don't take the anecdotes compiled and presented in this context by Ibn Hayyan at face value as "objective" historical accounts of Ibn Firnas, then how are we to understand them? Should we, rather, approach them as literary constructions meant to entertain, amuse, and instruct an eleventh-century Andalusi audience?[24] These anecdotes probably should not be understood as factual, "eyewitness" historical accounts, as the laudatory tone of the chronicle seems common in medieval Arabic biographies of intellectuals. I will leave it to others to speak to this issue and the significance of the laudatory tone. For my purposes, I have pointed out the identity of Ibn Hayyan's informants to emphasize their roles as prominent Córdoban religious elites, intellectuals, and court administrators. In other words, these were not anonymous informants, or sources with little credibility on matters to do with the court and its intellectual circles. Rather, they were leading figures in Córdoban society who either knew Ibn Firnas personally or who would have known those who had. Despite the eleventh-century date of Ibn Hayyan's compilation, the sources that he drew together to shape his portrait of Ibn Firnas are quite early. This is not to say, however, that they are transparent and objective sources. To learn from them and from the chronicle as a whole, we read in relation to context, in relation to other texts and other kinds of evidence, but to do so thoroughly is beyond the scope of this study.

Historical writing in the Arabic tradition certainly drew on or incorporated elements from *adab*, which were indeed meant to entertain and instruct. Ibn Hayyan's own eleventh-century context must be kept in mind as we try to understand the portrait of Ibn Firnas that he constructed. Ibn Hayyan was writing from a perspective shaped by the still-fresh memories of the social and political turbulence of the period leading up to the *fitna* that marked a dramatic end to the earlier ninth and tenth centuries of Córdoban Umayyad rule, which by his time was viewed through a nostalgic lens, taking on an almost mythic character that was further elaborated in subsequent centuries until it became a veritable golden age.[25] He crafted the Córdoban court chronicle having lived through the sack and destruction of some of the city's most notable monuments: Madinat al-Zahra' and royal villas such as Rusafa, and other traumatic incidents that marked the civil unrest (*fitna*) in the eleventh century and its devastating consequences for the celebrated urban, intellectual, and social fabrics of the city. His historical moment and the dissolution of Córdoban Umayyad political power and the subsequent cultural diaspora of its intellectuals, the rise of communities of intellectuals in the *taifa* courts and the burgeoning of the exact sciences, and the advances in precision instrumentation are all part of the backdrop that informed Ibn Hayyan's view of the Umayyad past, and hence his view of Ibn Firnas.

A Portrait

Ingenious, inventive, creative, original, resourceful, unorthodox, and possessed of a sense of humor that was at times bawdy and sarcastic and wielded as a weapon against rivals, the personality of 'Abbas Ibn Firnas that emerges from the voices preserved in the Córdoban chronicle is a vibrant one indeed. Ibn Hayyan and his informants describe him as a man who was handsome, much admired, and someone who was the subject of anecdotes and gossip during his lifetime and for many generations after. According to the chronicler, the poet 'Ubada wrote this of 'Abbas Ibn Firnas:

> He excelled in all the sciences, ancient and modern (*al-'ulumi al-qadimati wa-l-muhdathati*). He dominated Arabic and was adept at making good poetry, excelling as well in philosophy, astronomy, and astrology; he also knew enchantments, occult powers, and magic (*ṣahiba nayranjatin wa-alṭafin wa-asharin*). About this stories and anecdotes are told.[26]

Ibn Hayyan himself calls our polymath no less than "the sage of al-Andalus" (*al-hakim*), while his tenth-century predecessor, the court historian 'Isa b. Ahmad al-Razi, judged 'Abbas Ibn Firnas to be "exemplary in his skill and mastery of every field of instruction, new and old."

What do we know about the fields to which these early Iberian intellectuals are referring?[27] In ninth-century Islamic intellectual and religious circles, the "modern sciences" encompassed those matters related to religion and to the study of Arabic, above all poetry and prosody. The fields of knowledge with which early Islamic intellectuals of the Abbasid period (roughly mid-eighth to mid-thirteenth centuries), the "classical" moment of Islamic civilization that forms the broader context for Ibn Firnas and his peers in Córdoba, would have been educated from childhood included Arabic grammar, history, poetry, theology, and law. By the time

'Abbas Ibn Firnas began his career in the Córdoban court, scholars had developed a rigorous system of grammar that allowed for the systematic analysis of the Qur'an and the Arabic language.[28]

Among medieval intellectuals 'Abbas Ibn Firnas seems to have been particularly known for his poetry, which may also explain why so many of the sources of anecdotes about him were composed by other poets or literary figures.[29] Later authors—among them such luminaries as the Córdoban court poet Ibn 'Abd Rabbih (d. 940); the Eastern connoisseur and literary critic al-T̲h̲a'alibi (d. 1038); the Murcian scholar al-Ḍabbi (d. 1203), author of an important biographical dictionary of Andalusi intellectuals; and the Maghribi historian Ibn 'Id̲h̲ari (fl. 1312)—preserved and transmitted fragments of Ibn Firnas's compositions.[30] An anecdote preserved by the Córdoban court intellectual al-Zubaydi (d. 989) underscores 'Abbas Ibn Firnas's long-lived reputation as musician and poet extempore. Said to have taken place in the final years of the reign of 'Abd al-Rahman II, the anecdote has him outdo the famous Ziryab's son (and musical successor) at a reception hosted by one Mahmud Ibn Abi Jamil, a wealthy provincial governor of Sidonia:

> When [the son of Ziryab] had finally finished, 'Abbas Ibn Firnas took the lute in his hands and sang the song once more, finishing it off with two improvised verses in praise of Mahmud [the host of the reception] which said:
> In Mahmud I have strengthened my hand, which was defenceless,
> In a time that was barren of hope.
> For generosity and glory he has built a pavilion (*qubba*, or alternatively *al-qibla*)
> Before which the most generous men are left prostrate.[31]

His ability to not only perform the same song, but also to add to it two additional verses, was so well received by the company that the admiring host made a gift to 'Abbas Ibn Firnas of the pavilion, completion of which the feast and reception were meant to celebrate, and on which he is said to have spent the sum of 500 dirhams.[32] This was not an insignificant sum; in Umayyad al-Andalus a worker earned 1–1.5 dirhams per day. Other fragments of his poetry preserved by later biographers illustrate his handling of popular poetic genres of the time, including those devoted to flowers, gardens, and romance, and that were part and parcel of the villa culture of the Umayyad court:

> The roses appear in the garden with the daisies,
> Like the red lips of a smiling mouth.[33]

And

> She is beautiful like a houri: there is no escape from her love
> For the eyes that look upon her,

> Though the happiness that it offers is a lie sweeter than the truth.
> In her cheeks shines a perennial sun of beauty
> And a full moon that never wanes.
> Life consists only in killing absence and loneliness,
> In the company of a beauty who ceaselessly grants us her love.[34]

Besides composing the floral and romantic poetry favored in court intellectual circles of the ninth century, 'Abbas Ibn Firnas also wrote verses declaiming the military undertakings of his royal patron, in keeping with the role of court poets as the medieval equivalent of publicity or advertising figures; these verses are likewise preserved in the chronicle.[35]

The newly discovered volume of Ibn Hayyan's chronicle augments our knowledge of how 'Abbas Ibn Firnas' contemporaries and later Arabic authors remembered the polymath. As mentioned in the chronicle, according to the poet 'Ubada, 'Abbas Ibn Firnas "dominated Arabic and was adept at making good poetry." Likewise, the vizier 'Abdalhamid Ibn Basil noted that he "dominated poetry and developed well in its paths," while Ibn Hayyan describes him as a brilliant poet, and the first in al-Andalus to explain the contents of what seems to have been a proverbially difficult treatise on poetry, al-Khalil's *al-Mital min -al-'arid* (*Model of Meter*). Ibn Hayyan also notes that 'Abbas Ibn Firnas was the first to study and understand the *Kitab al-Furush*, which presumably was another work on grammar/prosody, and to explain its significance to his contemporaries, which earned him 300 dinars and a present of clothing from the emir himself. In fact, it was his skill with prosody, according to the tenth-century Córdoban Umayyad court historian 'Isa b. Ahmad al-Razi, that provided a path into the ruler's inner circle:

> Prosody was the means [of his influence] with the emir 'Abd al-Rahman. He broke into his circles, and in this, his flattery [of the emir] helped him more than a little. . . . He was given an allowance so that, in praising ['Abd al-Rahman] and giving him reason to pause, he recited his choice poetry for the emir . . . [who] admired this poetry of his.

The chronicle also makes clear that 'Abbas Ibn Firnas was much admired for his abilities as a musician as well as a poet and that his reputation in these two realms was great. Thus, the vizier 'Abdalhamid Ibn Basil noted that 'Abbas Ibn Firnas played the 'ud and composed beautiful melodies. Terés had observed that 'Abbas Ibn Firnas's skill as a musician and a poet must have been formidable indeed, given how much the Arabic texts emphasize it. This impression is compounded by the new information provided in the chronicle. An anecdote found in it sheds light on 'Abbas Ibn Firnas's initial entry into the emir's inner circle, an anecdote that indicates that the most famous musician in the whole of Islamic civilization, Ziryab, not only was our polymath's contemporary and colleague in the court but also played a role in

'Abbas Ibn Firnas's big break into the ruler's inner circle by performing one of his compositions. The anecdote, which Ibn Hayyan attributes to al-Razi, states:

> Ziryab sang ['Abbas Ibn Firnas' verses] to ['Abd al-Rahman II] in a voice that delighted him. [The emir] then . . . had ['Abbas Ibn Firnas] admitted to his circle. He gave him the allowance due to boon companions and he became one of his intimates].

Moreover, Ibn Hayyan preserves the verses of the *qasida* that had provided Ibn Firnas with his big break, yielding additional examples of his poetic oeuvre, such as:

> The creature of the Merciful has reached the point where he has settled down,
> Granted sustenance by the generosity of the Servant of the Compassionate
> He is the one for whom it is difficult to ever imagine,
> In regards to glorious deeds, as having been surpassed,
> His heavens pour silver, when
> The sundered sky has been mended
> O, heir to justice after four,
> Who proved to be true to the religion of right guidance,
> The chosen one, the one who sealed prophecy, the second
> Of two, was a righteous man,
> As were the two 'Umars, who together won [a reward in paradise]
> And thus were called a good [caliph] and a savior.[36]

Ibn Hayyan adds to our portrait a more nuanced sense of 'Abbas Ibn Firnas's early years in the court, and the personal and professional difficulties he may have had to overcome in its competitive atmosphere. There are hints in the chronicle that 'Abbas Ibn Firnas's entry into the ruler's inner circle was neither as smooth nor as inevitable as his later elevated reputation might lead us to assume. According to 'Isa ibn Ahmad al-Razi, he was seen at first as having got in because of his ability to flatter the emir and was not at first accepted as a peer by the other court intellectuals: "['Abbas Ibn Firnas broke into ['Abd al-Rahman II's] circles, and in this, his flattery [of the emir] helped him more than a little. His acceptance by us came later." What al-Razi doesn't explain is why the other court intellectuals did not immediately accept as an equal someone for whom they later came to have such a high regard. Here is where the chronicle suggests some possibilities. For instance, might we speculate that his perceived Berber identity posed a social hurdle for 'Abbas Ibn Firnas? The possibility that he was of Berber origins was apparently still a subject of speculation by the eleventh century, according to Ibn Hayyan. Another anecdote suggests that, besides the problem of a perceived Berber ethnicity, a humble economic situation might have been a stumbling block for the ambitious newcomer in the ninth-century court.

What is it that gives us a sense that ʿAbbas Ibn Firnas suffered from financial difficulties? The vizier ʿAbdalhamid Ibn Basil after all notes that the polymath was "a person of many merits and enormous advantage [and] splendid qualities," while the poet ʿUbada remarked that he lived in Córdoba's western suburb, which by the tenth century was the desirable address among the city's wealthy and refined. Yet this anecdote is one Ibn Hayyan relates on the authority of ʿUbadah Ibn Ma' al-Sama', who in turn had received the anecdote from a ninety-year-old sheikh, one Muhammad Ibn ʿUtbah al-Shaffaq, who had been a contemporary of ʿAbbas Ibn Firnas and a friend of his great rival, the court poet Mu'min Ibn Saʿid. The story is meant to explain the origins of the enmity between Mu'min and ʿAbbas Ibn Firnas, an enmity that manifested itself in poetry against the meteorological chamber and the aviation experiment, and about which I will say more in the following chapters.

The anecdote portrays ʿAbbas Ibn Firnas riding an emaciated mule, "more emaciated than any other," during a customary visit to his then-friend Mu'min.[37] After the visit, as ʿAbbas Ibn Firnas is riding away on his mount, the mule apparently stumbled, leading Mu'min to clap his hands and to laughingly ask, "Do you know why your mule stumbled, Abu al-Qasim?" (this being another name by which ʿAbbas Ibn Firnas was known). When the latter responded that he didn't know, Mu'min is said to have held up a piece of straw or a bit of clay and to have delivered the punch line, "By God, this is what it stumbled on. It wore itself out on it. Take the mule for food or sell it." ʿAbbas did not appreciate the joke; he is said to have

> fumed and grown very angry toward Mu'min. . . . He told him, "Mu'min, you catamite! Is this now how you think of me? Do you bring me down to the level of someone who is ridiculed? Surely, you know the consequence of this." He turned away from him in anger. He then began from that day on to satirize him. The ill will spread between them. They did not reconcile until the end of their lives. Some of the most obscene satirical verse composed by ʿAbbas [about Mu'min, included] "You would think the impression of hard penises in Mu'min's kind/ Is like the impressions of an egg in sifted ashes."

Besides alerting the reader that ʿAbbas Ibn Firnas could not afford a better mount, and providing an interesting context for the later poetic attacks that these two waged against one another, the story suggests that Ibn Hayyan and perhaps ʿAbbas Ibn Firnas's own contemporaries saw him as self-conscious about his limited means, as possessed of a personality that could not suffer a perceived insult, and as one who was vengeful enough to use his celebrated skills as a poet to turn against a friend because of the hurt to his pride.

In the same section of the chronicle, Ibn Hayyan includes another story in a similar vein. This story has one Ahmad Ibn Abdallah al-Habibi, on the authority of Ishaq Ibn Salama, relating how ʿAbbas Ibn Firnas—who in the aforementioned anecdote responded to the joke by calling Mu'min "catamite" (a boy kept by a pederast)—used another overtly homosexual reference to humiliate Mu'min in public:

> I was . . . walking one day during the time of the emir Muhammad on the bank of the river in Cordoba to watch the ships coming from Seville, when I saw 'Abbas Ibn Firnas. He was yelling at Mu'min Ibn Sa'id who was in front of him,
> "Hey, Abu Marwan!"
> Mu'min then replied turning his face toward him. He asked him,
> "How do you know who I am, Abu al-Qasim, without looking at my face?"
> Abbas replied, "Why wouldn't I? Wouldn't I know the nape of your neck better than I know your face?"
> This struck him dumb.

This is meant to be a lampoon, a type of poetic exchange with a long history in Arabic literature.[38] The joke is at Mu'min Ibn Sa'id's expense, as it casts him in a passive and therefore inferior role to Ibn Firnas. 'Abbas and Mu'min were continuing an Arabic literary fashion for a type of crude satirical poetry, *naḳa'iḍ*, in which personal insults, often grossly obscene, were traded in the form of poems.[39] The genre had been established much earlier by the celebrated Umayyad poets al-Farazdaḳ (d. ca. 728) and his rival Dj̲arir, who famously abused one another in poetry over a period of some forty years.[40] The poetic jabs exchanged between the two Córdoban poets were circulated by their contemporaries and by later authors, as 'Utbah al-Shafiq alludes when he notes that after the initial falling out between the two, Mu'min

> did not cease with his foul mouth and maliciousness. He picked quarrels with 'Abbas until ['Abbas'] judged him to be loathsome. They each found fault in and severed ties with the other. The relations between them grew worse. They ridiculed and attacked each other in satirical verse, and traded vitriolic and obscene poetry.

In any case, the anecdote indicates that such exchanges between the two had a long duration, since the mule anecdote occurred at the beginning of 'Abbas Ibn Firnas's career, before he attained great wealth and status, presumably around the 820s, while the later episode occurred at least thirty years later, during the reign of Muhammad I (sometime between 852 and 886). This brings up again the theme of transmission of knowledge between the Islamic West and the preeminent Eastern Islamic cultural centers, a process in which Ibn Firnas was given a leading role by Ibn Hayyan and the other Andalusi intellectuals, as observed previously. It is but another example of how the intellectuals of Umayyad al-Andalus evoked deliberate parallels and connections between the court at Córdoba and that of the dynasty's Syrian forebears.[41]

As we will see in the chapters that follow, the poetry exchanged between the two men also has a bearing on the flight experiment and his wondrous astronomical-meteorological creation, and on how his work was received by other intellectuals in the Córdoban court.

In any case, 'Abbas Ibn Firnas's financial success, once it came, can be gauged by his having been allotted not one but two salaries. 'Isa ibn Ahmad al-Razi notes that 'Abd al-Rahman II "gave 'Abbas one salary for poetry and another for astrology (*al-tanjim*)."[42] Was the receipt of two salaries for two such seemingly divergent realms of activity unusual in the ninth century?[43] Apparently not, given the presence of another poet-astrologer, Ibn al-Shamir, in the Córdoban court of 'Abd al-Rahman II.[44] It may tell us at least that Ibn Hayyan in the eleventh century, and possibly al-Razi in the tenth century, perceived that the astrology was officially recognized and valued in the ninth-century Córdoban court, in the form of remunerated positions. While we may dismiss it as superstition today, astrology was highly valued in the caliphal era, as is apparent in the works of well-known texts of the period. Abu-Hayyan al-Tawhidi, for example, mentioned only astrology, arithmetic, logic, and medicine as the spheres of ancient knowledge most relevant in his day.[45] This recognition of the value of astrology and the attendant financial and official support for its practice are thus crucial to understanding his inquiry into the exact sciences and the connections with design and visual and material culture, which are the focus of the following chapters.

His Intellectual World

For now, the reference to 'Abbas Ibn Firnas being given a second salary for astrology (*al-tanjim*) brings us back to the "sciences of the ancients," which the Arabic authors are keen to emphasize as the other sphere in which he excelled.[46] In the ninth century, these included such topics as Greek philosophy, as well as mathematics, engineering, and astronomy.[47] In the same breath in which he wrote that 'Abbas Ibn Firnas dominated Arabic and poetry, 'Ubada remarks that the polymath was known for "excelling in philosophy, astronomy, and astrology."[48] The modern and ancient fields in which 'Abbas Ibn Firnas made his mark illustrate what today we might call the multidisciplinary atmosphere of caliphal Islamic courts, in which the most successful courtier-intellectuals were those who could move between what today we have divided into two realms, with the arts, humanities, and social sciences in one, and the exact sciences in another.

In addition to the intellectual network of the Umayyad court, and of early Islamic Iberia, 'Abbas Ibn Firnas's broader context included an international intellectual network, which was in place by the time he entered 'Abd al-Rahman II's inner circle. As in the history of science in Europe, it is important to remember that "science" during the ninth century should more properly be thought of as various branches of philosophy, which in the early Islamic context was much broader than our conception of philosophy today. A brief word about the philosophical contexts of the ninth century may help us understand this Andalusi polymath's intellectual formation and how it may have impacted his career and the way he and other early Islamic intellectuals chose to give material and visual form to scientific knowledge.

In the ninth century, the early Peripatetic school of Islamic philosophers, which combined Aristotelian and Neoplatonic elements and attempted to harmonize faith and reason—notably, its founder al-Kindi (d. ca. 873) was famed in the medieval period as the "Philosopher of the Arabs" and held to be second only to Aristotle—are instructive in regard to the intersecting realms of the exact sciences and philosophy.[49] As was the case with other early Islamic philosophers, al-Kindi was a practitioner of what today we call science (or natural philosophy) as well as philosophy. What we see in the ninth-century Islamic courts, and what has to be thought of in relation to the translation movement of Abbasid Baghdad (the crucial movement of the early Islamic period that witnessed the translation of works from Greek and Persian traditions), is an intellectual milieu in which (to put in our own contemporary terms) science was philosophy and philosophers were scientists.[50] Of course this was also the case centuries later, notably with the French mathematician-philosopher Descartes, whose work stands at the beginning of the trajectory that historians of science have traditionally conceived of as the Scientific Revolution in early modern Europe.[51]

Early Islamic scientist/philosophers had an interest not only in the theoretical but also in the applied, material dimensions of philosophy and the natural or exact sciences, which constituted important branches of philosophical knowledge.[52] This applied, material dimension is striking in the case of ʿAbbas Ibn Firnas—his aviation experiment, his meteorological chamber, his inventions, and the precision instruments he created—all of which will be discussed in the following chapters. For now, I would like to point out that this concern with the applied, the material, and the visual is not unique to ʿAbbas Ibn Firnas but is also evident in the work and careers of early Islamic intellectuals such as al-Kindi and his students, who form ʿAbbas Ibn Firnas's larger intellectual context in the caliphal period. For example, al-Kindi's treatise "On Swords and Their Kinds" is concerned with the technical details of steel.[53] Likewise, medieval Arabic treatises on precious and semiprecious stones, such as that by Jabir ibn Hayyan, include information on the medicinal properties of the stones in question (as well as their magical properties).[54]

There are relatively few extant Arabic technical treatises from before the Mongol invasions of the thirteenth century. The most famous of the medieval treatises is the *Book of Knowledge of Ingenious Devices* of Ibn al-Razzaz al-Jazari, written in 1206.[55] I will discuss two from the early caliphal era that are key to contextualizing ʿAbbas Ibn Firnas's intellectual worldview in a later chapter. Most important for understanding the ninth century and the intellectual currents that ʿAbbas Ibn Firnas would likely have known and participated in is the *Book of Ingenious Devices* of the Banu Musa, three brothers who were key members of the Abbasid court elite and its administration structure in ninth-century Baghdad.[56] They offer the most important contemporary Eastern parallels to ʿAbbas Ibn Firnas. Also courtiers, they formed part of the Abbasid caliph's inner circle, and they were notable intellectuals and scientific practitioners known for their work in astronomy, mathematics, and engineering.

That the Banu Musa and their patrons and contemporaries, like ʿAbbas Ibn Firnas and his court circle in Córdoba, were interested in visualizing and making concrete aspects of philosophical and scientific knowledge is suggested by their treatise on automata, which contains an abundance of fine machines.[57] In al-Jazari's later treatise, which builds on the engineering knowledge of the Banu Musa, the combination of highly advanced technical and craft skill and the implicit court tastes and concerns is epitomized in surviving manuscript copies whose paintings suggest the aesthetic dimensions of the automata.[58]

Al-Jazari, as James Allan observes, raises questions about the extent to which we can understand him as either unusual or representative of a tradition of intellectuals working in design and craft: "how common were scholar-craftsmen like Jazari is unfortunately unknown, but his existence raises many interesting questions about the craft industries, and indeed about the view of artisans."[59] The view that Allan refers to is the general one that holds that artisans were illiterate and operating at a remove from elite social and intellectual circles. The textual and material evidence from Islamic civilizations over the *longue durée*, as Milwright points out, shows that men and women who produced visual and material culture have been accorded a low status in Islamic societies in general, as was also often the case in other premodern contexts.[60] Yet ʿAbbas Ibn Firnas's career, when considered alongside that of the Banu Musa (who were intellectuals but who were also designing works of Islamic visual and material culture), suggests that such scholar-craftsmen or scientist-designers may have been more common in the early Islamic period than the overall portrait of artisans as low-status illiterates might suggest.

As we consider the portrait of ʿAbbas Ibn Firnas that the Arabic authors are concerned to construct, humor, curiosity, creativity, and an impulse to innovation are other traits that come to the fore. The vizier ʿAbdalhamid Ibn Basil noted that ʿAbbas Ibn Firnas "devised all his life subtle inventions and marvelous innovations in more than one art, in jest and in seriousness." The reference to jest refers to the literary contrast between "seriousness and joking" (*al-dj̲idd wa'l- hazl*), or the aspects of a person's life that were not about serious matters such as religion.[61] As we have seen, Ibn Firnas's satirical wit, as mentioned above, could also serve as a weapon against detractors such as his nemesis, the poet Mu'min. The characterization of his inventions as subtle suggests a keen and clever mind behind objects whose workings would not have been immediately apparent to observers, and that is characteristic of the desired effects of medieval automata, which were meant to amaze and delight those who saw them. Likewise, the reference to ʿAbbas Ibn Firnas's "marvelous innovations" suggests a curious, creative personality driven to create new and improved designs and processes. This is implicit in the inventions that Ibn Hayyan and others attribute to ʿAbbas Ibn Firnas. For instance, Ibn Hayyan asserts that ʿAbbas Ibn Firnas fabricated (*ṣanʿa*) a clock "with neither plan (*ʿala ghayri rasmin*) nor model (*wa-la mithalin*)."[62] This may underscore the creativity and innovative nature of the polymath's design process in particular, since it implies that the normal method of making such a device would have been to follow a preexisting plan or model.

The chronicler likewise credits him as being the first in al-Andalus to develop an industry for the production of glass: "He was the first to develop in al-Andalus the manufacture of glass from stones (*ṣinaʿata al-zujaji min al-hajarati*)," which seems to be the source for later assertions that Ibn Firnas invented lead crystal.[63] It may be that this refers to manganese dioxide, which was an Islamic innovation that produced clear transparent glass, or one of the mineral oxides used to color glass.[64] Or, perhaps it refers to natron or some similar substance, which was used in glass production in the central Islamic lands. It has been argued that the use of plant ashes combined with silica was a major technological innovation in glass production.[65]

While ʿAbbas Ibn Firnas fits the pattern of intellectual-scientists like al-Kindi and his students, and that of scholar-engineer-craftsmen like the Banu Musa and later al-Jazari, the personality constructed by the Arabic authors might diverge from these other figures, pertaining to his engaging in activities regarded in some quarters with suspicion. His wide-ranging interests led him into realms that some of his contemporaries in Córdoba perceived as heterodox. The poet ʿUbada, for instance, observed that in addition to his mastery of the sciences, ancient and modern, ʿAbbas Ibn Firnas "knew enchantments, subtleties and magic; about this stories and anecdotes are told." Ibn Hayyan further remarks:

> He [Muhammadb. ʿUmar b. Lubabah] says:
>
> [ʿAbbas] was so full of ingenuity (sahiba nayranjatin), creativity, originality, invention (kathira al-ibdaʿi / al-ikhtiraʿi wa-l-tawlidi wa-l-istinbaṭi) and resourcefulness (wasiʿa al-hiyali) that he was attributed with the knowledge of magic and alchemy (al-sihra wa-ʿamala al-kimiya'), and was often challenged on religious grounds.[66]

He then goes on to relay an anecdote that makes clear the dangerous consequences that such activities could engender:

> The learned Muhammadb. Ismaʿil said:
>
> Against ʿAbbas b. Firnas were written acts of irreligiosity (*bi-l-zandaqati*), attested by a group from the town in front of Sulayman b. Aswad [*qadi* of Cordoba under the emir Muhammad]; some of these saying: "He has been heard to say, "He did this and that (*mafaʿilun mafaʿilun*)." Others said, "I saw blood welling

> from the drainpipe of his house at the beginning of January," and other such foolishness typical of these poor witnesses, ignorant and foolish (*dhawi jahlin wa-fidamatin*), with whom the *qadi* in vain discussed the matter in order to enlighten them (*kashafahum*). Nothing was found. The jurists (*al-fuqaha'u*) took counsel regarding what of this had been noted. Nothing was discovered with which he could be punished, and 'Abbas escaped by the skin of his teeth.[67]

This anecdote is fascinating for the way it presents a perspective that we don't often see in the chronicle; that of the broader, nonelite population, and its suspicion of the activities and experiments that were held in such esteem by the intellectuals in 'Abbas Ibn Firnas's circle. Muhammad b. Isma'il, the source of the anecdote, is noteworthy. He seems to have been a companion of 'Abbas Ibn Firnas, and his reputation as a grammarian and mathematician earned him the nickname al-Hakim al-Qurtubi (the Córdoban Sage).[68] Indeed, his reputation as an intellectual can be gauged by his having later been appointed by 'Abd al-Rahman III, the first caliph of Córdoba, to serve as tutor to his son and heir al-Hakam II, whose own reputation as an intellectual is considerable. This anecdote reveals a tension between elite intellectual and religious circles in Córdoba and some segment of the general population, brought on by this polymath's investigations.

Note that the story mentions townspeople appealing to Sulayman b. Aswad,[69] who was twice appointed chief judge of Córdoba during the reign of the emir Muhammad, and to an otherwise anonymous group of "the learned." The story reports that these religious and intellectual elites dismissed the concerns of the accusers as "foolishness" typical of ignorant people. This account is quite fascinating in that it reveals tensions between high intellectual circles and an urban population unfamiliar with the kinds of activities that gave rise to rumors that 'Abbas Ibn Firnas was a practitioner of magic and alchemy.

Equally striking is the indication that these members of the religious elite sought to explain the intellectual merit or basis of 'Abbas Ibn Firnas's activities "in order to enlighten" the accusers, with its suggestion that reasoned discussion and debate about such matters was possible and desirable. The anecdote points to the potential consequences (social and political indictment, up to execution) of being judged guilty of heresy in the caliphal period.[70] But, it also reminds us of a key point about a commensurability that often existed between scientific, philosophical inquiry and religion in medieval Islamic civilization. The fact that 'Abbas Ibn Firnas's defense to these charges was mounted by none other than the chief religious authority of the capital, in consultation with other intellectual/religious elites, underscores that faith and scientific, philosophical inquiry were not perceived as opposing viewpoints. As George Saliba and many other scholars have pointed out, in medieval Islamic societies the leading astronomers and mathematicians were often also leading religious figures.[71]

Conclusion

Given how few biographies of men and women engaged in the production of early Islamic material and visual culture exist, the vibrant portrait of ʿAbbas Ibn Firnas that Ibn Hayyan and his early Arabic sources provide is a rare gem indeed. As he, and possibly his predecessors, were keen to show, ʿAbbas Ibn Firnas was an outsized personality. Brilliant, innovative, ingenious, inventive, the object of great admiration as well as disapproval, scandal, and opprobrium at times—he was obviously a person about whom his contemporaries and those who came after for many subsequent generations liked to tell stories and anecdotes.

As a historical figure today ʿAbbas Ibn Firnas is widely cited, but the significance of his contribution has been contested. One might rightly ask: Why, if Ibn Firnas was such an acclaimed intellectual, is he barely mentioned in the biographical dictionaries that are such an important source on medieval Islamic intellectuals? Why is it that his fame as a scientist endures despite the uncertainty and ambiguity that surrounds his intellectual production and impact, in contrast to other Andalusi intellectuals such as Maslama al-Majriti, Ibn al-Zarqulluh, or Ibn Baso, who also wrote treatises and made fine precision instruments that have survived to the present day? These are important questions but lie beyond the scope of my expertise, so I hope others better equipped to do so will address such questions in future work. Nevertheless, earlier authors and historians of science and technology were disposed to see him as a genius, and his reputation as an early aviator is popularly lauded, though more recently historians of science and technology have doubted the possibility that he could have achieved a successful flight. This is an issue to which I will return, but for now I think it is reasonable to conclude from our Arabic sources that ʿAbbas Ibn Firnas was portrayed as an exceptional intellectual by his Andalusi intellectual peers and successors—truly, the sage of al-Andalus. Yet, even as it is tempting today to see him as a kind of Islamic precursor to Leonardo da Vinci, it is more important to acknowledge ʿAbbas Ibn Firnas as a product of his time and place in the early Islamic lands.

Among the caliphal intellectuals of the ninth century, he was not unique in his interests, in his professional mastery of diverse disciplines, or even in his application of theoretical knowledge to visual and material culture. He was able to conduct his experiments over the course of a long career that spanned the reigns of three successive Córdoban rulers (al-Hakam I, r. 796–822; ʿAbd al-Rahman II, r. 822–52; Muhammad II, r. 852–86). In large part this long career was possible because of the royal patronage system that funded his activities as a poet, as an astronomer-astrologer, and as an intellectual-designer, and thanks to the support of other intellectuals and elites who supported and defended him when, as we have seen, his activities pushed the boundaries of what was deemed acceptable and orthodox.

But while it is important to acknowledge his embeddedness in early Andalusi intellectual and court contexts, he also stands out from his contemporaries in the Abbasid and other courts of the time, as an innovator who designed and made mechanical devices for the Córdoban court, and who sought to replicate and visualize scientific phenomena—namely, soaring flight and meteorological phenomena—which others either could not or did not imagine was possible.

2
Mind and Hand

Having established that by the eleventh century Andalusi intellectuals perceived Ibn Firnas as having inaugurated a tradition of fine scientific instrumentation, this chapter turns to the implications of this reputation.[1] It begins by considering the polymath as Ibn Hayyan portrays him—as an inventor, designer, and maker of innovative instruments for the Umayyad emirs. It begins by considering what the chronicle says about these instruments, including Ibn Firnas's poetry that was purportedly inscribed upon their surfaces. It then moves to consider some extant medieval Islamic instruments that likewise bear poetic inscriptions. The chapter discusses how, when we consider the Arabic account of Ibn Firnas as instrument maker alongside the early instruments from al-Andalus and elsewhere, much is revealed about connections between elite intellectual culture and craft, about science and art making, in Umayyad Córdoba and the early Islamic lands. By considering the early surviving instruments and other surviving works of visual culture in tandem with our Arabic text, this gives us a clearer sense of Ibn Firnas and other scientists and intellectuals as makers of Andalusi visual culture.

Inventor, Designer, Maker

Ibn Hayyan begins his account of Ibn Firnas's career by mentioning his skill as an inventor, designer, and maker, and emphasizing his ability to invent and to innovate in particular:

> In the time of the emir al-Hakam appeared ʿAbbas b. Firnas, the wise man (*hakimu*) of al-Andalus who superseded all others in the number of skills and arts (*al-adawati wa-l-fununi*). He was . . . full of inventiveness (*hasana al-ikhtiraʿi*) and of the capacity for innovation (*kathira al-ibdaʿi*).[2]

Later in the passage he returns to this theme of the polymath's inventiveness and innovative tendencies as evidenced by instruments Ibn Firnas is said to have designed and made. Reporting the words of a tenth-century Córdoban court poet, regarding these objects, he writes:

> I read the following words of the poet ʿUbada, handwritten by the poet himself: He was the one who made in al-Andalus the clepsydra (*alladhi ʿamila bi-l-Andalusi*

A Bridge to the Sky. Glaire D. Anderson, Oxford University Press. © Oxford University Press 2024.
DOI: 10.1093/oso/9780190913243.003.0003

> *al-minqanata*) for knowing the hour, which he sent to the emir Muhammad, grandson of the emir Al-Hakam. . . . Before that 'Abbas had also made an armillary sphere (*wa-'amila 'Abbassun ayḍan min qablu, dhata al-halaqi* . . .) for the emir 'Abd al-Rahman b. Al-Hakam, which he sent . . . [3]

The anecdote establishes a chronology, albeit a skeletal one, for considering 'Abbas Ibn Firnas's activities as a maker. It tells us that Ibn Firnas was creating instruments sometime in the three decades between 822 and 852, which is when 'Abd al-Rahman ibn al-Hakam ('Abd al-Rahman II) reigned as emir of al-Andalus. It was for this ruler that Ibn Firnas made the first of the instruments, an armillary sphere. Armillary spheres were an important type of astronomical tool known from antiquity that were used to model the heavenly spheres and to carry out various celestial observations and calculations. The earliest armillary spheres that have survived are European examples dated to the fifteenth century or later, centuries after Ibn Firnas's time. It is therefore difficult to gauge how a medieval Islamic armillary sphere might compare in terms of appearance, scale, materials, or visual language, although the device is discussed in textual sources, including Ptolemy, whose writings were available and revered in the medieval period.[4] The armillary's significance as a tool for understanding celestial motion is clearly articulated in a treatise by the Abbasid astronomer al-Farghani (Baghdad, ca. 856) on the astrolabe, which is the earliest Arabic work on the topic. In this work, al-Farghani states that "the observational instrument with which they [scholars of mathematical astronomy] achieved most was the instrument that is called the armillary sphere (*dhat al-halaq*)."[5] Al-Farghani emphasized the utility of the instrument as a means to understand the celestial spheres and their motion. He also discusses the origins of its design in both mathematical theory and observation, making clear the interconnectedness of mathematics, astronomy, and design. One of the notable features of al-Farghani's treatise is that it provides the information that medieval intellectuals would have needed in order to draw the circles and arcs on astrolabes—in other words, to design a crucial aspect of their visual program. In the preface to his treatise on the astrolabe, al-Farghani explains that he wrote the work in order to provide visual, graphic proof of the astrolabe's correctness, and to refute any doubts regarding the design of the instrument. He states:

> I wrote a comprehensive book in which I demonstrate the correctness of the form of the astrolabe . . . the obtaining of the sizes of all the circles that are formed on the astrolabe to replace the sphere of the heavens, the description of their construction . . . [6]

Here, al-Farghani emphasizes the application of geometry to the design of a two-dimensional representation of the universe. It takes great creativity and imagination to conceive of representing the universe in the form of an instrument that can be held in the palm of one's hand. The link between mathematics, imagination, three-dimensional space, and geometrical objects evident in such texts illuminates how intellectuals working in the exact sciences were able to translate that knowledge into craft and architecture.[7]

The tenth-century philosopher al-Farabi discusses the Arabic term *takhyil*, which designates the imaginary in classical Arabic poetics, and which like mathematics, can be related to medieval Islamic understanding of the imagination and creativity.[8] Al-Farabi identifies two modes of verbal representation encompassed by the term. The first mode discussed by al-Farabi is a direct representation (in other words, a representation that aspires to realism), while the second mode is one that is removed from the object it represents potentially by multiple levels. According to al-Farabi,

> many people believe that the more removed the imitation is from its subject matter the better and more complete it is in comparison with a more direct representation of a subject matter. They also hold that the creator . . . of this [latter] description is more entitled to the act of imitation, more skilled in the craft and more proficient in its practice."[9]

Al-Farabi was speaking about literary representation, and one could argue therefore that the realm of literature and the realm of the material and the visual, as pertain in the case of these precision instruments, may not be entirely commensurable.[10] Yet, if we entertain the notion that crafting poetry and crafting visual and material models and representations of the heavens were compatible pursuits for caliphal intellectuals, perhaps al-Farabi's observations provide a valuable clue as to how scientific instruments and wondrous devices may have been understood and valued by those who designed, made, and used them in their own day.

Returning to the Córdoban chronicle, it might seem strange that the source for our information about Ibn Firnas's scientific instruments was a court poet, but in fact science and poetry are very closely connected in the account of our polymath's career. At the very outset of the account, Ibn Hayyan characterizes Ibn Firnas as "a brilliant poet" (*sha'iran mufalliqan*) and an "inspired and truthful astrologer" (*munajjiman maṭbu'an muwaffaqan*)—and here it is important to bear in mind that in the ninth century, astronomy and astrology were nearly indistinguishable.[11] Ibn Hayyan cites the tenth-century Córdoban historian 'Isa ibn Ahmad al-Razi (d.?), who likewise observed that our polymath was remunerated for his skills in both science and poetry: "The emir 'Abd-al-Rahman ['Abd al-Rahman II] gave 'Abbas two allowances: one for poetry and another for astrology (*li-l-tanjimi*)[12] and drew him close as a boon companion."[13] Likewise, the poet 'Ubada begins his anecdote about Ibn Firnas and the instruments he made by noting that the polymath was known for having "excelled in all the sciences, ancient and modern (*al-'ulumi al-qadimati wa-l-muhdathati*). He dominated Arabic and was adept at making good poetry, excelling as well in philosophy, astronomy, and astrology."[14] But it is the lines of poetry preserved in 'Ubada's anecdote—lines that Ibn Firnas is said to have composed and engraved himself on the two instruments—that fully illustrate the close links between science, intellect, and craft in the court at Córdoba:

> ʿAbbas had also made an armillary sphere (*wa-ʿamila ʿAbbassun ayḍan min qablu, dhata al-halaqi*) for the emir ʿAbd al-Rahman ibn Al-Hakam, which he sent, inscribing upon it (*wa-kataba maʿaha*):
>
> "Complete is the instrument (*min alatin*) that was commissioned of me
> That great philosophers could not achieve, save for me;
> If Ptolemy had been successful in doing so,
> I wouldn't be occupying myself with the tables of the *Qanun*[15]
> And if the sun was seen on its horizon,
> It would be sending its measured light,
> And the lunar mansions (*manazilu al-qamari*), hidden to all eyes with the horoscope of each moment (*duna al-ʿuyuni li-kulli ṭaliʿ hini*),
> They would see during the day, the same as they appear
> In the night, in its deep darkness."[16]
>
> The poetry inscribed on the armillary sphere thus presents the instrument as speaking in the voice of its maker. In these lines, the personality of Ibn Firnas shines through vividly in his boast that in the instrument's creation he had achieved something of which "great philosophers," including Ptolemy himself, were incapable.

ʿUbada tells us that the next instrument for which ʿAbbas Ibn Firnas was known in court was a water clock, which he made for Muhammad I (r. 852–86), the ruler who succeeded al-Hakam I as emir of al-Andalus. At the beginning of his account of Ibn Firnas's career, Ibn Hayyan notes that Ibn Firnas was the first "to discover intricate issues, fabricating with neither plan nor model the instrument known as clepsydra (*minqanah*) to tell the time." The implicit emphasis here is on the ingenuity and technical know-how Ibn Firnas possessed in order to have been able to design and build the water clock without a model.[17] Although it is only from this Arabic text that we know of Ibn Firnas's instrument, and therefore of an early Andalusi engagement with the technology, the allusion to the instrument in the text is in itself notable. Ibn Hayyan's chronicle is the earliest Arabic textual reference to water clocks, which arguably became the most important device in the medieval Islamic technological landscape.[18] I will have more to say on medieval Andalusi water clocks in Chapter 3, but they operated by means of transferring water, or in some cases mercury, via large outflow clepsydras (instruments known from antiquity that measured time using the flow of water) with concentric siphons, which in turn transferred power to automata via mechanisms that included complex gearing.[19]

Whereas the armillary sphere is made to speak with the voice of its maker, the poetry that the chronicle tells us Ibn Firnas engraved on the water clock is composed as if the instrument itself were addressing the beholder:

> He sent to the emir Muhammad, grandson of the emir Al-Hakam, engraving on it (*wa-naqasha fiha*) some verses of his that said (*tawil*):
>
> "I am the best instrument (*khayru adati*) for religion,
> When you don't know the moment of each prayer,
> When one can not see for oneself the sun in the day, nor
> the stars in nights of deep darkness;
> For the blessing of Muhammad, imam of the Muslims,
> With me the moments of prayer are clear."[20]

Thus, the inscribed poetry has this water clock claim for itself a useful religious function: it can ascertain correct prayer times without celestial observation.

The poems Ibn Firnas composed and inscribed on these two instruments constitute a striking early example of Andalusi "speaking" objects.[21] The poetic conceit of a speaking object has a rich history in the art and architecture of al-Andalus.[22] The most celebrated example is the carved ivory pyxis on display in the Metropolitan Museum of Art, whose inscription has the object describing its own beauty and function to the viewer: "The sight I offer is the fairest, the firm breast of a delicate girl. Beauty has invested me with splendid raiment, which makes a display of jewels. I am a receptacle for musk, camphor, and ambergris."[23]

The same use of inscriptions to give voice to instruments, allowing them to "speak" with their own voice as well as with the voice of their makers, appears in two unique thirteenth-century devices made later in the eastern reaches of the empire. The first is a geared astrolabe, preserved in Oxford, and likely made in Isfahan. The rear face of the geared astrolabe bears a carefully worked Kufic signature inscription that gives the name of its maker: "Made by Muhammad b. Abi Bakr b. Muhammad al-Rashidi al-Ibari [or al-Abiri] al-Isfahani. 618 [A.H./ 1221–1222]."[24]

The inscription bordering its rear face continues, and the instrument—like those made and inscribed by Ibn Firnas—speaks with the proud voice of the maker, explaining its functions and features to the viewer/user and then proclaiming, "this disc is the product of the endeavour of someone learned in the technical arts, which are based on precision and scientific proof."[25] Indeed, the instrument is worthy of the maker's pride; it is a very finely crafted piece of thirteenth-century metalwork, beautifully inlaid with silver, and incorporating an abundance of animal and human imagery (including images of the zodiac).

Besides this instrument's high aesthetic value as a fine metalwork object, it is likewise a masterful piece of precision engineering. Its internal gearing was designed to show the lunar phases, which were displayed in a small round opening

Figure 2.1. Inscription on obverse. Astrolabe with geared calendar, Muhammad Ibn Abi Bakr Isfahan, 618 AH, 1221/2 CE. Inv. 48213. © History of Science Museum, University of Oxford.

on the instrument's obverse face. As the world's oldest complete geared device, it shows how scientists in the medieval Islamic lands adapted ancient astronomical technologies such as those represented by the ancient Greek Antikythera mechanism, to create new and innovative devices fully embedded in caliphal social and intellectual currents.[26]

Just as Ibn Firnas's water clock inscription juxtaposed theological sentiments side by side with scientific concerns, the inscription on the geared astrolabe likewise alludes to the inextricability of medieval Islamic science and faith, stating, "Behold the disc! It will show you many of the wonders that prove the wisdom of the Merciful; its different motions are by virtue of a single mover, and it has meanings going beyond all meanings."

A second extant device of the caliphal age that "speaks," as Ibn Firnas's creations did, is an instrument for the divinatory practice of geomancy (*'ilm al-raml* ["the science of the sand"]) preserved in the British Museum.[27] Besides inscriptions on its front and rear faces composed so that the object "speaks" to the viewer, it includes a signature inscription: "The work of Muhammad ibn Khutlukh al-Mawsili in the year 639 [1241–42]."[28] Along with numerous inscriptions explaining how to use the device for divination, the maker decorated this device with poetic inscriptions that allude to religious and supernatural themes. Framing the central dial at the lower left and right, respectively, are the following poetic inscriptions, in which the device speaks in the first person: "I am the revealer of secrets; in me are marvels of wisdom and strange and hidden things." In these lines the object speaks directly to the viewer about its own efficacious power. Most striking indeed are these words, inscribed just below the central dial: "From my intricacies there comes about insight superior to books concerned with the study of the art." Here the device speaks in order to insist on its own superiority to books, to the written word, as a means of obtaining knowledge.

Despite having been crafted later and in courts and contexts far removed from those of ninth-century Córdoba, these two "speaking" objects, when considered together with 'Ubada's anecdote on Ibn Firnas's armillary sphere and water clock, make it clear that caliphal intellectuals could and did design and craft objects of science, which participated in (or indeed shaped) Islamic court literary as well as visual modes.

The Earliest Andalusi Instruments

Turning to the earliest extant objects from Córdoba and al-Andalus, these likewise offer a clear sense of scientific instruments as works of art as well as intellect.[29] The earliest precision instruments that have survived from Islamic Spain, comprising several astrolabes and one celestial globe, were made at approximately the same historical moment that Ibn Hayyan was compiling his account of Ibn Firnas's career in the Córdoban court chronicle. These early astronomical

Figure 2.2. Geomantic tablet. Signed by Muhammad ibn Khutlukh al-Mawsili. 1241–1242 (AH 639), probably Damascus (Syria). Brass alloy, inlaid with silver and gold. 26.8 × 33.6 cm. The British Museum, London (1888,0526.1). ©The Trustees of the British Museum. All rights reserved.

instruments confirm the impression that in al-Andalus, science and visual culture were closely intertwined by the opening decades of the eleventh century. As Azucena Hernández has established, of the thirty-four astrolabes that have survived from medieval al-Andalus, four date to the Umayyad period, with an additional nine from the *taifa* period (so-called in reference to the eleventh-century *muluk al-tawaif*, independent kingdoms of Iberia that came to prominence following the abolishment of the Córdoban caliphate in 1031).[30] These instruments have been thoroughly studied by historians of science, notably Julio Samsó, and most recently and authoritatively, Hernández.[31]

The objects I will discuss below are preserved today in museums in Edinburgh, Madrid, Oxford, and Florence. Along with other early astrolabes and other precision instruments preserved in museum collections elsewhere in Europe, the United States, and the Middle East, they provide the clearest visual evidence of the intimate connections between science, court culture, design, and craft. These objects bear eloquent witness to an early Andalusi tradition of design and invention. The wellspring of that tradition, according to Andalusi intellectuals of the tenth and eleventh century as conveyed in the court chronicle, was ʿAbbas Ibn Firnas.

Astrolabes are analog computers, meant to make it easier for the user to carry out a variety of mathematical functions related to astronomical timekeeping.[32] They are related to armillary spheres in that they represent a model of the heavens and can be used for some of the same mathematical and astronomical observations and calculations. Historians of science describe astrolabes as models of the universe that can be held in the hand. This sense of the object as an abstract representation is key to keep in mind in considering the creativity and formal, visual choices—quite apart from the technical knowledge—that a maker would bring to the task of designing and creating such an object.[33]

Astrolabes constitute the earliest and most abundant type of instrument to survive from the medieval Islamic lands. Indeed, the fact that so many finely crafted metalwork astrolabes survive—preserved today in both scientific and art collections around the globe—deserves comment, since there is no particular reason why astrolabes have to be crafted as fine metalware objects. They could also be constructed in a utilitarian mode out of less durable and expensive materials, such as paper or wood, as early and modern examples of other types of instruments suggest.[34] It may be that the abundance of extant instruments reflects the limited period—about seventy years—for which an astrolabe could function with precision, due to the motion of celestial bodies over time.[35] But astrolabes can be updated to keep the instruments accurate, and there are other examples of astrolabes fitted with new retes or otherwise altered after their initial facture in order to address this issue.[36]

The abundance of medieval Islamic examples bears witness to a deep engagement on the part of early Islamic instrument makers and users with materiality and visuality. Brass, the alloy used for Islamic astrolabes, is a perfect material for precision instrumentation due to its hardness and the precision with which it could be engraved. But besides these practical considerations, the golden appearance of a fine brass object is part of its visual appeal. The abundance of astrolabes speaks as much to the intimate connections between the intellect and craft that the chronicle's account of Ibn Firnas's career likewise reveals. As Paul Kunitschz has observed, "an instrument is the sort of curiosity that attracts the attention of a wider audience than tables in learned treatises which may even shy people off."[37]

While the chronicle does not state that Ibn Firnas himself made or designed astrolabes, his official salaried position as court astronomer makes it highly likely that he knew and used such instruments, which draw on much the same mathematical and astronomical knowledge as that used to construct armillary spheres. In any case, because astrolabes constitute our earliest examples of precision instruments that are also works of art, it is worth examining the earliest Andalusi examples closely, and considering what they reveal about the entanglements between science and craft exemplified in Ibn Firnas's career.

On display in the Museo Arqueológico Nacional in Madrid is an eleventh-century astrolabe whose age, monumental size, fine craftsmanship, and elaborate decoration are outstanding, especially given the relative rarity of fine Islamic metalwork before the twelfth century.[38] This instrument is arguably the most impressive work of science and art to have survived from the early Islamic West. The Madrid instrument measures 24.2 cm in diameter and is constructed from three layers of brass measuring 1.9 cm.

The surfaces of the astrolabe are inscribed throughout with elegant Kufic inscriptions. Most important for this discussion is the inscription placed in a prominent position at the top and center of the rear face of the astrolabe's body (*mater*). Historians of science understand this inscription to be the signature of the instrument's maker, and it also provides the exact time and place of its creation: "Made by (*sanaʿa*) Ibrahim b. Saʿīd al-Sahli, in the city of Toledo in [the month of] Shawwal AH 459 [June/July 1067 AD]."[39] The Arabic inscription is carefully worked in Kufic calligraphy, which was favored before the twelfth century for important official inscriptions, as well as in the luxurious tenth-century Qur'an manuscripts produced across the Islamic lands. Along with the signature inscription, the rear face of the astrolabe is inscribed with calendar scales, four quadrants, circles representing signs of the zodiac in Arabic, and circles indicating days of the month. Adding to the visual appeal of the instrument's elegantly worked inscriptions, the brass alloy would have had the rich appearance of gold when new.

Six interchangeable plates, which fit within the body, or mater, of the astrolabe, are inscribed front and back with the names and latitudes of important Islamic cities, both east and west: Mecca, Medina, Baghdad, and Mosul appear along with Córdoba, Toledo, Seville, and Zaragoza, among others. Besides the names of the cities and their latitudes these plates are inscribed with carefully worked arcs indicating prayer times and unequal hours.

The rete, or movable grid, used to mark the positions of stars, features elegantly curved pointers for twenty-eight stars and is engraved with the names and symbols of the constellations of the zodiac circle. These are normally not found on the earliest Eastern astrolabes, but they do appear on later European instruments. The rete also features a striking framework of cusped arches to enclose and highlight slender, curved pointers for three important stars: Rigel, Sirius, and Alfard.

The cusped frames that al-Sahli created for the three major star pointers is particularly striking, in that they introduce in miniature scale certain artistic and architectural forms that were commonly used in the court of the Córdoban Umayyads, the ʿAmirids, and subsequently by the independent *taifa* kingdoms that emerged after 1031 in the wake of the dissolution of the Córdoban Umayyad caliphate.[40] As Hernández has observed, the connections to architectural forms, such as the arcades of the reception hall at the Aljafería palace in Zaragoza, are an important visual aspect of the medieval Iberian astrolabes.[41]

Figure 2.3. Al-Sahli astrolabe, Madrid. Front. Museo Arqueológico Nacional, Madrid. Photo: Ángel Martínez Levas.

Figure 2.4. Al-Sahli astrolabe, Madrid. Back. Museo Arqueológico Nacional, Madrid. Photo: Ángel Martínez Levas.

The presence of these cusped arches, or miniaturized architecture, as part of the visual language of the astrolabe might serve simply as a visual referent to court settings, connecting this object to contemporary visual culture in the Taifa court.[42]

Yet there are three other ways that we might interpret the presence of this heightened visual aesthetic on the face of the astrolabe. First, perhaps their inclusion

Figure 2.5. Al-Sahli astrolabe, mater. Museo Arqueológico Nacional, Madrid. Photo: Ángel Martínez Levas.

in the visual program of a highly complex mathematical instrument is indicative of an intellectual appreciation for the mathematics that also undergird these cusped and polylobed forms. In this sense, the astrolabe's rete recalls the first appearance of such forms in Umayyad Córdoba during the reign of the intellectual al-Hakam II, where they likewise gesture to mathematics, cognition, and visual culture.[43] Indeed,

Figure 2.6. Al-Sahli astrolabe, Madrid. Signature inscription. Museo Arqueológico Nacional, Madrid. Photo: Juan Carlos Quindós de la Fuente.

Figure 2.7. Al-Sahli astrolabe, detail of plate. Madrid. Museo Arqueológico Nacional, Madrid. Photo: Juan Carlos Quindós de la Fuente.

Figure 2.8. Al-Sahli astrolabe, Madrid. Rete. Museo Arqueológico Nacional, Madrid. Photo: Ángel Martínez Levas.

the polylobed and cusped arches and the ribbed domes of al-Hakam II's expansion to the prayer hall, built between 960 and 965, may be symptomatic of what Felix Arnold has described as a new "mathematical turn" in architectural design, in which designers employed geometry to compose a "spatial web in which all parts are equal to each other and part of a single unified space."[44]

A much smaller astrolabe preserved in the Museum of the History of Science in Oxford bears an inscription that identifies it as the work of the same maker, Ibrahim b. Saʿīd al-Sahli.[45] It is sized to be comfortably held in the hand of a user, but despite

Figure 2.9. Cusped and polylobed arches. Aljafería Palace, taifa Zaragoza, last half of the eleventh century. Photo: Glaire Anderson.

its comparatively diminutive dimensions, the heightened visual elaboration of its rete further attests to the maker's virtuosity in creating instruments that are both works of art and works of science. Like its much larger counterpart, this instrument offers the viewer the same impression of carefully worked mathematical precision coupled with a luxurious sense of materiality and design.

While the instrument of al-Sahli preserved in Madrid is perhaps the most spectacular of the early astrolabes from al-Andalus, it is not the oldest. That distinction has long been held by an instrument preserved in the National Museum of Scotland, in Edinburgh.[46] Made of cast brass, this astrolabe was made some forty years prior to the Madrid astrolabe. Measuring 15.5 cm in diameter, it is much smaller than the instrument preserved in Madrid. In contrast to the outsize dimensions of that astrolabe, this earlier instrument fits comfortably in the hands of a user. Like the others, this astrolabe features a carefully worked program of Kufic Arabic inscriptions, including the one prominently engraved on its rear face that names its maker and

Figure 2.10. Polylobed arches at the Great Mosque of Córdoba. Photo: Daniel C. Waugh. Image courtesy of Aga Khan Documentation Center, MIT Libraries (AKDC@MIT).

Figure 2.11. Astrolabe, Ibrahim b. Saʿīd al-Sahli, Toledo, 1068. Front. Inv. 55331, © History of Science Museum, University of Oxford.

Figure 2.12. Astrolabe, Ibrahim b. Saʿīd al-Sahli, Toledo, 1068. Obverse. Inv. 55331, © History of Science Museum, University of Oxford.

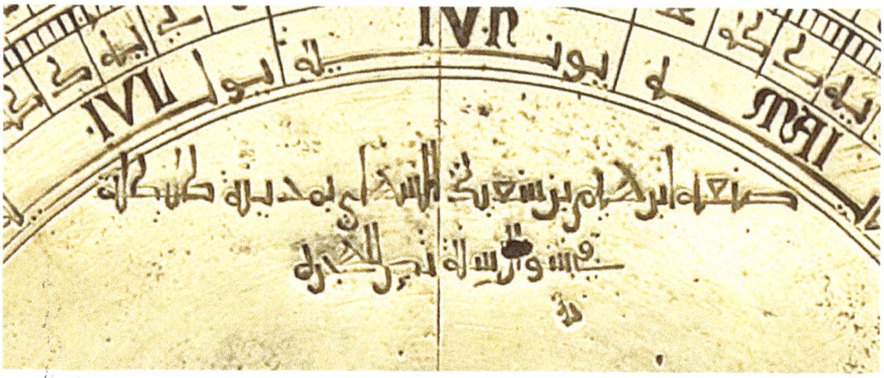

Figure 2.13. Astrolabe, Ibrahim b. Sa'īd al-Sahli, Toledo, 1068. Signature Inscription. Inv. 55331, © History of Science Museum, University of Oxford.

provides the time and place of its creation: "work of (*'amala*) Muhammad ibn al-Saffar in Córdoba in the year 17 and 400 (417 AH or 1026/27 CE)."[47]

The body (mater) of the astrolabe, its inscribed rim, and seven interchangeable plates housed within the mater are original, though the rete is a later medieval replacement.[48] The interior of the mater is engraved with ecliptic coordinates, the ecliptic being a great circle on the celestial sphere representing the sun's apparent path during the year. The plates are inscribed with the names of cities whose latitudes would have been appropriate for the use of that particular plate: these are San'a and Mecca; Medina and Samarra; Kairouan and Córdoba; Zaragoza; Saba' and Misr (Egypt); Qulsum and Tanja (Tangier); Toledo and Constantinople. Each plate also provides the latitude for those cities, the hours in the longest day, *azimuths* (the direction of a celestial object from the observer), *almucantars* (a circle on the celestial sphere parallel to the horizon), and lines indicating times of prayer. The choice of cities for which these plates were to be used offers some clues about the intended recipients and functions. They might indicate places to which their user might have traveled. The reasons for including plates suitable for Mecca and Medina, the two holy cities of Islam, is understandable, as these two cities are the goal of pilgrimage for any Muslim able to carry out the journey. The other cities represent important centers in the Iberian Peninsula and North Africa, or farther east. Kairouan, in present-day Tunisia, and Córdoba—where the instrument was made—were the two major political and intellectual centers of the Islamic West.

Founded during the Umayyad conquest of North Africa in the eighth century, Kairouan became the premier religious, political, and cultural capital of Ifriqiyya under the Aghlabid dynasty (r. 800–909) and retained its importance long after.[49] Zaragoza was one of the major cities of al-Andalus beginning in the eighth century.[50] Its flourishing intellectual reputation was stimulated by the migration of Córdoban scholars to the city following the dissolution of the Córdoban Umayyad dynasty.[51] Toledo was likewise one of the earliest and most important of the independent *taifa* dynasties, ruled by the Dhu'l-Nunid dynasty until the Castilian

Figure 2.14. Astrolabe, Muhammad ibn al-Saffar, Córdoba, 1026–27. Front. T. 1959.62, © National Museum of Scotland.

conquest in 1085.[52] The D̲h̲u 'l-Nunid court was famous for its wealth and luxury. In the decades immediately following the construction of the astrolabe now in the National Museum of Scotland, Toledo would become famous for its astronomers and other scientist-intellectuals, notably Ibn Saʿid (d. 1070), author of the medieval history of science, *Kitab ṭabaqat al-umam* (Categories of Nations), and the astronomer al-Zarkala (d. 1087).[53]

Figure 2.15. Astrolabe, Muhammad ibn al-Saffar, Córdoba, 1026–27. Back. T. 1959.62, © National Museum of Scotland.

At first glance the size and the visual language of al-Saffar's astrolabe appear consistent with the earliest instruments made in the Abbasid East beginning in the eighth century.[54] However, the analysis of al-Saffar's astrolabe in Edinburgh indicates that the rete and part of its suspension device (throne) were not original to the instrument but, rather, are later replacements. The difference in the coloration of the metal and the coarser workmanship, in comparison with the original body

Figure 2.16. Astrolabe, Muhammad ibn al-Saffar, Córdoba, 1026–27. Signature inscription. T. 1959.62, © National Museums Scotland.

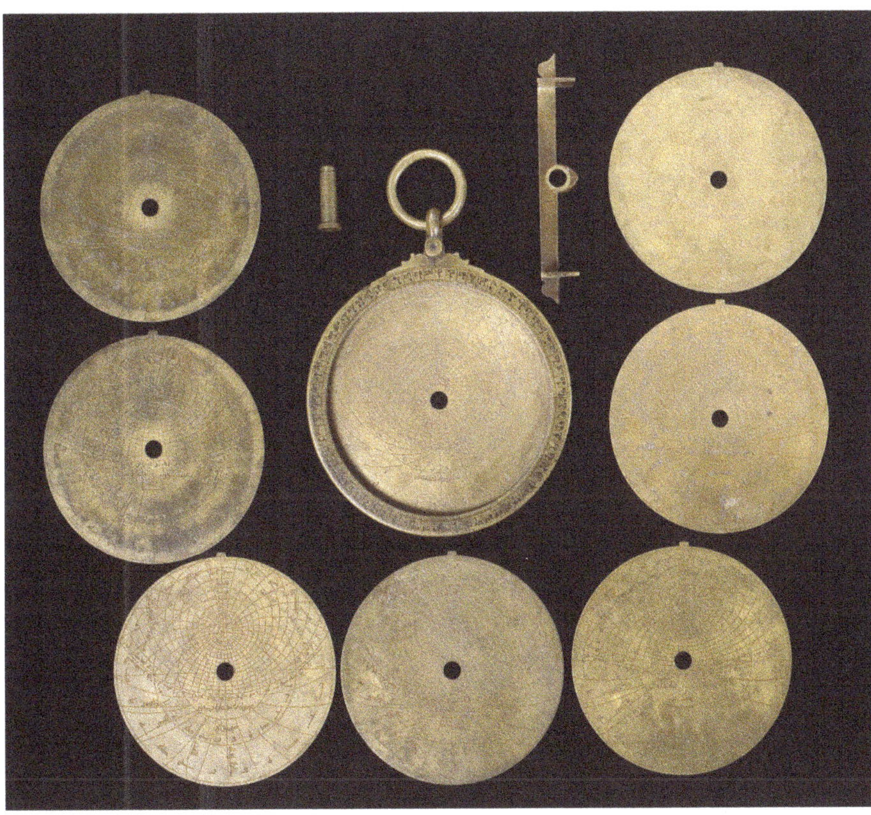

Figure 2.17. Astrolabe, Muhammad ibn al-Saffar, Córdoba, 1026–27. Mater (front) and plates, T. 1959.62, ©National Museums Scotland.

and plates, are apparent to the naked eye, but scientific analysis of the astronomical calibration and the metallurgy confirm different phases of facture for the body and the rete. Astronomical analysis of the star positions on the rete suggest that it was made around 1320 CE (plus or minus 126 years).[55]

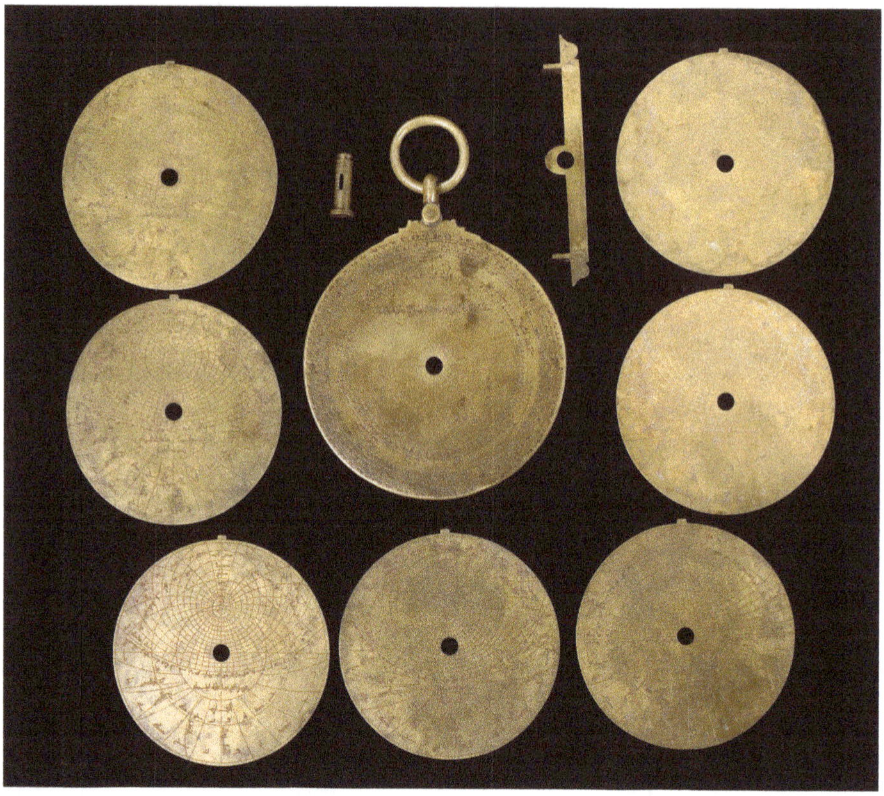

Figure 2.18. Astrolabe, Muhammad ibn al-Saffar, Córdoba, 1026–27. Mater (back) and plates. T. 1959.62, © National Museums Scotland.

Although we cannot know for certain what al-Saffar's original rete design looked like, a second instrument, preserved in Berlin and bearing a signature inscription also identifying al-Saffar as the maker, provides the best indication.[56] The inscription reveals that the astrolabe was made in 1029/30 in Toledo. Crafted only three years after al-Saffar's instrument preserved in Edinburgh, its rete is original, thus offering the best indication of the earlier instrument's original rete. While the instrument in Berlin shows a heightened aesthetic impulse also evident in Eastern astrolabes beginning in the tenth century, when considered in tandem with the other early Andalusi instruments it nevertheless suggests an Iberian visual approach to astrolabe design that is distinct from the formal appearance of Eastern examples.[57]

Instead of using the dagger-shaped star pointers typical of the earliest Eastern instruments, al-Saffar designed the slender, curving star pointers in the Berlin astrolabe that al-Sahli would also use in his instruments slightly later. The rete diverges in its formal visual language from the earlier Eastern retes as known from examples such as the elegant astrolabe signed by the celebrated instrument maker Khafif, likely made in the late ninth century.[58] The oldest astrolabe preserved in the History of Science Museum at the University of Oxford, it is a rare example of

Figure 2.19. Astrolabe, Muhammad ibn al-Saffar, Córdoba. Replacement rete (probably fourteenth century). T. 1959.62, © National Museums Scotland.

a fine precision instrument from Ibn Firnas's time. Made of brass and measuring 11.2 cm in diameter, it is inscribed on the front of its throne in a rounded *nashkhi* script with "by order of (*bi-rasm*) Ahmad al-Munajjim (the astronomer) of Sinjari," while the inscription on the back identifies its maker: "Made by Khafif the apprentice (*ghulam*) of 'Ali ibn 'Isa."[59]

Like Ibn Firnas, Khafif (active ca. 875–900) was remembered by later intellectuals as an early instrument maker whose abilities were deemed worthy of mentioning in Arabic literary and scientific texts.[60] As David King has discussed, the tenth-century *Kitab al-Fihrist* (The Catalogue) of Ibn al-Nadim, which is a key source on Abbasid literary culture, devotes a special section to Khafif, along with several other well-known "makers" of scientific instruments who moved in tenth-century court circles, including one father–daughter pair.[61] He observed that the text indicates Khafif was connected, mainly as a teacher, to more than half of the sixteen ninth- and tenth-century instrument makers that al-Nadim mentions in his work. Moreover, King points out that the distinguished eleventh-century Egyptian astronomer Ibn Yunus also specifically mentions Khafif and his skill in astrolabe making; indeed, he asserts that Khafif's eminence as an astrolabe maker was comparable to Ptolemy's status in demonstrative sciences and to Galen's in medicine.[62]

The formal similarities between the rete decoration in the star pointers of both the Berlin and Madrid instruments suggest that a distinct Iberian visual language

Figure 2.20. Astrolabe, Muhammad ibn al-Saffar, Córdoba. Front. Staatsbibliothek zu Berlin - Preussischer Kulturbesitz, Orientabteilung, Sprenger 2050.

had been formulated by the early eleventh century, which diverged from the one that is evident on the surviving instruments made in the Islamic East. It is therefore remarkable that the designer of the fourteenth-century replacement rete emulated the early Eastern Islamic astrolabes, rather than those of eleventh-century Iberia.[63]

Signatures, Makers, and Making

This brings us back to the signatures on the astrolabes in Madrid, Oxford, Edinburgh, and Berlin, which provide further clues about the connection between intellect, making, and visuality in early Islamic courts. Their importance to this discussion hinges on what we know about the identity and reputation of their makers. Historians of early Islamic art are usually frustrated by the lack of artisans' signatures, or any substantive information about those artisans whose signatures have survived. By contrast, we actually do know something about the identity of these early Andalusi astrolabe makers, thanks to the eminent Toledan scientist and intellectual Sa'id al-Andalusi (d. 1070), who flourished at the same time.[64]

Figure 2.21. Astrolabe, Muhammad ibn al-Saffar, Córdoba. Obverse. Staatsbibliothek zu Berlin - Preussischer Kulturbesitz, Orientabteilung, Sprenger 2050.

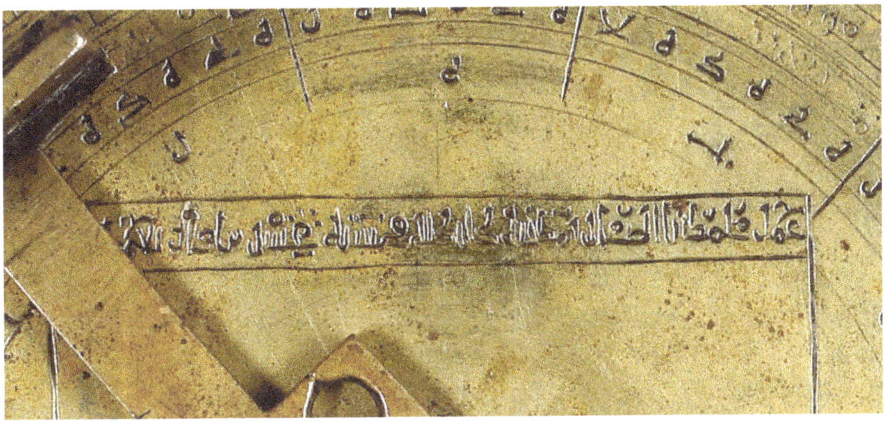

Figure 2.22. Astrolabe, Muhammad ibn al-Saffar, Córdoba. Signature inscription. Staatsbibliothek zu Berlin - Preussischer Kulturbesitz, Orientabteilung, Sprenger 2050.

Figure 2.23. Astrolabe, Muhammad ibn al-Saffar, Córdoba. Rete. Staatsbibliothek zu Berlin - Preussischer Kulturbesitz, Orientabteilung, Sprenger 2050.

Like many other contemporary intellectuals, Saʿid al-Andalusi had studied law, religion, grammar, and literature and was appointed the qadi of Toledo by that city's *taifa* ruler, Yahya ibn Dhi'l-Nun. Later in his life he focused on the exact sciences, especially mathematics and astronomy, and divided his time between his legal duties, teaching, and research in the history of science, theology, and literature. As a leading religious scholar as well as a scientist and intellectual, Saʿid al-Andalusi might have known these astrolabe makers personally. In his famous Arabic treatise on the sciences and scientists of his time, *Ṭabaqat al-umam* (Categories of Nations), Saʿid al-Andalusi tells us that the maker of the Edinburgh instrument, Muhammad al-Saffar, was "famous for his skill in building the astrolabe. No one before him, in al-Andalus, had known how to build this instrument better . . . "[65] About al-Sahli, maker of the aforementioned instrument in Madrid, the same author has this to say:

> During our present time, there are many young scholars who have distinguished themselves in the study of philosophy and demonstrated great energy and ability

Figure 2.24. Astrolabe, Khafif, Syria, late ninth century (?) Inv. 47632, © History of Science Museum, University of Oxford.

> to acquire a knowledge of most of its branches. Those of them who live in Toledo or around it include . . . Ibrahim al-Sahli, the constructor of astrolabes.[66]

That an intellectual as eminent as Sa'id al-Andalusi categorizes al-Sahli as a scholar who had distinguished himself in the branches of philosophy underscores the close relationship between high intellectual culture and the practice of design and making. Mathematics and astronomy were considered branches of philosophy in the ninth century, when 'Abbas Ibn Firnas was carrying out his activities in the Córdoban court, as well as in the eleventh century, which was the era of our chronicler Ibn Hayyan, the Toledan intellectual Sa'id al-Andalusi, and our astrolabe makers Muhammad Ibn al-Saffar and Ibrahim al-Sahli. There is an issue that arises when considering Sa'id al-Andalusi's important treatise. Given that the *Kitab tabaqat al-umam* is arguably the most significant text on the development of the exact sciences that survives from medieval al-Andalus, what are we to make of the absence in it of any reference to Ibn Firnas? The question lies beyond the scope of this work, but perhaps others will take it up and further illuminate our understanding of science in al-Andalus.

While there are examples of ceramic and metalwork objects bearing signatures in early Islamic art, for the caliphal period we tend to know little about the artists, even when their names are painted or inscribed on the objects. Precision instruments that are also works of art, such as the astrolabes discussed earlier, are the major exception to this rule, in that they are very often signed by their makers.[67] The makers of such instruments may have enjoyed a prestige similar to that of calligraphers due to the intellectual expertise and the craft skill required to produce these objects.

Umberto Bongianino has studied a twelfth-century manuscript in the Qarawiyyin Library in Fes, which offers evidence that artistic ability and social status were sometimes conjoined in al-Andalus. The manuscript, copied after 1109 in Marrakesh, features beautiful calligraphy and preserves the signature of the copyist, who was none other than a member of the royal family of Abbadid Seville, Abu Bakr Yahya Sharaf al-Dawla (d. after 1109).[68] This prince is remembered in Arabic sources as an intellectual and well-known book collector, who was also a talented copyist and calligrapher.[69] We might wonder whether this is mere hyperbole, or a literary convention or trope, but the evidence of the manuscript itself confirms the portrait of a royal who was also an intellectual with significant artistic skill in calligraphy. Indeed, he notes that following this prince's exile to North Africa, he earned his living as a copyist and became the personal copyist for the Almoravid ruler 'Ali ibn Yusuf ibn Tashfin (r. 1106–43).

If we look at the Kufic style of the signature inscription on the earliest instrument, the Edinburgh astrolabe, it appears distinct from the style used to inscribe the scientific information that makes up the bulk of the writing on the rear of the mater. Whereas the scientific information is written in a plain Kufic without any decoration, the letters of the signature inscription are embellished with pointed flaglike flourishes at the terminal points of individual letters. Although the difference between the treatment of the signature inscription and the scientific information is less apparent in al-Saffar's slightly later instrument, the inscription on his earlier work certainly lends a greater visual importance to the name of the maker, and to the place and time of the object's creation.

Al-Saffar employed the term *'amala* (maker) in his signature inscriptions on the instruments he made in Córdoba and Toledo, and the same term is used in signature inscriptions from Umayyad Córdoba in the caliphal period—for example, on the Córdoban ivories and architectural inscriptions.[70] However, on al-Sahli's slightly later instruments he seems to have preferred the term *ṣana'a* over the earlier *'amala*.[71] The same root (*ṣ-n-'*) is used to derive the noun, *ṣani'*, which is sometimes translated as "artisan," but which I have translated as "maker," following the lead of David A. King, who uses the term in his translation of Ibn al-Nadim's passage on famous instrument makers of the tenth century.[72] The translation "maker" also conforms with Therese Martin's recent attempts to broaden our understanding of how medieval works of architecture, as well as visual and material culture, came into being.[73]

That makers of fine instruments were recognized and esteemed as intellectuals is not only suggested by the consistency and style with which makers signed their instruments but also evident in key Arabic texts of the early medieval period. For example, the *Kitab al-Fihrist* of Ibn al-Nadim, a key source on Abbasid literary culture, contains a section devoted to well-known makers of scientific instruments who moved in Abbasid-era court circles, including the aforementioned Khafif.

It seems, then, that the designer-makers of these scientific instruments that are such striking works of art were in some cases also highly regarded intellectuals who were recognized as expert scientific practitioners in their own time, and who were connected to, or part of, elite learned and court circles. Leo Mayer, in his foundational book on Islamic astrolabists, observes that the choice of phrases habitually inscribed on astrolabes alongside the names of the instrument makers reveals an unusual pride in the work. Examples of such phrases include: "among the objects skillfully made by [so and so] . . . " "[so and so] . . . constructed and invented it"; "[so and so] . . . calculated as well as constructed it himself."[74] Significantly, Mayer found that the vocabulary used in the astrolabe inscriptions is consistent with terminology normally used to designate the creation of literary works—for example, "he composed" (*allafa*) or "he wrote" (*katabahu*)—whereas this is not the case for the inscriptions on other types of Islamic metalwork objects.[75]

The Celestial Globe of Ibrahim ibn Sa'īd al-Sahli al-Wazzan

Besides the Edinburgh and Madrid astrolabes, there is one more early instrument that survives from al-Andalus, which places Ibn Firnas's reputation as the maker

Figure 2.25. Celestial globe, Ibrahim Ibn Said al-Sahlì, 1080 or 1085. Antarctic pole with inscription. Inv. 2712. Museo Galileo, Firenze - Photographic Archives.

of the emir's armillary sphere in context and likewise reveals early intellectuals as makers of early Islamic visual culture. This is the celestial globe preserved today in the Museo Galileo, Florence, the oldest extant celestial globe to survive from any culture.[76] The globe's careful Kufic inscription, which rings the Antarctic polar circle, has been read as follows:

> Ibrahim ibn Sa'īd al-Sahli al-Wazzan in Valencia together with Muhammad his son made (*sana'a*) this globe with stand (*al-kurah dhat al-kursi*) for the holder of the dual office of wazir, the supreme commander-in-chief (*qa'id*) Abu 'Isa ibn Labbun, may God prolong him and sustain him. And the fixed stars were placed on it in proportion to their magnitude and sizes. It was completed the first of the month of Safar in 473 H [22 July AD 1080]. God bless him and give him secure peace.[77]

Thus, the globe's Arabic inscription tells us that it was also made by al-Sahli, the same maker of the magnificent astrolabe preserved in Madrid. Made some

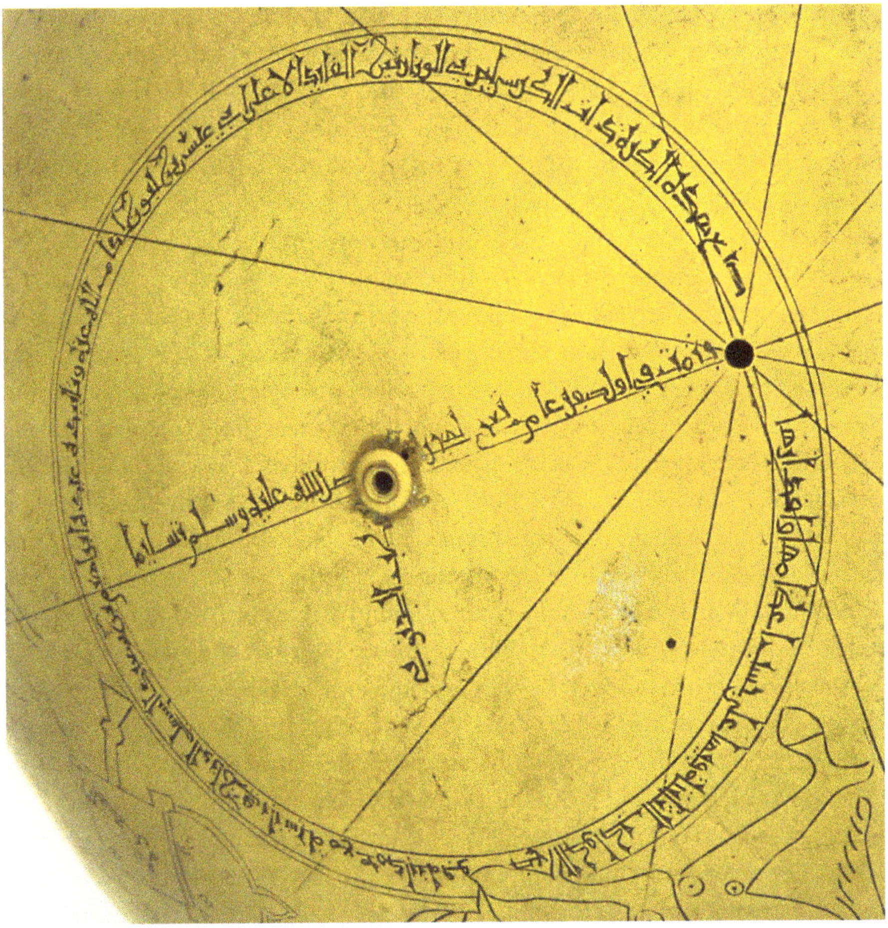

Figure 2.26. Celestial globe, Ibrahim Ibn Said al-Sahlì, 1080 or 1085. Signature inscription. Inv. 2712. Museo Galileo, Firenze - Photographic Archives.

seventeen years after the astrolabe now in Madrid, the globe is likewise made of brass and formed of two uniform and precisely joined hemispheres, connected at the equator. It measures 209 mm in diameter and represents 1015 of the 1025 stars cataloged by Ptolemy, which are indicated by a dot inside an engraved circle, and is inscribed with many star and constellation names, along with other types of astronomical information. The inscription also states that al-Sahli's son collaborated with him on the globe, which accords with other instances of intellectual-makers within the same family. Such practices were not unique to al-Andalus but shared by other Islamic courts of the caliphal era.[78]

Fragments of the lid of an early thirteenth-century metalwork box, preserved in the David Collection in Copenhagen, offers further evidence to support a view of astronomers as makers of medieval visual culture. The fragment, measuring 4.4 cm high, 23.5 cm wide, and 18.5 cm deep, is made of cast and hammered brass and beautifully inlaid with silver and copper.[79] Notably, the lid of this metalwork box incorporates an early combination lock, of a type described by al-Jazari (d. 1206) in his *Book of Knowledge of Ingenious Mechanical Devices*.[80] The box features a signature inscription placed prominently above the dials of the lock, framing the large central roundel. This inscription, consisting of two lines and bisected by the roundel, has been read: "Work of Muhammad ibn Hamid al-Asturlabi al-Isfahani in the year seven and ninety and five hundred (1200/1201 CE), and I tested it (?) (*fa-jarrabtuhu*)."[81] The signature inscription thus tells us that the person who created this finely crafted and technologically sophisticated locking box was a maker of astronomical instruments from Isfahan. Maddison observed that this same maker may have also created a second box with a combination lock, preserved in Boston, and four extant astrolabes preserved in Istanbul, Tehran, Kuwait, and Paris.[82] Moreover, the statement that this astrolabe maker "tested" the mechanism himself is perhaps suggestive of a kind of medieval "research and development" mindset, combined here with the design and craft processes. The lid's locking mechanism consists of four double combination dials. Each of the dials can be set to sixteen different positions, allowing for a staggering number of potential combinations—some four million. A movable dial and the larger concentric ring in which it is contained feature the characters for the possible combinations, inlaid in silver. Besides providing material evidence that astrolabe makers also crafted other types of fine objects, the box predates al-Jazari's treatise (written in 1206) and therefore allows us to situate al-Jazari within a broader context of craft practices and technology that existed by the thirteenth century. We should not regard al-Jazari as a lone genius, then, but, rather, as a representative of broader practices uniting craft and intellect that were already established in courts across the empire in the ninth century.

The passing down of astronomical and technical knowledge within families was not limited to fathers and sons. The aforementioned Ibn al-Nadim also mentions a father and daughter among the famous instrument makers of his time: the father's name was al-ʿIjli and the daughter was al-ʿIjliyya.[83] This female astrolabe maker, according to Ibn al-Nadim, was an astronomer in the court of the famous Hamdanid ruler Sayf al-Dawla (d. 967), well known for cultivating an outstanding circle of intellectuals at his court in Aleppo, including the great tenth-century philosopher al-Farabi (d. ca. 961), whom medieval Arabic intellectuals considered second only to Aristotle.

Siblings, too, could be collaborators in this respect. The aforementioned Saʿid al-Andalusi, in his *Categories of Nations*, describes the brother of the Córdoban astrolabe maker al-Saffar as an intellectual who was well known "for his precise knowledge of arithmetic, geometry, and astronomy," who taught those subjects in Córdoba—presumably at the Great Mosque—and who was notable as the author of the earliest Andalusi treatise on the astrolabe.

Unlike the astrolabe inscriptions, which name their maker but do not tell us for whom the instruments were intended, the inscription on al-Sahli's globe also names the recipient of this object, Abu ʿIlsa ibn Labbun. Ibn Labbun was one of

Figure 2.27. A thirteenth-century box lid with combination lock, whose signature inscription states that it was made by an astrolabist. Inventory number 1/1984, The David Collection, Copenhagen. Photo: Pernille Klemp.

the most prominent intellectuals in the *taifa* court at Toledo during the reign of its most celebrated ruler, al-Ma'mun (d. 1074–75), a ruler famous as a patron of learning. His dynasty's capital was Toledo, but al-Ma'mun also came to control Córdoba as well as Valencia, where the globe was produced. Ibn Labbun was one of al-Ma'mun's boon companions, and one of the three most-cited poets associated with al-Ma'mun's court. He was a very well-known court intellectual, whose biography and selections of his poetry were transmitted by later Andalusi authors. A.R. Nykl, scholar of Hispano-Arabic poetry, described Ibn Labbun as "a poet of true feeling" whose compositions showed him to be "a great lover of flowers and wine, a faithful companion, and an affectionate brother."[84] The globe's inscription identifies him as the holder of two important official administrative positions within the court at Toledo: supreme commander-in-chief (*qa'id*) and holder of the dual office of wazir.

The globe provides additional evidence for an early Andalusi intersection between science and visual culture that complements that represented by the astrolabes. Al-Sahli's globe features an extensive program of figural imagery representing forty-seven of the forty-eight classical constellations. The figural imagery engraved on its surface is important in the history of Islamic art. One reason is that it is rare to have astronomical (or—closely related—astrological) figural imagery in Islamic art generally, and on metalwork specifically, before the twelfth century.

Figure 2.28. Celestial globe, Ibrahim Ibn Said al-Sahlì, 1080 or 1085, view with line of the ecliptic. Inv. 2712. Museo Galileo, Firenze - Photographic Archives.

As Carey has argued, depictions of the constellations on the al-Sahli globe seem indicative of a specifically Western Islamic visual repertoire, distinct from a standard Eastern iconography.[85] Al-Sahli may have combined Islamic materials with a late classical source, such as illustrated manuscripts of the ancient Greek poet Aratus, whose poem on constellations and celestial phenomena was widely copied and circulated in late antiquity and the medieval period. This seems likely, as numerous painted Aratus manuscripts survive (thirteen in the ninth century alone, which is twice the number that survive from the tenth and eleventh centuries combined). These have been attributed to the major Carolingian centers and seem to have circulated widely in Western Europe.

In an Aratus manuscript made in France, perhaps in Rheims around 820–840 and preserved in the British Library, the heads of Antecanum (Sirius?) and Cetus, with their long pointed snouts, are similar to those depicted on the globe. Likewise, a similar treatment of the mythical animals and the human figures—notably the wavy short hair and the forms of the heads, noses, and eyes—is evident in the famous Iberian manuscript known as the Morgan Beatus of 962.

Figure 2.29. Celestial globe, Ibrahim Ibn Said al-Sahlì, 1080 or 1085. Equator. Inv. 2712. Museo Galileo, Firenze - Photographic Archives.

It may be that al-Sahli and his son were composing the globe's figural imagery within a visual frame of reference that encompassed Frankish as well as Iberian manuscript-painting traditions (as known from surviving manuscripts).[86] Such similarities between the manuscripts circulating in Iberia and Frankish courts—considered in tandem with the globe's figural decoration—suggest that al-Sahli and his son were inspired by themes and modes of representation across a variety of religious and political borders, not only from the Iberian Peninsula, but Europe north of the Pyrenees, and elsewhere in the Islamic lands.[87]

When examined alongside the instruments and other works discussed in this chapter, ʿAbbas Ibn Firnas's reputation as the pioneering instrument maker of al-Andalus and a leading intellectual of the ninth-century court alerts us to close connections between science and medieval Islamic visual culture. Fine scientific instruments make clear the complex relationship between Islamic science and visual culture, in which aesthetic and intellectual agendas were linked through specific visual strategies, as Martina Müller-Wiener, Moya Carey, Persis Berlekamp,

Figure 2.30. Celestial globe, Ibrahim Ibn Said al-Sahlì, 1080 or 1085. Arctic pole. Inv. 2712. Museo Galileo, Firenze - Photographic Archives.

and Gulru Necipoglu have demonstrated.[88] These strategies aided the users of scientific instruments and illustrated manuscripts in the acquisition of knowledge.[89] Astrolabes and other fine scientific instruments such as globes, armillary spheres, and water clocks, as well as illustrated scientific texts, combined aesthetic and intellectual agendas that required their users to engage in a visual, physical, and mental process of close looking that led to an intellectual engagement with complex scientific information.

ʿAbbas Ibn Firnas's reputation as the pioneering instrument maker tells us that high social and intellectual status and the practices of design, making, and science were commensurable in medieval Islamic societies. Our polymath, and other intellectual-makers in al-Andalus and elsewhere, epitomize what Margaret Graves has described as a medieval Islamic "intellect of the hand."[90] One final example of a surviving instrument, made later and in a different court context, illustrates the point that high social or intellectual status and design or craft ability may not have been mutually exclusive. This is an astrolabe in the Metropolitan Museum

Figure 2.31. Illustration of the sea-monster Coetus (Cetus) from an Aratus manuscript made in France, perhaps in Rheims around 820–840. Harley 647, f.10 c13507-40, © The British Library Board.

of Art, whose inscription states that its maker was a prince of the Rasulid dynasty of thirteenth-century Yemen.[91] It suggests that even those with royal blood were sometimes renowned for combining intellectual and craft skills: "This astrolabe is the work of ʿUmar ibn Yusuf ibn ʿUmar ibn ʿAli ibn Rasul al-Muzaffari directly [by himself] and by his instruction in the year A.H. 690 (1291 CE)."

Given the royal identity of the named maker, one might reasonably ask whether in this case "maker" might indicate the patron or intended recipient of the instrument, rather than the person who designed and fashioned it. But that does not seem to be the case here. As scholars have pointed out, besides the attestation of the

Figure 2.32. Illustration of Anticanis from an Aratus manuscript made in France, perhaps in Rheims around 820–840. Harley 647, f.13 c13507-41, © The British Library Board.

maker's inscription on the instrument itself, a singular piece of written evidence exists to confirm the identity of its maker as the prince. This is a manuscript copy of a treatise on the construction of astrolabes, written in ʿUmar Ibn Yusuf's own hand, and demonstrating his interest in and technical knowledge of the subject.[92] Moreover, this manuscript also contains attestations from his teachers that the prince was in fact a competent maker of astrolabes, and it includes a description

Figure 2.33. Four beasts. The Morgan Library & Museum. MS M.644, fol. 40r. Purchased by J.P. Morgan (1867–1943) in 1919. Photographic credit: The Morgan Library & Museum, New York.

Figure 2.34. Angel of the abyss and locusts. The Morgan Library & Museum. MS M.644, fol. 142v. Purchased by J.P. Morgan (1867–1943) in 1919. Photographic credit: The Morgan Library & Museum, New York.

Figure 2.35. Astrolabe signed by prince ʿUmar ibn Yusuf of Rasulid Yemen, dated AH 690 / AD 1291. Brass; cast and hammered, pierced, chased, inlaid with silver. Accession Number: 91.1.535a–h. Edward C. Moore Collection, bequest of Edward C. Moore, 1891. Metropolitan Museum of Art, New York.

Figure 2.36. Obverse, astrolabe signed by the Rasulid prince 'Umar ibn Yusuf of Yemen, dated AH 690 / AD 1291. Brass; cast and hammered, pierced, chased, inlaid with silver. Accession Number: 91.1.535a–h. Edward C. Moore Collection, bequest of Edward C. Moore, 1891. Metropolitan Museum of Art, New York.

of the instrument preserved in the Metropolitan Museum. The Rasulid astrolabe and its accompanying manuscript treatise thus offer clear visual and material evidence that medieval Islamic intellectual and social elites were at times actively engaged in design and craft, and that such skills could be visibly demonstrated and acknowledged—even celebrated—in Islamic court societies.

3

Visualizing Science at Home

The previous chapter considered Ibn Firnas's reputation as a maker of fine scientific instruments. Having established a clearer sense of the polymath as a maker of works that were both science and art, in this chapter I turn to a creation that he designed and made not for the Córdoban ruler, but for himself, which he displayed to other intellectuals at his home. I begin by considering some of the ambiguity around this famous creation, which has been imagined as a kind of early planetarium. I argue that what Ibn Firnas designed and presented to other intellectuals in his residence might best be understood as a large-scale mechanical device, or automaton, housed within a chamber, and designed to dramatically visualize astronomical, astrological, and meteorological information and phenomena to other intellectuals in his circle. My intent in speculating about the nature of his creation is to further flesh out our picture of Ibn Firnas as a maker of science and visual culture, and to use the creation as an example of the important connection between science, art, and courtly patronage in ninth-century Córdoba and elsewhere.

I consider surviving works of visual culture from the Islamic lands and neighboring territories, in tandem with the account of this wondrous chamber in Ibn Hayyan's text, for clues to better understand the creation's functions and its potential visual program. I then turn to a unique medieval Andalusi engineering treatise, exploring what this important text and the mechanical devices it describes might suggest about the nature of Ibn Firnas's creation as a work of architecture and science. From there the chapter takes up issues around science, architecture, and design raised by the account of Ibn Firnas's creation, chiefly what this account reveals about intellectuals' involvement simultaneously in the exact sciences and in architectural design and construction during the caliphal era. I consider a brief and somewhat puzzling reference that the eleventh-century Toledan intellectual Saʿid al-Andalusi included in his famous treatise on medieval science and scientists, which states that a court intellectual participated in the design and execution of al-Hakam II's expansion of the Great Mosque of Córdoba and that his role was commemorated in the monument's mosaic inscriptions. To unpack this reference I take a small detour to ninth-century Egypt to discuss parallel textual evidence for the participation of Abbasid intellectuals in the design and construction of the Nilometer of Cairo, a monument that also combines architecture and the visualization of scientific information and phenomena. The chapter concludes that Ibn Firnas's creation underscores the innovative character of the devices he designed and created and the distinctive way in which he combined the visual and

A Bridge to the Sky. Glaire D. Anderson, Oxford University Press. © Oxford University Press 2024.
DOI: 10.1093/oso/9780190913243.003.0004

technological to create a spectacular visualization of natural scientific phenomena. This is a departure from the otherwise similar use of mechanical devices in the contemporaneous Abbasid and Byzantine courts, which similarly used technology to spectacular effect, but which used automata and figural imagery mainly to convey political statements about a ruler's power and prestige, or to stage visual narratives derived from literature. What emerges is a clearer sense of the connections between science, visual culture, and court patronage in early medieval Córdoba and beyond.

Representing the Heavens at Home

Besides the armillary sphere and the water clock that he designed and created for the Córdoban ruler, Ibn Firnas, according to the chronicle, crafted something wondrous that he displayed within his own residence, which he showed to an audience of his audience. As Ibn Hayyan states:

> Muhammad b. Yahya b. ʿAbd al-ʿAziz related:
>
> "As ʿIbn Firnas had manufactured a reproduction of the heavens (*hayʾata al-samaʾi*) in his house, which he assembled in scientific fashion (*rakkabaha ʿala minhaji al-hikmati*), representing the stars and setting up mechanisms that appeared (*wa-aqama fiha alatin tukhayyilu*) to its viewer as though they were stars, clouds, thunder and lightning, he showed it often to the notables among the people, boasting of his wisdom. News and talk of it spread."[1]

Many historians have alluded to this device, but scholars have not considered it fully in light of what the early text reveals about its character, nor in relation to the later aeronautics experiment. Yet this passage, with its emphasis on the representation of the celestial realm and meteorological phenomena, suggests that this creation marked an important phase in the intellectual and artisanal journey that eventually inspired the later aeronautics experiment.

The passage raises a number of questions. What exactly was this celestial representation? Was it another precision instrument, similar to the armillary sphere, or was it something else entirely? Was it a celestial globe that Ibn Firnas could turn clear or cloudy at will?[2] Given our polymath's reputation as the pioneer of Andalusi precision instrumentation, a small, portable instrument would be a reasonable assumption. Armillary spheres, celestial globes, and astrolabes would all to some extent fit with the Arabic text's description of "a reproduction of the heavens (*hayʾata al-samaʾi*)" "assembled in scientific fashion (*rakkabaha ʿala minhaji al-hikmati*)." But the text goes on to say that this creation encompassed "mechanisms that appeared (*wa-aqama fiha alatin tukhayyilu*) to its viewer as though they were stars, clouds, thunder and lightning." The reference to "mechanisms" suggests a type of apparatus, an object with parts that moved together to create specific visual and auditory effects. Artist Michael Grimsdale's rendering of Ibn Firnas's device, created for *AramcoWorld*, depicts what appears to be a monumental armillary sphere, which fits the impression of an object with moving parts (Fig. 3.1). However, while the Arabic text tells us that Ibn Firnas did make an armillary sphere for ʿAbd al-Rahman II, the creation he designed and made for his own home suggests something rather different.

One can imagine the representation of such celestial objects and visual phenomena as stars, clouds, and even lightning on the surface of an instrument such

Figure 3.1. Imagining Ibn Firnas's wondrous creation: here the artist's rendering resembles a monumental armillary sphere set in a courtyard. Image: Michael Grimsdale / Saudi Aramco World / SAWDIA.

as a celestial globe. Stars might be indicated through the use of distinct materials, as exemplified in the use of silver and gold inlay on the globe made for the Ilkhanid observatory at Maragha that Moya Carey has discussed.[3] We can imagine too how clouds might have been visually evoked, either through surface decoration or through the use of visual effects, but the reference to thunder signals something entirely different. This tells us that there was an auditory element to the creation, in addition to the visual ones, which suggests that this was probably neither a celestial globe nor an armillary sphere, at least not in the way we know such instruments from extant examples. Here we can speculate that some types of visual and auditory effects were in play, such as those described in a later medieval treatise on white magic, *Fi 'l-hiyal al-babiliyya li 'l-khizana al-kamiliyya* (The Complete Bag of Babylonian Tricks), by one al-Hasan b. Muhammad al-Iskandari al-Kūshi al-ʿAbdari.[4] The chapters devoted to "Tricks involving the air and atmospherical vapours" and "IV. Tricks with fire and the illusions produced in the minds of the spectators" seem particularly apropos in conceptualizing Ibn Firnas's device.[5] Magic and its associated literary works were popular in medieval Islamic intellectual and literary culture.[6] The text that may best represent the interest in this topic is the *Kitab al-Khawaṣṣ al-kabir* (The Great Book of Properties) of Djabir b. Hayyan, a corpus believed to have been composed around the late ninth century, which concerns alchemy as an experimental science based on philosophical theory.[7] Given ʿAbbas Ibn Firnas's reputation as a master of occult knowledge, including alchemy, and the date of this corpus of alchemical knowledge, we can suppose that Ibn Firnas may have been familiar with this literature and the techniques and operations detailed in it. This type of knowledge seems to have been part of the "*ʿulum al-awail*" (sciences of the ancients) associated with learned elites in the early medieval Islamic period.[8]

Further along in this passage of the chronicle, the impression of a large construction that involved not only sight but also sound and that engaged the viewer's body in a holistic way is confirmed by lines of poetry penned by Ibn Firnas's rival, the court poet Mu'min b. Saʿid, in reaction to Ibn Firnas's creation. This poetry immediately follows the statement that "news and talk" of the polymath's spectacular creation had spread. The chronicle states:

> [*Regarding this talk*], the poet Mu'min b. Saʿid opposed those who spoke of him [Ibn Firnas] by criticizing his actions and challenging him on religious grounds. He recited many verses on this [subject] in which mockery degenerated into obscenity. Among these was his remark:
> [131v]
>
> I sat under a firmament (*sama'in*) of Ibn Firnas,
> And fancied that a windmill revolved (*rahan darat*) around my head:
> It is the heavens fabricated (sawwaha) by a silly fellow, encircled
> By a serpent with fangs and teeth;

> It has stars that will tell you that its creator,
> if you looked at [this firmament], is the biggest fool.
> Come morning and afternoon he works (*min shughlin*) on his creation
> Secretly preoccupied, [with the] reflection and suggestion of Satan:
> He deserves someone to raise him to the top [of the building/structure]
> And then make him jump head-first[9]

As a literary evocation of an emotional and intellectual response to Ibn Firnas's creation, the passage gives us a rare sense of how one intellectual of Ibn Firnas's acquaintance reacted to his creation. Clearly, while it caused a stir ("news of it spread," we are told) not everyone welcomed the spectacular creation, and its ascription of the inspiration behind the device to the "reflection and suggestion of Satan" resonates with other passages in the chronicle that allude to Ibn Firnas's reputation for heterodox behavior and beliefs.

Visualizing Ibn Firnas's Celestial Creation: A Painted Astronomical Vault?

If we speculate that the poetry bears some relation to the appearance of Ibn Firnas's creation, these lines provide additional clues as to its nature of the device, its scale, and its visual features. The poet says, "I sat *under* a firmament (*sama'in*)," indicating that the device was of a sufficient size that the speaker or viewer could be seated beneath the representation of the celestial vault.[10] This indicates that the device was not a small portable instrument but, rather, a construction that was architectural in scale. Indeed, the final two lines of this poem—"he deserves someone to raise him to the top / and then make him jump head-first"—suggest a creation of sufficient height that a person who jumped from the top of the structure might suffer bodily injury.

That the construction incorporated a visual program of astronomical and astrological information is indicated by the poet's lines that allude to the representation of this celestial vault as "encircled by a serpent with fangs and teeth." Such a serpent encircling the heavens would have represented to ninth-century viewers the constellation Draco (Ar. *al-Tinnin*), known in Ptolemy's *Almagest* as the third of the twenty-one northern constellations, and one that regularly appears in the Arabic astronomical and astrological literature.[11] If Ibn Firnas's celestial vault was indeed decorated with a representation of the constellation Draco and other celestial features, we might start to imagine possibilities for its appearance by looking at an example of such a decorated vault that existed by his time. This is the well-known caldarium vault of the eighth-century Umayyad bathhouse at Qusayr 'Amra, in present-day Jordan, which offers the best example of a medieval Islamic architectural space decorated with a representation of the heavens (Fig. 3.2). The curved interior surface of the caldarium vault in Qusayr 'Amra's bath is famously painted with frescos of the constellations. Significantly, historians of science have argued that the artisan(s) who painted the Qusayr 'Amra vault copied the depictions of constellations from the surface of a celestial globe, transferring late antique Greek star imagery to the interior surface of this early Islamic dome.[12] As a domed space decorated with constellation imagery likely taken from an early scientific instrument, Qusayr 'Amra's painted caldarium vault may therefore provide a significant precursor to Ibn Firnas's celestial creation as we can imagine it from these lines of poetry.

In the Andalusi context there is no evidence from the ninth century that provides a sense of the imagery decorating Ibn Firnas's creation. Rather, we find the nearest Iberian comparison to the serpent encircling Ibn Firnas's vault in the sinuous, fanged creatures depicted on the celestial globe (discussed in Chapter 2), crafted later, in the eleventh century, by the astronomer and instrument maker al-Sahli in collaboration with his son. Inscribed on the surface of the metal, each creature has a long, thick body along which the stars comprising the constellation have been indicated in the form of a dot within an engraved circle (Fig. 3.3). Rounded bulging nodules at intervals represent the monsters' coiling bodies, with heads presented in profile. They have tiny, pointed ears, pointed snouts, and open jaws that display sharp tongues and rows of jagged teeth. Elsewhere in the Islamic lands, explicitly

Figure 3.2. Zodiac fresco, caldarium vault, Qusayr Amra, Jordan. Umayyad, eighth century. Photo: Marlena Whiting / Manar al-Athar: http://www.manar-al-athar.ox.ac.uk. Creative Commons Attribution-NonCommercial-ShareAlike 2.0 UK: England and Wales (CC BY-NC-SA 2.0) Licence.

Figure 3.3. The head of a serpent visible where it crosses the ecliptic latitude circle at top left. Celestial globe, Ibrahim Ibn Said al-Sahli, 1080 or 1085. Inv. 2712. Museo Galileo, Firenze - Photographic Archives.

zodiacal imagery does not become a feature of Islamic art generally until around the twelfth century.[13] Another work with which we can compare the sinuous creatures found on al-Sahli's globe is found in the Doha illustrated copy of al-Ṣūfi's *Treatise on the Fixed Stars*, made in 1125 in Baghdad.[14] Its depiction of Draco illustrates an Eastern iconographic tradition for representing constellations that Moya Carey has established as distinct in its visual iconography from the al-Sahli globe (Fig. 3.4).[15]

The most celebrated medieval Islamic automata treatise, al-Jazari's *Book of Knowledge of Ingenious Devices*, provides a thirteenth-century example of the combination of a device combining astronomical and astrological imagery that seems to have featured in Ibn Firnas's wondrous creation. This is the first device described in al-Jazari's treatise, the "castle water-clock," which was a monumental timepiece twice the height of a man and combining the architectural form of a castle or palace with figural representations of drummers and trumpeters, the whole composition "rising from the ground a distance of about twice the height of a man, comprising

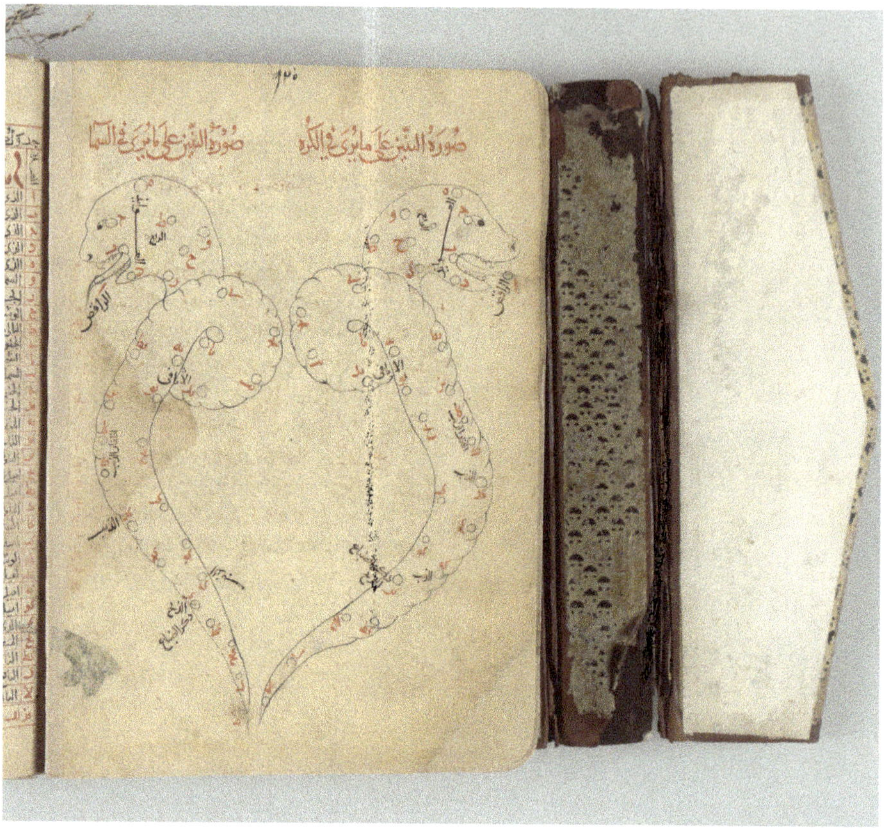

Figure 3.4. Folio with drawings of the constellation Draco (*al-tinnin*), the dragon. By the manuscript copyist, ʿAli ibn ʿAbd al-Jalil ibn ʿAli ibn Muhammad, Baghdad, 1125. Al-Ṣufi's astronomical treatise, *Kitab Ṣuwar al-kawakib (al-thabitah)* (*Book of pictures of the [fixed] stars*), folio 20v. Photo: The Museum of Islamic Art, Doha, Qatar.

all that is required for telling the passage of the hours."[16] Surmounting the composition was a rotating component with the sun, moon, and representations of the zodiac, which al-Jazari describes in these words:

> [The zodiac appears in] a semi-circle with its convexity towards the top. Around its circumference are six of the 12 Zodiacal signs [i.e., visible at a given time], and below this is a sphere carrying the sun, a golden roundel and, below this, a sphere carrying the moon, a glass roundel.[17]

We can visualize this device thanks to two paintings of the clock preserved in later copies of al-Jazari's treatise. The manuscript painting from a copy preserved in Boston depicts the castle clock's facade surmounted by the roundel showing six of the zodiac signs, richly rendered in gold on a deep blue ground (Fig. 3.5). On a page preserved in Washington, D.C., the artist depicted the clock's entire roundel, with the twelve zodiac signs painted in gold on a blue ground, along with the representations of the sun and moon roundels, rendered in gold and silver, respectively (Fig. 3.6).

If we look beyond al-Andalus and Islamic territories, however, star paintings in Frankish and Byzantine astronomical manuscripts offer a near-contemporary visual and intellectual context that could help us imagine the appearance of Ibn Firnas's celestial vault. Surviving examples provide the closest comparanda near Ibn Firnas's lifetime for the kind of imagery with which he and his peers were likely to have been acquainted. Byzantine astronomical manuscripts were conceived and used as practical handbooks for experts in astronomy and astrology and were possibly made by imperial astrologers.[18] I have already mentioned the ninth-century Carolingian Aratus painted manuscript (see Chapter 2), in the context of the decoration of al-Sahli's celestial globe. The manuscript's illustrations provide evidence for the persistence of ancient and late antique cosmological visual culture in ninth-century Frankish territory, and thus relatively near to Ibn Firnas's own time and place.[19]

Art, Science, and Medieval Diplomacy

But how likely is it that he and those in his intellectual and court circles would have been familiar with such depictions? Diplomatic connections between early medieval courts are one channel by which scientific visual culture, in the form of instruments and illustrated manuscripts, may have circulated in intellectual circles by Ibn Firnas's time.[20] The issues of diplomacy and visual culture and the extent to which intellectuals from various religious backgrounds participated in design and transfer of visual culture from one place or context to another are worth considering briefly before returning to our main discussion on Ibn Firnas and his wondrous creation. A drawing of an Andalusi Umayyad astrolabe of circa 976–1000, preserved in a manuscript in Paris, for example, attests to the transfer of scientific instruments and astronomical information from al-Andalus to Europe north of the Pyrenees.[21] Likewise, several texts refer to Córdoba's diplomatic exchanges with contemporary non-Muslim courts.[22] The first Córdoban embassy to Constantinople took place in 839–40, a time when Ibn Firnas was active in the Umayyad court. His colleague, the prominent Córdoban court poet al-Ghazal, was charged with representing the Córdobans at the court of the Byzantine emperor Theophilus (r. 829–42).[23] According to the Córdoban chronicle, the ambassador thoroughly charmed Theophilus and the Byzantine empress. In the tenth century, Umayyad Córdoba exchanged three embassies alone with the Byzantine court of Constantine VII in 945–46, 949–50, and 955–56, and in the 950s the Ottonian court likewise sent an embassy to Córdoba. Against this backdrop of intensified diplomatic exchange, the medieval sources attest to the circulation of scientific manuscripts as gifts.[24] Famously, the Byzantine emperor Romanos II is said to have sent a copy of Dioscorides's pharmaceutical

Figure 3.5. Al-Jazari's "Book of Knowledge of Ingenious Mechanical Devices": The Castle Water Clock. Egyptian, Mamluk period, 1354. Object place: probably Cairo, Egypt. Ink, opaque watercolor, and gold on paper. Height × width: 39.8 × 27.5 cm (15 11/16 × 10 13/16 in.) Francis Bartlett Donation of 1912 and Picture Fund 14.533. Photograph © 2019 Museum of Fine Arts, Boston.

Figure 3.6. The zodiac roundel that surmounted the Castle Water Clock. Detached folio from a dispersed copy of al-Jazari's "Book of Knowledge of Ingenious Mechanical Devices": Freer Gallery of Art, Smithsonian Institution, Washington, D.C.: Purchase—Charles Lang Freer Endowment, F1930.74.

treatise to 'Abd al-Rahman III. The Córdoban chronicle discusses the arrival of the manuscript in Córdoba, and the subsequent collaboration that ensued between Córdoban and Byzantine intellectuals in order to translate the work from Greek into Arabic.

As S.M. Stern has discussed, a letter from an unnamed Byzantine emperor to al-Hakam II, preserved in a circa fifteenth-century Arabic manuscript in Madrid, suggests the transfer of another manuscript from the Byzantine to the Córdoban court, providing an additional example to add to that of the Dioscorides manuscript.[25] The letter indicates that either al-Hakam II or another intellectual in his court, presumably an ambassador, specifically requested manuscripts of a scientific, philosophical nature from the Byzantine emperor, and the author emphasizes their shared interest in such topics. The manuscript that apparently accompanied the letter was a copy of *The Book of Causes*, by the first-century author Apollonius of Tyana. Stern has described Apollonius as an "antique sage and magician," to whom various works were attributed, including the one sent to al-Hakam II, whose variant titles hint at its subject matter: it was also known as the *Book of the Secrets of Creation* and *Assembly of Wisdom*.[26] If authentic, the letter suggests how manuscripts (and other works of visual and material culture) traveled via diplomatic channels. It also suggests that in the tenth century the court intellectuals of Umayyad Córdoba were still interested in the kind of occult and philosophical material with which Ibn Firnas was so strongly associated, and that Byzantium had access to such material and shared it with its Córdoban ally.

That Ibn Firnas's construction was not only visual but also kinetic, incorporating moving components that made possible rotating motion is suggested by the lines that say that the poet, sitting under the vault, "fancied that a windmill revolved (*rahan darat*) around" his head. This suggests a large-scale device, housed within an architectural space as I have discussed earlier, capable of producing visual effects suggestive of perceived or actual rotating movement. The earliest extant objects that attest to a medieval Islamic tradition of moving mechanisms are those that I have already discussed: the geared astrolabe and the geomantic tablet used for divination (see Chapter 2) (Figs. 3.7, 3.8).[27] Like Ibn Firnas's wondrous creation and the geared astrolabe, the geomantic tablet is also an innovative caliphal machine with moving parts. The instrument has numerous dials and knobs that the user would manipulate to obtain a divinatory reading by activating the inner workings of the machine. This consisted of a series of disks bearing geomantic markings that could be read through the openings on the object's face. Thus, like Ibn Firnas's creation, it too was a kinetic device that brought together ingenious craft, science, occult knowledge, and religion.

Figure 3.7. The world's oldest complete geared mechanism, an astrolabe with geared calendar. Signed by Muhammad Ibn Abi Bakr, Isfahan, 618 AH, 1221/2 CE. Inv. 48213. © History of Science Museum, University of Oxford.

Figure 3.8. Interior gearing, astrolabe with geared calendar. Signed by Muhammad Ibn Abi Bakr, Isfahan, 618 AH, 1221/2 CE. Inv. 48213. © History of Science Museum, University of Oxford.

Andalusi Automata: Al-Muradi's *Kitab al-Asrar Fi Nata'ij al-Afkar*

A unique thirteenth-century copy of the earliest medieval Arabic engineering treatise from al-Andalus provides the best evidence for understanding Ibn Firnas's wondrous creation as likely a type of automaton, a mechanical device, capable of motion and executed on a large scale.[28] The manuscript is preserved in the Medici Library in Florence (Codex Medicea Laurenziana Or. 152) and has been studied as part of a project led by Massimiliano Lisa, Eduardo Zanon, and Mario Taddei (Fig. 3.9). Their team published a facsimile of the treatise, a translation of its text, and dramatic digital and physical reconstructions of the devices described in the text.[29] The models were exhibited at the inauguration of the Museum of Islamic Art in Doha in 2008 and subsequently featured in the "Allah's Automata" exhibition held in 2015–2016 at the Zentrum für Kunst und Medientechnologie in Karlsruhe, Germany.[30] As Julio Samsó has discussed, internal evidence within the manuscript text suggests that its author, al-Muradi, was a specialist in *'ilm al-handasiyya* (applied geometry, engineering, architecture), most likely working in the eleventh-century court of Toledo when it was the most important center of science in al-Andalus.[31] He furthermore points out that the manuscript is notable for several reasons. Besides being the only

Figure 3.9. The first folio of al-Muradi's *Kitab al-Asrar Fi Nata'ij al-Afkar*, the earliest engineering treatise from al-Andalus. Firenze, Biblioteca Medicea Laurenziana, Ms. Or. 152, f. 1v–2r. By permission of MiBAC. Any further reproduction by any means is prohibited/Su concessione del MiBAC E' vietata ogni ulteriore riproduzione con qualsiasi mezzo.

known extant example of al-Muradi's text, it may be the only surviving Arabic manuscript copied in Toledo during the reign of Alfonso X, known as The Wise (r. 1252–84), who was famous for his interest in the natural sciences. Indeed, according to Samsó, the manuscript's copyist was himself a well-known court intellectual, Ishaq b. al-Sid, a famous Jewish translator and intellectual in Alfonso X's court.

The manuscript contains descriptions and diagrams of mechanical devices—especially water clocks, but also calendars, war machines, and large complex automata, which combine precise engineering with figural imagery and visual effects, and which Donald Hill analyzed.[32] The diagrams accompanying the descriptions of the machines are highly schematic and illustrate features of the inner workings of the machines. Understandably, Hill's focus was the gearing and other components that comprised the advanced technologies embodied in these medieval devices. Yet, significantly for our understanding of what Ibn Firnas's creation might have looked like, the Arabic text of the al-Muradi manuscript makes it clear that the machines described in it featured elaborate figural imagery that helped a viewer understand the information the machine was meant to convey. In contrast with later painted manuscripts that depict devices described in other surviving engineering treatises, namely, that of al-Jazari, the scribe who drew the diagrams in the al-Muradi manuscript chose to leave out depictions of the representational elements—human and animal figural imagery and architecture—described in the texts (Fig. 3.10).[33] The scribe was not concerned with illustrating the finished machines to delight the eye of an elite viewer but, rather, was focused on diagramming the innovative mechanisms to a reader who could use them to construct the machine described.[34]

The copyist's diagram for the tenth device, for instance, whose description is titled "A clock, a man with an astrolabe and a maiden," provides no hint that the machine's action actually depended on the movements of the figures of the two protagonists (Fig. 3.11). But as the text makes clear, it is their movements that mark the passing of the hours: "when an hour is completed, he looks at her and, once he looks at her, she throws a pebble from her mouth. Then the man with the astrolabe turns his head back [until the beginning of] another hour."[35] It would be a mistake to assume that the men, women, and animals that decorated the clocks and other machines were merely ornamental, as their movements and motions translated the device's mechanical functions into meaningful information. In other words, the viewer of the clock could *see* the passage of time, through the movements of the woman and the astrologer. The imagery made the hidden mechanical actions apprehensible.

While other medieval engineering treatises have survived in multiple manuscript copies, there are no other known copies of al-Muradi's treatise that could provide information missing in this one. The manuscript illustrations are obviously important as a visual record of the gearing and the engineering innovations described in the accompanying text, and though to an art historian's eye they might suffer by comparison with the lavishly painted copies of al-Jazari's treatise, they are nevertheless incredibly significant as medieval diagrams, and as schematic representations of the mechanical devices that were so important in medieval Islamic court life.

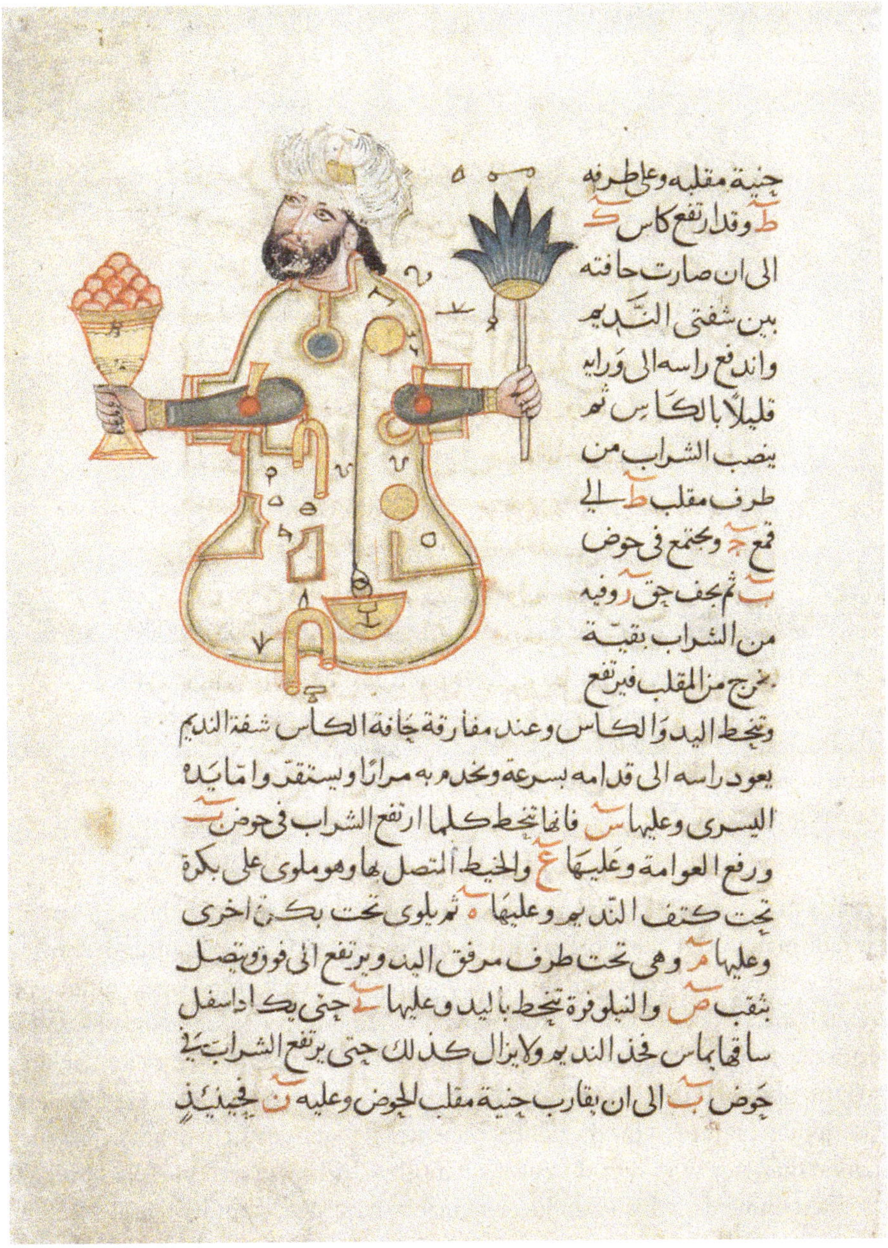

Figure 3.10. An automaton designed to "drink" and then unexpectedly drench an unsuspecting guest with the liquid. The manuscript painting is by Farkh ibn Abd al-Latif, who was also the manuscript's scribe. Folio from a *Book of the Knowledge of Ingenious Mechanical Devices* by al-Jazari, dated AH 715 / AD 1315. Syria (?). Ink, opaque watercolor, and gold on paper. Height × width: 11.62 in. × 7.94 in. (29.5 cm × 20.2 cm). Accession number: 55.121.12. The Metropolitan Museum of Art, New York, Rogers Fund, 1955.

Figure 3.11. Folio with diagram and description of al-Muradi's tenth device, a water clock with figures of a maiden and a man holding an astrolabe, presumably an astrologer. Firenze, Biblioteca Medicea Laurenziana, Ms. Or. 152, cc. 18v–19r. By permission of MiBAC. Any further reproduction by any means is prohibited / Su concessione del MiBAC E' vietata ogni ulteriore riproduzione con qualsiasi mezzo.

Such drawings are rare in the medieval Islamic context, and those in the al-Muradi manuscript therefore offer important evidence for design and drawing practices that complement other surviving diagrams related to visual culture and architecture.[36] Rather than the diagrams providing information about the architectural settings and figures that comprise the visual program of each machine, it is the titles and descriptive texts that convey the information. These titles and descriptions allude to how the figures were meant to move and to interact, and they suggest that they were meant to evoke narratives, perhaps from popular literature or entertainments, which would presumably have been familiar to al-Muradi's contemporaries and to the viewers of these complex devices. Al-Muradi's treatise may therefore help us understand the impression of Ibn Firnas's wondrous creation as a type of large-scale apparatus or mechanism that could produce movement (or the sensation of movement) as well as visual and auditory effects.[37]

The first machine that al-Muradi describes is a large clepsydra, and it may therefore provide the best sense of the type of apparatus that Ibn Firnas is said to have designed and created for the Umayyad ruler, which I introduced in the previous chapter.[38] The Arabic text that accompanies the diagram describes the device as "a love fairy tale and the evil snakes," which suggests a narrative that unfolded through the movements of the machine's figural images, and that included a man and woman, snakes, and gazelles (Fig. 3.12).[39]

Figure 3.12. Folio with diagram of al-Muradi's first device, a water clock (*clepsydra*) that featured figures of a man, a woman, snakes, and gazelles. Firenze, Biblioteca Medicea Laurenziana, Ms. Or. 152 cc. 2v–3r. By permission of MiBAC. Any further reproduction by any means is prohibited / Su concessione del MiBAC E' vietata ogni ulteriore riproduzione con qualsiasi mezzo.

The al-Muradi treatise's emphasis on narrative, and the centrality of the human and animal automaton figures enacting the tale, reminds us of the signal importance of the automaton's figural imagery to medieval audiences. While it was the mechanical features of al-Muradi's machines that brought them to the attention of modern scholars of science and technology, to viewers in Ibn Firnas's time, the immediate impact of these fantastic devices would have been visual, auditory, and kinetic. They were subtly crafted in wood and metal, with miniature architectural settings within which people, animals, and objects moved and made sounds by invisible means. Prior to the aforementioned project led by Lisa, Zanon, and Taddei, scholars in Spain had collaborated on reconstructions of al-Muradi's devices in an attempt to understand them as working machines and objects of visual culture. As Samsó has discussed, one reconstruction was crafted in 1990 by the expert craftsman Eduard Farré, in collaboration with Juan Vernet and Rafael Casals, with the aim of discovering whether it was possible technically to produce a working mechanism as described in the manuscript.[40] "The Clepsydra of the Gazelles," as it was called, was exhibited in the Museo Arqueológico Nacional, Madrid, as part of a landmark 1992 exhibition on science in al-Andalus and is preserved today in the Museo Nacional de la Ciencia y de la Técnica in Madrid.[41] A second version, originally in the museum of the Institut für Geschichte der Arabisch-Islamischen Wissenschaften (Frankfurt), is preserved today in Istanbul in the Museum of History of Science and Technology (Figs. 3.13–3.15).[42] While Silke Ackermann has

Figure 3.13. Clepsydra of the Gazelles, reconstruction by Eduard Farré, Istanbul. Photo courtesy of İstanbul İslam Bilim ve Teknoloji Tarihi Müzesi

questioned the historical veracity and ultimate utility of such reconstructions, they are useful in offering today's viewers some sense of the performative, visual, and material qualities of the medieval automata in the absence of surviving artifacts.[43] That such devices can still capture the eyes and imaginations of twenty-first-century viewers alerts us to the power that automata like Ibn Firnas's wondrous creation may have had to capture the imaginations of his peers in the Córdoban court.

The Arabic text accompanying the diagram tells us that the visual focus of the fifth device described in al-Muradi's text is a scene of combat, with an architectural setting providing a frame for the human combatants. In terms of its engineering features, Donald Hill noted that Machine Five is also the most complex of the first five automata described in the treatise, containing all the mechanisms presented in the other four either singly or in combination.[44] As interpreted by Hill, the diagram's vertically oriented rectangle represents the box that housed the gears and pulleys that powered the moving parts, and that would not have been visible to the machine's viewers (Fig. 3.16). Moreover, as Hill explained, the diagram shows the interior workings of the machine and its complex gearing system. Within the rectangle a gridlike arrangement provides a visual order to the components within: in the center are two concentric circles with doubled perimeters whose outer edges are marked with sixty-four triangular teeth, representing the machine's central cogwheel. A smaller cogwheel, likewise featuring a toothed perimeter, is connected to the large central one, and above and below the central one are two additional small cogwheels of thirty-two teeth each.

Figure 3.14. Female figures. Clepsydra of the Gazelles, reconstruction by Eduard Farré, Istanbul. Photo courtesy of İstanbul İslam Bilim ve Teknoloji Tarihi Müzesi.

Figure 3.15. Gazelles and figure hiding in a well. Clepsydra of the Gazelles, reconstruction by Eduard Farré, Istanbul. Photo courtesy of İstanbul İslam Bilim ve Teknoloji Tarihi Müzesi.

Figure 3.16. Folio with diagram for al-Muradi's fifth device, which presented viewers with a scene of combat. MS Orient. 152. Firenze, Biblioteca Medicea Laurenziana, Ms. Or. 152 cc. f. 11v. By permission of MiBAC. Any further reproduction by any means is prohibited / Su concessione del MiBAC. E' vietata ogni ulteriore riproduzione con qualsiasi mezzo.

The other elements of the diagram consist of lines and circles at the top and bottom of the rectangle representing a central axle, bearings to which the cogwheels and axle were connected, and to the right and left of the three cogwheels, lines and small rectangular forms representing the ropes, pulleys, rings, tubes, columns, rods, and cross-shaped components detailed in the description, which transferred the power to the moving components on the exterior of the box. To the left of the rectangle is a circle with a double perimeter, divided into quadrants by two lines, of which the horizontal one extends to connect this circle to the perimeter of the rectangle at right, and to a thick vertical line at left. Strikingly, this circle represents a waterwheel, and the connecting line is the means by which it was attached to the central axle within the main body of the machine. Hill noted that the use of a full-size waterwheel to power the machine is particularly significant, indicating the sheer size and power of al-Muradi's machines.[45] I will return to this point later, when I discuss the architectural and spatial implications of Ibn Firnas's creation.

Less than a century after Ibn Firnas's death, we can discern a similar conjunction of wondrous creations combining human and animal figures displayed in the Córdoban court. For instance, al-Maqqari wrote that the Córdoban caliph ʿAbd al-Rahman III commissioned twelve spectacular metalwork animals that were affixed to a beautiful green marble basin, brought to Madinat al-Zahraʾ from either Syria or Constantinople:

> The figures, which were all made in the arsenal of Cordova [sic], represented various animals; as for instance one was the likeness of a lion, having on one side an antelope, and on the other a crocodile; opposite to these stood an eagle and a dragon; and on the two wings of the group a pigeon, a falcon, a peacock, a hen, a cock, a kite, and a vulture. They, moreover, were all ornamented with jewels and the water poured out of from their mouths.[46]

The setting is unspecified, and one wonders who the audience for this work may have been, and what significance such specific animal imagery may have had for them. Might the animals have alluded to the information contained in scientific works such as Jahiẓ's treatise on animals, the *Kitab al-Hayawan*?[47] Or might they have represented astronomical information, perhaps a combination of Greek and Bedouin constellation imagery, as is the case with the imagery on the al-Sahli celestial globe? Or could they have alluded to animal fables, such as those in the Khalila wa Dimna?[48] The vulture, which might seem an odd choice in this rather extensive group of birds, may have evoked the most celebrated sage of the early Islamic tradition, Luqman, and I will have more to say about him in relation to Ibn Firnas in the following chapter. Allegra Iafrate has proposed that surviving medieval hollow bronze animal figures, and the Byzantine and Abbasid ones mentioned in texts, were rudimentary water-powered automata.[49] Antonio Vallejo-Triano, Anna Contadini, and Calvo Capilla have likewise discussed the famous bronze "deer" fountainheads

Figure 3.17. Bronze deer, attributed to Córdoba. Museo Arqueológico Nacional, Madrid. Photo: Glaire D. Anderson.

from Madinat al-Zahra', and their significance to understanding caliphal metalwork and court culture, including as part of diplomacy and gift giving, and as elements of a "multisensory" and theatrical ensemble of fountains and sound-making zoomorphic figures, such as the Pisa Griffin (Fig. 3.17).[50]

If we look beyond Córdoba to the Abbasid court, by contrast, animal figures are specifically mentioned in only three of the one hundred devices in the Banū Mūsa treatise: these are the fifth, sixth, and seventh devices, which are described as featuring the figures of lions, bulls, and smaller wild animals.[51] Interestingly, both animals and human figures feature in the illustrations that accompany the textual descriptions of the devices in what Hill judged to be the finest surviving illustrated copy of the Banu Musa manuscript, preserved in the Topkapi Palace Museum. Examples include those of device 85 (featuring two horned animals) device 23 (featuring a duck), and device 46 (featuring a human figure holding what appears to be a small tree or shrub) (Figs. 3.18–3.20).[52]

'Abd al-Rahman III is said to have had a second basin, slightly different from the aforementioned one in its appearance but no less wondrous in its effects, which was installed in a reception space at the palace city of Madinat al-Zahra':

> Another of the wonders of al-Zahra' was the hall called Qasru-l-Khulafa (the hall of the caliphs) . . . according to Ibn Bashkuwal, there was in the center of the room a large basin filled with quicksilver; on each side of it eight doors fixed on arches

Figure 3.18. Folio with diagram of device 85, with animal imagery (gazelles). Banu Musa manuscript. Photo, © Topkapi Palace Museum. TSMK. A.3474.47v.

of ivory and ebony, ornamented with gold and precious stones of various kinds, resting upon pillars of variegated marble and transparent crystal. When the sun penetrated through these doors into the apartment, so strong was the action of its rays upon the roof and walls of this hall that the reflection only was sufficient to

Figure 3.19. Diagram of device 23 with animal imagery (duck), Banu Musa manuscript. Photo, © Topkapi Palace Museum. TSMK. A.3474.19r.

Figure 3.20. Diagram of device 46 with human figural imagery, Banu Musa manuscript. Photo, © Topkapi Palace Museum. TSMK. A.3474.59r.

> deprive the beholders of sight. And when al-Nasir wished to frighten any of the courtiers that sat with him, he had only to make a sign to one of Sclavonians to set the quicksilver in motion, and the whole room would look in an instant as if it were traversed by flashes of lightning; and the company would begin to tremble, thinking that the room was moving away, his sensation and their fears continuing as long as the quicksilver was in motion.[53]

In this case the architectural space and its interactions with natural elements—sunlight and mercury—created the dramatic visual effect. Here sunlight reflecting on the surface of a basin of mercury frightened and awed viewers by simulating flashes of lightning. This anecdote suggests one method by which Ibn Firnas may have been able to produce the effect of lightning for his own creation in the ninth century.

An International Taste for Automata

If we consider the broader context of the ninth century, Ibn Firnas's spectacular chamber with its representation of the heavens, and the water clock he created for the Umayyad ruler that I discussed previously, fit within a larger landscape of mechanical devices that were a feature of early medieval courts in the Dar al-Islam and elsewhere. In contrast to Ibn Firnas's creation, however, other wondrous chambers appear to have been primarily an expression of imperial power, and to have been situated within a palace or other specifically royal architectural setting. Al-Khatib al-Baghdadi's account of the Byzantine embassy to Baghdad in 917, discussed by Grabar, for example, alludes to a striking automaton in the form of a tree, situated in the caliphal palace. Al-Khatib describes the tree as having stood in the midst of a large circular pond filled with clear water, and as having been crafted mainly of silver weighing 500 dirhams, and to a lesser extent of gold. Its eighteen twigged branches, al-Khatib tells, featured leaves and birds that moved and whistled in the wind, which the author claims greatly astonished the Byzantines.[54] This splendid tree was flanked on two sides by the figures of thirty mounted horsemen, clothed in brocade and brandishing long-poled javelins, one line at the other.

One wonders about the reference to a weight of 500 dirhams and an unspecified amount of gold. What does this suggest about the size and scale of this precious metal tree? Was this enough silver and gold to construct something on a large scale? In any case, the architectural setting is potentially suggestive of a large installation, and clearly one that was meant to deploy mechanical and visual arts to impress viewers with a message of imperial power. A few decades later we see a similar type of automata in the service of an imperial image in Byzantine Constantinople. Writing in the context of his 949 reception by Constantine Porphyrogenitus, Liudprand of Cremona famously described the Byzantine emperor's throne in the Great Triclinium of the Magnaura palace in Byzantine Constantinople in this way:

> A tree made of bronze but covered with gold leaf stood in front of the emperor's throne. Its branches were filled with similar golden birds of various types, which emitted various notes according to their species. The emperor's throne was cleverly constructed so that at one moment it was on the floor level, at the next it seemed raised to a great height. It was guarded by lions of enormous size, which may have been made of bronze or wood but were gilded. They swept the floor with their tails, opened their mouths, moved their tongues and emitted a roar.[55]

Besides the Byzantine emperor's throne room there are also Carolingian sources that mention Frankish chambers said to have produced meteorological effects. However, those seem not to have been set in private residences of intellectuals, but in palaces, and seem to have been meant to enhance the image of the ruler, rather than to visualize scientific knowledge. These are not exclusive possibilities, however. These were wondrous devices rooted in technological knowledge and know-how, but different in intention from Ibn Firnas's chamber.[56] Such works were designed specifically for royal or imperial spaces, where the display of technological prowess served to underscore the cosmological power and the authority and magnificence of the emperor or the caliph.[57] In Ibn Firnas's creation these particular conjunctions of architectural space and automata combined engineering and visual representations of natural things (trees, lions, birds) with kinetic and auditory effects (the lions' moving tails and roars, the chirping of the birds).[58]

We can therefore understand Ibn Firnas's creation as having been conceived primarily as a space of scientific visualization, not imperial power, and one that may have evoked connections with occult literature and knowledge. The overall impression that we take away from the description in Ibn Hayyan's text is that while the creation was dramatic, it was not primarily meant to convey a message of imperial or cosmological power, as would have been the case had the setting been the Umayyad palace in Córdoba, or Rusafa, or one of the other Umayyad suburban villas. Because it was constructed and housed within the polymath's own residence, and because it depicted astronomical, astrological, and meteorological information for other intellectuals, Ibn Firnas's creation stands apart from the automata of the early medieval period. While, like those of the Byzantine and Abbasid courts, his device was presented in a theatrical, spectacular way meant to evoke wonder in the viewer, ultimately it is notable as a dramatic visual expression of scientific knowledge, primarily meant for an audience of intellectuals.

Benjamin Anderson has made an instructive comparison between Islamic and Frankish courts.[59] He finds a similarity between the roles of astronomical experts in Islamic and Frankish contexts, and a shared conceptualization of astronomical/astrological experts who operated within the orbit of the ruler. According to Anderson this stands in contrast to the contemporaneous Byzantine notion, which positioned the ruler as the astronomical/astrological expert. This way that Islamic and Frankish courts may have differed from the Byzantine court makes it less surprising that Ibn Firnas would construct his meteorological chamber within his own residence, rather than in a royal setting.

Having argued that Ibn Firnas's creation was an architectural space housing a large-scale mechanical device like the machines featured in al-Muradi's treatise, and featuring celestial imagery, this may also help us better understand the water clock that Ibn Firnas made for the ruler (see Chapter 2), which Ibn Hayyan's text does not, unfortunately, describe in any detail. The machines described and diagrammed in al-Muradi's treatise, and the recreations that today's scholars have created, reveal how in early Islamic Iberia water clocks existed at the intersection of visual culture, science, and technology. Of the thirty-one mechanical devices described and illustrated with diagrams, more than half are clocks, whose measuring devices were powered through hydraulic systems and which used gears and other mechanisms to produce the movements and the accompanying noises and visual effects—most often the dropping of pebbles or some type of hard marker—which marked the passage of time.[60]

As with the first five automata, most of the clock designs include figures of women and men, which appear singly or in combination with one or more humans and animals, such as snakes, goats, and lions. In several of the vignettes the male figures hold astrolabes, suggesting that by the eleventh century these devices exercised a strong hold on the way science and technology were visualized. Margaret Graves has delineated a prehistory for this, observing how astrolabes are held up as the epitome of human craft and technical ingenuity by the Ikhwan al-Safa, or Brethren of Purity.[61] Those clocks that did not feature figural automata manipulated light to indicate the passage of time. Several use mirrors, and others some form of illumination, whether sunlight or lanterns. Some were designed to be used at any time of day; others are specifically designed to operate during the night or during the day. The twenty-ninth device, a specifically nocturnal clock, used lanterns to mark the passage of time and was meant to be constructed on a scale large enough to be legible from a distance; a viewer could tell the hour by observing how many of the lanterns were lit. In some cases dimensions are provided, such as in device number 20, which is specified as 3.2 feet in height, with an automata roughly 8 inches tall. In other cases al-Muradi's notes indicate the possibility of adjusting the scale of the clocks through the use of waterwheels and ropes, which indicates that the clocks, as in the first five automata, could be built at significant size and with mechanisms of considerable power.

As was the case in antiquity, monumental clocks played a role as notable fittings elsewhere in the Islamic lands and beyond, where they appeared in important architectural and urban contexts, including in Umayyad Syria, as Flood has discussed.[62] These mechanical devices were spectacular creations whose visibility to viewers was a tangible expression of the connections between the cosmos and the ruler, underscoring political and religious legitimacy.[63] From the eighth century, and certainly by the tenth, however, court architecture, court and urban viewing publics, and clocks seem to have been features of important cities.[64]

In Iberia, the water clock constructed on the bank of the river in twelfth-century Toledo served as a monumental urban expression of the trajectory of automata design and construction. Ibn Hayyan and his sources likewise traced this important aspect of Andalusi intellectual and design culture back to ʿAbbas Ibn Firnas in the ninth century. Like the Antiochene clock the Toledo water clock did not survive, but the evidence for this key conjoining of architecture and engineering in the Islamic West did persist in Fes and can be seen in the traces of the fourteenth-century clocks constructed at the Bu' Inaniyya Madrasa and the Qarawiyyin mosque.[65] The clock at the Qarawiyyin consisted of a chamber that would have contained the machinery, and from which a beamlike structure extended, supporting a row of twenty-four hinged wooden doors. A system of concealed tubes would have discharged balls at specific intervals onto a row of metalware bowls or gongs (now missing), one per door, to mark the hours.[66] We can see Ibn Firnas's creation as linked to ancient and late ancient precedents in important ways, but new and distinctive in others. Fusing architecture and technology to dramatic visual effect, Ibn Firnas's meteorological chamber resonated deeply within a framework of medieval Islamic intellectual, religious, and social currents.[67]

Science, the Occult, and Intellectual Culture

There are more esoteric aspects of Ibn Firnas's creation, which speak to its target audience of court intellectuals, and which underscore the difficulty of distinguishing the exact sciences from the related occult knowledge with which intellectuals in medieval Islamic courts were also engaged. The visual and auditory effects to which these texts allude underscore the kind of knowledge Ibn Firnas was famed for possessing, which extended into the realm of the occult arts. According to Ibn Hayyan, Ibn Firnas was "a master of white magic (*sahib nairanjat*)."[68] The term *nirandj* in Arabic and Persian encompasses "prestidigitation, fakery and counter-fakery, the creating of illusions and other feats of sleight of hand (*hiyal*)," and it refers to a body of knowledge and a literary genre popular since antiquity and the Hellenistic period.[69]

By the tenth century in al-Andalus, based on the text known as *G͟hayat al-hakim*, also known as the *Picatrix*, the term *nirandj* also denoted a type of object: amulets with power over men and natural phenomena, whose crafting required *perfect precision* and precautions against the poisonous substances involved in their creation.[70] In other words, the creation of such amulets called for both occult and philosophical knowledge and craft skill.[71] Maribel Fierro has proposed that the author of this important text was none other than the tenth-century Córdoban intellectual Maslama b. Qasim al-Qurtubi (d. 964), suggesting a continuity in interests and activities—or at least, a perceived continuity by Ibn Hayyan's time—from ʿAbbas

Ibn Firnas's occult practices in the ninth-century court into the second half of the tenth century.[72] Fierro also observes, recommending further investigation, that this same intellectual, Maslama b. Qasim al-Qurtubi, was identified as the architect of Madinat al-Zahra'.[73] Intersections between occult knowledge, design, and making existed by the tenth century, to which the writings of the Brethren of Purity allude, and which Margaret Graves has discussed in the context of what she understands as a medieval Islamic culture of craft and intellect.[74]

A similar connection between design, architecture, and intellectuals in Umayyad Córdoba is signaled by Ṣaid al-Andalusi', writing about one of the leading intellectuals in the caliphal court:

> There was also Muhammad ibn Tamlyh [sic], a scholar of dignity and respect having a deep knowledge of medicine, grammar, language, poetry, and history. He served al-Nasir and al-Mustansir bi-Allah . . . he was also the orator of al-Hakam [al-Mustansir bi-Allah], who charged him with the supervision of the addition to the south side of the mosque of Cordoba. The work was completed under his direction and responsibility. I have seen his name written in gold and pieces of mosaic on the wall of al-mihrab of that section. This structure was completed under his direction by the order of Caliph al-Hakam in AH 358 [AD 969].[75]

In this instance Ṣaʿid tells us that he himself saw the visual and material evidence for this court intellectual's participation in one of the caliphal era's major architectural projects: his name executed in gold mosaic in the mihrab zone of the Córdoba mosque. Ibn Saʿid's passage attests to a perception among eleventh-century intellectuals that men of learning in the Córdoban Umayyad court actively participated in the making of Umayyad visual culture.

Ṣaʿid's account is corroborated by the epigraphic evidence at the Great Mosque of Córdoba, as read by Levi-Provençal, who noted the connection between this intellectual and Saʿid al-Andalusi's reference in 1931, and later by Ocaña Jiménez.[76] Levi-Provençal identified the intellectual as Abu ʿAbd Allah Muhammad b. Tamlih al-Tamimi (d. Ramadan 361 / June–July 972), a Córdoban jurist and qadi of Córdoba.[77] He records no less than three inscriptions from al-Hakam II's expansion at the Great Mosque in which this intellectual's name appears in the mosaic inscriptions and carved in white marble within the mihrab.[78] The Kufic inscription is carved in relief on eight bands encircling the interior of the mihrab, for example (Fig. 3.21):

> [Qur'an II:239 . . .] At the order of the Imam al-Mustansir bi'llah, the slave of God, al-Hakam, the Commander of the Faithful. . . . This work was completed under the guidance of his freedman and *hajib* Ja'far, son ʿAbd al-Rahman—may Allah be pleased with him!—and under the supervision of Muhammad b. Tamlih, Ahmad b. Nasr, Hald b. Hashim, his police prefects, and Mutarrif b. ʿAbd al-Rahman the

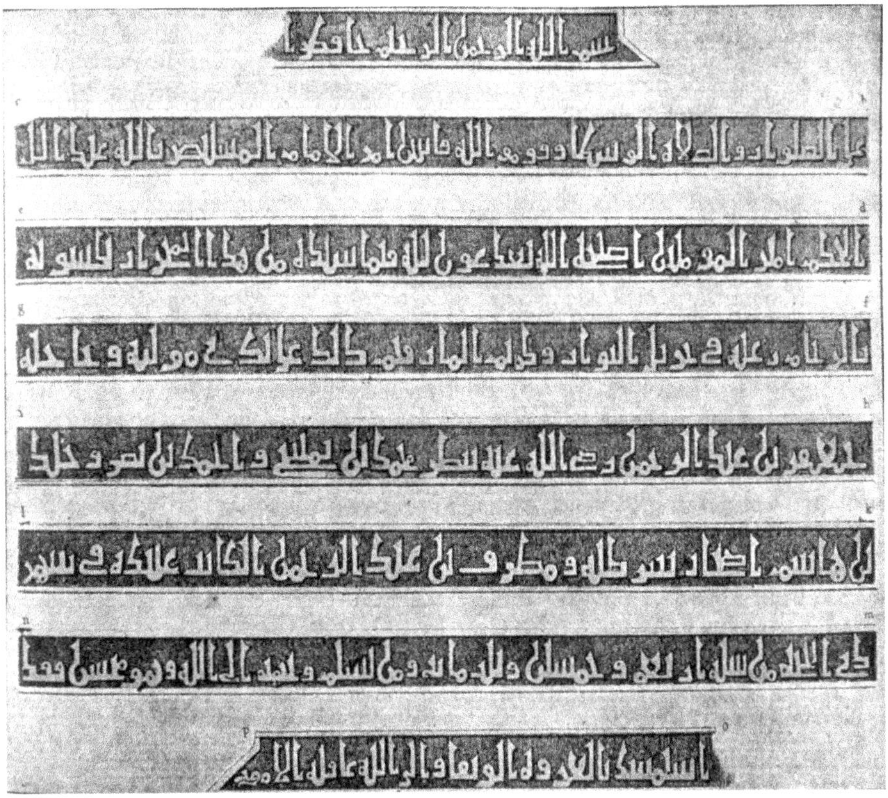

Figure 3.21. Mihrab, interior inscription band (marble), Great Mosque of Córdoba expansion of al-Hakam II, 965 CE. Drawing: Girault de Prangey, published in Lévi-Provençal, Inscriptions arabes d'Espagne, p. 11.

secretary (*katib*), his servants, in the month of du'l-hijja of the year 354 (November 28–December 27, 965). [Qur'an XXXI:21][79]

Muhammad b. Tamlih's role according to the inscription was that of "supervision" (*naẓar*). The Arabic root of the term (n-ẓ-r) has connotations of vision and looking, but also discernment, inspection, control, and competence. While it is difficult to say, based on the inscription alone, whether Muhammad b. Tamlih played a role in the design process, if we consider the possibility that court intellectuals such as Muhammad b. Tamlih in the tenth century were not disinterested bureaucrats, removed from the design process, but, rather, intellectuals who may have competently applied their knowledge of geometry and arithmetic to such projects, in collaboration with the unfree Slav elites like Ja'far and Durri al-Saghir, who supervised the state's arts and architectural production, this could help us understand what Felix Arnold has described as a revolutionary "mathematical turn" in tenth-century Córdoban architecture, and its evocation in the formal language of the early Andalusi astrolabes designed by intellectuals such as al-Sahli, as I discussed in Chapter 2.[80] Ocaña Jimenez, in his discussion of the mosaics and the inscriptions, pointed out the "extraordinary correctness" of the contents of the inscriptions from al-Hakam II's addition, elaborated in both mosaic and marble, noting as significant in this respect the involvement of Mutarrif b. 'Abd al-Rahman, the *katib* (secretary) who is named in the inscriptions, and who was responsible for their content.[81] Calvo Capilla has proposed that the qadi of Córdoba Mundhir ibn Sa'id al-Ballut may also have contributed to the content of the mosque's epigraphic program.[82] This indicates that in Córdoba by the tenth century there was collaboration between intellectuals-mathematicians and those who designed and carried out architectural projects, providing a precursor to what Alpay Özdural has argued occurred slightly later in medieval Iran, as evidenced by the collaboration between the celebrated Persian mathematician and poet Omar Khayyam (born 1048) and artisans working on the Great Mosque of Isfahan.[83] It seems likely that in Córdoba by the tenth century mathematical and other exact sciences became another arena in which to compete with other contemporary cultural centers.[84]

Architecture as Scientific Instrument: The Abbasid Nilometer

Looking beyond al-Andalus, in Ibn Firnas's own century one of the great monuments of early Islamic architecture, the Nilometer of Cairo, illustrates similar interconnectivity between architecture, science, and intellectuals. Although its significance and history are well known, as a roughly contemporary extant Islamic monument that embodies the themes I am concerned with here, I'd like to discuss the Nilometer in some detail, before returning to Ibn Firnas, Córdoba, and the main topic of the chapter.

In Umayyad Córdoba the practice and display of science was linked to specific spatial contexts. We have seen how the private residence of 'Abbas Ibn Firnas served as a setting for the design and creation of a scientific visualization within an architectural space, and how the royal villa of Rusafa served the ninth-century Córdoban ruler as a space for scientific experiment and display. The Nilometer resonates with some of the issues that have arisen from considering his wondrous creation that fused architecture, science, and instrumentation. Completed in 861—at the peak of Ibn Firnas's career in Córdoba—the Nilometer parallels the impression of Ibn Firnas's creation in that it combined architecture and the visualization of scientific information.[85] Its purpose was to measure the annual Nile flood in August-September, which was vital to Cairo's rulers as a means to predict flooding or drought and famine, and to regulate distribution of water and levy of taxes paid as tribute to the Caliph (Fig. 3.22).

Within the shaft that comprises the main interior space is a marble column resting on millstone, topped with a Corinthian capital and used to measure the water levels (Fig. 3.23). In days spent waiting for the flood, the column was anointed with saffron and musk "to induce a good water level." It is significant in the history

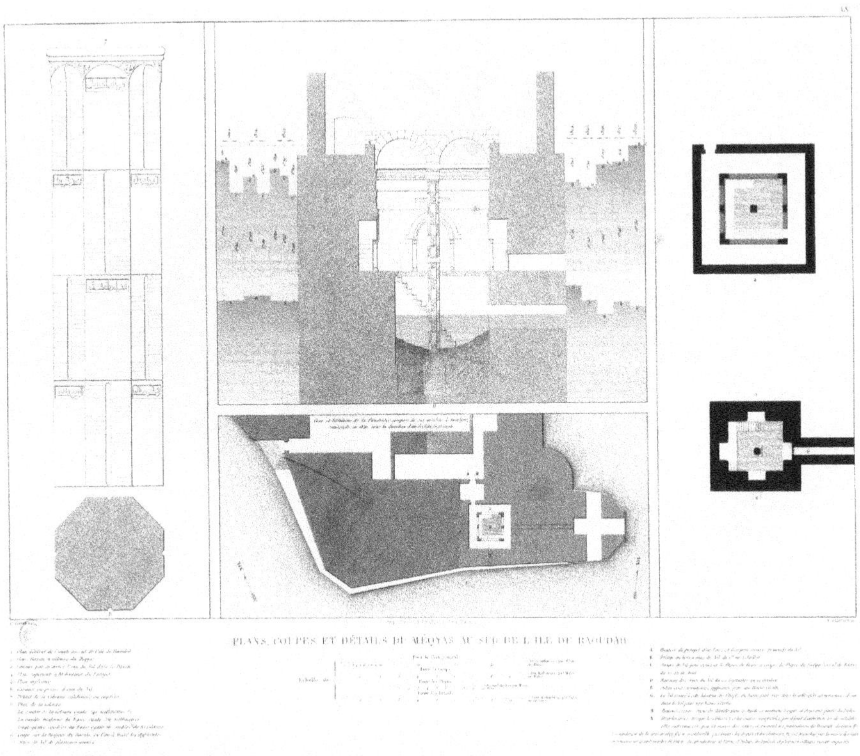

Figure 3.22. Cairo, Nilometer. Section, 1818 lithograph showing plan, section, and detail. Pascal Coste, *Architecture arabe; ou, Monuments du Kaire, mesurés et dessinés, de 1818 à 1826*, published in 1839. Image courtesy of Aga Khan Documentation Center, MIT Libraries (AKDC@MIT).

of architecture as an early Islamic example of the use of pointed arches, and because its carved stone inscriptions are the earliest monumental Kufic inscriptions in Egypt.[86]

In Creswell's extensive discussion of the medieval Arabic texts on the Nilometer he notes several Abbasid intellectuals as having been involved in the project to construct it, attributing to them its design, its construction, and the execution of its important inscription program.[87] These intellectuals include several men of science, identified by their names or titles as mathematicians, engineers, and astronomers. For example, Eutychius, writing in 939—less than a century after the construction of the Nilometer—stated that Muhammad (d. 873), the eldest of the three brothers collectively known as the Banū Mūsa, chose an architect (*muhandis*) from Iraq that the caliph al-Mutawakkil then sent to Egypt to carry out the works. Muhammad himself was known as a specialist in geometry and astronomy, and in addition to the scientific tasks that he carried out for the Abbasid caliph al-Ma'mun, the Arabic sources state that he was involved in architectural and major civic projects, notably the construction of canals for al-Mutawakkil.[88]

Figure 3.23. Cairo, Nilometer interior view. Photo: Yasser Tabbaa, courtesy of Aga Khan Documentation Center, MIT Libraries (AKDC@MIT).

The Banū Mūsa's *Book of Ingenious Devices* is pertinent here, in that as the earliest Arabic treatise on automata and mechanical devices, it is also all about the manipulation of water. Most of the hundred or so machines that are described are small machines, fine devices in the form of trick fountains and drinking vessels, which use a variety of pneumatic and technological innovations in devices that were mainly meant to surprise and delight viewers. Some would release water when wine was poured in, for example, while others bore figures of humans or animals that moved and even produced sounds. The description of the sixth device in their treatise, for instance, describes it as featuring "a figure of a bull [who], when offered a vessel containing water, drinks it and his voice and clamour are heard, so that anyone looking at him thinks that he was thirsty."[89]

The descriptions of the devices indicate that they could be built at a scale suitable for large exterior spaces, or for interior use in either religious or secular contexts. Model 91, for instance, describes a trick fountain that produced one jet of water in the shape of a shield and one in the form of a lance or a lily of the valley and then reversed the two shapes once a specific period of time had elapsed (Fig. 3.24). Its description states that the device could be constructed "in places of ritual ablutions or in some places by some rivers," implying a device of large scale whose water would be supplied from the nearby river. In the case of the former it would be suitable for ritual ablutions. In the latter, it would serve in a bath or porch and could be ornamented with a figurehead in the form of an animal or human to discharge either water or wine.[90]

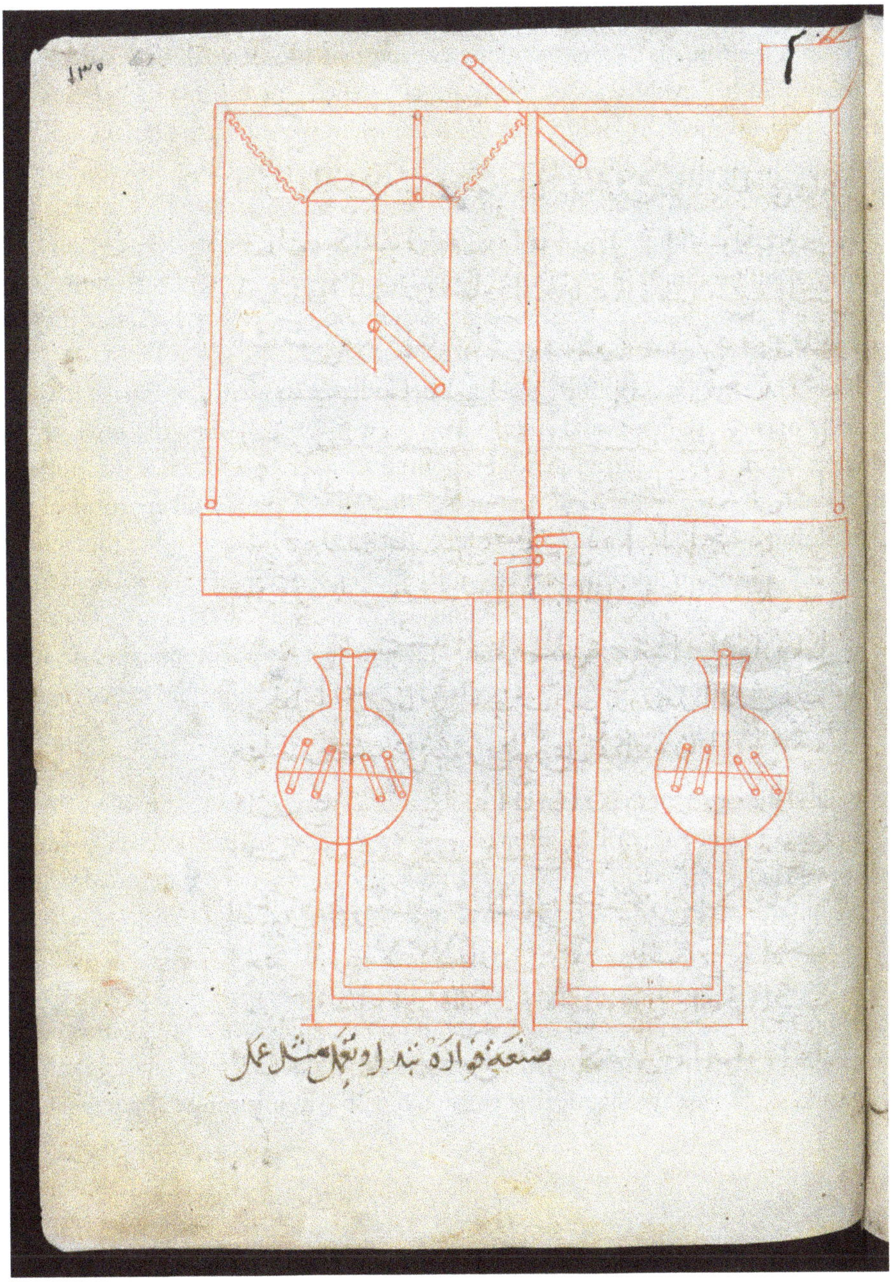

Figure 3.24. Folio with diagram of Model 91, a fountain that produced two jets shaped like a shield and lance, or lily of the valley. Banu Musa, *Kitab al-Ḥiyal*. Collection of the Staatsbibliothek zu Berlin, Stiftung Preußischer Kulturbesitz, Oriental Department, Folio 61r, MS or. Quart. 739, 1210.

Given the engagement with water and its manipulation at various scales, as indicated in their treatise, we can understand why someone like Ahmad of the Banū Mūsa would be involved in choosing other intellectuals capable of working on urban projects involving water, like the Nilometer. According to Donald Hill another medieval author, Ibn al-Day'a (Abu Ja'far Ahmad ibn Yusuf al-Katib) stated that the Abbasid astronomer al-Farghani executed the work on the Nilometer. The aforementioned Muhammad was a colleague of al-Farghani's; according to another medieval author Ibn Abi Usaybi'a, the Banū Mūsa had collaborated with the astronomer on a civic project in Iraq, subcontracting him to excavate a canal, a project that al-Mutawakkil had charged them to oversee.[91]

The Nilometer's inscription program offers further evidence of intellectuals as makers of early Islamic visual culture (Fig. 3.25).[92] Ornamenting the walls of the shaft in which the measuring column is housed are a series of Quranic inscriptions that allude to water, vegetation, and prosperity (Sura XIV: 37), all appropriate for a monument used to measure the water levels that would determine the annual yield. Ibn Khallikan, the thirteenth-century biographer, preserves a detailed first-person account by one Ahmad ibn Muhammad al-Hasib al-Qarasani, an otherwise unknown figure, but whose name indicates that he was a mathematician.[93] In this account Ahmad al-Hasib describes his role in designing and executing the Nilometer's inscription program at some length:

> I chose the verses of the Quran the best and most appropriate to the Nilometer. I carved what I had written on marble in the position fixed beforehand, with straight letters as thick as the finger, stiff, the background colored with waxed lapis lazuli, so that they could be read from a distance.[94]

Ahmad al-Hasib's account, as relayed by Ibn Khallikan, has been accepted as a credible historical source, and it gives an illuminating glimpse of an intellectual at work on an artistic commission and putting into practice various types of knowledge and skills. He says that he first consulted with administrators about what the

Figure 3.25. Nilometer, inscription detail. Photo courtesy of Bernard O'Kane.

inscriptions should say, that he expressed his opinion about the desirability of using Quranic passages and including the name of the ruler as patron, and that once he received a general agreement from the caliph, he took on the responsibility of ultimately selecting the specific Quranic verses, choosing their placement, and designing the inscriptions.

In passages of his account Ahmad al-Hasib emphasizes his active involvement in making the inscriptions, stating repeatedly that he "wrote" (*kataba*), carved, engraved, and painted the inscriptions in blue and gold on the walls: "the upper walls I entirely engraved, carved and painted in waxed lapis lazuli . . . I have engraved all of this in gold and lapis lazuli (*bi'l-dhahab wa'l-lazaward*).[95] The remaining inscriptions seem to corroborate the accuracy of the account. Creswell noted that the first part of al-Hasib's inscription, eighteen pieces of whitish marble on which the inscriptions are carved in a bold Kufic script, was still visible in the monument's interior, on the east and north sides of the pit, and above the arched recesses, and that the Quranic content of the inscriptions agreed with the description given in the account.[96] Likewise, traces of a dark blue ground have been documented, and Alain George has observed that it is plausible that its letters may indeed have once been painted in gold, as al-Hasib describes, which is in keeping with other early Islamic inscriptions in this color scheme.[97]

The Abbasid mathematician's account continues with further explanation of the placement of these inscriptions:

> First of all I engraved four verses of the same length, in four lines, on the four sides of the pit of the Nilometer, at a level corresponding to 17 cubits on the column. On the east side, that is opposite the entrance, I wrote on the four faces of the monument—[gives the Quranic verses according to the cardinal directions of the walls on which they appear]. These verses become lines on the face of the water when it reaches 17 cubits, which is the average height of the inundation.

Notably then, according to the mathematician, he designed the lines of text and carefully chose their placement, not simply to be decorative, but to function as the measuring indicators for the rising water levels. The inscriptions therefore are intrinsic to the functionality of the monument as a scientific instrument.[98] Elsewhere in the account, Muhammad al-Hasib gave further details of the wording of his inscription, which emphasized his participation in the monument's inscriptions, both those on the interior that aided the water measurements, and those on the exterior that announced his role in the architectural project, in effect rendering him visible as a maker of this monument to a ninth-century viewing public.

I have been at pains to discuss the Nilometer as a work from Ibn Firnas's time, which like his creation combined architecture and the visualization of scientific information, and which moreover offers clear evidence for an intellectual's active participation in its visual program. Al-Hasib's role in the Nilometer's inscription program, and the potential connections to the Banu Musa and other Abbasid intellectuals may help us better understand a broader Islamic context for Ibn Firnas's involvement in the exact sciences and design.[99] Al-Hasib's account of his role in the Nilometer's inscription program also illuminates Sa'id al-Andalusi's allusion to the Córdoban intellectual Ibn Taymih's involvement in the tenth-century expansion of the Great Mosque of Córdoba and the attestation of his involvement in the inclusion of his name in the mihrab inscription program (Fig. 3.26). Like Ahmad al-Hasib at the Nilometer, might this future qadi of Córdoba have put his theological expertise to work by selecting the most appropriate Quranic verses to decorate the innovative new mihrab and also drawn upon his knowledge of calligraphy and mathematics to design its justly celebrated inscription program? If we take the mathematician Ahmad al-Hasib's involvement in the Nilometer as suggestive of how other caliphal intellectuals were working across disciplines and

Figure 3.26. Mihrab, mosaic inscriptions. Great Mosque of Córdoba, expansion of al-Hakam II. Visible beyond the arch is a partial section of the interior marble inscription, one of three in the mihrab zone that includes the name of the Córdoban jurist Muhammad b. Tamlih. Photo: Glaire Anderson.

applying mathematical, scientific knowledge to designing and crafting objects and monuments, this makes more plausible the possibility that Ibn Taymih likewise may have put his knowledge to work in the design and execution of al-Hakam II's expansion of the Great Mosque of Córdoba.

Conclusion

As I hope to have shown, Ibn Firnas's spectacular creation was a work of architecture and science that combined astronomical, astrological, meteorological, and kinetic effects with visual and auditory ones is an innovation partly arising out of an interest in meteorological phenomena that he shared with others of his time, and that was evident in early Islamic intellectual circles and in writings by figures such as al-Kindi.[100] Ibn Firnas's creation fused material spatiality, engineering, and striking visuals in a fashion that finds numerous parallels in the royal spaces of Córdoba and al-Andalus, in the medieval Dar al-Islam and beyond. Perhaps, like Qusayr 'Amra, it boasted a painted celestial vault and human and animal figural imagery. Perhaps both the vault and figures of men, women, and animals were set in motion by hidden devices, similar to the machines described in al-Muradi's treatise, thus aiding his audience's apprehension of his device's mechanical movements and rendering those movements meaningful. Ibn Hayyan's account of this creation may therefore be important as the earliest reference to a distinct Andalusi automata tradition that would subsequently be documented in al-Muradi's treatise.

Ibn Firnas's wondrous scientific chamber stands, it seems, at the beginning of a longer Andalusi trajectory combining engineering and visual culture, which subsequently was codified by al-Muradi in the *Book of Secrets and Results of Ideas*. The powerful and complex machines in the al-Muradi treatise offer the best indication as to the nature of what it was that Ibn Firnas labored to design and build within his own residence, his spectacular "representation of the heavens." At the beginning of the al-Muradi treatise, the author (or is it the scribe?) states that by his time the arts of engineering were falling into disuse compared with their flourishing earlier in al-Andalus. That earlier flourishing points perhaps to a tradition in which Ibn Firnas's creation was the progenitor, at least in the minds of Ibn Hayyan and his eleventh-century audience. In any case, the large and complex machines described in the al-Muradi treatise point to a longer Andalusi tradition of engineering wondrous automata that may have begun with Ibn Firnas. Combining visual, kinetic, and auditory effects, our polymath suggests a Western Islamic counterpart to the automata designed by his contemporaries, Banū Mūsa in Baghdad. As recounted by Ibn Hayyan in the eleventh century, Ibn Firnas's activities as a designer and maker of early automata, and the impact this may have had on subsequent intellectuals and Andalusi technologies may anticipate al-Muradi's work in *taifa* Toledo and, indirectly perhaps, medieval European interest and developments in such technologies.[101]

Wondrously animated, capable of producing sounds and moving, Ibn Firnas's device would not only have engaged the eyes and ears of medieval viewers, but also their intellects. The intellectuals who comprised ʿAbbas Ibn Firnas's audience shared an education and background that enabled them to appreciate the "sciences of the ancients." His chamber spoke to such adepts, who were well positioned to intellectually grapple with the complex inner workings of the machines—gears, pulleys, balances, weights, counterweights, and other mechanisms—that produced the marvelous effects that made his "representation of the heavens" the talk of intellectual circles and the subject of admiration as well as controversy.

If we think about the overall trajectory of Ibn Firnas's career we can discern in the meteorological chamber significant connections between his various activities and interests: those pertinent to the history of art and architecture, to design and craft; those having to do with the natural, exact sciences of astronomy, mathematics, and aeronautics; and also those deeply engaged with ninth-century intellectual culture, including the occult sciences. The reference to astronomical representation (stars)—in addition to meteorological phenomena (clouds, thunder, lightning)—combined and represented to spectacular visual and auditory effect in this space is illustrative of all of the spheres of knowledge that informed the chamber. The poetry composed about this wondrous creation suggested that Ibn Firnas's peers were eager to see and experience it as an unusual, indeed spectacular, sight, for themselves, even if not all of them approved of what he had constructed within that chamber of his home.

The derisive poetry composed by Ibn Firnas's rival about the latter's wondrous representation suggests that scientific knowledge was at times a field of competition between intellectuals in the Córdoban court. Similarly, the aforementioned manuscripts with their star imagery have been interpreted as constituting "medieval communities of knowledge" within and beyond Byzantine, Frankish, and Islamic courts of the time, and this notion is perhaps instructive for understanding Ibn Firnas's creation and its intellectual contexts, including competition, in the Umayyad court.[102] For Islamic as well as Frankish courts of the time, such celestial imagery in particular may be seen as a vehicle by which intellectuals competed for status within the social landscapes of the courts.[103] In fact, competition among intellectuals vying for status within Islamic court environments may have been a major catalyst of the early Islamic scientific revolution.[104] Such competition subsequently became an important part of the social landscape in which rulers and court intellectuals developed science in the Islamic lands.[105]

Attitudes regarding the connection between craft and intellect seem to have varied across the Islamic lands in the caliphal period. For example, Jahiz, writing in the ninth-century Abbasid milieu, contrasted ancient Greek intellectual achievements against that of the Byzantines (Rum), noting that the Greeks were scientists while the Byzantines mere artisans who were simply clever with their hands.[106] Nevertheless by the eleventh century Ibn Hayyan and his sources seem to have celebrated the union of craft and intellect, and to have been keen to characterize

Ibn Firnas as an innovative maker, as well as an intellectual: someone who could imagine, design, create, build—and whose creations subsequently inspired wonder, admiration, excitement, but also opprobrium among his contemporaries. Thus, it seems that in the tenth and eleventh centuries, Andalusi intellectuals looked back at Ibn Firnas not only as the pioneering instrument maker of al-Andalus, but also as its leading figure in the design and creation of automata. His chamber and its wondrous celestial representation alert us as well to a complex dialogue between architecture, science, occult knowledge, and visual culture in the intellectual atmosphere of the Córdoban court by the ninth century, which resonated for centuries after.

All of these surely would be profoundly important to the intellectual journey that culminated in the aeronautics experiment at the end of Ibn Firnas's long and illustrious career in the Umayyad court. Long-term, careful observation of weather would have been part and parcel of a ninth-century astronomer's work, and knowledge of winds, clouds, and seasonal weather patterns would certainly have informed the design of the aeronautics experiment and have been a key factor in its success. The representation of the heavens, finally, fleshes out our portrait of a man with the artisanal skill, the expansive intellectual breadth, and the flair for the dramatic to think up something as audacious as an aeronautics experiment.

4

Where Eagles and Vultures Dare

When now the finishing touches had been put upon the work, the master workman himself balanced his body on two wings and hung poised on the beaten air.

(Ovid, *Metamorphoses*)[1]

If I flew up to the starry vault / And joined the heavens' westward flow / I would learn, as I traversed the sky / The fate of all things here below.

(Al-Ma'mun, Abbasid caliph, d. 813)[2]

Having established a portrait of Ibn Firnas's intellectual qualities and his reputation as a maker of early scientific instruments, this chapter turns to the part of his career about which Arabic authors say relatively little in comparison with other aspects of his persona and activities, but which has resulted in this polymath's most enduring legacy for modern and contemporary audiences—his purported aeronautics experiment. It begins by considering how people in the medieval Islamic lands imagined flight and depicted it in medieval literature and visual culture. It then compares the Arabic sources for the aeronautics experiment, beginning with the later and most familiar one of al-Maqqari along with the nineteenth-century English version, before moving to consider Ibn Hayyan's text. As the earliest Arabic account of the experiment, this text offers more detail than the later brief and somewhat garbled version penned by al-Maqqari, and so the chapter spends some time considering what the earlier and more substantial text reveals about the experiment: its witnesses, the circumstances, the setting, and the details of the flight device. I consider the possibility that an experiment may have taken place at the Umayyad villa (*munya*) of Rusafa. I argue that this villa functioned as a site of scientific experimentation for the court during Ibn Firnas's lifetime, and that aspects of its topography and natural surroundings may have inspired curiosity about, and subsequent investigation into, the possibility of gliding flight. From there the chapter imagines the possible nature of a ninth-century flight device according to details in Ibn Hayyan's Arabic text and concludes by considering the significance of Ibn Firnas's experiment.

A Bridge to the Sky. Glaire D. Anderson, Oxford University Press. © Oxford University Press 2024.
DOI: 10.1093/oso/9780190913243.003.0005

Imagining Flight—Early Visual Sources

The notion of human flight was already present in Islamic court societies by Ibn Firnas's time. This should not surprise us, given the prevalence of the notion around the globe in ancient and late antique societies.[3] One might wonder whether Islamic intellectuals in the ninth century knew the myth of Daedalus, the ancient Greek inventor who fashioned wings for himself and his ill-fated son Icarus, and whether such a tale could have been one source of inspiration for an experiment in gliding flight.[4] Perhaps. But while scholars long viewed the ninth century as a moment in which Islamic intellectuals were engaging deeply with the works of ancient Greek authors, and translating many of those works into Arabic, current scholarship has emphasized that the Abbasid translation movement had much more to do with pre-Islamic Iranian and early Arabic lore than it did with ancient Greek sources.[5]

Of potential allusions from ancient and late ancient religious, mythic, and literary traditions, to which Islamic intellectuals saw themselves as heirs, they created new interpretations and stories of divine flight. The most obvious example is Muhammad's *miraj*, his ascent to the heavens, on the human-headed flying horse, Buraq, and the angels that appeared to Muhammad. As in the other monotheistic traditions, angels appear in the Qur'an with specific reference to their wings; for example, Surah 35:1 refers to them as multiwinged beings: "[All] praise is [due] to Allah, Creator of the heavens and the earth, [who] made the angels messengers having wings, two or three or four." The artist or artists who illustrated the scene of Muhammad, Buraq, and angels in the sixteenth-century *Bustan* depicted the angels mostly with two wings, but the crowned angel depicted just above Buraq's head boasts four wings: a red pair seemingly at rest and a second pair outstretched, as if in flight (Fig. 4.1). In contrast to the angels' wings, Buraq's one visible wing is so small as to be vestigial.

Writers and artisans in early Islamic societies developed the repertoire of images of winged beings, natural as well as supernatural, which they continued from the ancient and late ancient world. If we look to the genesis of Islamic art, among the famous Umayyad frescos decorating the bathhouse of Qusayr Amra is a fresco painting of a winged figure on the tympanum leading to the caldarium (Fig. 4.2). The figure is poised with one arm stretched to its right, where its gaze is also directed, and its wings outspread as if poised to ascend to the sky. The wings, though somewhat small in proportion to the body, are carefully drawn, with lines suggesting overlapping feathers.

Winged figures likewise appear in al-Ṣufi's *Treatise on the Fixed Stars*.[6] The manuscript, copied and illustrated by the astronomer 'Ali ibn 'Abd al-Jalil ibn 'Ali ibn Muhammad in Baghdad in 1125, is preserved today in the Museum of Islamic Art, Doha, Qatar, and includes three winged figures that depict the constellations Aquila, Virgo, and Pegasus.[7] The treatment of each of the figures, specifically the manner in which the wings are depicted, is of interest, as they were drawn by the manuscript's scribe, who was an astronomer. They illustrate a subtle difference in

Figure 4.1. "The Miʿraj or the Night Flight of Muhammad on his Steed Buraq," by Sultan Muhammad Nur (ca. 1472–ca. 1536). Folio 3v from a *Bustan* of Sa`di, ca. 1525–35. Attributed to present-day Uzbekistan and Afghanistan, probably Bukhara and Herat. Ink, gold, and colors on paper. Accession Number: 1974.294.2. The Metropolitan Museum of Art, New York; Purchase, Louis V. Bell Fund and The Vincent Astor Foundation Gift, 1974. (CC0 1.0)

one intellectual's approach to picturing both natural and supernatural appendages for flight. He rendered the wings of the constellation Aquila, the eagle, in a different fashion than he did for his representation of the mythical flying steed Pegasus, or for Virgo, winged here in accordance with Islamic astronomical convention.[8] The eagle features outstretched curved wings and individually drawn feathers that, along with the curved talons and beak, while abstracted are still relatively natural and might imply observations from nature (Fig. 4.3). The eagle's relative naturalism contrasts with the treatment of the wings of Pegasus and Virgo, articulated with greater abstraction, terminating in curving forms that are distinct from the more naturalistic treatment of the eagle's wings (Figs. 4.4, 4.5).

Comparing the Sources

While it is easy to imagine flight and even to depict it, it is another thing altogether to attempt it. Much of the debate surrounding Ibn Firnas's contribution to the history of flight stems from the fact that until the rediscovery of the long-lost volume of Ibn Hayyan's chronicle, scholars relied on al-Maqqari's and Gayangos's texts as sources for the experiment. Before examining what new light Ibn Hayyan's early account of our polymath's career can shed on the flight experiment, it might therefore be useful to review how those later sources portray the event. This is how al-Maqqari described ʿAbbas Ibn Firnas's feat, for his seventeenth-century audience:

> Among their accounts about intelligence and scientific deduction and discovery, writers mention that Abu al-Qasim ʿAbbas b. Firnas, the philosopher of Andalus . . . demonstrated ingenuity in launching his body in flight. He covered himself in feathers, provided himself with a couple of wings and flew a considerable distance in the air. However, he did not prove very ingenious in his landing. He hurt himself in the rear. He did not know that a bird lands on its tailhead, and did not make a tail for himself. About this, the poet Mu'min b. Saʿid said in verse:
>
> He soars above the phoenix in flight,
> When he covers his body with eagle feathers.[9]

Following al-Maqqari's account relatively closely, Gayangos's English version for his audience in Victorian England reads as follows:

> Among other very curious experiments which [Ibn Firnas] made, one is his trying to fly. He covered himself with feathers for the purpose, attached a couple of wings to his body, and getting on an eminence, flung himself down into the air, when according to the testimony of several trustworthy writers who witnessed the performance, he flew to a considerable distance, as if he had been a bird, but in alighting again on the place whence he had started his back was very much hurt, for not

Figure 4.2. Fresco of winged figure, Qusayr ʿAmra, eighth century, Jordan. Photo: Daniel C. Waugh. Image courtesy of Aga Khan Documentation Center, MIT Libraries (AKDC@MIT).

Figure 4.3. Constellation of Aquila, the Eagle, from an authoritative copy of al-Sufi's astronomical treatise, *Kitab Ṣuwar al-kawakib (al-thabitah)* (*Book of pictures of the [fixed] stars*), folio 54v. The drawings were done by the manuscript copyist, 'Ali ibn 'Abd al-Jalil ibn 'Ali ibn Muhammad, Baghdad, 1125. Photo: The Museum of Islamic Art, Doha.

> knowing that birds when they alight come down on their tails, he forgot to provide himself with one. Mumen Ibn Sa'id has said, in a verse alluding to this extraordinary man, "He surpassed in velocity the flight of the ostrich, but he neglected to arm / his body with the strength of the vulture."[10]

Both Gayangos's and al-Maqqari's accounts confuse rather than clarify details of the incident. Given their content and the fact that these two accounts were composed more than eight hundred years after Ibn Firnas's lifetime, it is not surprising that definite statements about the exact nature of the "flight" and its ultimate significance to aeronautics and aviation history have been elusive at best. Conflicting opinions about Ibn Firnas's achievement abound in the science and technology literature, which have been intractable until now due to the lack of alternative historical sources. For instance, historian Lynn White, Jr., whose *Medieval Technology and Social Change*, published in 1962, had a profound influence on history of technology studies that continues up to the present, discussed Ibn Firnas and concluded, on the

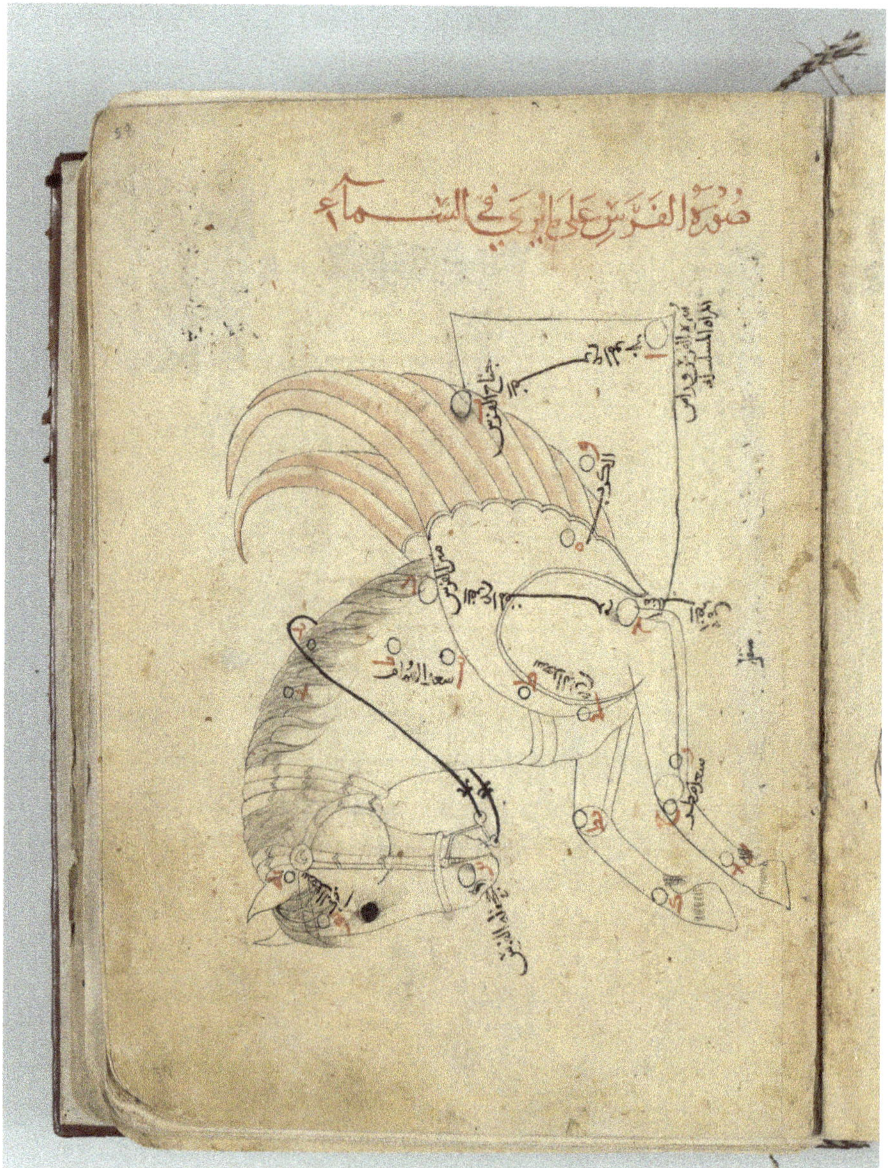

Figure 4.4. Constellation Pegasus, from an authoritative copy of al-Sufi's astronomical treatise, *Kitab Ṣuwar al-kawakib (al-thabitah)* (*Book of pictures of the [fixed] stars*), folio 59r. The drawings were done by the manuscript copyist/astronomer, ʿAli ibn ʿAbd al-Jalil ibn ʿAli ibn Muhammad, Baghdad, 1125. Photo: The Museum of Islamic Art, Doha, Qatar.

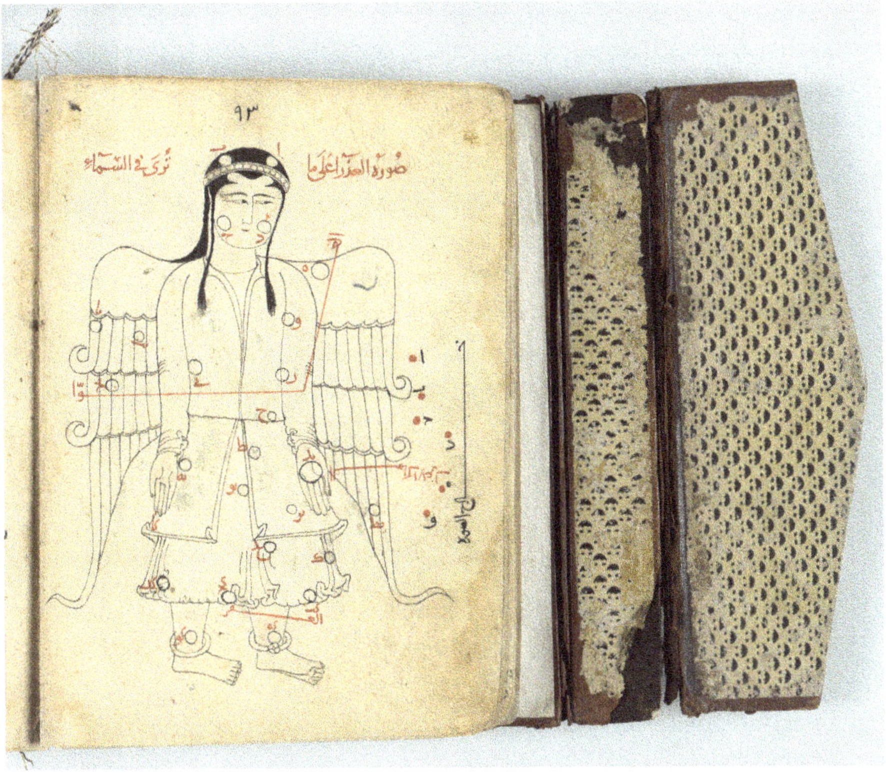

Figure 4.5. Constellation Virgo, from an authoritative copy of al-Sufi's astronomical treatise, *Kitab Ṣuwar al-kawakib (al-thabitah)* (*Book of pictures of the [fixed] stars*), folio 93v. The drawings were done by the manuscript copyist/astronomer, ʿAli ibn ʿAbd al-Jalil ibn ʿAli ibn Muhammad, Baghdad, 1125. Photo: The Museum of Islamic Art, Doha, Qatar.

basis of al-Maqqari's text and despite its limitations as a historical source, "although the evidence is slender, we must conclude that b. Firnas was the first man to fly successfully."[11] The eminent Arabist and science historian Juan Vernet also stated that Ibn Firnas attempted to fly and managed to glide for a distance, and he noted that the flight was mentioned in numerous Arabic and non-Arabic sources.[12] More recently historians of science and aviation have been more skeptical, relegating the anecdote to the realm of legend and pointing to the limitations of the same historical evidence.[13]

The Earliest Source

Now we can turn to the passage describing the flight in the Madrid manuscript of Ibn Hayyan's chronicle. It offers details absent in the later accounts, which may clarify some of the otherwise puzzling aspects found in the later versions. This is what Ibn Hayyan's passage states about Ibn Firnas's experiment:

> Some sheikhs said that he [once] managed to launch himself into flight. He clothed himself in feathers [fastened to *light colored*] silk and spread for himself (*madda*) two wings of calculated structure (jinaḥayni ʿala wazni taqdirin qaddarahu), with which he was able to rise in the air (istaṭara fi al-jawwi). He flew (ṭara) from the vicinity of Rusafa, moved through the air and then circled until he landed in a place far away from where he departed. But this landing went poorly when he hurt his tailbone. He had not managed the landing very well. He did not take into account that a bird, when landing, does so on its tailhead, which he [*neglected*]. He was more frightening than [*the clamor*] of the scattered places of Saharan nomads who [*ruminated*] at length over what they had witnessed, without knowing what it was all about. For this reason, the poet Mu'min b. Saʿid, his equal in some of what transpired between them, said:
>
> He soars above the phoenix in flight
> When he covers his body in [*vulture/eagle*] feathers[14]

The passage about the flight is immediately preceded by the following statements:

He [Muḥammad b. ʿUmar b. Lubaba] says:

> [ʿAbbas] was so full of ingenuity (saḥiba nayranjatin), creativity, originality, invention (kathira al-ibdaʿi / al-ikhtiraʿi wa-l-tawwaludi wa-l-istinbaṭi) and resourcefulness (wasiʿa al-ḥiyali) that he was attributed with the knowledge of magic and alchemy (al-siḥra wa-ʿamala al-kimiya'), and was often challenged on religious grounds.

Despite its brevity, a close examination of this earliest account of Ibn Firnas's flight suggests some clarifications about the informant, the audience and setting for the experiment, and some of the meanings it may have held for Córdoban intellectuals by Ibn Hayyan's time.

Who is Ibn Hayyan's informant for this event? The chronicle identifies the source of this passage as Muhammad b. ʿUmar b. Lubabah (d. 926 or 942), a learned Córdoban theologian renowned for his *fatwas* and for transmitting fundamental Maliki texts of juridical opinion.[15] If ʿAbbas b. Firnas's experiment took place twelve years before his death in 876, Ibn Lubabah would have been twenty-six years old at the time. Thus, we are provided here with an account purportedly from one of ʿAbbas b. Firnas's own contemporaries. Although Ibn Lubabah was not himself an eyewitness, according to the passage, his status as a leading jurisconsult of the day and a contemporary of ʿAbbas would have lent his account weight among the chronicle's eleventh-century readers, who would have perceived him as an important and reliable authority. We therefore see Ibn Hayyan, writing in the eleventh century, using his earlier tenth-century source to contextualize the account of the aeronautics experiment by underscoring Ibn Firnas's reputation as a resourceful, ingenious, creative, and inventive intellectual, different and distinctive from his peers because of these qualities.

The passage also says that Ibn Lubabah did not witness the experiment himself but, rather, that he received the anecdote from "some sheikhs." The choice of "sheikhs" as a term may also be significant, as it suggests that these informants—the unnamed eyewitnesses to the feat—were figures of some authority, prestige, and a certain level of scholarly attainment.[16] We have already seen Ibn Firnas's reputation for dramatic flair and showmanship in the account of his wondrous meteorological chamber, with its emphasis on its status as a spectacle among notable people of the day. We might therefore assume that if 'Abbas was planning to carry out something as unusual as an experiment in gliding flight, he would desire an audience for what would undoubtedly have qualified as a spectacular event. The same witnesses who came to see and experience his meteorological chamber, learned men who enjoyed authority and prestige as scholars in the Córdoban court and intellectual society and who were engaged with the exact sciences, may likewise have made up the audience for this experiment as well.

Palace of Science: Al-Rusafa

Here I would like to bring the setting for the experiment to the fore, as architecture and landscape, or to put it another way, the spatialization of science, emerges as a crucial but as-yet-overlooked factor in the flight. Ibn Lubabah's account situates the incident in a specific locale: "he flew from the site (*fatara min nahiyati*) of al-Rusafa." Al-Rusafa was the first suburban estate, or *munya*, founded by the transplanted Syrian Umayyad prince, 'Abd al-Rahman I, sometime during that ruler's reign between 756 and 788.[17] The villa was the premier setting for court gatherings, and thus it would have been a place where 'Abbas would have spent a great deal of time participating in court gatherings (*majalis*), and in the court's intellectual and scientific activities.[18] Rusafa was a major court node for much of the Umayyad period. For instance, in 795 it was where the question of the succession was decided at the death of 'Abd al-Rahman I. During the reign of 'Abd al-Rahman II (822–852), when 'Abbas Ibn Firnas entered the circle of boon companions, Rusafa became a favored setting for Córdoban court life.

The topographical and natural setting of the *munya* may have played a key role in inspiring the idea for the experiment. Today substantial archaeological remains from the Roman period as well as from the ninth and tenth centuries have been uncovered in the zone north of the walled center (Fig. 4.6). Remains that the archaeologist Juan Murillo has proposed may be those of al-Rusafa have been discovered in the northwest suburban area of the city, which is the site today of the eponymous Arruzafa hotel, or parador, located on one of the parcels identified with Rusafa since the medieval period (Fig. 4.7).[19] Today the area is a prosperous suburb of Córdoba, with a relatively dense development of houses, neighborhoods, and businesses. One has to drive about twenty minutes north of the medieval city center to reach the Arruzafa hotel, but the change in the elevation from the center

Figure 4.6. Remains of substantial stone walls unearthed north of Córdoba's walled urban center, possibly datable to the tenth century. Photo: Glaire Anderson.

to the suburb is gradually noticeable. The Arruzafa bills its grounds as the site of "Europe's first botanical garden," a reference to the cultivated gardens that 'Abd al-Rahman I is said to have established around the Rusafa *munya*.[20] Palm trees grow in the gardens below the sweeping terrace that stretches across the hotel's facade and that overlooks the Guadalquivir River and Córdoba's center to the south. Immediately behind the hotel are the ruins of an early modern monastery, which sit at the highest point of the hillside on which the hotel is perched. From this vantage point, and especially from the hotel terrace, a viewer today gains a clear sense of the site's marked elevation over the landscape below. The site enjoys sweeping views over the whole expanse of the Guadalquivir River valley that spreads out below and a steady breeze, all of which make abundantly clear why a site in this territory would have been a desirable setting for a space of leisure and retreat, as the Umayyad villas were.

Just south of the hotel's current location Murillo has identified the remains of an extensive late antique complex with an extensive hydraulic infrastructure, constructed in the first century AD, which supplied a square courtyard structure (Fig. 4.8).[21] This edifice has been identified through geophysical prospection, which indicates a rectangular structure of some 50 meters per side, with a wide peripheral wall with buttresses in its facades, and several rooms arranged around a large courtyard (Fig. 4.9). Murillo notes that the walls were rebuilt with buttresses in a construction technique characteristic of the ninth century. The ancient and medieval remains that have been unearthed in this part of the Córdoban suburban landscape, and the extent to which the exact site on which the hotel is situated corresponds to the Córdoban Umayyad *munya*, remain uncertain.[22]

Figure 4.7. View south toward Córdoba, from the elevated terrace of La Arruzafa, Córdoba's parador. The Ibn Firnas Bridge is visible in the distance. Photo: Glaire Anderson.

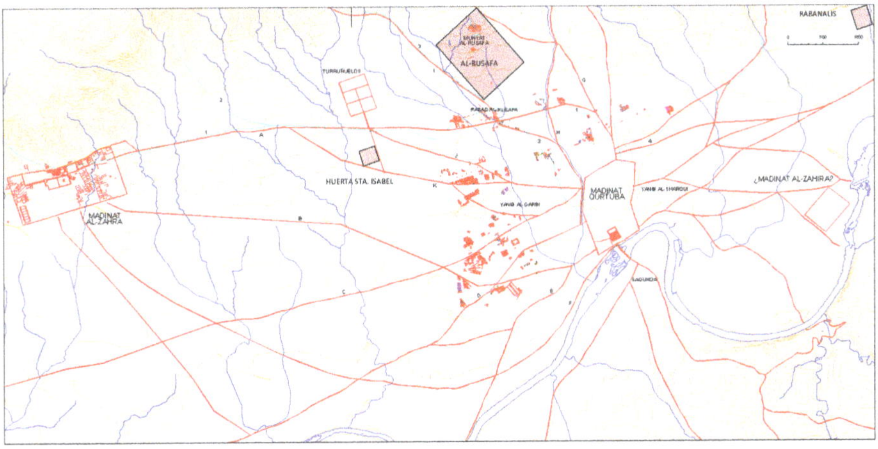

Figure 4.8. Territory around medieval Córdoba, with proposed area of Rusafa demarcated northwest of the urban center. Image courtesy of Alberto León and Juan Fco. Murillo.

But if Rusafa was situated in this general area of greater suburban Córdoba, the topography of the site and its suitability for gliding flight may have inspired the idea for an experiment and informed possible approaches to the problems it presented. The higher elevation of this zone—the same feature that made it attractive as a pleasurable villa retreat—creates atmospheric conditions favorable to gliding flight.[23] Higher elevation means cooler temperatures, and indeed today one

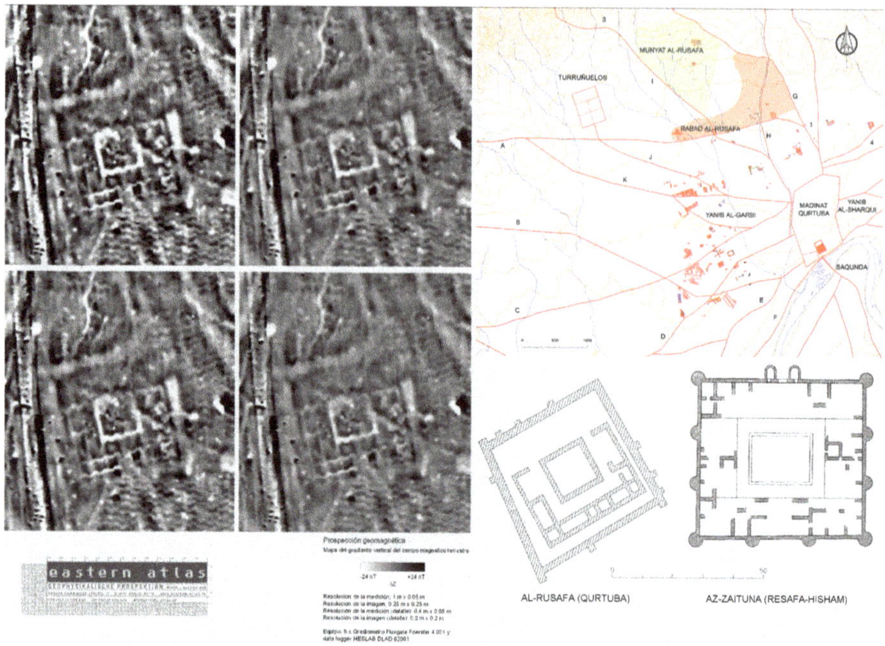

Figure 4.9. Remains identified through geomagnetic survey, in the vicinity of the Arruzafa parador. Vestiges of the Umayyad suburban villa (*munya*) of al-Rusafa? Image courtesy of Alberto León and Juan Fco. Murillo.

of the attractions of the hotel is that the temperature in its locale in the hills north of the city remains several degrees cooler than in the urban center to the south. The combination of the higher elevation, the shape and forms of the land as it rises toward the Sierra Morena mountain range, and the cooler temperatures all affect air currents in this zone. The effect of sunlight warming the earth may have created warm currents of air in this particular area that would have been conducive to soaring flight of the sort favored by vultures and other birds of that type. Moreover, this process would presumably have created a more or less regular seasonal pattern. In effect, the topography of the Rusafa villa site may well have created ideal conditions for an aeronautics experiment.[24]

Over a career spanning decades, during which ʿAbbas would have visited the Rusafa villa and spent significant time there as one of the boon companions of two successive rulers, it seems very likely that the soaring flight of eagles and vultures over the skies of Rusafa, and the seasonal wind currents that made such soaring flight possible, would not have escaped the notice of as keen an observer as ʿAbbas Ibn Firnas, who was, after all, a court astronomer. Even in our own time meteorological knowledge and its effects on gliding flight are still considered key to aviation.[25] It seems likely that his observations of the winds and the soaring flight of birds at Rusafa could have inspired the idea for an aeronautics experiment. Given the scientific interests that the chronicle attributes to both of his patrons, ʿAbd al-Rahman II and Muhammad I, and the resources and patronage both rulers provided to the polymath, it is no far cry to imagine ʿAbbas conceiving the notion following a period of observation and experimentation. The chronicle provides the date of Ibn Firnas's death as 887, while other sources mention that he died some twelve years after the flight. This puts the approximate year of the purported experiment around 875, squarely within the period during which Muhammad I ruled in Córdoba and was active at the villa of al-Rusafa. We might therefore speculate that if ʿAbbas was interested in an aeronautics experiment, he could have been working on it by the year 864 at least. This date falls squarely within the reign of Muhammad I, and it fits with what the chronicle has to say about that ruler's scientific activities at the villa of Rusafa. Elsewhere in Ibn Hayyan's chronicle he mentions other scientific activities in connection with Rusafa, which helps us further understand why it may have been perceived as a suitable setting for such an experiment.

In a passage about Muhammad I's predilection for architecture, the chronicle relates the following:

> Muʿawiya b. Hisham said:
> The emir Muhammad was naturally disposed to the love of building, was enamored with the fortification of his buildings, *designed their mechanical devices* (*ala*), chose their workers, was extraordinary in his mastery of them, was generous in his expenditure on them. . . . He loathed the economy to which his fathers had adhered in furnishing them. To the contrary, he enhanced them, raised their finery and proceeded with furnishing, decoration, carpeting and *mechanical devices* as was agreeable and appropriate for them. Every masterpiece among the king's vessels, *noble contrivance among his mechanical devices* (*ala*), and precious ornament among his decoration was acquired by Muhammad, deduced from his cleverness, and invented by his genius.[26]

The multiple references in this passage to "mechanical devices" (*ala*) juxtapose residential architecture, technology, and science, paralleling the way the polymath's celestial automaton discussed in the previous chapter fuses an apparatus and an architectural space. The term *ala* literally means "an instrument," and it bears related grammatical and philosophical, as well as scientific, meanings: "in the classification of sciences, *alat* is the name of such attainments as are acquired not for their own sake, but 'as a means to something else'; while in philosophy, it refers to logic, considered by the philosophers of the period as the instrument of philosophy."[27] We might speculate that in this context *ala* referred to water technologies or infrastructure, or perhaps other types of scientific instruments and devices found within or around the villa, such as the celestial globe and the clepsydra that Ibn Firnas made and presented to the ruler. Given Rusafa's centrality to court intellectual life in the ninth century, and Ibn Hayyan's desire to situate the Córdoban ruler's scientific activities in that locale, it seems reasonable to suppose that those instruments may have been housed, used, and displayed at Rusafa. If so, in Rusafa and its mechanical devices and instruments we have a Córdoban Umayyad parallel to the fountains, vessels, and machines described by ʿAbbas Ibn Firnas's ʿAbbasid contemporaries, the Banu Musa, in their *Book of Ingenious Devices.*[28] Susana Calvo has discussed the likely spaces of science and other intellectual activities at the palace city of Madinat al-Zahra in the tenth century.[29] In the ninth century Rusafa, it seems, may have been its precursor as a royal space of science.

Besides a potentially lengthy period of thought and preparation, substantial physical, material, and human resources would likely have been necessary to construct a winged device that might achieve what Ibn Lubabah described. Besides the silk and feathers, Ibn Firnas would have needed wood or other rigid materials necessary to construct the framework of the device. ʿAbbas would also have required space in which to construct a device, and perhaps other artisans and craftsmen to help him in its construction and, given what likely would have to be a substantial wingspan, to help him move a device into place for testing. In terms of space and the material and human resources that would have had to go into the creation of a garment and a flight device, Rusafa makes sense as the favored setting for royal scientific activities, experiments, and the display of mechanical devices and other material and visual manifestations of science.

ʿAbbas composed a lengthy poem on Rusafa, which Ibn Hayyan also preserves in the Arabic text, and which further strengthens the connections between the polymath and this space of medieval science. The poem appears in a section of the chronicle devoted to the *munya* and follows the account of the villa's significance during the reign of ʿAbd al-Rahman I and the attention it subsequently received during the reign of the emir Muhammad I (r. 852–886) when it was enlarged with a reception hall (*majlis*). Ibn Hayyan relates that the emir had allotted ten thousand dinars for the expense of constructing this hall, but that his vizier, one Hashim, elected to pay for it himself, as a gift to the ruler, and he mentions a feast that was held there for Muhammad and his boon companions.[30]

> He [the emir Muhammad] summoned the words of his poets in describing it [Rusafa] in congratulating him in what of it was there for him. Their master, the great orator ʿAbbas b. Firnas b. [Wa]rda[s], his peerless poet, said concerning this what [all of them] agreed was the best of what has been said in its substance.

In the verses celebrating Rusafa, Ibn Firnas combines astronomical and other scientific imagery with garden and floral imagery popular in Córdoba and in the Abbasid court in the ninth and tenth centuries. The poem opens with imagery of the villa's lofty heights, so elevated that celestial bodies appear beneath it. The lofty heights can be read as standard poetic tropes, of course, but the reference is interesting in this context because it also evokes the elevated topography of the landscape in which Rusafa was purportedly situated:

> [How lovely is the palace of] Al-Rusafa with its gold,
> . . . and the magic (*wa-l-sihri*),

/ and its lofty heights, under which appears
the stars of the Pleiades (al-Thurayya) and al-Semakayni [Arcturus and Spica Virginis] and al-Ghafri [one of the stations of the moon],
If the abundant gold reached its height, and then poured down, it wouldn't reach the ground for a month
It has white chambers (*laha al-ghurafu al-biḍu*) at whose light the morning sun laughs,
These chambers encompass the heights with their light, as if by the brilliance of bright faces
It is as though the palaces of the world after its [Rusafa's] completion,
are just tiny specks [literally "bumps on a {camel's} hump"], that are more obscure than dust

Further along, the poem evokes the radiant spaces of the villa with respect to celestial bodies again.

They [the courts] are like a dawn sleeper, dignified and glowing,
they cast light without exposure to the sun or moon

Astronomical allusions and metaphors, in combination with religious allusions, also feature regularly in the Córdoban court poetry composed in the tenth century, and in these lines we see how Ibn Hayyan and his eleventh-century readers may have traced that practice back to Ibn Firnas and the ninth century. Following the opening lines with their reference to the various stars, the sun, and the moon, Ibn Firnas's poem then goes on to allude to the villa's immediate landscape of gardens and water features:

O, how excellent are its green plants around it,
And its white rivers which flow beneath it,
You could see the tall majestic trees spreading their branches,
swaying from the weight of their fruit

At this moment in the poem he then introduces materials, objects, and themes associated with alchemy, another realm in which 'Abbas was considered expert:

It is as though a goldsmith had forged clusters of dates from fiery gold over their branches
They changed into three states
The molten vessel of [the two hands full of gold pieces] and in the jewels the radiant,
They began as pearls and then transformed into emerald,
Which turns back into gold after the plucking of dates

In short, ʿAbbas's poem on Rusafa not only pays homage to this locus of ninth-century Córdoban court social and intellectual life; it also epitomizes the aestheticization of science in Córdoban Umayyad court culture that is a major theme of this polymath's career.

Returning to the experiment, if we assume Ibn Firnas undertook it, his approach would likely have relied on a long period of prior observations and experiments. As a boon companion to the Córdoban ruler, ʿAbbas would have spent substantial time at the villa and in its environs, and his activities as a court astronomer are pertinent to this point. As noted in the previous chapter, medieval Islamic astronomers were careful, systematic observers of meteorological phenomena of the kind that would directly impact gliding flight.[31] Winds, clouds, seasonal weather patterns, and the like are all factors that, even in today's computer-driven environment, pilots are still required to know.[32] And the writings on precisely such meteorological phenomena by none other than the great ninth-century Abbasid philosopher and scientist al-Kindi tell us that such knowledge of wind, clouds, and weather patterns would also have been part of the purview of intellectuals like Ibn Firnas, which helps contextualize his incorporation of those meteorological phenomena in the celestial representation he created and displayed in his home.[33] During Ibn Firnas's lifetime, intellectuals like al-Kindi elsewhere in the Islamic lands were translating, commenting upon, and composing new works in a variety of topics in the exact sciences.[34] But their intellectual activity did not end at writing about science. This was also the historical moment in which scientific principles were tested through experiment. For example, the diameter of the earth was calculated by the Banu Musa, his Abbasid contemporaries in ninth-century Bagdad. Observation of the natural world and the expectation that human beings would seek to learn from those observations are in keeping with religious sentiments such as Qur'an 31:20, which exhorts, "See ye not how Allah hath made serviceable unto you whatsoever is in the skies and whatsoever is in the earth."[35] Such sentiments, attributed to the wise and aged sage Luqman, may have resonated deeply and meaningfully with Ibn Firnas and other intellectuals of the time, whose scientific activities were inspired by direct observation of the natural world. The details about ʿAbbas b. Firnas offered in the chronicle may therefore indicate that Ibn Hayyan, in the eleventh century, was keen to represent the "sage of al-Andalus" in terms analogous to those of his intellectual peers in the Abbasid court, even as he was just as committed to insisting on the Andalusi polymath's distinctiveness.

But Ibn Lubabah's account makes it clear that there was another group of eyewitnesses to ʿAbbas's experiment besides the "sheikhs" who, it seems, were gathered at the Rusafa villa or in its vicinity to witness the experiment. The passage states that there were also "Saharan nomads" (Berbers?) scattered about the Córdoban countryside who also observed the event. Here Ibn Lubabah seems to be referring to ordinary people, inadvertent eyewitnesses removed from Córdoban court and intellectual circles. Like the fisherman and shepherd who were stupefied by the flight of Daedalus and Icarus in Ovid's myth, lacking a context in which to place such a sight, those witnesses in the fields and hills around Córdoba would naturally have been startled and disturbed enough to exclaim over it, and to discuss at length such a strange sight, one for which they would not have been prepared.[36]

Returning to the first audience discussed above, the term "sheikh" can have another sense in Arabic, referring to the heads of trade and professional guilds, including artisanal and craft guilds.[37] If by "sheikh" Ibn Lubabah meant the heads of Córdoban artisanal workshops, this underscores the visual and material, as well as the logistical, aspects of planning and conducting such an experiment and creating and attempting to test a flight device. Ibn Lubabah provides some details about Ibn Firnas's flight garment and device that can help clear up some of the puzzling aspects of the later texts, with respect to the material dimensions of the experiment.

For instance, while al-Maqqari and Gayangos have Ibn Firnas covering himself with feathers, an absurd image to be sure, Ibn Hayyan's account states that Ibn Firnas *clothed himself* in silk and feathers. According to the poetry composed by Ibn Firnas's contemporary Mu'min b. Sa'id, the feathers seem to have been specifically those of eagles or vultures. The word used in the Madrid manuscript to refer to the feathers (*qshjm*) is unknown, though orthographically similar to *qsh'm*, which the *al-Munjid* dictionary identifies with *nasr*, referring to "an eagle or vulture."[38] The term refers in particular to an animal or human reaching a great age, which might weigh the balance toward translating the term as "eagle," as these birds normally live longer than the vulture. This is the reading that Dozy provides in his edition of al-Maqqari. Eagles and vultures belong to the same family (*accipitridae*), and it is often difficult to distinguish whether one or the other is meant in premodern sources.[39] Yet, as I hope to show, the association with vultures is perhaps stronger and more significant in this context.

Vultures

The cultural significance of vultures in Islamic societies also gives some further context to their evocation in the Arabic text. Vultures evoked a plethora of specifically Islamic religious and cultural associations with which Ibn Firnas and the intellectuals of the Córdoban court, as in other courts of the time, would have been familiar. By contrast to largely negative Anglo-European attitudes toward vultures, which persist today, in 'Abbas b. Firnas's time and in cultural contexts vultures were regarded in a very positive light. In Arabic the vulture has been known as the "Lord of the Birds," specifically because of its prowess in flight, which it accomplishes through gliding, rather than the flapping movement of the wings.[40] Old World vultures were likely to have been a common sight in the skies around Córdoba in Ibn Firnas's time, and their large size would likely have drawn the eye (at the upper range they can achieve lengths of up to 59 inches with a wingspan of around 9 feet) (Fig. 4.10, 4.11).[41] If so, over the course of decades as a court astronomer, during

Figure 4.10. An Old World vulture (*Gyps fulvus*) in flight. Photo: Stefan Krause, Germany, CC BY-SA 3.0 (https://creativecommons.org/licenses/by-sa/3.0), via Wikimedia Commons, no changes made. https://upload.wikimedia.org/wikipedia/commons/b/b8/Gyps_fulvus_in_flight.jpg

which his eyes were trained on the skies to carry out the astronomical observations that were part and parcel of his job, Ibn Firnas's eye may naturally have been drawn by these magnificent natural gliders, and he would have had ample opportunity to observe them in flight.

The significance of vultures in the modern history of aeronautics may be instructive in this regard. The insights of the nineteenth-century aeronautics pioneer Louis Mouillard, which he described in *L'empire de l'air* (1881) and which had a formative impact on Wilbur Wright, were based on his observations of the gliding flight of North African vultures.[42] Reflective of the importance of these birds to the early aviation pioneer, the monument erected in 1912 in Cairo to celebrate Mouillard's achievements prominently featured a sculpture of a vulture in flight (Fig. 4.12). Inspired by Mouillard's example, the Wright Brothers closely observed the birds of the Outer Banks on the southeast coast of the United States and derived innovative design ideas from their observations. One of their most significant innovations in glider design, flexible box construction, was inspired by their observation of the motion of the wings of geese. Thus, it seems likely that close observation of vultures and eagles in the skies above Córdoba could have inspired Ibn Firnas to conceive of an aeronautics experiment and might have informed the design and the materials of any garment or device he might have created to test his ideas (Fig. 4.13).

Besides their reputation as masters of gliding flight, vultures held great significance in medieval Islamic societies, relating to notions of wisdom and longevity.[43]

Figure 4.11. An Old World vulture (*Gyps fulvus*) in the Natural History Museum of London. Photo: I, Drow male, CC BY-SA 4.0 (https://creativecommons.org/licenses/by-sa/4.0), via Wikimedia Commons. No changes made. https://upload.wikimedia.org/wikipedia/commons/8/8b/Gyps_fulvus.002_-_Natural_History_Museum_of_London.JPG

They were intimately associated with the Quranic sage Luqman, a prophet known for his great age (similar in this respect to Methuselah), held to be the equivalent of the life spans of seven vultures.[44] Most of all, for intellectuals like Ibn Firnas, Luqman was famous for his wisdom and intellect. Luqman, as Dmitri Gutas has observed, was considered "the *hakim* [learned or wise man] par excellence in Islamic tradition, the best known pre-Islamic sage whose sayings were in circulation in Arabic both during the Jahiliyya and afterwards."[45] There are six verses in the Qur'an in which Luqman's sayings are quoted, beginning with 31:12: "verily We gave Luqman wisdom, saying: Give thanks unto Allah; and whosoever giveth thanks, he giveth thanks for (the good of) his soul."[46] Moreover, Luqman's intellectual reputation had an architectural and technological dimension as well; he was said to have been one of the architects, or the architect, of the ancient Maʾrib dam. Luqman may very well have been a cultural figure with whom Ibn Firnas would have identified.

Ibn Firnas's own historical moment marked a major stage in the transmission into Arabic of wisdom literature attributed to Luqman. This literature was compiled in the milieu of Abbasid Baghdad by the Arab Christian intellectual Hunayn b. Ishaq (d. 877) in his *Nawadir al-falasifa*, which contains a section devoted to Luqman's sayings.[47] One can certainly imagine ʿAbbas b. Firnas identifying with this ancient

Courtesy of the Aero Club of America "Bulletin," New York.

A GREAT MISSIONARY OF THE FLYING CAUSE.

The statue erected to Louis Pierre Mouillard at Heliopolis.

Figure 4.12. A vulture, its wings outstretched, figures prominently on the memorial (no longer extant) to aeronautics pioneer Louis Pierre Mouillard at Cairo. The memorial was designed by Guillaume Laplagne (1912) and was located in Heliopolis, Cairo, Egypt. Source: Wikimedia Commons (work in the public domain), after Anonymous, "A prophet of aviation." *The Literary Digest*, April 27, 1912, 879.

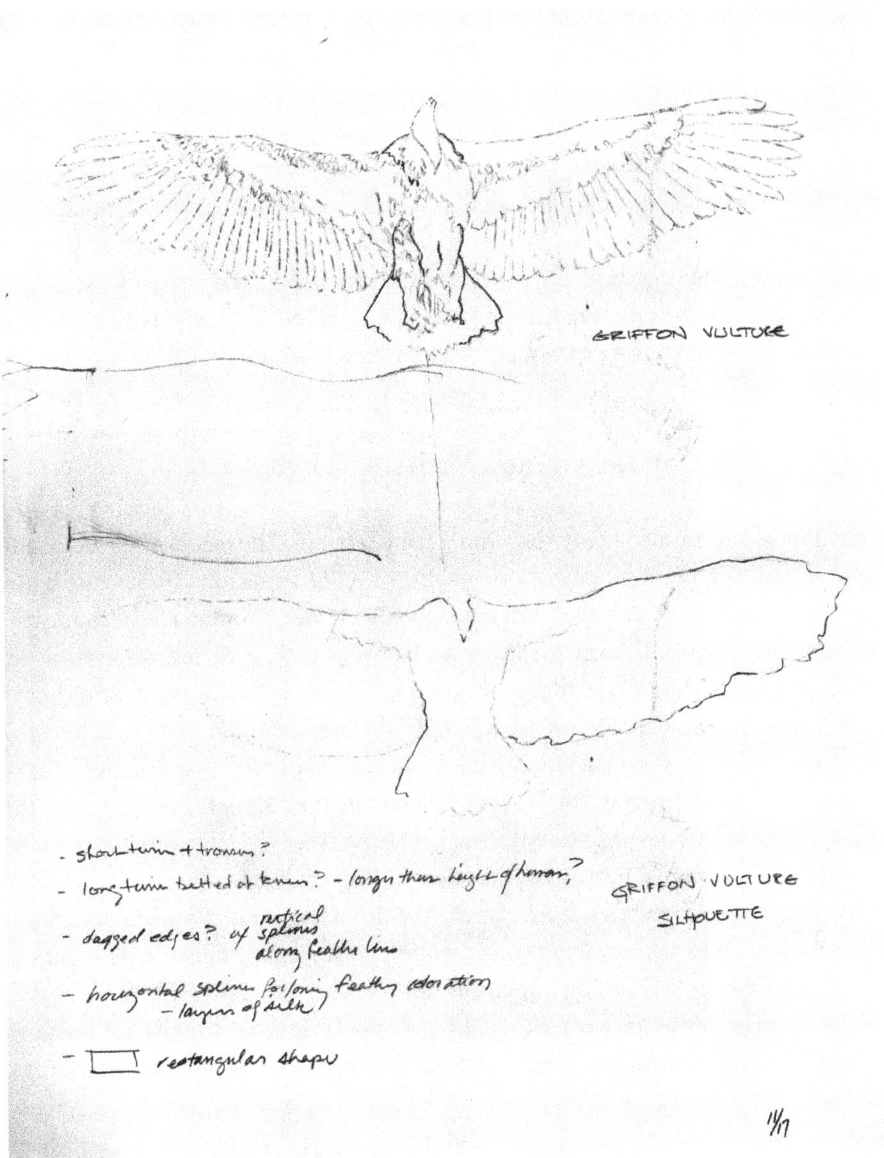

Figure 4.13. Imagining a medieval garment inspired by a vulture in flight. Jan Chambers, Resident Set and Costume Designer for Playmakers Repertory Company, and coinvestigator on the "Medieval First in Flight" project, brought her creative sensibilities to the challenge of imagining and visualizing a garment rooted in the social, visual, and material contexts of Ibn Firnas's time and place.

sage, given that our polymath is said to have carried out his aeronautics experiment in his old age and near the end of his life. And if Ibn Firnas was inspired to conceive an aeronautics experiment and to design a flight device from close observations of vultures in the skies above Córdoba, that too would have been in keeping with an association with the sage Luqman.

Besides their association with Luqman and their fame in Islamic cultural contexts as lords of the air due to their natural skill as gliders, vultures' bodies had numerous talismanic and medicinal properties in medieval Islamic medicine.[48] In this context one might well understand why the talismanic protection of a creature especially admired for its skills in gliding flight may have seemed a desirable addition to a flight device or garment, and one that would have been deeply meaningful and appropriate to Ibn Firnas and his ninth-century audience. As discussed in the previous chapter, magic and science were often entwined in medieval Islamic societies, and such connections may have been more apparent to the court intellectuals who witnessed his aeronautics experiment than they are to us today.

Imagining a Medieval "Flight"

It is impossible to know whether Ibn Firnas actually designed or created any type of flight garment or device, or whether he did in fact carry out any aeronautics experiments. And even if we imagine for a moment that the account and testimonials that Ibn Hayyan wrote down in his chronicle do bear witness to an experiment in gliding flight that took place in Umayyad Córdoba, it would nevertheless be impossible to know what a flight garment would have looked like, the precise materials from which it may have made, or the specifics of how it might have functioned.[49] Nevertheless, Ibn Hayyan's Arabic text, as the earliest account of the incident, provides a few additional details missing from the later versions penned by al-Maqqari and then Gayangos that allow us to speculate further.

Turning to Ibn Lubabah's reference to ʿAbbas having clothed himself in silk for the occasion, for instance, we can consider the availability and characteristics of silk in Córdoba during ʿAbbas's own lifetime and consider in a general way the sort of garment he is likely to have worn (Fig. 4.14).[50] Available in al-Andalus by the ninth century,[51] among courtiers and elite society silk was one of the most favored fabrics for garments; a normal male outfit would have consisted of two or more garments, such as a lined coat, a sleeved robe, and a body shirt.[52] ʿAbbas would have been around sixty years old when this experiment took place, and given what we know of his high status in the court, a silk garment would have corresponded to elite tastes of the time. White silk was particularly favored as a material for garments for specific medical reasons, and this may explain why it seems to have been particularly associated with Muslims in Byzantine texts. For instance, silk does not tend to stick to wounds, it is lightweight and breathable, and vermin (such as fleas) were easy to spot on white or light-colored silk.

Aside from elite consumption in the form of clothing, silk had other applications in medieval Islamic (and Byzantine) societies. For example, it was used for royal tents, banners, and bowstrings. A plain, tabby weave (the simplest form of woven interlace) silk would be a logical choice, as it would have been widely available in the ninth century—indeed the technology to produce it had existed for centuries by

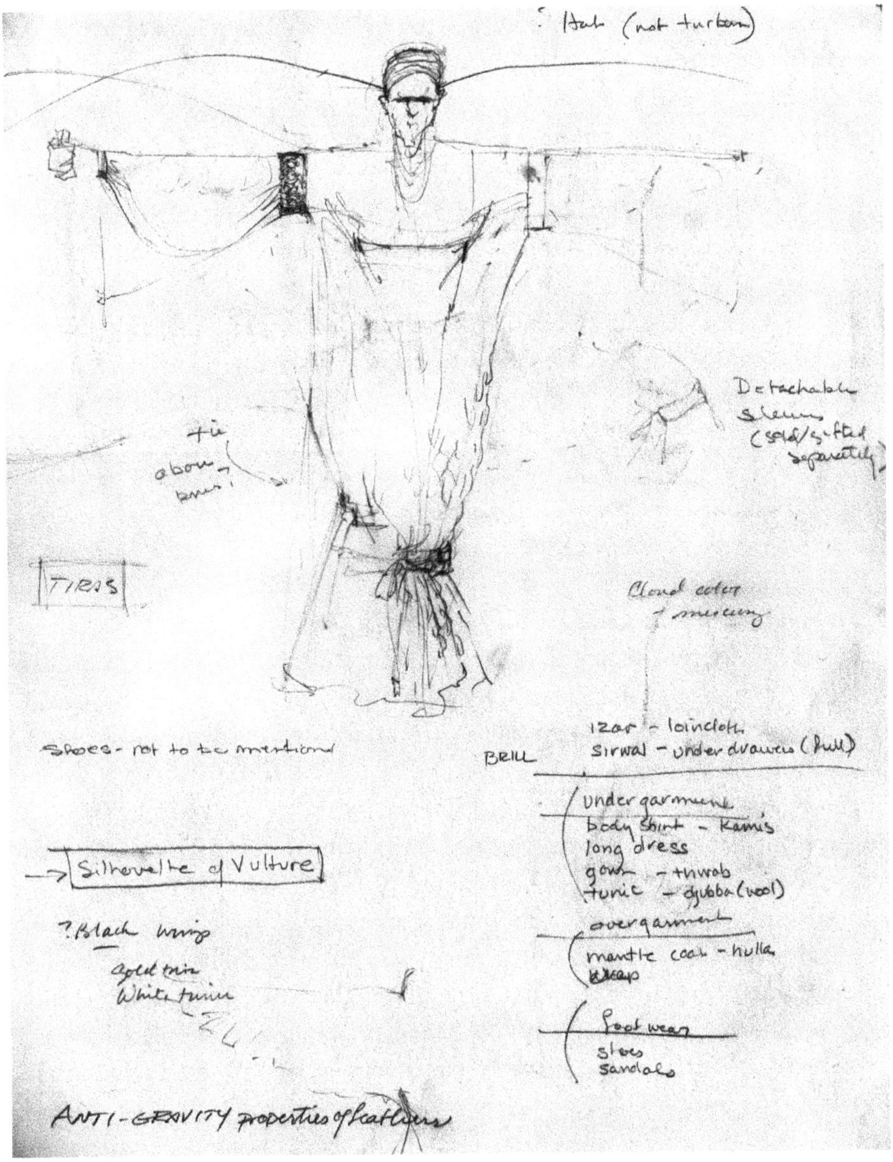

Figure 4.14. Chambers's evolving creative interpretation of Ibn Firnas and an imagined ninth-century silk flight garment, based on collaborative research into medieval Islamic costume, materials, forms, and sociohistorical contexts. Sketch, Jan Chambers for *A Medieval "First in Flight."*

'Abbas's lifetime. A plain-weave silk would have had strength and rigidity, thanks to an up-and-down weave. Spun silk was widely available and was not confined to royal workshops, nor were there significant technical differences between silk produced in royal or imperial workshops and silks attributed to other producers. The medieval Jewish manuscripts found in Old Cairo and known as the Geniza documents mention some sixteen varieties of silk and overall show great sophistication in silk circulation, specifications, demand, and informed consumption, with real evidence of standards and professional conventions in production.[53] For my collaborative project, *A Medieval "First in Flight,"* costume and set designer Jan Chambers imagined Ibn Firnas in a garment of silk appropriate for a leading medieval court intellectual, but that anticipates practicalities that would have needed to be taken into account if it were to be worn during an aeronautics experiment; in this case she visualized a garment bound just below the knees to prevent the silk from billowing in the wind, as an alternative to a tunic and trousers.

Now that we have imagined possibilities for the garment in which Ibn Lubabah tells us 'Abbas was clothed, its materials, and the meanings and associations that it may have held for courtiers in ninth-century Córdoba, we can turn our attention to what the Arabic text says about the flight device proper. Here the chronicle is again more illuminating than the later accounts. Here are what the later accounts say: al-Maqqari, writing in the seventeenth century, wrote that Ibn Firnas "provided himself with a couple of wings and flew a considerable distance," while Gayangos, in his nineteenth-century version, wrote that Ibn Firnas "attached a couple of wings to his body." Both statements are cryptic and reveal little about the device beyond it having two wings. Turning to Ibn Hayyan's chronicle, he records Ibn Lubabah's statement that the polymath spread for himself (*madda*) two wings of calculated structure (*jinahayni 'ala wazni taqdirin qaddarahu*), with which he was able to rise in the air (*istaṭara fi al-jawwi*).

These details, while still brief, nevertheless offer slightly more information. Ibn Lubabah's observation that there were two wings, and that they were of "calculated" structure or weight, is especially illuminating. Calculation implies a knowledge of mathematics and engineering sufficient to design and construct a device capable of what the account describes as rising in the air, movement through the air, and a landing at a distance from the starting point. In other words, the earliest account describes lift and a sustained, controlled glide, to use modern aeronautical terms. To design and construct the precision instruments and machines discussed in the preceding chapters, 'Abbas would certainly have had a sound knowledge of geometry and other branches of mathematics of the time. To construct a water clock, which he did without using a preexisting plan or model, according to the text, he would also have needed to understand astronomy and mathematics as well as principles of engineering, including pneumatics. Such knowledge and skills would have been integral to any design Ibn Firnas may have imagined and executed for a winged device for an aeronautics experiment.

Ibn Hayyan's reference to rising in the air implies that any such device incorporated material to catch the air currents that would provide the initial lift, and this brings us back to the reference to silk.[54] The two wings of a device might have consisted of a rigid, yet flexible, framework to which silk was attached. Silk has a long history of use in aeronautics—used since antiquity in Chinese kites, and in the modern era for hot air balloons and parachutes, of course. Models that would have been available and that 'Abbas could have adapted for his purpose might have included sails, as utilized in windmills or on ships, either of which may have provided inspiration for the idea of covering a wing framework with fabric. In fact, if we remember the meteorological chamber, as we have seen, Mu'min's poem specifically compares the rotating components of Ibn Firnas's device to the arms of a windmill.[55]

For the structural framework, materials and techniques used for constructing tents and bows used for hunting and as weapons also come to mind. Tents, which are regularly mentioned in Ibn Hayyan's chronicle, would have combined light yet flexible rigid frames with silk. Likewise, bows would have needed to be both rigid and flexible, and the materials and techniques involved in their construction could have been adapted for 'Abbas's needs. Bows in this period were generally constructed of a wooden core, to which a strengthening layer of horn could be applied. Indeed, the tenth-century text *Kitab fi tafṣil al-zaman wa-maṣalih al-abdan*, known as the *Calendar of Cordoba*, which contains valuable information about daily life in the Umayyad capital, refers to gazelle horn being sourced from the hinterland and sent to the city precisely for that purpose.[56]

We can therefore speculate that the two wings of any device would have been created out of a rigid yet flexible frame, to which silk was then attached, given that these are materials and craft techniques that were known and commonly employed in early al-Andalus (Fig. 4.15). Finally, we can speculate as well that the size of any winged gliding device would have been considerable—spanning at least 18 feet—but likely even larger, if 'Abbas had in mind vultures as the model for calculating the proportions of the wings to that of his own body. The construction of a large device implies a space in which to construct and house such a device, and the assistance that would have been necessary to move it from the place of construction to an elevated site from which to harness the wind currents that are necessary to achieve lift and glide.

In sum, although we can't know whether such an aeronautics experiment actually took place, the description of it in Ibn Hayyan's text is commensurate with the picture he and his informants, notably the learned Ibn Lubabah, provide of Ibn Firnas's activities and reputation as an inventor, and an unusually ingenious and creative one at that. Moreover, the experiment purportedly took place near the very end of Ibn Firnas's career, by which time he had already achieved a high reputation in the court as an inventor known for being able to conceptualize new and original designs, as we are specifically told by Ibn Hayyan with respect to the water clock Ibn Firnas designed for the ruler and created "without plan or model."

Considering possibilities for the materials and forms that would have been available to Ibn Firnas and that would have been in keeping with his time, place, and sociohistorical contexts allows scope for imagining what may have been possible and available to Ibn Firnas. In contrast to the humble craftsman image that circulates in popular culture, we could imagine a different vision—that of an elite intellectual carrying out a sophisticated experiment using materials and designs in keeping with the visual culture of the ninth-century Córdoban court. In Jan Chambers's sketches

Figure 4.15. In this set of drawings Chambers began to imagine the two wings of Ibn Firnas's device, and potential options for attaching it to the body. Among the inspirations—vulture feathers, basketry, carved wood, leatherwork, and on the right, an ancient Roman cuirass, or piece of armor with a chest plate and backplate. Sketch, Jan Chambers for *A Medieval "First in Flight."*

the flight device is portrayed as a framework of flexible, but sturdy, reinforced wood to support stretched silk, attached to the body with a leather harness (Fig. 4.16). Rather than the tunic and trousers, and the modern glider form provided in the Ibn Firnas model that is displayed in the Ibn Battuta Mall, Chambers imagined the sage in a silk garment decorated with vulture feathers, in acknowledgment of these masters of gliding flight that held so much cultural and religious significance for Ibn Firnas and his peers (Fig. 4.17). Chambers's sketch for a flight device adopts a more fanciful approach, imagining a biwinged device with rounded forms inspired by medieval Islamic astrolabes, a creative nod to Ibn Firnas's eleventh-century reputation as the pioneering instrument maker of al-Andalus.

In recent decades historians of science and of aviation have questioned the nature of Ibn Firnas's experiment and its significance to the history of human flight. For example, aviation historian Richard Hallion has suggested that Ibn Firnas's flight device would have lacked the proper form necessary to achieve flight: "it is unlikely that Ibn Firnas' wings were cambered—curved—like a bird's. Instead, they probably resembled a cloak-parachute rather than a real wing." Yet, why should we assume this? Design based on close observation of natural phenomena, such as the celestial

Figure 4.16. Chambers's final creative visualization of Ibn Firnas with a flight garment of silk ornamented with vulture feathers, and a biwinged flight device whose form was inspired by the rounded lines and forms of astrolabes, the medieval Islamic precision instruments par excellence. Sketch, Jan Chambers for *A Medieval "First in Flight."*

observations that informed the design of armillary globes, celestial spheres, and astrolabes—and even the shape and form of a bird's wing—was commensurate with the scientific activities of medieval Islamic intellectuals.

As Hallion has discussed, textual and material evidence for the close observation and design from nature survives from ancient Greece and from Hellenistic Egypt.[57] The former was a wooden dove, said to have been capable of flight through use of some type of pneumatic means, and whose design and construction texts are attributed to one Archytas, a Greek intellectual and politician of circa 400 BC. Hallion points out that the Sakkara Bird, preserved among tomb artifacts in Egypt in 1898 and dated to the Ptolemaic period of the third century BC, provides visual evidence of close study and emulation of a bird's anatomy for the purpose of understanding flight. The scientific and technological accomplishments of ancient Greek and Hellenistic Egyptian societies were integral to the ninth-century Islamic scientific revolution, and Ibn Firnas's effort may perhaps be best understood as a continuation of this experimental mindset, applied to the problem of flight. The aviation experiment would be comparable in this sense, therefore, to his design and construction of armillary spheres, water clocks, and mechanical devices, creations that also had precedents in ancient and late ancient traditions that were adapted and transformed by medieval Islamic intellectuals.

Figure 4.17. Detail, conjectural model of Ibn Firnas and glider, Ibn Battuta Mall, Dubai. Photo: Dick Doughty / Saudi Aramco World / SAWDIA.

Lacking Ibn Hayyan's chronicle, Hallion proposed that Ibn Firnas did not achieve a glide, but, rather, survived a fall: "Thus it is in all likelihood more accurate to envision him sinking earthwards at a high—though fortunately not terminal—rate of descent rather than gently settling downward in a true glide."[58] This is a reasonable supposition, given a late twelfth-century account of one unnamed Muslim's attempted flight in Byzantine Constantinople, which was recounted by the Byzantine chronicler Niketas Choniates, who described the flight device, or garment, as follows:

> A certain descendant of Agar [Muslims are termed Hagarenes in Niketas's chronicle], who posed as a conjurer [announced] that he would fly through the stadium. He stood on the tower . . . dressed in an extremely long, wide white robe, on which twisted withes, gathering the garment all around, made ample folds.[59]

Although in this case the attempt ended in tragedy, with the would-be aviator plummeting to his death, the account indicates that interest in the possibility of human flight existed on the eastern shores of the Mediterranean by the twelfth century. In Choniates's case the flight device was not a device but a garment incorporating twisted withes meant to serve as wing structures, but that were incapable of achieving lift or glide. Unlike Ibn Firnas's device, which the chronicle implies was a carefully calculated and calibrated fixed-wing structure, the garment described by Choniates was apparently meant to work by raising the arms and beating the air. Hallion's proposal that Ibn Firnas's experiment was likely to have been a kind of medieval parachute drop, as this one was, is not supported by Ibn Lubabah's account as preserved in Ibn Hayyan's chronicle.

The closest comparable medieval aviation experiment to Ibn Firnas's as Ibn Hayyan describes it is also the one that both Hallion and White have accepted as credible. This is the flight of the English monk Eilmer, about whom the historian William of Malmesbury wrote in his *De gestis regum Anglorum* (*The History of the Kings of England*) that he had "fastened wings to his hands and feet so that . . . he might fly like Daedalus, and, collecting the breeze on the summit of a tower, he flew for more than the distance of a furlong.[60] In this account architecture and topography emerge as key factors in any experiment that might have taken place, just as they do in Ibn Firnas's case. Unlike the villa of Rusafa, however, the Abbey at Malmesbury survives. Based on the medieval account's description of Eilmer's glide as having covered a furlong (approximately 600 feet), the height of the Abbey tower, and the topographical and average meteorological conditions of its region (Western Wiltshire and its damp, constant, wind blowing from the southwest), Hallion proposed the following: Eilmer would have needed a stable glide, accomplished at a ratio of 4:1, or over 4 feet forward for every 1 foot in descent.[61] He would have launched into the wind, following the example of birds such as jackdaws within the vicinity of the Abbey, and the entire flight would have been rapid, taking between 12 and 15 seconds. Regarding the materials and design of Eilmer's glider, Hallion posited that its wings would likely have been made of ash or willow wands; that they may have been braced across the back of the shoulders, covered with a stretched, light cloth; and that they would been positioned relatively far aft on his body in order to prevent stalling and a deadly drop.

The way in which ʿAbbas is described by Ibn Lubabah and the other intellectual informants of the Córdoban chronicle suggests that Ibn Firnas's design could have taken inspiration from natural forms that he observed around him. As we have seen, the Arabic text is emphatic about Ibn Firnas's outstanding intellectual qualities and his capacity to innovate in the realm of design: "he was full of ingenuity (*ibdaʿi*) and creativity (*ikhtiraʿi*) and the capacity for invention (al-*tawlidi)*, and the capacity to observe and to derive rules and principles from his observations (*instinbat)*." Such intellectual qualities would have served him well as an observer of natural phenomena and as a scientist. In other words, he was a person quite capable of deriving knowledge from his observations of the natural world, including observations about flight such as one could take away from close attention to eagles and vultures, whose superior gliding abilities derive from their utilization of air currents. It was this ability to observe birds in flight and to learn from those observations through repeated experiments that modern aviation pioneers such as Louis Mouillard and the Wright Brothers made their breakthroughs. Ultimately, those better equipped to judge will have to decide whether the Córdoban chronicle renders Ibn Firnas's experiment and its significance any clearer. The Arabic text certainly seems no more and no less significant as an indicator of medieval interest and experimentation in aeronautics than William of Malmesbury's account of Eilmer's feat.

As I hope to have shown, a host of factors likely came together to inspire Ibn Firnas's purported experiment. Chief among these were 'Abbas's own intellectual gifts and craft ability, celebrated by his peers and developed over the course of a long career. Beyond his personal attributes, just as crucial were the social and intellectual environment of the Umayyad court, and its natural and built surroundings of what I have called the *munya* landscape, for the villas that Umayyad patrons favored in Ibn Firnas's time as the spaces for scientific experimentation and display. The same topographical features that made the suburban area north of the walled city particularly desirable as the setting for the Umayyad villa of al-Rusafa—elevated views and cooler temperatures—are also conducive to thermal soaring and therefore attractive to birds such as vultures that are masters of gliding flight, and that would have provided a first-hand model from nature for anyone interested in the mechanics of flight. An elevated topography also lends itself to conducting astronomical and meteorological observations of the kind in which Ibn Firnas had a professional interest as court astronomer. He had many years to observe those features of his natural surroundings firsthand, and the knowledge such observations would have provided would also have had a direct bearing on interest in the possibility of gliding flight.

5
Epilogue
Echoes

As I hope to have shown in the previous chapters, Ibn Firnas's career illuminates science, design, and making as interconnected intellectual practices in the ninth century, during the first flowering of the Islamic scientific revolution. This polymath's career, alongside the early precision instruments and illustrated scientific treatises I have discussed in the preceding chapters, helps us better appreciate the intense connections between science and visual culture in the medieval Islamic lands. What has emerged is a rare portrait of an early Islamic polymath who in many ways represents what would come to be known as a "Renaissance Man," and the court culture that produced such polymaths, and in which design and making were central to scientific intellectual pursuits.

Having established that Ibn Firnas's activities as an intellectual and a maker represent neither an aberration nor something peculiar to al-Andalus, and that his career alerts us to widespread sympathies between the fields of science, architecture, and the plastic arts during the caliphal period, in this epilogue I turn to a later place and time in which we can perhaps see the impact of the cultural practices of caliphal science as represented by Ibn Firnas: sixteenth-century Europe. I depart from the medieval Islamic lands to consider two drawings of an early Abbasid astrolabe by the architect Antonio da Sangallo the Younger. I then consider the questions raised by these intriguing drawings before moving to consider the significance of this evidence for the apparent transfer to and reception of medieval Islamic scientific objects in Medici Florence during the sixteenth century, engaging with some of the topics raised by George Saliba in his 2007 *Islamic Science and the Making of the European Renaissance* and Ana Contadini and others on the circulation of Islamic visual culture in Renaissance Europe.[1]

I consider the possibility that the fruitful dialogue between the exact or rational sciences and Islamic visual culture for which I have been arguing in the preceding chapters was carried beyond Iberia and beyond the Dar al-Islam, to be adapted by new designers, makers, and patrons who embraced the links between craft and intellect and who applied the exact sciences and precision instruments to create new visual cultures in the Renaissance, and that new patrons such as Cosimo de' Medici deployed to express their princely aspirations, much as the rulers of the caliphal Islamic courts had done in previous centuries. The centrality of Islamic civilization

A Bridge to the Sky. Glaire D. Anderson, Oxford University Press. © Oxford University Press 2024.
DOI: 10.1093/oso/9780190913243.003.0005

to the formation of the European Renaissance is by now firmly established, thanks to scholarship that has grappled with long-standing problematic notions that have created a divide between Islamic and European territories of the Mediterranean. For instance, Flood and Necipoglu have discussed the notions that the classical Mediterranean heritage belonged exclusively to Europe in the postmedieval period, and that fixed Islamic civilization into an essentializing medieval state, excluded from a modernity perceived as exclusively European.[2] Even so, we probably still do not yet fully appreciate the extent to which European designers and patrons were deeply engaged with medieval Islamic science, including its visual and material expressions in the form of precision objects and illustrated scientific treatises. For this reason the chapter briefly considers the relevance of such expressions to Europe's Scientific Revolution, before concluding that the entwining of craft and intellect, epitomized by Ibn Firnas's career and embodied in the works that I have discussed in these pages, can be added to the many and varied cultural transmissions from the medieval Islamic lands to later European contexts.

I would like to begin with two drawings by the Florentine architect Antonio da Sangallo the Younger (1484–1546) preserved today in the Uffizi's Gabinetto dei Disegni e delle Stampe, which George Saliba identified as the representation of an actual ninth-century Abbasid instrument (Fig. 5.1).[3] Made in 1520, the drawings depict the front and rear faces of an astrolabe. The drawings are of interest to what I have discussed in the preceding pages because they suggest that Antonio da

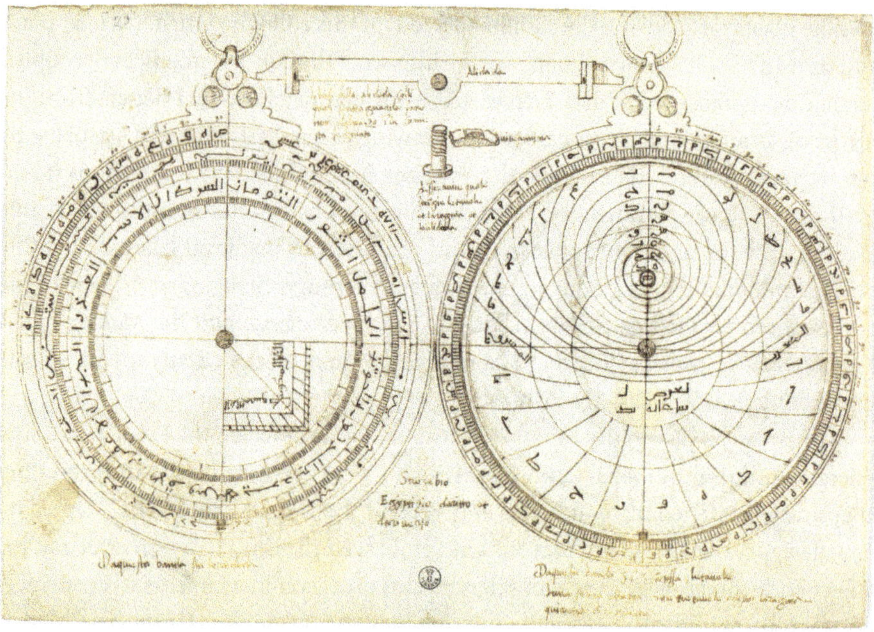

Figure 5.1. Drawing of an ʿAbbasid astrolabe made by Khafif (fl. ninth c.), by Antonio da Sangallo the Younger (1484–1546), 1520 CE. Inv. U 1454A. Image courtesy of Gabinetto dei Disegni e delle Stampe, Uffizi, Florence.

Sangallo was sensitive to the close interconnections between the exact sciences and the Islamic visual culture that flourished through the activities of polymaths like Ibn Firnas and the courts that encouraged and supported their work. Antonio da Sangallo is in some ways representative of the multidisciplinary artist-intellectuals of the Italian Renaissance. He was one of the most distinguished architects of the Italian High Renaissance, having worked on such important projects as St. Peter's, for which he became the sole architect in 1536, and the Villa Madama, for instance.[4] In true Renaissance fashion he can also be described as an engineer, a landscape architect, an urban strategist, and an early industrial designer.[5] His interest in this early Islamic astrolabe, conveyed in the precision and detail of his drawing, therefore suggests that there was something significant about these objects of science for figures such as da Sangallo, an intellectual who worked across disciplines, and who shaped the artistic culture of Renaissance Florence.[6]

The astrolabe inscriptions, masterfully rendered in detail by the designer, reveal it to be the work of the celebrated Abbasid instrument maker Khafif (see Chapter 2) (Fig. 5.2). Sangallo drew the front of the instrument on the right side of the sheet, and the back of the instrument on its left side. Sangallo drew the astrolabe's rete on the back of the sheet, oriented at a 90-degree rotation, so that one has to turn the sheet to portrait orientation to read the Arabic text. The dagger-shaped star pointers and the Arabic inscriptions throughout are rendered overall with clarity and a sense of confidence, for the most part. Sangallo filled in the Arabic inscriptions on the

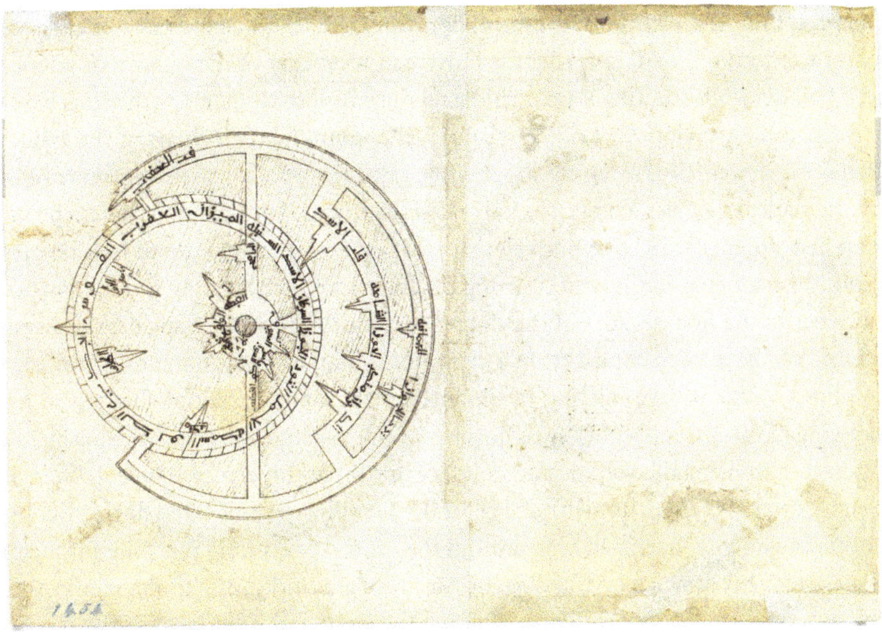

Figure 5.2. Rete, drawing of an ʿAbbasid astrolabe made by Khafif (fl. ninth c.), by Antonio da Sangallo the Younger (1484–1546), 1520 CE. Inv. U 1454A. Image courtesy of Gabinetto dei Disegni e delle Stampe, Uffizi, Florence.

top left quadrant of the instrument and drew in the numbers for all of the top right quadrant and part of the lower right quadrant. His rendering of the Arabic on the two inner rings has a much sketchier quality than the other Arabic inscriptions, which elsewhere are rendered with a sure hand, perhaps suggesting that those on the two inner rings were done first. Close examination reveals the tiny holes, marks, and points of darkened ink that show Sangallo's use of a compass in laying out the design, and this is especially clear when one looks closely at the circles that make up the instrument's obverse face.

There are a number of questions raised by this drawing. Was Sangallo drawing from life or was he working from another drawing? If he was drawing from life, how and why did an instrument made by the most celebrated maker of the 'Abbasid intellectual milieu come to be in sixteenth-century Florence? And why would Sangallo, a skilled and masterful architect and designer, have been interested enough in this medieval Islamic scientific instrument to render it with such care and attention to its most minute details? Saliba, Ana Contadini, and others have discussed the adoption of medieval Islamic astrolabes as part of a wider transfer of Islamic learning into early modern European contexts.[7] An interest in and receptivity to the exact sciences that had been developed in the Islamic lands, extending to the instruments of science, even one like this one that had been made centuries before, go some way toward explaining the artist's interest in capturing it on paper, but there is more at play here than a sixteenth-century intellectual's appreciation of the exact sciences as these had developed in the Islamic lands.

On the one hand Sangallo's drawing provides an important material evidence of the reception of astronomical information from the Islamic lands in Renaissance Europe, offering a visual parallel for European reception of the culture of science as it had developed in the Islamic lands; medieval Islamic planetary theories likely informed the development of Copernican astronomy.[8] Intellectuals of the Italian Renaissance were thus receptive to scientific information, such as astronomical and mathematical treatises, coming to Italy from the Islamic lands, and to Islamic precision instruments.[9] This drawing offers further evidence that medieval Islamic precision instruments (or at least drawings of them) were circulating in Renaissance Florence in the first decades of the sixteenth century. However, Sangallo's drawing could itself have been copied from a drawing, as manuscripts containing drawings of objects were also circulating in Florence at the time.[10] Careful shading of his drawing of the rete and other specific parts of the instrument reveals the designer's interest in showing the volume and depth of this three-dimensional object. There is a suggestion of perspective with the central hole, showing as if tilted down slightly, and in the intense, dark hatching around the central part of the rete. The throne of the astrolabe is drawn as if tilted slightly to the right, indicating to the viewer that this is a three-dimensional object, whereas the front and back faces of the instrument are drawn flat, with no indication of volume or depth of an object in space.

Beyond the interest in the astrolabe as a useful object with which to experiment with depicting a three-dimensional subject on a flat surface, Sangallo's drawing reflects an awareness and an appreciation on the part of Italian designers, artists, and architects of the interconnected relationship between the exact sciences and visual culture, as these had developed in the Islamic lands since at least the ninth century.[11] Not only were intellectual-designers like Sangallo and other great Renaissance figures aware of those medieval Islamic science/art connections, but the astrolabe drawing suggests that they were adapting that approach in their own practices and that this was a strand in the development of the artistic culture of Renaissance Florence from the fifteenth century, one that was fully embraced in the mid-sixteenth century under the patronage of Cosimo I de' Medici, the first Duke of Florence.

The famous Accademia del Disegno in Florence was central to this dialogue between the exact sciences and art. It received its official recognition in January 1563, some forty years after Sangallo made his drawing of the Abbasid astrolabe. Cosimo I de' Medici (d. 1574) was its head, along with Michelangelo.[12] As Filippo Camerota has discussed, Cosimo I, who became Duke of Florence from 1537, through his patronage used the exact sciences in combination with the arts to develop an image of power and prestige in his Florentine court.[13] Cosimo's close connection with the Accademia speaks to his interests in the exact sciences and their application to design and visual culture in support of Medici political interests.[14] The institute sponsored the ideals of excellence in painting, sculpture, and architecture as architecture, but the exact sciences were fundamental to the training provided there; alongside the sculpture and drawing lessons designers and artists had lessons in perspective, practical geometry or mechanics, and mathematics.

An Islamic astrolabe owned by Cosimo I de' Medici and displayed in his palace in Florence suggests that at least one medieval Islamic instrument was present in the city in the second half of the sixteenth-century, and that the interest in Islamic science and visual culture, revealed by Sangallo's astrolabe drawing some forty years earlier, extended to the collecting habits and patronage of the Medici themselves.[15] It was apparently displayed in Cosimo I de' Medici's new Sala della Guardaroba (Wardrobe Room), constructed in 1567 in the Palazzo Vecchio.[16] The room was meant to be both an architectural space and a wondrous chamber whose ceiling was meant to open, and from which two great globes would descend—a celestial one, lost or perhaps never built, and a terrestrial one that still stands in the room today. Cosimo I's interest in the exact sciences was thus given architectural and visual expression in this project, which was a collaboration between designers who were also practitioners of exact sciences: Giorgio Vasari (who designed the room's architecture); Miniato Pitti, a cosmographer who designed the cartographic decoration; and Egnazio Danti, (1536–1586), Cosimo's instrument maker, who drew the Ptolemaic maps that decorated its interior, and who was responsible for creating a display of scientific instruments within the new chamber. Danti described the astrolabe as Arabian in his 1569 treatise on astrolabes, referring to it as "a very ancient astrolabe that belonged to . . . [Cardinal Ferdinando de' Medici], made perhaps 500 years ago in Arabia, which is at present in my hands . . . "[17]

Besides the Islamic astrolabe the chamber included a magnificent armillary sphere and a mechanical clock.[18] Danti himself designed and built portable scientific instruments, including instruments that were designed with specific architectural contexts: these included a marble quadrant for the facade of Santa Maria Novella and a bronze equatorial armilla, as well as anemoscopes for palaces and gardens in Bologna and Perugia.[19]

Sangallo's drawing and perhaps the Islamic astrolabe displayed in Cosimo's collection are intriguing because they provide a material counterpart to the evidence that intellectuals from the Islamic lands were introducing receptive European courts to the exact sciences as these had developed in Islamic contexts. These intellectuals included figures such as Leo Africanus (al-Hasan b. Muhammad Ibn al-Wazzan, d. ca. 1550), his student Jean-Albert Widmanstadt, (1506–c.1559), and Nehemias (d. 1590), the Syriac Jacobite Patriarch from Diyar Bakr, whose Arabic mathematical treatises were published by the Medici Oriental Press under the patronage of Cardinal Ferdinand de Medici.[20] Such international networks seem also to have included Jewish intellectuals involved in international trade. Such figures mediated between the Turkish Ottoman Empire and Italy and may have introduced Islamic scientific texts to European audiences.[21] Another context for Italian patrons' and architects' interests in the exact sciences as developed in the Islamic lands was the reform of the Papal Calendar, which was manifested architecturally in projects such as the Tower of the Winds in the Vatican, under Gregory XIII.[22]

But even before such sixteenth-century encounters between Italian patrons and designers, and medieval Iberian and Islamic science and visual culture, one can discern connections between the exact sciences and Florentine design and architecture that recall those that occurred earlier in medieval Islamic contexts. Take, for example, the sculptural program of Giotto's Campanile in Florence. Designed before his death in 1337, the program includes personifications of architecture, astronomy, and engineering as part of a cycle representing the Liberal Arts. Here Daedalus, representing the mechanical sciences, is depicted wearing what appears to be a garment covered with feathers, a distant echo, perhaps, of accounts that mention Ibn Firnas's silk garment (Figs. 5.3, 5.4).[23]

Other early points of potential congruence may be found in the career of the great Florentine architect Filippo Brunelleschi, who may have known and used the astrolabe to develop his system of perspective, in projects that included sculpture, architecture, and civil waterworks.[24] Brunelleschi, the epitome of the Renaissance architect, combined the exact sciences and design and worked across media and at a range of scales. Long before his work as an architect tasked with the challenge of designing a massive new dome for the Florence cathedral, he was a master goldsmith and sculptor of the celebrated bronze panels for the doors of the Florence Baptistry.[25] Later in his career he worked as an engineer and collaborated with astronomers and engineers in his architectural and urban projects: with the astronomer Paolo dal Pozzo on the dome of the Florence cathedral, and with Mariano di Jacopo da Siena, author of an engineering treatise

Figure 5.3. Sculpture of Daedalus (at right), by Andrea Pisano (d. ca. 1348–49). Pisano, a sculptor, goldsmith, and architect, created this as one of a series of allegorical scenes of the *Sciences and Arts* and *Trades* decorating the base of the Campanile, Florence. The original has been removed to the Mus. dell'Opera di S Maria del Fiore. Photo: Glaire Anderson.

that includes images depicting the use of an astrolabe to determine changes in the levels of water courses.[26]

The connections that I have tried to make in these pages between science and visual culture; between making and knowing; and between philosophy, science, and arts are not unique to medieval Islamic courts, nor to Renaissance Italy. Ibn Firnas's activities as a designer and maker of precision instruments bring up a broader question that could be of interest to historians of material culture and science in other times and places: namely, how do we understand the intersection of philosophical and intellectual issues, with the development of sophisticated precision instrumentation and other visual and material expressions of science?[27] If the astrolabe, celestial globes, and sundials were the cutting edge technologies and coveted devices of the caliphal era, a similar role may have been played later in Europe by the telescope, and subsequently the microscope.[28]

Just as Ibn Firnas and other court intellectuals were designing and creating precision instruments and devising and carrying out scientific experiments as participants in high court and intellectual culture, so too can we discern a similar connection between design, making, and knowledge when we examine the activities of some of the

Figure 5.4. Daedalus, by Andrea Pisano (d. ca. 1348–49). Mus. dell'Opera di S Maria del Fiore, Florence. Pisano has depicted his body covered with feathers. Photo: Glaire Anderson.

great figures of the European Scientific Revolution. For instance, Galileo made a fine telescope for his Medici patron, which is preserved today in the Museo Galileo collection in Florence. Luxurious in appearance and finely crafted, apparently Galileo ignored requests for detailed information about it from his contemporary colleagues, preferring to reserve this important new technology as a means to attract a wealthy patron whose support would further his scientific work. Just as Ibn Firnas found an interested patron with the considerable resources to support his activities in the rulers of the caliphal courts, so too did Galileo and the great scientists of Europe find that designing and crafting sophisticated new technological devices could attract interest and necessary support from wealthy and powerful patrons. Tycho Brahe, for instance, made a large celestial globe (no longer extant) for the royal observatory at

Copenhagen and was also commissioned by the King of Denmark to make other precision instruments and to build an astronomical observatory.

Like Ibn Firnas and his contemporaries in the caliphal era, later European scientist-intellectuals such as Galileo, Brahe, Descartes, and Newton all placed great importance on designing and making instruments as an important part of the intellectual enterprise of the scientific process.[29] In his introduction to the *Principles*, for instance, Descartes wrote of designing telescopes and sets out the notion that the careful study of philosophy was a requirement before a scientist could build that instrument, which he describes as "one of the most difficult tasks ever undertaken."[30] Likewise, Newton's writings suggest that his experiments with telescopes led to his important conclusions about optics.[31] As was the case in Ibn Firnas's era, seventeenth-century European natural philosophers did not distinguish between theoretical and applied or experimental concerns as we currently do but did the theorizing alongside the making and experimenting.

Conclusion

When we look at monuments and objects made elsewhere in the early Islamic lands we can glimpse the same conjoining of science, intellectual culture, and visual culture to which the chronicle's account of Ibn Firnas's career alerts us. The impression, gleaned from the account, that astronomers and other intellectuals with a knowledge of mathematics and other exact sciences applied that knowledge to creating works of visual culture is corroborated by many extant works made between the ninth and thirteenth centuries across the Islamic lands: manuscript illustrations, scientific instruments and other fine metalwork objects, and architecture. Singly and as a group these works suggest that the sketch of Ibn Firnas that has come down to us in the Córdoban chronicle, of a court intellectual who could and did design and craft works of visual culture and was remembered and celebrated for this by Andalusi court intellectuals of the eleventh century, is symptomatic of a broader intersectionality of science and art in the caliphal lands.

In medieval Islamic visual culture, between the ninth and thirteenth centuries, intellect and craft went hand in hand. By considering the Arabic texts alongside the physical and visual evidence, we can see that across the Islamic lands, Ibn Firnas and other court intellectuals such as the Banu Musa, and specialists in mathematics such as al-Farghani and Ahmad al-Hasib, applied their knowledge and expertise in the exact sciences of astronomy, geometry, and mathematics to designing and making at all scales, from precision instruments to automata to architectural monuments and urban infrastructure.

The preceding chapters will not satisfy those wishing for clear, unambiguous historical evidence of our polymath's impact on the intellectual developments in al-Andalus. I have not presented new written sources about Ibn Firnas. Nor have I discovered surviving objects that could be clearly linked with Ibn Firnas.

Nevertheless, I do hope to have shown that his career as recounted by Ibn Hayyan, and the texts and objects that point to the activities of others like him in caliphal era courts, helps us better understand how the boundaries between design, the practice of science, and other intellectual pursuits were not mutually exclusive, but in fact closely interconnected in Umayyad Córdoba and elsewhere. For intellectuals such as ʿAbbas Ibn Firnas it was the usual practice to work across different areas of knowledge. This contrasts with our own contemporary academic intellectual practices that separate the exact sciences and technology from the humanities, and the "fine arts" from "craft" and "decorative arts." It is, however, very much in keeping with the usual practices of intellectuals of the European Renaissance. Ibn Firnas's career as it was remembered by his contemporaries and by Ibn Hayyan and his eleventh-century audience, and the astrolabes, celestial globes, and other works I have discussed in the previous pages, tells us that caliphal intellectuals operated in a very different environment. They valued the fruitful dialogue between craft and intellect and esteemed the intellectual who could demonstrate his intellectual skills through the processes of design and making that produced elegant, skillful, creative works with which they could observe and better understand wondrous Creation. Our polymath's activities in Córdoba throw into relief a role for mathematicians, astronomers, engineers, and other scientists as makers of Islamic visual culture in the caliphal era.[32] The portrait of Ibn Firnas as a medieval intellectual, and a designer and maker of early Islamic objects and spaces of science, reveals that visuality, design, and making have been central to the practices of science, and to high intellectual and social cultures in Islamic societies.

Ibn Firnas's career and the objects of science and art that I discuss in this book may therefore further nuance the reception and appreciation of the medieval Islamic intellectual and visual culture in later times and places beyond the Islamic lands. Considering visual culture and texts together, the intellectual currents of the early Islamic courts may reveal new contexts for Europe's engagements with Islamic science and visual culture, and with ways of design, making, and thinking.

Notes

ʿAbbās Ibn Firnas and His Career: Selected Passages from Ibn Ḥayyān

1. Ibn Ḥayyān, *Crónica de Los Emi-res Alḥakam I Y ʿAbdarraḥmān II*, pp. 137–42. This is the Spanish translation of Makki's critical Arabic edition of Ibn Ḥayyān, *al-Muqtabis II-1*, published as Ibn Ḥayyān, *Al-Sifr Al-Thānī Min Kitāb Al-Muqtabas*.
2. Ibn Ḥayyān, *Crónica de Los Emires Alḥakam I Y ʿAbdarraḥmān II Entre Los Años 796 Y 847 (Almuqtabis II-1)*, pp. 140–41.
3. Translation from Mamoun Sakkal's transcription of the folio in the Real Academia de la Historia manuscript in Madrid, published in facsimile as Ibn Ḥayyān, *Muqtabis II: Anales de los Emires de Córdoba*, p. 131r.
4. Ibn Ḥayyān, *Al-Sifr al-Thānī min Kitāb al-Muqtabas*, ed. Maḥmūd ʿAlī Makkī, Al-Ṭabʿah 1 (al-Riyāḍ: Markaz al-Malik Fayṣal lil-Buḥūth wa-al-Dirāsāt al-Islāmīyah, 2003).
5. This reading clarifies the Madrid manuscript's "*ʿalā [sadfi] al-harīri*."
6. Clarifies *matāriḥa* "places" followed by [d-n], in the Madrid manuscript.
7. Transcribed by Stuart and Irina Sears from Ibn Ḥayyān, *Muqtabis II: Anales de los Emires de Córdoba*, 131v.
8. Ibn Ḥayyān, *Crónica de los Emires Alḥakam I y ʿAbdarraḥmān II entre los Años 796 y 847 (Almuqtabis II-1)*, 140.
9. Ptolemy's "Handy Tables," later revised by Theon of Alexandria. My thanks to Julio Samsó.
10. Ibn Ḥayyān, *Crónica de los Emires Alḥakam I y ʿAbdarraḥmān II*, 140–41.
11. Ibn Ḥayyān, *al-Muqtabas min anbāʾ ahl al-Andalus* (Bayrūt: Dār al-Kitāb al-ʿArabī, 1973), 227–34.

Introduction

1. On Leonardo's sketches of birds and flying devices, see Leonardo da Vinci, *Il codice sul volo degli uccelli nella Biblioteca reale di Torino*. Edizione nazionale dei manoscritti e dei disegni di Leonardo da Vinci (Firenze: Giunti-Barbera, 1976); Edoardo Zanon, *Il libro del Codice del volo: Leonardo da Vinci: dallo studio del volo degli uccelli all'aeroplano* (The book of the Codex on flight: Leonardo da Vinci: from the study of bird flight to the airplane), 1st ed. (Milan: Leonardo3, 2009).
2. Lynn White Jr., "Eilmer of Malmesbury, an Eleventh Century Aviator: A Case Study of Technological Innovation, Its Context and Tradition," *Technology and Culture* 2, no. 2 (April 1, 1961): 97–111. doi:10.2307/3101411.
3. Antonio R. Acedo del Olmo, *Abbas Ibn Firnās: El sabio de al-Andalus* (Granada, Spain: El Legado Andalusi, 2016); Julio Samsó, "ʿAbbās Ibn Firnās," in *The Oxford Encyclopedia of Philosophy, Science, and Technology in Islam*, ed. Ibrahim Kalin (Oxford: Oxford University Press, 2014), 1–2; Mónica Rius, "El sabio total Ibn Firnás," in *Jábega* 97 (2008), 9–13; M. Aragón Huerta, "Ibn Firnās, ʿAbbas," in *Biblioteca de Al-Andalus*, ed. Jorge Lirola Delgado and José Miguel Puerta Vílchez (Almería, Spain: Fundación Ibn Tufayl de Estudios Árabes,

2004), 168–72; Elías Terés, "Sobre el vuelo de Abbas Ibn Firnās," *Al-Andalus* 29, no. 2 (1964): 365; Elías Terés, "'Abbas Ibn Firnās," in *The Formation of al-Andalus*, ed. Manuela Marin, Maribel Fierro, and Julio Samsó, vol. 2, Formation of the Classical Islamic World: vols. 46–47 (Aldershot, U.K.: Ashgate, 1998), 235–44; Lévi-Provençal, E., "ʿAbbās b. Firnās," in *Encyclopaedia of Islam*, 2nd ed., ed. P. Bearman, Th. Bianquis, C.E. Bosworth, E. van Donzel, and W.P. Heinrichs. Consulted online on September 27, 2021 http://dx.doi.org.ezproxy.is.ed.ac.uk/10.1163/1573-3912_islam_SIM_0021. First published online: 2012. First print edition: ISBN: 9789004161214, 1960–2007.

4. David McCullough, *The Wright Brothers* (New York: Simon & Schuster, 2015), 1.
5. Jim Al-Khalili, *Pathfinders: The Golden Age of Arabic Science* (London; New York: Allen Lane, 2010), 196.
6. Glaire Anderson, *The Islamic Villa in Early Medieval Iberia: Architecture and Court Culture in Umayyad Córdoba* (Farnham, U.K.: Ashgate, 2013), 25–26.
7. For evocative introductions to the major figures, places, and times under consideration in this book, see Eduardo Manzano Moreno, *La corte del califa: cuatro años en la Córdoba de los omeyas*, 1st ed. (Barcelona: Crítica, 2019); Jerrilynn Denise Dodds, Abigail Krasner Balbale, and Maria Rosa Menocal, *The Arts of Intimacy: Christians, Jews, and Muslims in the Making of Castilian Culture* (New Haven, Conn.: Yale University Press, 2008); Maribel Fierro, *ʿAbd Al-Rahman III: The First Cordoban Caliph* (Oxford: Oneworld, 2005); Maria Menocal, *The Ornament of the World: How Muslims, Jews, and Christians Created a Culture of Tolerance in Medieval Spain* (Boston: Little, Brown, 2002); Manuela Marín, Julio Samsó, and Maribel Fierro, *The Formation of al-Andalus*, vols. 46–47 (Brookfield, U.K.: Ashgate, 1998).
8. On the notion of the caliphate, see Hugh Kennedy, *Caliphate: The History of an Idea* (New York: Basic Books, 2016); Robert Hoyland, "Making of Islamic Civilization," in *In God's Path: The Arab Conquests and the Creation of an Islamic Empire* (New York: Oxford University Press, 2015), 207–30. For an excellent social history of the caliphal era, see Amira Bennison, *The Great Caliphs: The Golden Age of the 'Abbasid Empire* (London: I. B. Tauris, 2009). Two classics on the history of the period are Marshall Hodgson, *The Venture of Islam; Conscience and History in a World Civilization* (Chicago: University of Chicago Press, 1974), and Albert Hourani and Malise Ruthven, *A History of the Arab Peoples* (Cambridge, Mass.: Belknap Press of Harvard University Press, 2002).
9. Christine Mazzoli-Guintard, "Córdoba," *In Encyclopaedia of Islam, THREE*, ed. Kate Fleet, Gudrun Krämer, Denis Matringe, John Nawas, and Everett Rowson. Accessed September 17, 2021. doi:http://dx.doi.org/10.1163/1573-3912_ei3_COM_25577; Robert Hillenbrand, "'The Ornament of the World': Medieval Córdoba as a Cultural Centre," in *The Legacy of Muslim Spain*, ed. Salma Khadra Jayyusi and Manuela Marín (Leiden: Brill, 1992), 112–35. On the palace city of Madinat al-Zahrāʾ, see Antonio Vallejo Triano, *La Ciudad Califal de Madinat Al-Zahrāʾ: Arqueología de Su Excavación*, 1a ed., Colección Naturaleza y Medio Ambiente (Córdoba, Spain: Editorial Almuzara, 2010); Antonio Vallejo Triano, *Madinat al-Zahra: Official Guide to the Archeological Complex* (Córdoba, Spain: Junta de Andalucía, Consejería de Cultura, 2006).
10. Maria Menocal, *The Ornament of the World: How Muslims, Jews, and Christians Created a Culture of Tolerance in Medieval Spain* (Boston: Little, Brown, 2002).
11. Glaire Anderson, "Remembering ʿAbbas Ibn Firnas: How a Medieval Polymath's Career Suggests a More Diverse History of Science, Technology, and Visual Culture," ed. P. Kitlas, *Spain-North Africa Project Bulletin* (October 21, 2021). http://www.spainnorthafricaproject.org/bulletin.
12. Photos and details of the Ibn Firnās crater are available on the International Astronomical Union (IAU) Working Group for Planetary System Nomenclature's Gazetteer of Planetary

Nomenclature at https://planetarynames.wr.usgs.gov/Feature/2634, accessed September 17, 2021.

13. See images of these representations in the interactive digital timeline of Ibn Firnās in popular culture at http://glairedanderson.com/medievalflight/ibn-Firnās-in-popular-culture/
14. For an overview of the early Islamic scientific revolution see Ahmad S. Dallal, "Beginnings and Beyond," in *Islam, Science, and the Challenge of History*, Terry Lectures (New Haven, Conn.: Yale University Press, 2010), 1–53.
15. On this false distinction, see Martina Müller-Wiener, "Puns and Puzzles: The Interplay between the Visual and the Verbal in 13th Century Mesopotamian Metalwork, Book Painting and Astrolabes," in *Siculo-Arabic Ivories and Islamic Painting, 1100–1300: Proceedings of the International Conference, Berlin 6–8 July 2007*, ed. David Knipp (München: Hirmer Verlag, 2011), 275–76.
16. Pamela Smith's work on early modern European science and making likewise is very much in keeping with the issues of craft and intellect in Islamic societies that concern me here: Pamela H. Smith, *The Body of the Artisan: Art and Experience in the Scientific Revolution* (Chicago: University of Chicago Press, 2004). It would be interesting to investigate possible congruences further, though such investigation is beyond the bounds of this book; see Ashley West, "Review of 'The Body of the Artisan: Art and Experience in the Scientific Revolution' by Pamela H. Smith," *CAA.Reviews*, 2004, https://doi.org/10.3202/caa.reviews.2004.102
17. See Sonja Brentjes and Robert G. Morrison, "The Sciences in Islamic Societies (750–1800)," in *Islamic Cultures and Societies to the End of the Eighteenth Century*, ed. Robert Irwin, vol. 4, The New Cambridge History of Islam (Cambridge: Cambridge University Press), 564–639, accessed August 26, 2017, /core/books/new-cambridge-history-of-islam/E32DFCAE452A7FB7247318D16723F1E6
18. Li Guo, *The Performing Arts in Medieval Islam: Shadow Play and Popular Poetry in Ibn Dāniyāl's Mamluk Cairo* (Leiden: Brill, 2012); J.M. Landau, s.v. "Ibn Daniyal," *Encyclopaedia of Islam*, 2nd ed. (Leiden, Brill, 2012).
19. R. Hillenbrand, '"The Ornament of the World': Medieval Córdoba as a Cultural Centre," in Jayyusi, *Legacy of Muslim Spain*, 112–35; Glaire Anderson, *The Islamic Villa in Early Medieval Iberia: Architecture and Court Culture in Umayyad Córdoba* (Burlington, Vt.: Ashgate, 2013).
20. Aragón Huerta, "Ibn Firnās, 'Abbas," *Biblioteca de al-Andalus.*
21. Muzaffar Iqbal, "Ahmad Dallal. *Islam, Science, and the Challenge of History*," *Islam & Science* 10, no. 2 (2012): 139.
22. On this issue, see Iqbal's comments in "Ahmad Dallal. *Islam, Science, and the Challenge of History*," 139. The notion that there was such a divide is represented, he notes, in George Makdisi, *The Rise of Colleges: Institutions of Learning in Islam and the West* (Edinburgh: University Press, 1981).
23. Emphasis added. Ahmad Dallal, *Islam, Science, and the Challenge of History* (New Haven, Conn.: Yale University Press), 48.
24. See, for example, Ikhwān al-Ṣafā', *Epistles of the Brethren of Purity: Sciences of the Soul and Intellect* (Oxford: Oxford University Press, in association with the Institute of Ismaili Studies, 2015).
25. Sonja Brentjes, *Teaching and Learning the Sciences in Islamicate Societies (800–1700)* (Turnhout, Belgium: Brepols, 2018); Jim al-Khalili, *The House of Wisdom: How Arabic Science Saved Ancient Knowledge and Gave Us the Renaissance*, 1st American ed. (New York: Penguin, 2011); Jim Al-Khalili, *Pathfinders: The Golden Age of Arabic Science* (London: Allen Lane, 2010); Dallal, *Islam, Science, and the Challenge of History.*
26. Thomas Kuhn, *The Structure of Scientific Revolutions* (Chicago: University of Chicago Press, 1962), 1–2.
27. Ibid., 42.

28. Sonja Brentjes and Robert G. Morrison, "The Sciences in Islamic Societies (750–1800)," in *Islamic Cultures and Societies to the End of the Eighteenth Century, The New Cambridge History of Islam. Volume 4: Islamic Cultures and Societies to the End of the Eighteenth Century*, ed. Robert Irwin (Cambridge: Cambridge University Press), 564–639.
29. The question of the social standing of scientists might be considered as a parallel one to the social status of intellectuals who were also "makers." For example, in considering the apparent high social standing that the tenth-century intellectuals Abu l-Wafa' and Abu Ja'far al-Khazin (well known to scholars for their scholarly work in mathematics and astronomy) enjoyed in the Buyid and Samanid courts of Iran and Central Asia, and the possibility that they achieved such status by climbing the ranks of the secretarial class, historian of Islamic science Sonja Brentjes posed the question of whether these two important mathematicians and astronomers were indeed members of the secretarial class and thus part of the social elite, and if so, whether that would change our perspective on the social and cultural meaning of the exact sciences in the tenth century. See Sonja Brentjes, "What Could It Mean to Contextualize the Sciences in Islamic Societies of the Past?," in *Les Sciences dans les Sociétés Islamiques* (Casablanca: Fondation du Roi Abdul-Aziz, 2007), 15–42, reflecting on the argument made in Joel L. Kraemer, *Humanism in the Renaissance of Islam: The Cultural Revival during the Buyid Age*, Studies in Islamic Culture and History Series, vol. 7 (Leiden: Brill, 1986), 10.
30. On competition as a catalyst for the translation movement, see George Saliba, *Islamic Science and the Making of the European Renaissance* (Cambridge, Mass.: MIT Press, 2007), especially 58–72.
31. On early artisans and intellectual circles, see Alain George, *The Rise of Islamic Calligraphy* (London: Saqi, 2010), 105–108. On Abu Zayd, perhaps the best-known potter of medieval Iran, and one who signed a number of his works, see Sheila S. Blair, "A Brief Biography of Abu Zayd," *Muqarnas* 25 (2008): 155–76; on post-Mongol metalworkers, see Julian Raby, "Mosul Metalworkers after the Mongols," in *Court and Craft: A Masterpiece from Northern Iraq*, ed. Rachel Ward, 56–67 (London: Courtauld Gallery, 2014).
32. Flood, Finbarr Barry, and Gulru Necipoglu, "Frameworks of Islamic Art and Architectural History: Concepts, Approaches, and Historiographies," in *A Companion to Islamic Art and Architecture: From the Prophet to the Mongols*, vol. 1 (Bognor Regis, U.K.: John Wiley & Sons, 2017), 20.
33. Margaret S. Graves, *Arts of Allusion: Object, Ornament, and Architecture in Medieval Islam* (New York: Oxford University Press, 2018), 27.
34. Ibid.
35. Julio Samsó, *On Both Sides of the Strait of Gibraltar: Studies in the History of Medieval Astronomy in the Iberian Peninsula and the Maghrib*, Handbook of Oriental Studies. Section 1, Near and Middle East (2014), vol. 144 (Leiden; Boston: Brill, 2020); Julio Samsó, *Astronomy and Astrology in al-Andalus and the Maghrib* (Ashgate, U.K.: 2007); Julio Samsó, "La astronomía en Toledo durante la etapa taifa (1031–1086)," in *Entre el Califato y la Taifa: mil años del Cristo de la Luz. Actas del Congreso Internacional, Toledo, 1999* (Toledo, Spain: Asociación de Amigos del Toledo Islámico, 2000), 125–34; Julio Samsó, "La ciencia en al-ándalus," in *¿Cómo entender al-Andalus? Reflexiones sobre su estudio y enseñanza. Coord. Manuela Marín* (Madrid: Ministerio de Educación y Cultura y Anaya, 1999), 95–107; Julio Samsó, "Originalidad en la ciencia andalusí de la época taifa," in *Los reinos de taifas: un siglo de oro en la cultura hispanomusulmana. Ciclo de conferencias in memoriam de D. Emilio García Gómez* (Madrid: Real Academia de la Historia y Fundación Ramón Areces, 1997), 115–36; Julio Samsó, *Las ciencias de los antiguos en al-Andalus*, Colección al-Andalus, vol. 7 (Madrid: Editorial MAPFRE, 1992); George F. Hourani, "The Early Growth of the Secular Sciences in Andalusia," *Studia Islamica*, no. 32 (January 1, 1970): 143–56, https://doi.org/10.2307/1595215

36. I'm thinking especially of the connections with mathematics and design practices that Gülru Necipoğlu and other scholars have discussed. See Necipoğlu, "Ornamental Geometries: A Persian Compendium at the Intersection of the Visual Arts and Mathematical Sciences," in *The Arts of Ornamental Geometry: A Persian Compendium on Similar and Complementary Interlocking Figures, Fī Tadākhul al-Ashkāl al-Mutashābiha Aw al-Mutāwafiqa (Bibliothèque Nationale de France, Ms. Persan 169, Fols. 180r–199r): A Volume Commemorating Alpay Özdural*, Muqarnas, Supplements, vol. XIII (Leiden; Boston: Brill, 2016), 11–78. I am grateful to Gülru Necipoğlu for sharing this volume with me in advance of its publication.

In thinking about issues of social status I have in mind especially Nasser Rabbat, "Architects and Artists in Mamluk Society: The Perspective of the Sources," in *Mamluk History through Architecture: Monuments, Culture and Politics in Medieval Egypt and Syria* (London: I. B. Tauris, 2010), 33–44, as well as Julio Samsó, "Is a Social History of Andalusī Exact Sciences Possible?," *Early Science and Medicine* 7, no. 3 (2002): 296–99; Sonja Brentjes, "What Could It Mean to Contextualize the Sciences in Islamic Societies of the Past?," in *Les Sciences dans les Sociétés Islamiques* (Casablanca: Fondation du Roi Abdul-Aziz, 2007), 15–42, reflecting on the argument made in Kraemer, *Humanism in the Renaissance of Islam*, 10.

37. I hope my indebtedness to the work of these scholars of Islamic art and science will be clear in the pages that follow. See Michael Yonan, "Toward a Fusion of Art History and Material Culture Studies," *West 86th* 18, no. 2 (2011): 232–48, https://doi.org/10.1086/662520

38. The exhibition was held from October 9, 2020–January 10, 2021. See https://www.hsm.ox.ac.uk/islamicmetalwork

39. On the gendered dimension of the European art/craft notion see Rozsika Parker and Griselda Pollock, *Old Mistresses: Women, Art and Ideology* (London: Pandora, 1995), 50.

40. On the historiographic issues of Islamic art, objects, and art history see Graves, *Arts of Allusion*, 12.

41. Marcus Milwright, *Islamic Arts and Crafts: An Anthology* (Edinburgh: Edinburgh University Press Ltd, 2017), 57; Avinoam Shalem, "What Do We Mean When We Say 'Islamic Art'? A Plea for a Critical Rewriting of the History of the Arts of Islam," *Journal of Art Historiography*, no. 6 (June 1, 2012):1–18.

42. Jules Prown, "Mind in Matter: An Introduction to Material Culture Theory and Method," *Winterthur Portfolio* 17, no. 1 (1982): 1–19, https://doi.org/10.1086/496065. My thanks to Lyneise Williams.

43. James Herbert, "Visual Culture / Visual Studies," in *Critical Terms for Art History*, ed. Robert Nelson and Richard Shiff, 2nd ed. (Chicago: University of Chicago Press, 2003), 452–64.

44. Oleg Grabar, "Islamic Atttitudes towards the Arts," in *The Formation of Islamic Art*, rev. and enl. ed. (New Haven, Conn.: Yale University Press, 1987), 72–98.

45. See Milwright, *Islamic Arts and Crafts*, 9.

46. Therese Martin, "Exceptions and Assumptions: Women in Medieval Art History," in *Reassessing the Roles of Women as "Makers" of Medieval Art and Architecture* (Boston: Brill, 2012), 1–36; Therese Martin, "The Margin to Act: A Framework of Investigation for Women's (and Men's) Medieval Art-Making," *Journal of Medieval History* 42, no. 1 (January 2016): 1–25, https://doi.org/10.1080/03044181.2015.1107751. Azucena Hernández has likewise adopted Martin's framework: Azucena Hernández Pérez, *Astrolabios en al-Andalus y los Reinos Medievales Hispanos* (Madrid: La Ergástula, 2018).

47. Glaire Anderson, *The Islamic Villa in Early Medieval Iberia: Architecture and Court Culture in Umayyad Córdoba* (Farnham, U.K.: Ashgate, 2013), 26.

48. This is a topic explored from a different angle by Susana Calvo Capilla in "The Reuse of Classical Antiquity in the Palace of Madinat al-Zahrā' and Its Role in the Construction of Caliphal Legitimacy," *Muqarnas* 31 (2014): 1–33.

49. Two recent explorations of Byzantine and Frankish science and visual culture are Benjamin Anderson, *Cosmos and Community in Early Medieval Art* (New Haven, Conn.: Yale University Press, 2017), and Eric Ramírez-Weaver, *A Saving Science: Capturing the Heavens in Carolingian Manuscripts* (University Park: Pennsylvania State University Press, 2017).
50. Martina Müller-Wiener, "Science as the Handmaiden of Power: Science, Art and Technology in Ayyubid Syria," in *Ayyubid Jerusalem: The Holy City in Context 1187–1250*, ed. Robert Hillenbrand and Sylvia Auld (London: Altajir Trust, 2009), 418–22.

Chapter 1

1. Manuela Marín, "El «halcón Maltes» del Arabismo Español: El Volumen II/1 de al-Muqtabas de Ibn Hayyán," *Al-Qanṭara: Revista de Estudios Árabes* 20, no. 2 (1999): 543–49. See also J. Viguera Molins, "El manuscrito del Muqtabas II-1," *Qurtuba: Revista de Estudios Andalusies* 2 (1997): 327–28.
2. The manuscript is published in facsimile as Ibn Ḥayyān, *Al-Muqtabas II: Anales de los Emires de Córdoba Alhaquém I . . . y Abderramán II . . .* (Madrid: Real Academia de la Historia, 1999).
3. See Joaquín Vallvé Bermejo's introduction in *Al-Muqtabas II*, ix–xii; Virgilio Martínez Enamorado, "Ibn Hayyan, el Abanderado de la Historia de al Ándalus," *Jábega* 97 (2008): 30–34.
4. See Martínez Enamorado, "Ibn Hayyan," 30–34, and Eduardo Manzano Moreno, "¿El fin de la historia? La historiografía árabe en torno al año 1000," in *Hommes et sociétés dans l'Europe de l'An Mil*, ed. Pierre Bonnassie and Pierre Toubert (Toulouse, France: Presses Universitaires du Mirail, 2004), 407–19.
5. The critical Spanish edition and translation of this manuscript is Ibn Ḥayyān, *Crónica de los Emires Alḥakam I y ʿAbdarraḥmān II entre los Años 796 y 847 (Al-Muqtabas II-1)*, ed. Federico Corriente, Serie Estudios Islámicos (Zaragoza, Spain: Instituto de Estudios Islámicos y del Oriente Próximo, 2001). The critical Arabic edition of this manuscript, which clarifies issues in the Madrid manuscript, is Ibn Ḥayyān, *Al-Sifr al-Thānī min Kitāb al-Muqtabas*, ed. Maḥmūd ʿAlī Makkī, Al-Ṭabʿah 1 (al-Riyāḍ: Markaz al-Malik Fayṣal lil-Buḥūth wa-al-Dirāsāt al-Islāmīyah, 2003). See the translations that preface the Introduction of the present work, "'Abbas Ibn Firnas and His Career: Selected Passages from Ibn Ḥayyān."
6. The manuscript is copied on parchment, and its pages measure 245 × 195 mm. On medieval manuscripts from the Islamic West, see Umberto Bongianino, "Quelques Remarques sur l'origine des Écritures Coraniques Arrondies en al-Andalus (Ve/XIe–VIe/XIIe Siècles)," *Al-Qanṭara* 38, no. 2 (2017): 153–87; Umberto Bongianino, "The Origin and Development of Maghribī Round Scripts: Arabic Palaeography in the Islamic West (4th/10th–6th/12th Centuries)" (PhD diss., University of Oxford, 2017). By way of comparison with tenth-century examples, see also Mustapha Jaouhari, "Les Manuscrits Datés en Écriture Maghrébine: Enquete en Cours," *Fondation Max Van Berchem Bulletin* 30 (2016): 3–5.
7. I am grateful to Umberto Bongianino for his observations on the script and for drawing my attention to possible comparanda preserved in Moroccan and Italian collections. In his judgment the script appears comparable to Nasrid scripts, but further examination of features such as the paper and its marks or watermarks, and the positions of chain and laid lines, would be necessary to determine whether the script is indeed from the Nasrid era or was a later creation that uses an archaizing style (personal communication, 2019).
8. C.F. Seybold, *Encyclopaedia of Islam*, 2nd ed. (*EI2*), s.v. al-Dabbi, Abu Dja'far; al-Dabbi, *Bug͟hyat al-multamis fī Taʾrīk͟h Ridjāl Ahl al-Andalus*, no. 1247.

9. Aḥmad ibn Muḥammad Maqqarī and Reinhart Pieter Anne Dozy, *Analectes sur l'histoire et la littérature des Arabes d'Espagne* (Amsterdam: Oriental Press, 1967); *Nafḥ al-Ṭīb Min Ghuṣn al-Andalus al-Raṭīb*, ed. Iḥsān Abbās (Bayrūt: Dār Ṣādir, 1968).
10. Translated by Stuart Sears from al-Maqqarī, *Analectes*, II: 254–55.
11. R. Sellheim, "al-K̲h̲alīl b. Aḥmad," in *Encyclopaedia of Islam*, 2nd ed., ed. P. Bearman, Th. Bianquis, C.E. Bosworth, E. van Donzel, and W.P. Heinrichs. Consulted online on October 11, 2021, http://dx.doi.org.ezproxy.is.ed.ac.uk/10.1163/1573-3912_islam_SIM_4161. First published online: 2012. First print edition: ISBN: 9789004161214, 1960–2007.
12. C. Brockelmann, "Ibn ʿAbd Rabbih," *Encyclopaedia of Islam*, 2nd ed.; Aḥmad ibn Muḥammad Ibn ʿAbd Rabbih, *The Unique Necklace / Al-ʿIqd Al-Farīd*, trans. Issa J. Boullata, 1st ed. (Reading, U.K.: Garnet, 2006).
13. Owen Jones's study on the Alhambra (1835–46) and his design for the Alhambra court in the Crystal Palace Exhibition of 1854 illustrate this fascination in nineteenth-century England, while Washington Irving's *Tales of the Alhambra* (1832) illustrate it in the American context. See Owen Jones, *The Alhambra* (London: Saqi Books, 1997); Kathryn Ferry, "Owen Jones and the Alhambra Court at the Crystal Palace," in *Revisiting Al-Andalus: Perspectives on the Material Culture of Islamic Iberia and Beyond*, ed. G.D. Anderson and M. Rosser-Owen, Medieval and Early Modern Iberian World 34 (Leiden: Brill, 2007), 227–45; Washington Irving, *The Alhambra* (New York: G.P. Putnam, 1851). For the problematic issues with the terms "Moors" and "Moorish," see Ross Brann, "The Moors?," *Medieval Encounters: Jewish, Christian and Muslim Culture in Confluence and Dialogue* 15 (2009): 307–18; Glaire D. Anderson and Mariam Rosser-Owen, "Introduction," *Revisiting al-Andalus: Perspectives on the Material Culture of Islamic Iberia and Beyond* (Leiden: Brill, 2007), 34.
14. Aḥmad ibn Muḥammad Maqqarī and Pascual de Gayangos, *The History of the Mohammedan Dynasties in Spain: Extracted from the Nafhu-t-Tíb Min Ghosni-l-Andalusi-r-Rattíb Wa Táríkh Lisánu-d-Dín Ibni-l-Khattíb* (London: Printed for the Oriental Translation Fund of Great Britain and Ireland, 1840–43).
15. On Gayangos see the studies in Cristina Alvarez Millán and Claudia Heide, *Pascual de Gayangos: A Nineteenth-Century Spanish Arabist* (Edinburgh: Edinburgh University Press, 2008).
16. Gayangos, *The History of the Mohammedan Dynasties in Spain*, vol. I, 148–49.
17. On the meaning of the term in the early period, see Hikmet Yaman, *Prophetic Niche in the Virtuous City: The Concept of Ḥikmah in Early Islamic Thought*, Islamic Philosophy, Theology, and Science, vol. 81 (Leiden: Brill, 2011). My thanks to Rodrigo Adem for his thoughts on the term and for pointing me to this source.
18. Samsó, *Las ciencias de los antiguos*.
19. Gayangos, *The History of the Mohammedan Dynasties*, vol. I, 148–49.
20. There are many pages devoted to him in II-2 as well. Eight of the pages appear in *al-Muqtabis* 11-1, and four appear in the *al-Sifr al-Thani*. My thanks to Julio Samsó.
21. On Ziryāb, see Dwight F. Reynolds, "Ziryāb in the Aghlabid Court," in *The Aghlabids and Their Neighbours: Art and Material Culture in Ninth-Century North Africa*, ed. Glaire D. Anderson, Corisande Fenwick, and Mariam Rosser-Owen (Leiden: Brill, 2017); Dwight F. Reynolds, "Al-Maqqarī's Ziryāb: The Making of a Myth," *Middle Eastern Literatures* 11, no. 2 (2008): 155–68; and Carl Davila, "Fixing a Misbegotten Biography: Ziryāb in the Mediterranean World," *Al-Masaq: Islam and the Medieval Mediterranean* 21, no. 2 (2009): 121–36. I would like to thank Dwight Reynolds for generously sharing material on Ziryāb, in advance of its publication, from *The Musical Heritage of al-Andalus* (Oxford: Routledge, 2021).
22. J. Sadan, "Nadīm," *Encyclopaedia of Islam*, 2nd ed. On boon companions in the eleventh-century Andalusi context, see Cynthia Robinson, *In Praise of Song: The Making of Courtly Culture in al-Andalus and Provence, 1005–1134 A.D.* (Leiden: Brill, 2002), 75; Anwar G.

Chejne, "The Boon-Companion in Early ʿAbbāsid Times," *Journal of the American Oriental Society* 85 (1965): 327–35; Nadia Maria el Cheikh, "To Be a Prince in the Fourth/Tenth-Century Abbasid Court," in *Royal Courts in Dynastic States and Empires: A Global Perspective*, ed. Jeroen Duindam, Tülay Artan, and Metin Kunt (Leiden: Brill, 2011), 199–216, 209.

23. Jaakko Hämeen-Anttila, "Multilayered Authorship in Arabic Anecdotal Literature," in *Concepts of Authorship in Pre-Modern Arabic Texts*, ed. L. Behzadi and J. Hämeen-Anttila, Bamberger Orientstudien, Band 7 (Bamberg, Germany: University of Bamberg Press, 2016), 184. Also see Stefan Leder, "The Use of Composite Form in the Making of the Islamic Historical Tradition,' in *On Fiction and adab in Medieval Literature*, ed. Philip F. Kennedy (Wiesbaden, Germany: Harrassowitz, 2005), 125–48; Stefan Leder, *Story-Telling in the Framework of Non-Fictional Arabic Literature* (Wiesbaden, Germany: Harrassowitz, 1998); Chase F. Robinson, *Islamic Historiography* (Cambridge: Cambridge University Press, 2003).
24. See Jaakko Hämeen-Anttila, "Multilayered Authorship in Arabic Anecdotal Literature."
25. Manzano Moreno, "¿El fin de la historia? La historiografía árabe en torno al año 1000," 407–19; Cyrille Aillet, "La 'Fitna,' Pierre de Touche du Califat de Cordoue (IIIe/IXe–IVe/Xesiècle)," *Médiévales* 60, no. 60 (2011): 67–83; Brigitte Foulon, "L'impact de la fitna chez les lettrés andalous," *Médiévales* 60, no. 60 (2011): 45–66; Emmanuelle Tixier du Mesnil, "La 'Fitna' Andalouse du Xie Siècle," *Médiévales*, no. 60 (2011): 17–28.
26. Passage II.
27. Sonja Brentjes, *Teaching and Learning the Sciences in Islamicate Societies (800–1700)* (Turnhout, Belgium: Brepols, 2018).
28. Michael Cooperson, *Al-Ma'mun* (Oxford: Oneworld, 2005), 22–36.
29. Elías Terés, "'Abbas Ibn Firnās." In *The Formation of al-Andalus*, ed. Manuela Marin, vol. 2, 235–44 (Brookfield, Vt.: Ashgate), 1998.
30. The sources and bibliography are surveyed by M. Aragón Huerta, "Ibn Firnās, 'Abbas," ed. Jorge Lirola Delgado and José Miguel Puerta Vílchez, *Biblioteca de al-Andalus* (Almería, Spain: Fundación Ibn Tufayl de Estudios Árabes, 2004), 168–72. On these authors, see E.K. Rowson, "al-T̲h̲aʿālibī," *Encyclopaedia of Islam*, 2nd ed., C.F. Seybold, "al-Ḍabbī, Abū D̲j̲aʿfar," *Encyclopaedia of Islam*, 2nd ed.; J. Bosch-Vilá, "Ibn ʿId̲h̲ārī," *Encyclopaedia of Islam*, 2nd ed. Many of these fragments of his poetry are translated in Elías Terés, "'Abbas Ibn Firnās," in Marin, *Formation of al-Andalus*, 242–43.
31. Al-Zubaydī, *Ṭabaḳāt*, 291–92, trans. in Elías Terés, "'Abbas Ibn Firnās," in Marin, *Formation of al-Andalus*, 242–43.
32. Terés, "'Abbas Ibn Firnās," in Marin, *Formation of al-Andalus*, 242–43.
33. Humaydi, Jadhwa, no. 731; Dabbi, Bughya, no. 1247, trans. in Terés, "'Abbas Ibn Firnās."
34. Tha'alibi, Yatima, 2, p. 16 (though Terés notes his likely misreading of the polymath's name as 'Abbas Ibn Qirmas). Trans. in Terés, "'Abbas Ibn Firnās."
35. A long *qasida* and some other of 'Abbas Ibn Firnās' verses inspired by Muhammad's military actions are translated in Terés, "'Abbas Ibn Firnās."
36. Translation, Stuart Sears; Ibn Ḥayyān, *Al-Sifr al-Thānī Min Kitāb Al-Muqtabas*. Al-Ṭabʿah 1. (al-Riyāḍ: Markaz al-Malik Fayṣal lil-Buḥūth wa-al-Dirāsāt al-Islāmīyah, 2003), 348.
37. Passage IV, trans. Stuart Sears; Ibn Ḥayyān, *Al-Sifr al-Thānī Min Kitāb al-Muqtabas*, ed. Maḥmūd ʿAlī Makki. Al-Ṭabʿah 1 (al-Riyāḍ: Markaz al-Malik Fayṣal lil-Buḥūth wa-al-Dirāsāt al-Islāmīyah, 2003), 347–50.
38. I am grateful to Jaakko Hämeen-Anttila for clarifying the lampooning nature of the anecdote for me, and for alerting me to the literary contexts and the Umayyad precedent in the exchanges between al-Farazdaḳ and D̲j̲arīr.
39. G.J.H. Van Gelder, "Naḳāʾiḍ," in *Encyclopaedia of Islam*, 2nd ed..

40. R. Blachère, "al-Farazdaḳ," *Encyclopaedia of Islam*, 2nd ed.; A. Schaade and H. Gätje, "Djarīr," *Encyclopaedia of Islam*, 2nd ed.. For a ninth-century parallel, see the obscene lampoons by the famous Abbasid poet Abu Nuwas: Geert Jan Van Gelder, "Waspish Verses: Abu Nuwas's Lampoons on Zunbūr ibn Abī Ḥammād," *Annali di Ca' Foscari: Rivista della Facoltà di lingue e letterature straniere dell'Università di Venezia* 35, no. 3 (January 1, 1996): 447.
41. On this textual conversation as a caliphal "idiom," see Gabriel Martinez-Gros, *L'idéologie Omeyyade: La Construction de la Légitimité du Califat de Cordoue (Xe–XIe Siècles)*, Bibliothèque de la Casa de Velázquez, vol. 8 (Madrid: Casa de Velázquez, 1992), and Janina M. Safran, *The Second Umayyad Caliphate: The Articulation of Caliphal Legitimacy in al-Andalus*, Harvard Middle Eastern Monographs, vol. 33 (Cambridge, Mass: Harvard University Press, 2000).
42. Passage II; trans. Stuart Sears. Ibn Ḥayyān, *Al-Sifr al-Thānī Min Kitāb al-Muqtabas*, 347–50.
43. On astrology in al-Andalus, see J. Samsó, "The Early Development of Astrology in al-Andalus," *Journal of the History of Arab Science* 3 (1979): 228–43; Julio Samsó, *Astronomy and Astrology in al-Andalus and the Maghrib* (Aldershot, U.K.: Ashgate, 2007).
44. Elías Terés, "Ibn al-Šamir, Poeta-Astrólogo en la Corte de ʿAbd al-Raḥmān II," *Al-Andalus* 24 (1959): 449–63.
45. Sonja Brentjes, "What Could It Mean to Contextualize the Sciences in Islamic Societies of the Past?," in *Les Sciences dans les Sociétés Islamiques* (Casablanca: Fondation du Roi Abdul-Aziz, 2007), 29.
46. Brentjes, *Teaching and Learning the Sciencies in Islamicate Societies*; Sonja Brentjes, "On the Location of the Ancient or 'Rational' Sciences in Muslim Educational Landscapes (AH 500–1100)," *Bulletin of the Royal Institute for Inter-Faith Studies* 4, no. i (2002): 47–71.
47. On astrology/astrologers and astronomy in the Islamic past more broadly, see George Saliba, "The Role of the Astrologer in Medieval Islamic Society," in *Magic and Divination in Early Islam*, ed. Emilie Savage-Smith (Burlington, Vt.: Ashgate/Variorum, 2004), 341–70; David King, "Islamic Astronomy," in *Astronomy before the Telescope* (New York: St. Martin's Press, 1997), 143–74.
48. Passage II. Ibn Ḥayyān, *Crónica de los Emires Alḥakam I Y ʿAbdarraḥmān II entre los Años 796 y 847 (Almuqtabis II-1)*, ed. Federico Corriente, Serie Estudios Islámicos (Zaragoza, Spain: Instituto de Estudios Islámicos y del Oriente Próximo, 2001), 140–41.
49. Peter Adamson, *Al-Kindī* (Oxford: Oxford University Press, 2007); "Philosophy," in *The Oxford Dictionary of Islam*, ed. John L.Esposito (New York: Oxford University Press, 2003).
50. See Ahmad S. Dallal, "Beginnings," in *Islam, Science, and the Challenge of History*, Terry Lectures (New Haven, Conn.: Yale University Press, 2010), 1–53; Dimitri Gutas, *Greek Thought, Arabic Culture: The Graeco-Arabic Translation Movement in Baghdad and Early ʿAbbāsid Society (2nd–4th/8th–10th Centuries)* (New York: Routledge, 1998), 133–36, and Ibrahim Kalin, "Review of Dimitri Gutas, *Greek Thought, Arabic Culture: The Graeco-Arabic Translation Movement in Baghdad and Early Ábbasid Society (Second–Fourth/Eighth–Tenth Centuries)*," *Isis* 94, no. 1 (March 2003), 138–140.
51. René Descartes, *Principles of Philosophy*, trans. Reese P. Miller and Valentine Rodger Miller (Dordrecht, the Netherlands: Reidel, dist. by Kluwer Boston, 1983).
52. A. Dallal, *Islam, Science, and the Challenge of History*, Terry Lectures (New Haven, Conn.: Yale University Press, 2010).
53. Robert Hoyland, trans., *Medieval Islamic Swords and Swordmaking: Kindī's Treatise "On Swords and Their Kinds"* (Warminster, U.K.: Gibb Memorial Trust, 2006).
54. Syed Nomanul Haq, *Names, Natures and Things: The Alchemist Jābir Ibn Hayyān and His Kitāb Al-aḥār (Book of Stones)*, Boston Studies in the Philosophy of Science, vol. 158 (London: Kluwer, 1994).

55. Al-Jazarī, *The Book of Knowledge of Ingenious Mechanical Devices*, trans. Donald R. Hill (Boston: Reidel, 1974).
56. Donald Hill, "The Banū Musā and Their Book of Ingenious Devices," in *Studies in Medieval Islamic Technology: From Philo to al-Jazarī, from Alexandria to Diyār Bakr*, ed. David A. King, vol. XII (Brookfield, Vt.: Ashgate, 1998), 39–76.
57. D.R.Hill, "al-Djazarī," in *Encyclopaedia of Islam*, 2nd ed.; Donald Routledge Hill, *The Book of Ingenious Devices (Kitāb al-Ḥiyal)* (Boston: D. Reidel Publishing Company, 1978).
58. Topkapı Saray MSS. H 414 and A 3350. On these and the other extant manuscripts, see Hill, *Book of Ingenious Devices (Kitāb al-Ḥiyal)*; A.K. Coomaraswamy, *The Treatise of al-Jazarī on Automata* (Boston 1924), discusses paintings from two of the manuscripts. The Metropolitan's watercolor and gold painting of the Elephant Clock (accession number: 57.51.23) comes from a Mamluk painted manuscript, dated AH 715/1315.
59. See James Allan, "Introduction," *Medieval Islamic Swords and Swordmaking: Kindī's Treatise "On Swords and Their Kinds"* (Warminster, U.K.: Gibb Memorial Trust, 2006), v–vii.
60. Marcus Milwright, "The Lives of Artisans and Artists," In *Islamic Arts and Crafts* (Edinburgh: Edinburgh University Press Books, 2017), 57–64.
61. My thanks to Jaako Hameen-Antilla for alerting me to this literary context as well. See Ch. Pellat, "al-Djidd wa 'l-Hazl," *Encyclopaedia of Islam*, 2nd ed.
62. See Passage I. Ibn Ḥayyān, *Crónica de los Emires Alḥakam I Y 'Abdarraḥmān II entre los Años 796 y 847 (Almuqtabis II-1)*, ed. Federico Corriente. Serie Estudios Islámicos (Zaragoza, Spain: Instituto de Estudios Islámicos y del Oriente Próximo, 2001), 137–42; Antonio Fernández Puertas, *Clepsidras y Relojes Musulmanes = Muslim Water Clocks and Mechanical Time Pieces* (Granada, Spain: Fundación el Legado Andalusí, 2010), 119.
63. See the translation of passage I of the Arabic texts that follows the Introduction. The reference to Ibn Firnās's inventing some kind of glass is often mentioned. The best-known references are in al-Maqqari, *Analectes*, vol. II, 254–55, and Gayangos, *History of the Mohammedan Dynasties in Spain*, vol. I, 148–49, but the best reference is Ibn Ḥayyān's passage, in *Crónica de los Emires Alḥakam I Y 'Abdarraḥmān II*, 137–42. provided in a new translation by Stuart Sears in the present work.
64. See David J. Govantes-Edwards and Chloë Duckworth, "Recipes and Experimentation? The Transmission of Glassmaking Techniques in Medieval Iberia—Brill," *Journal of Medieval Iberian Studies* I, no. ii (2016): 176–95; Ḥasan Aḥmad and Donald Routledge Hill, *Islamic Technology: An Illustrated History* (New York: Cambridge University Press, 1986), 151–53.
65. I would like to thank the anonymous reader for these suggestions and the references. See J. Henderson, J. Evans, and Y. Barkoudah, "The Roots of Provenance: Glass, Plants and Isotopes in the Islamic Middle East," *Antiquity* 83, no. 320 (June 2009): 414–29; Julian Henderson, Keith Challis, Sarah O'Hara, Sean McLouglin, Adam Gardner, and Gary Priestnall, "Experiment and Innovation: Early Islamic Industry at al-Raqqa, Syria," *Antiquity* 79, no. 303 (March 2005): 130–45. Nadine Schibille is leading a project, *Mapping the First Millennium Glass Economy*, which "explores the production, trade and consumption of glass as a major economic activity in the medieval Mediterranean" and which may illuminate the context for Ibn Firnās's purported innovations in Andalusi glass production. See https://cordis.europa.eu/project/id/647315
66. Passage Va.
67. Passage VIII. Ibn Ḥayyān, *Crónica de los Emires Alḥakam I y 'Abdarraḥmān II entre los Años 796 y 847 (Almuqtabis II-1)*, ed. Federico Corriente, Serie Estudios Islámicos (Zaragoza, Spain: Instituto de Estudios Islámicos y del Oriente Próximo, 2001), 141–42.
68. According to Corriente and Makki. See Ibn Ḥayyān, *Crónica de los Emires Alḥakam I y 'Abdarraḥmān II entre los Años 796 y 847 (Almuqtabis II-1)*, ed. Maḥmūd 'Alī Makkī, trans.

F. Corriente, Serie Estudios Islámicos (Zaragoza, Spain: Instituto de Estudios Islámicos y del Oriente Próximo, 2001), 141n289.

69. He is identified by Corriente and Makki. See Ibn Ḥayyān, *Crónica de los Emires Alḥakam I y ʿAbdarraḥmān II entre los Años 796 y 847 (Almuqtabis II-1)*, ed. Maḥmūd ʿAlī Makkī, trans. F. Corriente, 141n290.
70. See *EI2*, "*Zindīḳ.*"
71. See especially, ch. 5, "Science between Philosophy and Religion: The Case of Astronomy," in George Saliba, *Islamic Science and the Making of the European Renaissance* (Cambridge, Mass.: MIT Press, 2007), 171–92.

Chapter 2

1. A version of this chapter was published as "Mind and Hand: Early Scientific Instruments from al-Andalus and ʿAbbas Ibn Firnas in the Cordoban Umayyad Court," *Muqarnas: An Annual on the Visual Culture of the Islamic World* 37 (2020): 1–26.
2. See "ʿAbbas Ibn Firnas & His Career: Selected Passages from Ibn Ḥayyān," number I. Ibn Ḥayyān, *Crónica de los Emires Alḥakam I yʿAbdarraḥmān II*, 137–42. This is the Spanish translation of Makkī's critical Arabic edition of Ibn Ḥayyān, *Al-Muqtabis II-1*, published as Ibn Ḥayyān, *Al-Sifr al-Thānī Min Kitāb al-Muqtabas.*
3. See "ʿAbbas Ibn Firnas & His Career: Selected Passages from Ibn Ḥayyān, number VII. Ibn Ḥayyān, *Crónica de los Emires Alḥakam I yʿAbdarraḥmān II*, 140–41.
4. S. Schechner Genuth, "Armillary Sphere," in *Instruments of Science: An Historical Encyclopedia*, ed. Robert Bud and Deborah Warner (New York: Routledge, 1998), 28–31. On Andalusi science and instruments, see Samsó, *Las ciencias de los antiguos*. For medieval Islamic instruments, see King, *In Synchrony with the Heavens: Studies in Astronomical Timekeeping and Instrumentation in Medieval Islamic Civilization*. Islamic Philosophy, Theology, and Science, vol. 55 (Leiden: Brill, 2004). An Iberian painted manuscript from thirteenth-century Toledo, the *Libros del Saber de Astronomía* (Book of Astronomical Knowledge) preserved today in the Complutense University, Madrid, provides an important perspective on Iberian scientific instrumentation in the court of Alfonso X (d. 1284), including descriptions and painted diagrams of an armillary sphere and other scientific instruments. See Laura Fernández Fernández, "Astrolabes on Parchment: The Astrolabes Depicted in Alfonso X's Libro del Saber de Astrologia and Their Relationship to Contemporary Instruments," *Medieval Encounters* 23, nos. 1–5 (2017): 287–310. The manuscript has been digitized by the Biblioteca Complutense: http://alfama.sim.ucm.es/dioscorides/consulta_libro.asp?ref = B18550071&idioma = 0
5. *Al-Farghānī on the Astrolabe*, trans. Richard Lorch (Stuttgart: Steiner, 2005), 23.
6. Ibid., 25.
7. Shlomo Pines, "Philosophy, Mathematics and the Concepts of Space in the Middle Ages," in *Studies in Arabic Versions of Greek Texts and in Mediaeval Science*, ed. Shlomo Pines (Leiden: Brill, 1986), 75–90.
8. Graves, *Arts of Allusion*, 139; Yaron Klein, "Imagination and Music: Takhyīl and the Production of Music in al-Fārābī's Kitāb al-Mūsīqī al-Kabīr," in *Takhyīl: The Imaginary in Classical Arabic Poetics*, ed. G.J.H. van Gelder and Marlé Hammond, 179–95 (Cambridge: Gibb Memorial Trust, 2008). On al-Farabi's discussion of "mixed" mathematics, also useful for these issues, see Gülru Necipoğlu, "Ornamental Geometries: A Persian Compendium at the Intersection of the Visual Arts and Mathematical Sciences," in *The Arts of Ornamental Geometry: A Persian Compendium on Similar and Complementary Interlocking Figures, Fī Tadākhul al-Ashkāl al-Mutashābiha Aw al-Mutāwafiqa (Bibliothèque Nationale de France, Ms. Persan*

169, Fols. 180r–199r): A Volume Commemorating Alpay Özdural, Muqarnas, Supplements; Volume XIII (Leiden: Brill, 2016), 20. My thanks to Gülru Necipoğlu for alerting me to the publication.

9. Al-Farabi, "Treatise on Poetry," *Takhyīl: The Imaginary in Classical Arabic Poetics*, 18.
10. Valérie Gonzalez, *Beauty and Islam: Aesthetics in Islamic Art and Architecture* (London: I.B. Tauris, 2001).
11. Ibn Ḥayyān, *Crónica de los Emires Alḥakam I y'Abdarraḥmān II*, 137–42.
12. According to Stuart Sears, "predict the future from the stars, astrology."
13. Ibn Ḥayyān, *Al-Sifr al-Thānī Min Kitāb al-Muqtabas*, ed. Makkī, Al-Ṭab'ah 1. (al-Riyāḍ: Markaz al-Malik Fayṣal lil-Buḥūth wa-al-Dirāsāt al-Islāmīyah, 2003), 347–50.
14. Ibn Ḥayyān, *Crónica de los Emires Alḥakam I y'Abdarraḥmān II entre los Años 796 y 847 (Almuqtabis II-1)*, 140–41.
15. This refers to Ptolemy's work, the *Handy Tables* (2nd c.), which was later revised by Theon of Alexandria (fl. ca. 360–80); Julio Samsó, personal communication.
16. Trans. Stuart Sears. Ibn Ḥayyān, *Crónica de los Emires Alḥakam I y'Abdarraḥmān II*, 140–41.
17. Donald R. Hill, *Arabic Water-Clocks* (Aleppo: University of Aleppo, 1981). The earliest extant Islamic water clock is the Merinid clock constructed in 1357 over the portal of the Bu Inaniyya madrasa in Fès.
18. Ibid.
19. Aḥmad Ḥasan and Donald Routledge Hill, *Islamic Technology: An Illustrated History* (New York: Cambridge University Press, 1986), 55–7; Donald Hill, "Andalusian Technology," in *Studies in Medieval Islamic Technology: From Philo to Al-Jazarī, from Alexandria to Diyār Bakr*, ed. David A. King, XVIII (Aldershot, U.K.: Ashgate, 1998), 1–16.
20. Selection V. Ibn Ḥayyān, *Crónica de los Emires Alḥakam I y 'Abdarraḥmān II*, 140–41.
21. These may offer an interesting ninth-century Iberian counterpart to Byzantine epigrams that provided artisans, objects, and even spaces such as gardens and suburban estates with a speaking voice. See Kathryn Gutzwiller, "Art's Echo: The Tradition of Hellenistic Ecphrastic Epigram," in *Hellenistic Epigrams*, ed. Annette Harder, R.F. Regtuit, and G.C. Wakker (Leuven, Belgium: Peeters, 2002), 86, cited in Steven D. Smith, "Art, Nature, Power: Garden Epigrams from Nero to Heraclius," in *Greek Epigram from the Hellenistic to the Early Byzantine Era*, ed. Maria Kanellou, Ivana Petrovic, and Christopher Carey (Oxford: Oxford University Press, 2019), 343–44. Also see Ivan Drpić, *Epigram, Art, and Devotion in Later Byzantium* (Cambridge: Cambridge University Press, 2016). My thanks to Kirsty Stewart and Foteini Spingou for drawing my attention to Byzantine epigrams as a possible point of comparison.
22. On the notion of Islamic "speaking" objects, see, e.g., Avinoam Shalem, "If Objects Could Speak," in *The Aura of Alif: The Art of Writing in Islam*, ed. Jürgen Wasim Frembgen (Munich: Prestel, 2010), 127–47; Hana Taragan, "The 'Speaking' Inkwell from Khurasan: Object as 'World' in Iranian Medieval Metalwork," *Muqarnas* 22 (2005): 29–44.
23. On this object's inscription, see Olga Bush, "Poetic Inscriptions and Gift Exchange in the Medieval Islamicate World," *Gesta* 56, no. 2 (2017): 179–97; Olga Bush, "Prosopopeia: Performing the Reciprocal Gaze," *Muqarnas Online* 32, no. 1 (2015): 13–19. For an overview of the pyxis and the Córdoban ivories, see Glaire Anderson and Mariam Rosser-Owen, "Great Ladies and Noble Daughters: Ivories and Women in the Umayyad Court at Córdoba," in *Pearls on a String: Art in the Age of Great Islamic Empires*, ed. Amy Landau (Seattle: University of Washington Press, 2015), 28–51.
24. Oxford History of Science Museum, Inv. Number 48213. This object was presented to the museum by Lewis Evans in 1924 and recorded by Evans as having been "Bought from Heilbronner Paris 1913."
25. Translation by Dr. Afifi al-Akiti, 2010. Inv. 48213. Oxford History of Science Museum. King, *In Synchrony with the Heavens* II, 66–68; on al-Biruni's description of a similar type of device,

see Donald R. Hill, "Al-Bīrūnī's Mechanical Calendar," *Annals of Science* 42, no. 2 (March 1985): 139–63, https://doi.org/10.1080/00033798500200141

26. See Alexander Jones, *A Portable Cosmos: Revealing the Antikythera Mechanism, Scientific Wonder of the Ancient World* (New York: Oxford University Press, 2017). On new analysis of the inscriptions on the device see Ashkan Pakzad, Francesco Iacoviello, Andrew Ramsey, Robert Speller, Jennifer Griffiths, Tony Freeth, and Adam Gibson, "Improved X-Ray Computed Tomography Reconstruction of the Largest Fragment of the Antikythera Mechanism, an Ancient Greek Astronomical Calculator," *PLOS ONE* 13, no. 11 (November 9, 2018): e0207430, https://doi.org/10.1371/journal.pone.0207430. My thanks to Melissa Terras for alerting me to this work. I would also like to thank Marcus Milwright for first bringing the Mechanism to my attention.
27. British Museum Inv. No. ME OA 1888.5-26.1. Francesca Leoni, *Power and Protection: Islamic Art and the Supernatural* (Oxford: Ashmolean Museum, 2016); Emilie Savage-Smith and Marion B. Smith, "Islamic Geomancy and a Thirteenth-Century Divinatory Device: Another Look," in *Magic and Divination in Early Islam*, ed. Emilie Savage-Smith (Ashgate, U.K.: 2004), 211–76; Emilie Savage-Smith and Marion Bush Smith, *Islamic Geomancy and a Thirteenth-Century Divinatory Device* (Malibu, Calif.: Undena Publications, 1980). On geomancy and divination, see Pierre Lory, "Divination & Religion in Islamic Medieval Culture," in *Power and Protection: Islamic Art and the Supernatural*, 13–32; Emilie Savage-Smith, "Magic and Divination in Early Islam," in Savage-Smith, *Magic and Divination*, xiii–li; Emilie Savage-Smith, "Divination," in *Science, Tools & Magic. Part One. Body and Spirit, Mapping the Universe*, ed. Francis Maddison and Emilie Savage-Smith (Oxford: Nour Foundation, in association with Azimuth Editions and Oxford University Press, 1997),148–59.
28. The same maker signed a brass incense burner, inlaid with copper, which is preserved in Doha and provides further evidence of instrument makers' abilities to produce other types of fine objects. All translations from Savage-Smith and Smith, "Islamic Geomancy and a Thirteenth-Century Divinatory Device: Another Look," 211–76.
29. On medieval Iberian astrolabes, see Salvador García Franco, *Catálogo Crítico de Astrolabios Existentes en España* (Madrid: Instituto Histórico de Marina, 1945); and especially Azucena Hernández Pérez, *Catálogo razonado de los astrolabios de la España medieval* (Madrid: La Ergástula, 2018), which updates the previous literature on the instruments in question, providing a complete catalog and study of the instruments; also see "Astrolabios Andalusíes e Hispanos: De la Precisión a la Suntuosidad/Andalusi and Hispanic Astrolabes: From Precision to Sumptuousness," *Anales de Historia del Arte* 24 (2014): 289–305; Azucena Hernández Pérez, "El dragón en el astrolabio," *Revista Digital de Iconografía Medieval* 7, no. 13 (2015): 19–31; Azucena Hernández Pérez, "Astrolabes for the King: The Astrolabe of Petrus Raimundi of Barcelona," *Medieval Encounters* 23 (2017): 421–43.
30. Azucena Hernández Pérez, "Arte y ciencia en al-Andalus: el astrolabio nazarí de Alcalá la Real," *Boletín del Instituto de Estudios Giennenses* 215 (2017): 259–84; see the map of their geographic distribution on p. 260. I will not discuss the medieval drawing of the astrolabe preserved in Paris BN MS lat 7412, which Kunitschz ascribed to al-Andalus circa 1000 and which Hernández includes as the earliest in the list of Andalusi Umayyad astrolabes, as it does not bear an inscription identifying its maker, date, or place of facture. See Hernández, *Catálogo razonado*; Paul Kunitzsch, Menso Folkerts, and Richard Lorch, *Sic itur ad astra: Studien zur Geschichte der Mathematik und Naturwissenschaften: Festschrift für den Arabisten Paul Kunitzsch zum 70. Geburtstag* (Wiesbaden, Germany: Harrassowitz, 2000), 185. On the *taifa* kingdoms see Hugh Kennedy, *Muslim Spain and Portugal: A Political History of al-Andalus* (London: Longman, 1996), 146–69.
31. See previous note.

32. Besides the publications in the previous notes, see Graves, "The Intellect of the Hand," in *Arts of Allusion*; the essays in the special issue of *Medieval Encounters* 23, no. 1–5 (2017), including Silke Ackermann, "*Introduction Hic Sunt Dracones*—Astrolabe Research Revisited," *Medieval Encounters* 23, nos. 1–5 (2017): 3–7. See also R.T. Gunther and William H. Morley, *The Astrolabes of the World: Based upon the Series of Instruments in the Lewis Evans Collection in the Old Ashmolean Museum at Oxford: With Notes on Astrolables in the Collections of the British Museum, Science Museum, Sir J. Findlay, Mr. S. V. Hoffman, the Mensing Collection, and in Other Public and Private Collections* (London: Holland Press, 1976).
33. Graves, "Intellect of the Hand," in *Arts of Allusion*; L.A. Mayer, *Islamic Astrolabists and Their Works* (Geneva: A. Kundig, 1956); see also L.A. Mayer, "Islamic Astrolabists: Some New Material," in *Aus der Welt der islamischen Kunst: Festschrift für Ernst Kühnel zum 75. Geburtstag am 26.10.1957*, ed. Richard Ettinghausen (Berlin: Mann, 1959), 293–96.
34. For example, a thirteenth-century Mamluk quadrant made of wood in the Chester Beatty Library, Dublin. See King, *In Synchrony with the Heavens*, 2: 18.
35. Savage-Smith, "Most Authoritative Copy," 128.
36. Two Andalusi examples: the astrolabe preserved in Edinburgh, discussed in this chapter, and the astrolabe preserved in the collections of the Los Angeles County Art Museum (LACMA), made in Seville by Muhammad ibn ʿAbd al-ʿAziz al Khamaʾiri in 1226–1227/624. I would like to thank Linda Komaroff for bringing the LACMA instrument to my attention. It is not currently on view, but an image of it is available at https://collections.lacma.org/node/205855. See Linda Komaroff, John W. Hirx, Anke Scharrahs, Sandra Williams, Manal Alghannam, and Keelan Overton. *Beauty and Identity: Islamic Art from the Los Angeles County Museum of Art*. Los Angeles: Los Angeles County Museum Art, 2016.
37. Kunitzsch, Folkerts, and Lorch, *Sic itur ad astra*, 185.
38. MAN Madrid, Inv. No. 50762. On the maker and bibliography of the instrument, see Hernández Pérez, *Astrolabios en al-Andalus*, 70, 98–99, A6; Hernández Pérez, *Catálogo razonado*, 71–80; Mercé Viladrich, *El legado científico andalusí*, 64.
39. Hernández Pérez, *Astrolabios en al-Andalus*, 70; illustrated on p. 99.
40. Hernández Pérez, *Astrolabios en al-Andalus*, 183–85. On cusped arches in the ʿAmirid context, see Mariam Rosser-Owen, "Poems in Stone: The Iconography of ʿĀmirid Poetry, and Its 'Petrification' on ʿĀmirid Marbles," in *Revisiting al-Andalus: Perspectives on the Material Culture of Islamic Iberia and Beyond*, ed. Glaire D. Anderson and Mariam Rosser-Owen (Leiden: Brill, 2007), 83–98. Also see Mariam Rosser-Owen, *Articulating the Ḥijāba: Cultural Patronage and Political Legitimacy in al-Andalus: The ʿĀmirid Regency c. 970–1010 AD*, vol. 156, Handbook of Oriental Studies (Leiden: Brill, 2021).
41. On this monument, see Gonzalo M. Borrás Gualis and Bernabé Cabañero Subiza, eds., *La Aljafería y el Arte del Islam Occidental en el siglo XI. Actas del Seminario Internacional celebrado en Zaragoza los días 1, 2 y 3 de diciembre de 2004* (Zaragoza, Spain: Institución "Fernando el Católico," 2012); Bernabé Cabañero Subiza, *El Salón Dorado de la Aljafería: ensayo de reconstitución formal e interpretación simbólica*, Conocer Alandalús 1 (Zaragoza, Spain: Instituto de Estudios Islámicos y del Oriente Próximo, 2004); Cynthia Robinson, *In Praise of Song: The Making of Courtly Culture in al-Andalus and Provence, 1005–1134 A.D.* (Leiden: Brill, 2002); Cynthia Robinson, "The Aljafería in Saragossa and Taifa Spaces," in *The Literature of Al-Andalus*, ed. María Rosa Menocal, Raymond P. Scheindlin, and Michael Sells (Cambridge: Cambridge University Press, 2000), 233–34; Dorothea Duda, Gisela Kircher, and Christian Ewert, *Islamische Funde in Balaguer und die Aljafería in Zaragoza*, Madrider Forschungen 7 (Berlin: De Gruyter, 1971).
42. On miniaturization of architecture on objects, see Graves, *Arts of Allusion*, 13–22.
43. My thanks to Renata Holod for suggesting the idea; personal communication.

44. On the decorative motifs of Iberian astrolabes and their relation to architectural forms, see Hernández Pérez, *Astrolabios en al-Andalus*, 183–86. On the mathematical turn, see Felix Arnold, "Mathematics and the Islamic Architecture of Córdoba," *Arts* 7, no. 3 (2018): 35.
45. Oxford MHS Inv. 55331. On the maker and overview of the bibliography, see Hernández Pérez, *Astrolabios en al-Andalus*, 70, illustrated on p. 98, A7; see also ibid., 98, A8: a third astrolabe by the same maker, whose signature inscription indicates it was made in Valencia in 463 AH (1071 CE), is preserved in the Astronomical Observatory, Rome (inv. no. 157/688).
46. I would like to thank Margaret Wilson for kind assistance with the photographs. On the astrolabe, see Hernández Pérez, *Astrolabios en al-Andalus*, 68–70; 96–97, A3; Hernández Pérez, *Catálogo razonado de los astrolabios de la España medieval*, 43–50; Mercé Viladrich, *El legado científico andalusí*, 63–64; Angus MacDonald, A.D. Morrison-Low, Owen Gingerich, *A Heavenly Library: Treasures from the Royal Observatory's Crawford Collection: An Exhibition Held at the National Museums of Scotland, Chambers Street, Edinburgh, 8 October–31 December 1994* (Edinburgh: Royal Observatory, Edinburgh, 1994), 24; David A. King, "Some Medieval Astronomical Instruments and Their Secrets," in *Non-Verbal Communication in Science prior to 1900*, ed. Renato G. Mazzolini (Florence: Olschki, 1993), 29–52.
47. Or alternatively *ʿamila*, which Mayer notes is the second most common term, after *sanaʿahu*, used on astrolabes to introduce the makers.
48. On the rete, see David A. King, "Medieval Astronomical Instruments: A Catalogue in Preparation," *Bulletin of the Scientific Instrument Society* 31 (1991): 3–7; and Francis Maddison and Anthony Turner, "Catalogue: Science and Technology in Islam: An International Loan Exhibition, Held in the Science Museum, London 6 April–31 August 1976, as Part of the World of Islam Festival" [corrected typescript in National Museums of Scotland {NMS} object file] (Edinburgh: National Museums Scotland, 1976), 104–5.
49. See the essays in Glaire D. Anderson, Corisande Fenwick, and Mariam Rosser-Owen, eds., *The Aghlabids and Their Neighbours: Art and Material Culture in Ninth-Century North Africa* (Leiden: Brill, 2017).
50. On *taifa* arts and court culture, see the work of Cynthia Robinson cited in note 41 of this chapter, and also "Arts of the Taifa Kingdoms," in *Al-Andalus: The Art of Islamic Spain*, ed. Jerrilynn Denise Dodds (New York: Metropolitan Museum of Art, 1992), 49–61.
51. M.J. Viguera, "Saraḳusṭa," in *Encyclopaedia of Islam, Second Edition*. Consulted online on November 5, 2018, at http://dx.doi.org.ezproxy.is.ed.ac.uk/10.1163/1573-3912_islam_SIM_6621
52. On the city in the Umayyad and Taifa periods, see María Grego Gómez, *Toledo en la época Omeya (ss. VIII–X)* (Toledo, Spain: Diputación Provincial de Toledo, 2007); Clara Delgado Valero, *Regreso a Tulaytula: Guía Del Toledo Islámico: Siglos VIII–XI*, Conocer Castilla-La Mancha 23 (Toledo, Spain: Junta de Comunidades de Castilla-La Mancha, 1999). On the *taifa* rulers, see D.M. Dunlop, "D̲h̲u 'l-Nūnids," *Encyclopaedia of Islam, Second Edition*.
53. D.M. Dunlop, "D̲h̲u'l-Nūnids," *Encyclopaedia of Islam, Second Edition*.
54. On the oldest Islamic astrolabe, made of brass and measuring 8.5 cm, see King, *Instruments of Mass Calculation*, 422–33.
55. According to a document in the NMS object file.
56. My thanks to Kristina Münchow and Thoralf Hanstein for kind assistance with the photographs; Staatsbibliothek Zu Berlin - Preussischer Kulturbesitz, Orientabteilung, Sprenger 2050. On the maker and bibliography for the instrument see Hernández Pérez, *Astrolabios en al-Andalus*, 70; 96–97, A4; Hernández Pérez, *Catálogo razonado*, 51–58; Viladrich, *El legado científico andalusí*, 64.
57. *Astrolabios en al-Andalus*,188–91.
58. Formerly in Baghdad, the whereabouts of this astrolabe are now unknown. See King, *Instruments of Mass Calculation*, 422ff.

59. MHS, Oxford. inv. 47632. King, *In Synchrony with the Heavens*, 2:1005. I would like to thank Lee Macdonald for kind assistance with the photograph.
60. Ibid., 2:414, 418.
61. See King's translation and commentary on his text on astrolabe makers in ibid., 2:453–54, and for a discussion of female astrolabists, Hernández Pérez, *Catálogo razonado de los astrolabios de la España medieval* (Madrid: La Ergástula, 2018).
62. See translation and commentary of his text in King, *In Synchrony with the Heavens*, 2:455–56.
63. This is evident in the use of the simple dagger-shaped star pointers, rather than the elegant slender curves that distinguish the eleventh-century Iberian instruments. How the fourteenth-century designer came to be aware of the visual conventions of the early Eastern astrolabes and why the designer chose to evoke those, rather than the distinct visual forms shared among the eleventh-century Iberian astrolabes, are fascinating questions, but ones that require further research and lie beyond the boundaries of this study.
64. On Ṣā'id Al-Andalusī's background and reputation, see Jaakko Hämeen-Anttila, "Ṣā'id al-Andalusī, His System of Nations and the Progress of Science," *Zeitschrift für Geschichte der Arabisch-Islamischen Wissenschaften* 19 (2010–11): 2–4. Thanks to Professor Hämeen-Anttila for drawing my attention to this essay.
65. "Il avait un frère nommé Muhammad, célebre par son habileté dans la construction de l'astrolabe. Nul avant lui, en Andalousie, n'avait su mieux que lui construire cet instrument"; *Kitāb Ṭabaqāt al-umam*, trans. Régis Blachère. Manshūrāt Mahad Tārīkh al-Ulūm al-Arabīyah wa-al-Islāmīyah. Falsafah al-Islāmīyah 1 (Frankfurt: Institute for the History of Arabic-Islamic Science at the Johann Wolfgang Goethe University, 1999), p. 131 of the French translation; p. 70 of the Arabic text.
66. English translation, *Science in the Medieval World*, 69, though the French translation is preferred: "D'ailleurs, à l'heure actuelle, il existe de jeune savants qui, ça et là, étudient avec zèle la philosophie, dont l'entendement est sûr, les idées nobles, et qui ont déjà acquis la connaissance des diverses parties de cette science. . . . De ce nombre, parmi ceux qui résident à Tolède ou dans les environs, citons: . . . Ibrahîm ibn Sa'îd as-Sahlî, le Constructeur d'astrolabes [al-Asturlabi]," *Kitāb Ṭabaqāt al-umam*, 138–39; p. 75 of the Arabic text.
67. See Mayer, *Islamic Astrolabists and Their Works*, and Mayer, *Islamic Metalworkers and Their Works* (Geneva: A. Kundig, 1959).
68. Khizānat al-Qarawiyyīn - Fes, MSS. 605/1-2, discussed in Umberto Bongianino, "The Origin and Development of Maghribī Round Scripts: Arabic Palaeography in the Islamic West (4th/10th–6th/12th Centuries)" (PhD diss., University of Oxford, 2017), I:70, 132; and II:120–21 (item 39). Also see Yannick Lintz, Claire Déléry, and Bulle Tuil Leonetti, eds., *Le Maroc médiéval: un empire de l'Afrique à l'Espagne: album de l'exposition* (Paris: Musée du Louvre, 2014), 226, no. 129. Thanks to Bongianino for bringing the manuscript and its calligrapher to my attention.
69. Aḥmad ibn Muḥammad Maqqarī, *Nafḥ al-Ṭīb Min Ghuṣn al-Andalus al-Raṭīb*, ed. Iḥsān Abbās (Beirut: Dār Ṣādir, 1968), 4:96, cited in Bongianino, "The Origin and Development of Maghribī Round Scripts," 1:70.
70. Sheila S. Blair, "What the Inscriptions Tell Us: Text and Message on the Ivories from al-Andalus," *Journal of the David Collection* 2, no. 1 (2005): 74–99.
71. According to Mayer, *sana'ahu*, the most common term found on astrolabe signatures overall, indicated that the astrolabist in question was a professional astronomer and the actual maker of the instrument, whereas the meaning of the term *'amila* or *amal*, which is the second most common term found in the astrolabe signatures, is more difficult to determine: "with the exception of a sultan, not a single man who signed his astrolabe in this way is known from literature"; Mayer, *Islamic Astrolabists*, 13–14.

72. King, *Instruments of Mass*. Also see Yves Porter, "Les Art et les Sciences: Ars Gratia Ars," in *L'âge d'or des sciences Arabes: Exposition présentée à l'Institut du Monde Arabe, Paris, 25 Octobre 2005–19 Mars 2006*, 1st ed. (Arles, France: Actes sud, 2005), 243.

    For the occurrence of the term in the Geniza documents, see S.D. Goitein and Gustave E. von Grunebaum, *A Mediterranean Society: The Jewish Communities of the Arab World as Portrayed in the Documents of the Cairo Geniza*, 6 vols. (Berkeley: University of California Press, 1967–1993), 1:93, 410, 414, 415, 418; 2:478.
73. Therese Martin, ed., *Reassessing the Roles of Women as "Makers" of Medieval Art and Architecture*, Visualising the Middle Ages, vol. 7 (Leiden: Brill, 2012).
74. Mayer, *Islamic Astrolabists*, 14–15.
75. Mayer, *Islamic Astrolabists*, 15, where he observes that the use of such literary terms was "part and parcel of the desire of successful artists and artisans to appear as "gentlemen, and not as mere craftsmen."
76. Emilie Savage-Smith and Andrea P. A. Belloli. *Islamicate Celestial Globes, Their History, Construction, and Use* (Washington, D.C.: Smithsonian Institution Press, 1985); Carey, "Painting the Stars in a Century of Change."
77. Alternatively, it can be read as 478 AH / 28 May AD 1085, and this is the date used by the Museo Galileo; Filippo Camerota, *Museo Galileo: A Guide to the Treasures of the Collection* (Firenze: Giunti, 2010, 17).
78. For example, as Moya Carey has argued, the scribe and likely illustrator of the Bodleian's famous al-Ṣūfī manuscript was Ṣūfī's own son; Moya Carey, "Ṣūfī and Son: Ibn Ṣūfī's Poem on the Stars and Its Prose Parent," *Muqarnas* 26 (January 1, 2009): 181–204.
79. David Collection, inv. number 1/1984. I would like to thank Joachim Meyer and Mette Korsholm for kind assistance with information on the object, its inscription and photographs. For overview and bibliography, see *L'âge d'or des Sciences Arabes*, 277, catalog number 151.
80. Francis Maddison, "Al-Jazarī's Combination Lock: Two Contemporary Examples," in *The Art of Syria and the Jazīra, 1100–1250*, ed. Julian Raby, Oxford Studies in Islamic Art, vol. 1 (Oxford: Oxford University Press, 1985), 141–57.
81. The perimeter inscription states, "Glory and prosperity and wealth and happiness and well-being and [God's] support and success and power and strength and mercy and tranquility . . . health and grace and happiness and well-being and [God's] support and success and power and strength and gratitude and tranquility." Translated by Will Kwiatkovsky, courtesy of the David Collection.
82. Maddison, "Al-Jazarī's Combination Lock," 144–52.
83. On the daughter and father, see King, *In Synchrony with the Heavens*, 2:455. On examples in al-Andalus with an overview of the sources, see Hernández Pérez, *Astrolabios en al-Andalus*, 163–66. Maribel Fierro suggested that her name indicates enslaved or freed status; Personal communication.
84. A.R. Nykl, *Hispano-Arabic Poetry and Its Relations with the Old Provencal Troubadours* (Baltimore, 1946), 202.
85. Carey, "Painting the Stars in a Century of Change," 159–60. The previous dating of this manuscript to the early eleventh century has now been questioned and a later date proposed. See Savage-Smith, "The Most Authoritative Copy of ʿAbd al-Rahman al-Sufi's Tenth-Century Guide to the Constellations," in *God Is Beautiful and Loves Beauty: The Object in Islamic Art and Culture*, ed. Sheila Blair and Jonathan Bloom (New Haven, Conn: Yale University Press, 2013), 122–55.
86. Andreina Contessa, "A Geography of Learning: The World of the Presumed Map of Theodulphe of Orleans and Its Mid-Eleventh-Century Catalan Author," in *Miscellanea Bibliothecae Apostolicae Vaticanae*, XVIII:55–110 (Città del Vaticano: Biblioteca

Apostolica Vaticana, 2011). I would like to thank Mary Pardo for bringing this essay to my attention.

87. Three early extant Byzantine illustrated manuscripts also date from around the same period: late eighth to ninth century and are astronomical, notably Vatican 1296. I am grateful to Niels Gaul for bringing these to my attention, and for his observation that the eighth and ninth centuries are those in which there seems to be an emphasis on classical science (which then changes to an emphasis on rhetoric in the tenth century); personal communication, September 21, 2018.
88. Müller-Wiener, "Puns and Puzzles," 275–87; Moya Carey, "The Gold and Silver Lining: Shams al-Din Muhammad b. Mu'ayyad al-'Urdi's Inlaid Celestial Globe (C. AD 1288) from the Ilkhanid Observatory at Maragha," *Iran* 47 (2009): 97–108; Persis Berlekamp, "Visible Art, Invisible Knowledge," *International Journal of Middle East Studies* 45, no. 3 (August 2013): 563–65. On the intersection between mathematical sciences and visual arts, see Necipoğlu, "Ornamental Geometries," 11–78, especially the section titled "Mediating Art and Science," 57–62.
89. On the role of artisans and their activities in the production of knowledge and the emergence of the European Scientific Revolution, see Pamela O. Long, *Openness, Secrecy, Authorship: Technical Arts and the Culture of Knowledge from Antiquity to the Renaissance* (Baltimore: Johns Hopkins University Press, 2004); Pamela H. Smith, *The Body of the Artisan: Art and Experience in the Scientific Revolution* (Chicago: University of Chicago Press, 2004). Thanks to Jill Burke for bringing this work to my attention.
90. Graves, *Arts of Allusion*, 26–58.
91. David A. King, *Islamic Astronomy and Geography* (Farnham, U.K.: Ashgate, 2012), 156; Ellen Kenney, "Astrolabe of 'Umar Ibn Yusuf Ibn 'Umar Ibn 'Ali Ibn Rasul al-Muzaffari," in *Masterpieces from the Department of Islamic Art in the Metropolitan Museum of Art*, ed. Maryam Ekhtiar, Priscilla P. Soucek, Sheila R. Canby, and Navina Najat Haidar (New York: The Metropolitan Museum of Art, 2011), no. 107, 158–59, and online at The Metropolitan Museum of Art, accessed May 25, 2020, https://www.metmuseum.org/art/collection/search/444408; *L'âge d'or des sciences Arabes*, no. 26, 98–99.
92. This manuscript was apparently one of several scientific treatises that this prince compiled. See previous note.

Chapter 3

1. See passage IV.
2. Robert Hillenbrand, "'The Ornament of the World': Medieval Córdoba as a Cultural Centre," in *The Legacy of Muslim Spain*, ed. Salma Khadra Jayyusi (Leiden: Brill, 1992), 116. He does not provide a source.
3. Moya Carey, "The Gold and Silver Lining: Shams al-Din Muḥammad b. Mu'ayyad al-'Urdi's Inlaid Celestial Globe (C. AD 1288) from the Ilkhanid Observatory at Maragha," *Iran 47* (2009): 97–108, http://www.jstor.org/stable/25651466
4. T. Fahd, "Nīrandj," in *Encyclopaedia of Islam*, 2nd ed., ed. P. Bearman, Th. Bianquis, C.E. Bosworth, E. van Donzel, and W.P. Heinrichs. Consulted online on April 18, 2019, at http://dx.doi.org.ezproxy.is.ed.ac.uk/10.1163/1573-3912_islam_SIM_5922. First published online: 2012.
5. T. Fahd, *Sources orientales*, vii, Paris 1966, 184–85.
6. For overviews of magic in Islamic societies see Günther and Pielow, *Die Geheimnisse der Oberen und der Unteren Welt*; Emilie Savage-Smith, "Magic and Islam," in Francis Maddison and Emilie Savage-Smith, *Science, Tools & Magic. Part One. Body and Spirit, Mapping the*

Universe (London: Nour Foundation, in association with Azimuth Editions and Oxford University Press, 1997), 58–71.

7. Fahd, *EI2*, "s.v. Nīrandj."
8. Armand Abel, "La place des sciences occultes dans la décadence," in *Classicisme et déclin culturel dans l'histoire de l'Islam: actes du symposium international d'histoire de la civilisation musulmane, Bordeaux . . . 1956. Organisé par R. Brunschvig et G.E. von Grunebaum avec . . . [autres]*, ed. Robert Brunschvig (Paris: Éditions Besson-Chantemerle, 1957), 291–318, cited in Robert Irwin, "Review, *Magic and Divination in Early Islam, Edited by Emilie Savage-Smith*," *Magic, Ritual, and Witchcraft* 3, no. 1 (Summer 2008): 105–6.
9. See passage IV.
10. Emphasis mine.
11. Ibn Ḥayyān, *Crónica de los Emires Alḥakam I y'Abdarraḥmān II entre los Años 796 y 847 (Almuqtabis II-1)*, 139n284. Corriente and Makki also point out that Draco also appears in Ibn Quzmān (79/9/3 and 109/7/4) with the technical name of Jawzahar [sic]. Alternatively called al-Jawzahr in the Arabic literature, and associated with a mythological dragon or serpent, the constellation was linked to solar and lunar eclipses because the positions of its head and tail in the sky marked the points of the ecliptic toward north and south where eclipses are liable to occur. See P. Kunitzsch, "al-Tinnīn," *EI2*, and Stefano Carboni, *Following the Stars: Images of the Zodiac in Islamic Art* (New York: Metropolitan Museum of Art, 1997), 6ff.
12. J-P. Brunet, R. Nadal, and Cl. Vibert-Guigue, "The Fresco of the Cupola of Qusayr 'Amra," *Centaurus* 40 (1998): 97–123; Savage-Smith, *Islamicate Celestial Globes*, 16–17; Arthur Beer, "The Astronomical Significance of the Zodiac of the Qusayr 'Amra," in *Early Muslim Architecture*, 2nd ed., vol. 1, 2 vols. (Oxford: Clarendon Press, 1932), 289–303; Fritz Saxl, *The Zodiac of Quṣayr 'Amra.* (Oxford: Clarendon Press, 1932). However, if, as I have argued, the figural cycle on the ivory pyxis made for the Córdoban Umayyad prince al-Mughira were also meant to evoke astrological imagery for its tenth-century viewers, this would provide further evidence for a Western Islamic astronomical iconography already in place by the tenth century, from which al-Sahlī and his son could also have derived inspiration for the imagery on the globe. See Glaire D. Anderson, "A Mother's Gift? Astrology and the Pyxis of al-Mughīra," *Journal of Medieval History* 42, no. 1 (January 1, 2016): 107–30, https://doi.org/10.1080/03044181.2015.1103777
13. Carboni, *Following the Stars*, 1–7.
14. Savage-Smith, "The Most Authoritative Copy," 147–52.
15. On Eastern and Western treatments of constellation imagery see Carey, "Painting the Stars in a Century of Change," 159–60.
16. Jazarī, *The Book of Knowledge of Ingenious Mechanical Devices*, 17–41. Discussed in Martina Müller-Wiener, "Science as the Handmaiden of Power," 420–21.
17. On "the Castle Water-Clock," see Jazarī, *The Book of Knowledge of Ingenious Mechanical Devices*, 17–40; Section 9: "Construction of the spheres of the zodiac, the sun, and the moon," 35–39; Section 10: "On the place where the spheres are erected, and their functioning," 40–42.
18. Anderson, *Cosmos and Community*, 126. Byzantine conventions for representing celestial themes by the ninth century can be found in early illustrated manuscripts such as Ptolemy's *Handy Tables* (Vaticanus MS Graec. 1291) and the *Topographica* (Vatican Cod. Gr. 699). My thanks to Niels Gaul for bringing these to my attention.
19. Anderson, *Cosmos and Community in Early Medieval Art*, 114–26. On the Carolingian Aratus, British Library, Harley 647, see Helmut Gneuss, *Handlist of Anglo-Saxon Manuscripts: A List of Manuscripts and Manuscript Fragments Written or Owned in England up to 1100*, Medieval and Renaissance Texts and Studies, 241 (Tempe: Arizona Center for Medieval and Renaissance Studies, 2001), no. 423; *Treasures of the British Library*, ed. Nicolas Barker et al. (London: British Library, 2005), 51.

20. Maria Vaiou, *Diplomacy in the Early Islamic World: A Tenth-Century Treatise on Arab-Byzantine Relations: The Book of Messengers of Kings (Kitāb Rusul al-Mulūk) of Ibn al-Farrā'* (London: I.B. Tauris & Co. Ltd., 2015); Anthony Cutler, "Significant Gifts: Patterns of Exchange in Late Antique, Byzantine, and Early Islamic Diplomacy," *Journal of Medieval & Early Modern Studies* 38, no. 1 (Winter 2008): 79–101, https://doi.org/10.1215/10829636-2007-020
21. On BNF MS Lat 7411see Azucena Hernández Pérez, *Astrolabios en al-Andalus y los reinos medievales hispanos*, Colección Arte y contextos 3 (Madrid: Ediciones de la Ergástula, 2018); 96–97; Kunitzsch, Folkerts, and Lorch, *Sic Itur Ad Astra*, 185.
22. Elsa Cardoso, "The Scenography of Power in al-Andalus and the ʿAbbasid and Byzantine Ceremonials: Christian Ambassadorial Receptions in the Court of Cordoba in a Comparative Perspective," *Medieval Encounters* 24, no. 4 (2018): 390–434, https://doi.org/10.1163/15700674-12340007
23. Glaire D. Anderson, "Islamic Spaces and Diplomacy in Constantinople (Tenth to Thirteenth Centuries C.E.)," *Medieval Encounters: Jewish, Christian and Muslim Culture in Confluence and Dialogue* 15, no. 1 (2009): 86–113.
24. See Petros Bouras-Vallianatos, "Cross-Cultural Transfer of Medical Knowledge in the Medieval Mediterranean: The Introduction and Dissemination of Sugar-Based Potions from the Islamic World to Byzantium," *Speculum* 96, no. 4 (October 1, 2021): 963–1008, https://doi.org/10.1086/715838, and Paul Magdalino, "Pharmaceutical Diplomacy: A New Document on Fatimid-Byzantine Gift Exchange," in *Myriobiblos: Essays on Byzantine Literature and Culture*, ed. Theodora Antonopoulou, Sofia Kotzabassi, and Marina Loukaki, vol. 29, Byzantinisches Archiv 29 (Berlin: De Gruyter, 2015), 245–52, https://doi.org/10.1515/9781501501562.245. My thanks to Bouras-Vallianatos for drawing my attention to both essays.
25. Manuscript Gg. 153. The colophon gives the date of the text as 485/1092, but the copy has been dated to the fifteenth century based on the paper. See S.M. Stern, "A Letter of the Byzantine Emperor to the Court of the Spanish Umayyad Caliph al-Ḥakam," *Al-Andalus* 26, no. 1 (January 1, 1961): 37–42, cited in Cardoso, "The Scenography of Power," 426.
26. Stern, "A Letter of the Byzantine Emperor, 38.
27. On the description of such a device by al-Biruni see Donald R. Hill, "Al-Bīrūnī's Mechanical Calendar," *Annals of Science* 42, no. 2 (March 1985): 139–63, https://doi.org/10.1080/00033798500200141
28. Codex Medicia Laurenziana Or. 152. Published in facsimile with a new translation of the manuscript, as Massimiliano Lisa, Mario Taddei, and Edoardo Zanon, *The Book of Secrets in the Results of Ideas: Incredible Machines from 1000 Years Ago = Kitāb al-Asrār Fī Natā'ij al-Afkār: Ālāt Mudhhilah Min Alif ʿām*, trans. Ahmed Ragab, 1st ed. (Milano: Leonardo3, 2008). Samsó, *El legado científico andalusí*, 304–308.

    Samsó provides an overview of the main bibliography in "Reviews: Massimiliano Lisa, Mario Taddei & Edoardo Zanon, The Book of Secrets in the Results of Ideas. Incredible Machines from 1000 Years Ago, Ibn Khalaf al-Muradī," *Suhayl. International Journal for the History of the Exact and Natural Sciences in Islamic Civilisation* 9 (2009): 236–37, but some of the key works are A.I. Sabra, "A Note on Codex Medicea Laurenziana Or. 152," *Journal for the History of Arabic Science* 1 (1977), 276–283; Donald Hill, *Arabic Water-Clocks*, 33–45; M.V. Villuendas, "A Further Note on a Mechanical Treatise Contained in Codex Medicea Laurenziana Or. 152," *Journal for the History of Arabic Science* 2 (1978), 395–396.
29. Massimiliano Lisa, Mario Taddei, and Edoardo Zanon, *The Book of Secrets in the Results of Ideas: Incredible Machines from 1000 Years Ago = Kitāb Al-Asrār Fī Natā'ij al-Afkār: Ālāt Mudhhilah Min Alif ʿām*, trans. Ahmed Ragab, 1st ed. (Milano: Leonardo3, 2008). Images of the reconstructions can be seen at http://www.leonardo3.net/en/l3-works/publishing-house/1511-the-book-of-secrets-facsimile.html

30. On the Doha exhibition see http://www.leonardo3.net/en/exhibitions/1408-the-book-of-secrets.html. On the Karlsruhe exhibition see https://zkm.de/en/exhibition/2015/10/globale-allahs-automata
31. Samsó argues for placing al-Muradī in Toledo, not in Córdoba. See Samsó, "Reviews: Massimiliano Lisa, Mario Taddei & Edoardo Zanon, The Book of Secrets," 238.
32. Donald Routledge Hill, "An Andalusian Treatise of the 5th/11th Century," in *Arabic Water-Clocks*, vol. 4, Sources & Studies in the History of Arabic-Islamic Science (Aleppo: University of Aleppo, Institute for the History of Arabic Science, 1981), 36–46; Donald Hill, "Andalusian Technology," in *Studies in Medieval Islamic Technology: From Philo to al-Jazarī, from Alexandria to Diyār Bakr*, ed. David A. King (Aldershot, U.K.; Brookfield, Vt.: Ashgate, 1998), XVIII: 1–16.
33. This omission contrasts with illustrations included in the manuscript copies of the Banū Mūsā and al-Jazarī treatises, which furnished crucial information about the machines described in those texts. On the key manuscripts of the Banū Mūsā and al-Jazarī treatises, see Muḥammad Ibn Mūsá Ibn Shākir and Donald R. Hill, *The Book of Ingenious Devices (Kitāb Al-ḥiyal)* (Dordrecht, the Netherlands: D. Reidel Pub., 1979), 7–16; Ismāʿīl ibn al-Razzāz Jazarī, *The Book of Knowledge of Ingenious Mechanical Devices* (Dordrecht, the Netherlands; Boston: Reidel, 1974), 3–6.
34. Ibn Shākir, *Ingenious Devices*, 7–16.
35. Massimiliano Lisa, Mario Taddei, & Edoardo Zanon, *The Book of Secrets in the Results of Ideas: Incredible Machines from 1000 Years Ago = Kitāb al-Asrār Fī Natā'ij al-Afkār: Ālāt Mudhhilah Min Alif ʿām*, trans. Ahmed Ragab, 1st ed. (Milano: Leonardo3, 2008), 75.
36. Gülru Necipoğlu, *The Topkapı Scroll: Geometry and Ornament in Islamic Architecture: Topkapı Palace Museum Library MS H. 1956*, Sketchbooks & Albums (Santa Monica, Calif.: Getty Center for the History of Art and the Humanities, 1995); R. Holod, "Text, Plan and Building: On the Transmission of Architectural Knowledge," in *Theories and Principles of Design in the Architecture of Islamic Societies: A Symposium . . . Cambridge, Massachusetts . . . 1987* (Cambridge, Mass.: Aga Khan Program for Islamic Architecture, MIT, 1988), 1–12.
37. An accompanying catalog was published as Muḥammad ibn Mūsá Ibn Shākir et al., *Allah's Automata: Artifacts of the Arab-Islamic Renaissance (800–1200)* (Ostfildern, Germany: Hatje Cantz, 2015). Perhaps similar to the Pisa Griffin's intended auditory effects, see Anna Contadini, *The Pisa Griffin and the Mari-Cha Lion: Metalwork, Art, and Technology in the Medieval Islamicate Mediterranean* (Pisa, Italy: Pacini Editore, 2018), and Lamia Balafrej, "Saracen or Pisan?," *Ars Orientalis* 42 (2012): 31–40.
38. Juan Vernet, R. Casals, and M.V. Villuendas, "El capítulo primer del Kitab asrar fi nata'iy al-afkar," *Awraq: Estudios sobre el mundo árabe e islámico contemporáneo*, no. 5 (1982): 7–18.
39. al-Murādī, *The Book of Secrets in the Results of Ideas*, 33–36 of the English translation.
40. Samsó, *On Both Sides of the Strait of Gibraltar*, 124n307.
41. Samsó, "Review"; Julio Samsó, *El legado científico andalusí* (Madrid: Ministerio de Cultura, Dirección General de Cooperación Cultural, 1992), 304–309, with photograph of the reconstruction on p. 309.
42. In 2008 the collection was transferred from Frankfurt to the Museum of Science and Technology in Islam in Istanbul. See Samsó, "Review," 237. I would like to thank Esra Müyesseroglu, Çiğdem Yürür and the staff of the Museum of Science and Technology in Islam, Mira Xenia Schwerda, and Melis Taner for kind assistance in obtaining photographs of the Farré clepsydra.
43. Silke Ackermann, "Gerard Turner Memorial Lecture: In the Service of Religion? 'Islamic Science' in the Museum," *Bulletin of the Scientific Instrument Society* 139 (2018): 6. Ackermann also points in note 10 to the related issues raised by Nir Shafir in the essay "Forging Islamic

Science: Fake Miniatures Detract from the Real Work of Early-Modern Ottoman Scientists," *American Scientist* 107, no. 3 (2019): 156–161.

44. Hill, *Arabic Water-Clocks*, 40–43.
45. Ibid.
46. Maqqarī, *History of the Mohammedan Dynasties in Spain*, I: 236.
47. Jāḥiẓ, *Le livre des animaux: de l'étonnante sagesse divine dans sa création et autres anecdotes*, Bibliothèque Maktaba (Paris: Fayard, 2003).
48. On the imagery from the al-Mughira pyxis as evocative of these fables see Francisco Prado-Vilar, "Enclosed in Ivory: The Miseducation of Al-Mughira," *Journal of the David Collection* 2, no. 1 (2005): 138–63.
49. On al-Murādī and hollow bronze animals as a kind of rudimentary automata see Allegra Iafrate, *The Wandering Throne of Solomon: Objects and Tales of Kingship in the Medieval Mediterranean* (Leiden; Boston: Brill, 2016), 181–82; also see Antonio Fernández Puertas, *Clepsidras y Relojes Musulmanes = Muslim Water Clocks and Mechanical Time Pieces* (Granada, Spain: Fundación el Legado Andalusí, 2010).
50. See Contadini, "Wondrous Animals," 232–33; Antonio Vallejo Triano, "Piezas Metálicas Suntuarias del Periodo Califal de al-Andalus," in *The Pisa Griffin and the Mari-Cha Lion: Metalwork, Art, and Technology in the Medieval Islamicate Mediterranean*, ed. Anna Contadini, Damiano Anedda, and Rafael Azuar Ruiz (Pisa, Italy: Pacini Editore, 2018), 257–80; Susana Calvo Capilla, "Los Bronces Zoomorfos de al-Ándalus," in *Las Artes del Metal en al-Ándalus*, ed. Sergio Vidal Álvarez, Beatriz Campderá Gutiérrez, and Solène de Pablos Hamon (Madrid: Ministerio de Cultura y Deportes, 2020), 62–69. Also see Nadia Ambrosetti, "Wavering between the True and the False: A Short Excursion through Greek and Arab Automata," in *Allah's Automata: Artifacts of the Arab-Islamic Renaissance (800–1200)*, ed. Siegfried Zielinski and Peter Weibel (Ostfildern, Germany: Hatje Cantz, 2015), 44–45; D.F. Ruggles, *Islamic Gardens and Landscapes* (Philadelphia: University of Pennsylvania Press, 2008), 80.
51. Images and translations of the text describing the devices are in Hill, *The Banu Musa and Their Book of Ingenious Devices*, 50–55.
52. Topkapi Mss. A.3474.fols. 19r, 47v, and 59r. My thanks to Esra Müyesseroglu and Gülendam Karal for kind assistance and permission to publish the images. Donald Hill, *The Book of Ingenious Devices (Kitāb al-Ḥiyal)* (Dordrecht, the Netherlands; Boston: D. Reidel Pub. Co., 1978), 7–16. The duck appears in the illustration of model 23 (folio 19 recto).
53. Maqqarī, *The History of the Mohammedan Dynasties in Spain* I: 236–37.
54. Grabar, *The Formation of Islamic Art*, 159–61.
55. Cited in N.G. Wilson, *Scholars of Byzantium*. Duckworth Classical, Medieval, and Renaissance Editions (London: Duckworth, 1983), 81–82; Antonio Fernández Puertas, *Clepsidras y Relojes Musulmanes = Muslim Water Clocks and Mechanical Time Pieces* (Granada, Spain: Fundación el Legado Andalusí, 2010).
56. Gerard Brett, "The Automata in the Byzantine 'Throne of Solomon,'" *Speculum* 29, no. 3 (1954): 477–87; Ann Moffatt, Maxeme Tall, Ann Reiske, Johann Jacob, Philotheus, Pseudo-Epiphanius, Constantine VII Porphyrogenitus, Philotheos, and Australian Association for Byzantine Studies, *The Book of Ceremonies: With the Greek Edition of the Corpus Scriptorum Historiae Byzantinae (Bonn, 1829)*, Byzantina Australiensia; 18 (Canberra: Australian Association for Byzantine Studies, 2012).
57. Müller-Wiener, "Science as the Handmaiden of Power," 418–22.
58. I am grateful to Alex Brey for bringing these to my attention. See Iafrate, *The Wandering Throne of Solomon*, 190.
59. Anderson, *Cosmos and Community*, 146.

60. These are machines 6–15, 17–20, and 27–30. See Samsó, *Review*, 234. Machine 16, which he notes is missing in the manuscript, may have been a clock given its place within the sequence of machines.
61. Graves, *Arts of Allusion*, 42.
62. Alexander Jones and James Evans, *Time and Cosmos in Greco-Roman Antiquity* (New York: Institute for the Study of the Ancient World at New York University; Princeton University Press, 2016); Finbarr Barry Flood, *The Great Mosque of Damascus: Studies on the Makings of an Umayyad Visual Culture* (Leiden and Boston: Brill, 2001), 114–38
63. Flood, *The Great Mosque of Damascus*, 138. Besides the Syrian Umayyad clock at Damascus, the most famous timepiece of the early medieval period is arguably the water clock that the Abbasid caliph Harūn al-Rashid is said to have sent in 807 as a gift to Charlemagne. According to Eginard, this device was "a time-piece wonderfully constructed of brass with mechanical art, in which the course of the twelve hours was turned towards a clepsydra, with as many brass balls which fell down at the completion of the hour, and by their fall sounded a bell placed under them." ("Nec non et horologium, ex aurichalco arte mechanica mirifice compositum, in quo duodecim horarum cursus ad clepsydram vertebatur, cum totidem aereis pilulis, quae ad completionem horarum decidebant, et casu suo subjectum sibi cymbalum tinnire faciebant.") Eginard, *Annales Francorum: Chronicum Turonese*; quoted and translated in John Beckmann, *A History of Inventions, Discoveries and Origins*, 4th ed. (trans. William Johnstone, rev. and enl. by William Francis and J.W.Griffith), 2 vols. (London: H.G. Bohn, 1846), vol. 1, 343, and cited in Donald Hill, "Arabic Mechanical Engineering," in *Studies in Medieval Islamic Technology: From Philo to Al-Jazarī, from Alexandria to Diyār Bakr*, ed. David A. King, V (Aldershot, U.K.: Ashgate, 1998), 167–86, note 6.
64. An account from a Chinese embassy to Antioch of 945 describes a water clock (*clepsydra, finjan*) on a gate of the Qusiyan Church (cathedral of St. Peter), which combines the figural elements of the Abbasid piece sent to Charlemagne with a grand architectural setting. The Antiochene clock, which functioned in both day and night, is said to have been visible from the royal residence and to have featured a life-sized golden automaton and twelve golden balls, the dropping of which produced a chiming sound that marked the passing hours. See Friedrich Hirth, *China and the Roman Orient, Researches into Their Ancient and Medieval Relations as Represented in Old Chinese Records* (Leipzig, 1885). Reprinted, Paragon Book Reprint Corp., 1966. My thanks to Asa Eger for drawing my attention to both the clock and to Hirth's book.
65. On the two clocks of Fés, see Derek J. de Solla Price, "Mechanical Water Clocks of the 14th Century in Fez, Morocco," in: *Proceedings of the Tenth International Congress of the History of Science* (Ithaca, N.Y.; Paris: Hermann, 1962). 599–602; Hill, *Arabic Water-Clocks*, 123–24; Flood, *The Great Mosque of Damascus*, 116ff.
66. The display of clocks seems to have been an established phenomenon on both sides of the Straits of Gibraltar by the fourteenth century. As Olga Bush has discussed, monumental clocks were also regularly displayed in Nasrid court spaces and incorporated in court festivities marking the Prophet's birthday, and Arabic sources refer to clocks at Tlemcen and at the Alhambra in Granada, where the Nasrids displayed a polychrome wood clock approximately 1.65 m in height. See Olga Bush, *Reframing the Alhambra: Architecture, Poetry, Textiles and Court Ceremonial*, Edinburgh Studies in Islamic Art (Edinburgh: Edinburgh University Press, 2018), 266–67; Fernández Puertas, *Clepsidras y Relojes Musulmanes*, 59–77.
67. Bush, *Reframing the Alhambra*, 266–67.
68. Fahd, *EI2*, "s.v. Nīrandj." Fahd notes that the operations encompassed by the term are detailed in "*Fi 'l-ḥiyal al-bābiliyya li 'l-k͟hizāna al-kāmiliyya* (ms. Bursa, Haraççioğlu 1221, ff. 119, 18.5×14 cm, *nask͟hī*, copied in 881/1476 from another ms. of the same *K͟hizāna* dated 632/1234)."

69. Fahd, *EI2*, "s.v. Nīrandj"; Emilie Savage-Smith, "Magic and Divination in Early Islam," in *Magic and Divination in Early Islam* (Oxford, New York: Ashgate, 2004), xiii–li.
70. Emphasis mine.
71. On talismans see Persis Berlekamp, *Wonder, Image, and Cosmos in Medieval Islam* (New Haven, Conn.: Yale University Press, 2011); for an overview on amulets see Christiane Gruber, "From Prayer to Protection: Amulets and Talismans in the Islamic World," in *Power and Protection: Islamic Art and the Supernatural*, 33–52 (Oxford: Ashmolean Museum, 2016), and Karl Schaefer, *Enigmatic Charms: Medieval Arabic Block Printed Amulets in American and European Libraries and Museums. Enigmatic Charms* (Brill, 2006). Amulets and talismans are the subject of dissertations by Yasmine F. Alsaleh, "'Licit Magic': The Touch and Sight of Islamic Talismanic Scrolls" (PhD diss., Harvard University, 2014), and Lyla Halsted (in progress).
72. Maribel Fierro, "Batinism in al-Andalus. Maslama b. Qasim al-Qurtubi (d. 353–964), Author of the Rutbat al-Hakim and the Ghayat al-Hakim (Picatrix)," *Studia Islamica* 2 (1996): 87–112.
73. Fierro, "Batinism in al-Andalus," 112. On Maslama see "4.2.1. Abū l-Qāsim al-Qurṭubī (gest. 353/964) und Abū l-Qāsim al-Mağrīṭī (gest. 397/1007)," in *Die Geheimnisse Der Oberen Und Der Unteren Welt: Magie Im Islam Zwischen Glaube Und Wissenschaft*, ed. Sebastian Günther and Dorothee Pielow (Boston: Brill, 2018).
74. Graves, "Chapter One: The Intellect of the Hand," in *Arts of Allusion*, 26–58.
75. Ṣā'id Andalusī, *Science in the Medieval World*, 73. A similar situation pertained in Abbasid Baghdad. See Jacob Lassner, *The Topography of Baghdad in the Early Middle Ages; Text and Studies* (Detroit: Wayne State University Press, 1970). My thanks to Matthew Saba for drawing my attention to the parallel.
76. Evariste Lévi-Provençal, *Inscriptions Arabes d'Espagne: Avec Quarante-Quatre Planches en Phototypie.* (Leyde: E.J. Brill, 1931), 9–12; Manuel Ocaña Jiménez, "Las Inscripciones en Mosaico del Mihrab de la Gran Mezquita de Córdoba y la Incógnita de Su Data," in *Les Mosaïques de la Grande Mosquée de Cordoue*, ed. Henri Stern, Dorothea Duda, and Manuel Ocaña Jiménez, Madrider Forschungen, Bd. 11 (Berlin: de Gruyter, 1976), 48–52. For more recent overviews on the inscriptions of Umayyad Córdoba see the work of María Antonia Martínez Núñez, such as "Epigrafía Árabe e Historia de al-Andalus: Nuevos Hallazgos y Datos," *Xelb: Revista De Arqueologia, Arte, Etnologia e História* 9 (2009): 39–53, and "Sentido de la Epigrafía Omeya de al-Andalus," In *El Esplendor de los Omeyas Cordobeses: La Civilización Musulmana de Europa Occidental: Exposición en Madīnat al-Zahrā' . . . 2001. Estudios. Coord. Científica María Jesús Viguera Molins, Concepción Castillo* (Granada, Spain: Fundación el Legado Andalusí, 2001), 408–417.
77. Lévi-Provençal, *Inscriptions*, 12. He says, "un juriste cordouan, futur kadi de la capitale, avait été élevé aux memes fonctions. On trouve aussi une attesttion de la . . .dans une biographie de la Sila of Ibn Bashkuwal (n. 1339). Cette charge était sans doute celle du sahib al-mazalim, qui avait pour mission le radd al-mazalim ou 'redressement des griefs,' c'est-a-dire sans doute la répression de certains delits civils."
78. Ibn al-Faradi, *Ta'rikh 'ulama al-Andalus*, t. I, n. 1299, 366–67, cited in Lévi-Provençal, *Inscriptions*, 12.
79. Lévi-Provençal, *Inscriptions*, numbers 10, 12, and 13, 9–21.
80. Arnold, "Mathematics and the Islamic Architecture of Córdoba," 1–15. On the unfree elites see Mohamed Meouak, *Ṣaqâliba, Eunuques et Esclaves à la Conquête du Pouvoir: Géographie et Histoire des Élites Politiques "Marginales" dans l'Espagne Umayyade* (Helsinki: Academia scientiarum Fennica, 2004). On the Slav eunuchs' direct involvement in architecture and arts on behalf of the Córdoban Umayyad state see Glaire Anderson, "Concubines, Eunuchs, and Patronage in Early Islamic Córdoba," in *Reassessing the Roles of Women as "Makers" of Medieval Art and Architecture*, ed. Therese Martin (Leiden: Brill, 2012), 633–69, and Glaire Anderson, "Social Dimensions of Patronage," in *The Islamic Villa in Early Medieval*

Iberia: Architecture and Court Culture in Umayyad Córdoba (Farnham, U.K.: Ashgate, 2013), 33–37.

81. Manuel Ocaña Jiménez, "Las Inscripciones en Mosaico del Mihrab de la Gran Mezquita de Córdoba y la Incógnita de Su Data," in *Les Mosaïques de la Grande Mosquée de Cordoue*, ed. Henri Stern, vol. Bd. 11, Madrider Forschungen; Bd. 11 (Berlin: de Gruyter, 1976), 51. Also see Manuel Ocaña Jiménez, "Arquitectos y mano de obra en la construcción de la Gran Mezquita de Occidente," *Cuadernos de la Alhambra*, no. 22 (1986): 55–86.
82. Susana Calvo Capilla, "The Visual Construction of the Umayyad Caliphate in al-Andalus through the Great Mosque of Cordoba," *Arts* 7, no. 3 (2018): 18. https://doi.org/10.3390/arts7030036
83. Alpay Özdural, "Mathematics and Arts: Connections between Theory and Practice in the Medieval Islamic World," *Historia Mathematica* 27, no. 2 (May 2000): 171–201, https://doi.org/10.1006/hmat.1999.2274; Alpay Özdural, "Omar Khayyam, Mathematicians, and *conversazioni* with Artisans," *Journal of the Society of Architectural Historians* 54, no. 1 (1995): 54–71; Alpay Özdural, "A Mathematical Sonata for Architecture: Omar Khayyam and the Friday Mosque of Isfahan," *Technology and Culture* 39, no. 4 (1998): 699–715.
84. I am grateful to Matt Saba for the observation; personal communication, 2020. On Córdoba and caliphal competition see Glaire D. Anderson and Jennifer Pruitt, "The Three Caliphates, a Comparative Approach," in *A Companion to Islamic Art and Architecture*, ed. Finbarr Barry Flood and Gulru Necipoglu (Malden, Mass.: Blackwell Pub, 2017), 223–49. On the Great Mosque of Córdoba as part of broader caliphal discourses of legitimacy and power see Susana Calvo Capilla, "The Visual Construction of the Umayyad Caliphate in al-Andalus through the Great Mosque of Cordoba," *Arts* 7, no. 3 (2018): 36, https://doi.org/10.3390/arts7030036; Jerrilynn Denise Dodds, *Architecture and Ideology in Early Medieval Spain* (University Park: Pennsylvania State University Press, 1990); Nuha Khoury, "The Meaning of the Great Mosque of Cordoba in the Tenth Century," *Muqarnas* XIII (1996): 80–98.
85. Doris Behrens-Abouseif, *Islamic Architecture in Cairo: An Introduction* (Cairo: The American University in Cairo Press, 1989); K.A.C. Creswell and Marguerite Gautier-van Berchem, *Early Muslim Architecture*, 2nd ed. (New York: Hacker Art Books, 1979), 290–306.
86. Creswell, *Early Muslim Architecture*; on the pointed arches, 292; on the Kufic inscriptions, 302.
87. Ibid., 302.
88. Ibn Shākir, *The Book of Ingenious Devices (Kitāb al-Ḥiyal)*, 4–5.
89. Ibid., 52.
90. This is model number 78. Ibid., 198.
91. Ibid., 5.
92. Creswell, *Early Muslim Architecture* II, 200ff; William Popper, *The Cairo Nilometer; Studies in Ibn Taghrî Birdî's Chronicles of Egypt: I*, University of California Publications in Semitic Philology; v. 12 (Berkeley: University of California Press, 1951), 20–23.
93. Creswell identifies him as mathematician. A possible connection between Ahmad al-Hasib and Ibn Mudabbir is proposed by Popper, *The Cairo Nilometer*, 22–23. Ibn Mudabbir refers to two brothers, named Abu 'l-Ḥasan Aḥmad and Abū Isḥāḳ (Abū Yusr) Ibrāhīm b. Muḥammad b. ʿAbd Allāh b. *al-Mudabbir*, who were Abbasid "high officials, courtiers, and men of letters as well as poets" in Abbasid Samarra and in Egypt in the mid-ninth century and who were especially involved in the Abbasid tax and fiscal administration, which would have required significant mathematical expertise. H.L. Gottschalk, "Ibn al-Mudabbir," in *Encyclopaedia of Islam*, 2nd ed., ed. P. Bearman, Th. Bianquis, C.E. Bosworth, E. van Donzel, and W.P. Heinrichs.
94. Ibn Khallikān, *Wafayāt al-aʿyān wa-anbāʾ abnāʾ al-zamān* (Bayrūt: Dar Ṣādir, 1398), vol. 3, 113–14, translated in Alain George, "Calligraphy, Colour and Light in the Blue Qur'an," *Journal of Qur'anic Studies* XI, no. I (2009): 101–103, and Creswell, *Early Muslim Architecture*, 297–98.

95. Ibn Khallikān, *Wafayāt al-a'yān wa-anbā' abnā' al-zamān*, 113–14, translated in George, "Calligraphy, Colour and Light in the Blue Qur'an," 102–103, and Creswell, *Early Muslim Architecture*, 297–98.
96. Ibid., 298
97. George, "Calligraphy, Colour and Light in the Blue Qur'an," 103; Behrens-Abouseif, *Islamic Architecture in Cairo*, 51. On the color scheme also see Lawrence Nees, "Blue behind Gold: The Inscription of the Dome of the Rock and Its Relatives," in *And Diverse Are Their Hues: Color in Islamic Art and Culture*, ed. Jonathan Bloom and Sheila Blair (New Haven, Conn: Yale University Press, 2011), 153–73.
98. Indeed the mathematician recorded on the marble jambs of the Nilometer's entrance an inscription that ended by recording what might be regarded as an important bit of scientific data from the year in which the monument was built: "the water reached 17 cubits and 18 fingers in the year of construction (*bina'*) of the Nilometer of al-Mutawakkil the blessed"; Creswell, *Early Muslim Architecture*, 302.
99. The point would be worth investigating further for other instances of crossover activity on the part of intellectuals in astronomy engaging in design activities as well. For instance, it would be interesting to consider whether the Banu Munajjim, a family of Zoroastrian Iranian origin who became important figures in the Abbasid court, first as astrologers and then as courtiers, might have been involved in any design or planning activities. My thanks to Matt Saba for the suggestion. On the Banu Munajjim see M. Fleischhammer, "Munadjdjim," in *Encyclopaedia of Islam*, 2nd ed., ed. P. Bearman, Th. Bianquis, C.E. Bosworth, E. van Donzel, and W.P. Heinrichs. Consulted online on November 29, 2021, at http://dx.doi.org.ezproxy.is.ed.ac.uk/10.1163/1573-3912_islam_SIM_5501. First published online: 2012. First print edition: ISBN: 9789004161214, 1960-2007.
100. Gerrit Bos and Charles Burnett, *Scientific Weather Forecasting in the Middle Ages: The Writings of al-Kindī: Studies, Editions, and Translations of the Arabic, Hebrew and Latin Texts* (London: Kegan Paul International / Routledge, 2000); Charles, "Weather Forecasting in the Arabic World," in *Magic and Divination in Early Islam*, ed. Emilie Savage-Smith (London, New York: Ashgate, 2004), 201–10.
101. Julio Samsó, *Las Ciencias de los Antiguos* (Madrid, 1992), 249–57. For the later medieval European trajectory, see Elly Truitt, *Medieval Robots: Mechanism, Magic, Nature, and Art* (Philadelphia: University of Pennsylvania Press, 2015).
102. Anderson, *Cosmos and Community*, 145.
103. Ibid., 148.
104. Saliba, *Islamic Science and the Making of the European Renaissance*, 58–65.
105. Müller-Wiener, "Science as the Handmaiden of Power," 418–22.
106. I am grateful to Matt Saba for sharing, prior to its publication, a chapter from his forthcoming book on Abbasid palace architecture, which alerted me to the passage, and for his suggestion that the Arabic terms used by Jahiz to juxtapose intellectuals versus artisans may be *'ulama'* and *ṣunnā'*. See Jāḥiẓ, *Rasā'il al-Jāḥiẓ*, ed. 'Abd al-Salām Muḥammad Hārūn, vol. 3, 314–15. 4 vols. Cairo: Maktabat al-Khanjī, 1964–1979.

Chapter 4

1. Ovid, Metamorphoses, trans. Frank Justus Miller (Cambridge, Mass.: Harvard University Press, 1951), 442–43.
2. Diwan al-Amin wa l-Ma'mun, ed. Wadih al-Samad (Beirut: Dar Sadir, 1998), 75, cited in Michael Cooperson, Al-Ma'mun (Oxford: Oneworld, 2005), 88–89.
3. Richard Hallion, "Of Dreams and Desires," in Taking Flight: Inventing the Aerial Age from Antiquity through the First World War (New York: Oxford University Press, 2003), 4–23.

4. On the translation of ancient Greek texts into Arabic see Dimitri Gutas, Greek Thought, Arabic Culture: The Graeco-Arabic Translation Movement in Baghdad and Early ʿAbbāsid Society (2nd–4th/8th–10th Centuries) (London; New York: Routledge, 1998).
5. Dimitri Gutas and Kevin van Bladel, "Bayt al-Ḥikma," in *Encyclopaedia of Islam, THREE*, ed. Kate Fleet et al., consulted online on June 11, 2019, at http://dx.doi.org.ezproxy.is.ed.ac.uk/10.1163/1573-3912_ei3_COM_22882. First published online: 2009. First print edition: 9789004178533, 2009, 2009-2.
6. Long celebrated as the oldest illustrated Islamic manuscript, the Bodlein's copy of al-Ṣūfī's treatise (Marsh, 144) has been published in facsimile as ʿAbd al-Raḥmān ibn ʿUmar Ṣūfī, *Kitāb Ṣuwar al-kawākib*, Manshūrat Maʿhad Tārīkh al-ʿUlūm al-ʿArabīyah wa-al-Islāmīyah. Silsilah J, ʿUyūn al-turath; mujallad 29 (Frankfurt am Main: Jumhūrīyat Almāniyā al-Ittiḥādīyah: Maʿhad Tārīkh al-ʿUlūm al-ʿArabīyah wa-al-Islāmīyah fī iṭār Jāmiʿat Frānkfūrt, 1986). On the al-Ṣūfī illustrated manuscripts see Moya Catherine Carey, "Painting the Stars in a Century of Change: A Thirteenth-Century Copy of al-Sūfī's Treatise on the Fixed Stars"; Savage-Smith, "The Most Authoritative Copy," 122–55.
7. Ibid., 122–55.
8. Ibid.
9. Maqqarī, *Analectes*, II:254, trans. Stuart Sears. Translator's note: text has *rīḥ* without comment by the editor. This, nevertheless, seems to represent a mistake in the manuscript for *rīsh*, "feathers." The Madrid manuscript clearly has *rīsh*.
10. Maqqarī, *The History of the Mohammedan Dynasties in Spain*, I:148–49.
11. White Jr., "Eilmer of Malmesbury," 100–101. On White's importance to the history of technology studies see Shana Worthen, "The Influence of Lynn White, Jr.'s Medieval Technology and Social Change," History Compass 7, no. 4 (2009): 1201–17, https://doi.org/10.1111/j.1478-0542.2009.00615.x
12. Juan Vernet, "ʿAbbas Ibn Firnās," in Dictionary of Scientific Biography, ed. Charles Coulston Gillispie (New York: Scribner's, 1970), 5.
13. Hallion, *Taking Flight*, 11–12; Taner Edis and Sonja Brentjes, "A Golden Age of Harmony? Misrepresenting Science and History in 1001 Inventions," Skeptical Inquirer 36, no. 6 (2012): 49.
14. Passage III, Madrid Manuscript.
15. Janina M. Safran, Defining Boundaries in Al-Andalus: Muslims, Christians, and Jews in Islamic Iberia (Ithaca, N.Y.: Cornell University Press, 2013), 45.
16. E. Geoffroy, *EI2*, s.v. "shaykh."
17. On villas and palaces see Julio Navarro Palazón and José Miguel Puerta Vílchez, Almunias: Las fincas de la élite en el Occidente islámico: poder, solaz y producción (Granada: Universidad de Granada, 2018); Felix Arnold, Islamic Palace Architecture in the Western Mediterranean: A History (New York: Oxford University Press, 2017); D. Fairchild Ruggles, Gardens, Landscape, and Vision in the Palaces of Islamic Spain (University Park, Pa.: Pennsylvania State University Press, 2000).
18. On this villa's significance in Córdoban court culture see Glaire Anderson, The Islamic Villa in Early Medieval Iberia: Architecture and Court Culture in Umayyad Córdoba (Farnham, U.K.; Burlington, Vt.: Ashgate), 2013. Also see Felix Arnold et al., Munyat ar-Rummaniya: ein islamischer Landsitz bei Córdoba. Teil 1. Palastanlagen / Felix Arnold, Alberto Canto Garcia, Antonio Vallejo Triano; mit Beiträgen von Glaire D. Anderson . . . [et al.] (Wiesbaden: Reichert, 2015); Felix Arnold, Alberto Canto García, and Antonio Vallejo Triano, "Das islamische Landgut ar-Rumanīya bei Córdoba. Vorbericht einer Bauaufnahme," Madrider Mitteilungen *50* (2009): 503–23, 569–70; Felix Arnold, Alberto Canto García, and Antonio Vallejo Triano, "La Almunia de Al-Rummaniyya. Resultados de Una Documentación Arquitectónica," Cuadernos de Madinat Al-Zahra' 6 (2008): 181–204.

19. I would like to thank Juan Murillo of the Gerencia Municipal de Urbanismo of Córdoba for generously sharing his insights on the excavations undertaken in Córdoba's northern suburbs during my 2016 research in Córdoba, and for sharing the publications on the excavations associated with Rusafa. See Alberto León and Juan Fco. Murillo, "Advances in Research on Islamic Cordoba," Journal of Islamic Archaeology *1*, no. 1 (August 18, 2014): 15–16; J. F. Murillo et al., "La almunia y el arrabal de al-Rusāfa, en el Yanib al-Garbi de Madinat Qurtuba," in El anfiteatro romano de Córdoba y su entorno urbano: análisis arqueológico (ss. I–XIII d.C.), *ed.* Desiderio Vaquerizo and Juan F. Murillo, *Arqueología cordobesa, vol. 19* (Universidad de Córdoba, 2011), 565–614; Juan F. Murillo Redondo, "La Almunia de Al-Rusāfa en Córdoba," Madrider Mitteilungen, *des Deutschen Archäologischen Instituts. Abteilung Madrid 50* (2009): 449–568.
20. See Anderson, *The Islamic Villa*, 16–18, 115–16.
21. León and Murillo, "Advances in Research on Islamic Cordoba," 15–16.
22. I would like to thank Rafael Blanco of the University of Córdoba for generously showing me archaeological remains of walls, houses, water infrastructure, etc., unearthed during emergency excavations in Córdoba's northern suburban area during a 2016 research trip.
23. I would like to thank Frank Robasky of the MIT Lincoln Laboratory for kindly sharing these observations and insights into the connection between topography and wind currents relative to aviation at an early stage in the Medieval "First in Flight" project.
24. Research on thermals and flight of the mid-twentieth century may have first led to this conclusion. See M.A.R. Khan, "A Note on Ibn Firnās's Successful Attempt at Soaring Flight," Islamic Culture *21* (1947): 404–5.
25. In the Foreword to the World Meteorological Organization's technical handbook, the secretary-general of the organization pointed out that the pilot who successfully made an emergency landing in the Hudson River was able to do so thanks to his background as an experienced glider pilot; Weather Forecasting for Soaring Flight (Geneva: World Meteorological Organization, 2009).
26. Anderson, *The Islamic Villa*, 187.
27. R. Blachère and I. Goldziher, "Āla," in Encyclopaedia of Islam, 2nd ed., ed. P. Bearman et al.
28. Ibn Shākir and Donald Hill, *The Book of Ingenious Devices (Kitāb Al-ḥiyal)*; Hill, "The Banu Musa and Their Book of Ingenious Devices," 39–76.
29. Susana Calvo Capilla, "The Reuse of Classical Antiquity in the Palace of Madinat Al-Zahra' and Its Role in the Construction of Caliphal Legitimacy," Muqarnas *31* (2014): 1–33; see also Susana Calvo Capilla, "Ciencia y 'adab' en el islam. Los espacios palatinos dedicados al saber," Anales de Historia del Arte *23*, no. Esp. (II) (July 25, 2013): 51–78, https://doi.org/10.5209/rev_ANHA.2013.v23.42831
30. Anderson, *The Islamic Villa*, 16ff.
31. Bos and Al-Kindī, *Scientific Weather Forecasting in the Middle Ages.*
32. My thanks to Jillian Troftgruben for sharing her observations on the pilot training process.
33. Burnett, "Weather Forecasting in the Arabic World," 201–10.
34. Dallal, chap. 2, "Beginnings and Beyond," in *Islam, Science, and the Challenge of History*; al-Khalili, chap. 5, "The House of Wisdom," in *Pathfinders: The Golden Age of Arabic Science.*
35. Qur'an 31:20, Pickthall translation.
36. Ovid, *Metamorphoses*, 441.
37. Milwright, *Islamic Arts and Crafts*, 29–39.
38. I would like to thank Stuart Sears for his observations on eagle versus vulture with regard to this text, which I have reproduced here; personal communication.
39. Alan Kemp and Ian Newton, "Hawks, Eagles, and Old World Vultures," in The New Encyclopedia of Birds (Oxford University Press, 2003). https://www-oxfordreference-com.ezproxy.is.ed.ac.uk/view/10.1093/acref/9780198525066.001.0001/acref-9780198525066-e-63

40. F. Viré, "Nasr," in Encyclopaedia of Islam, *2nd ed.*, consulted online on July 13, 2019, at http://dx.doi.org.ezproxy.is.ed.ac.uk/10.1163/1573-3912_islam_SIM_5834
41. The likely species could be the Griffon vulture (*Gyps fulvus*), or the bearded vulture, Egyptian vulture, or Cinereous vulture. See Ingrid Seibold and Andreas J. Helbig, "Evolutionary History of New and Old World Vultures Inferred from Nucleotide Sequences of the Mitochondrial Cytochrome *b* Gene," Philosophical Transactions: Biological Sciences *350*, no. 1332 (November 29, 1995): 163–78. One can observe Old World vultures in Spain today at the Observatorio de aves Mas de Bunyol. I would like to thank Dr. Gianluigi Rossi of the Royal School of Veterinary Studies at the University of Edinburgh for kindly advising and bringing these to my attention. Also see D.W. Snow and C.M. Perrins, 1998, The Birds of the Western Palearctic, Volume 1: Non-Passerines (Oxford: Oxford University Press; Global Raptor Information Network, 2015). Species account: Griffon Vulture *Gyps fulvus*. Available at http://www.globalraptors.org/grin/SpeciesResults.asp?specID=8264
42. Louis-Pierre Mouillard, L'empire de l'air; essai d'ornithologie applique l'aviation (Paris: G. Masson, 1881); David G. McCullough, The Wright Brothers, 1st Simon & Schuster hardcover ed. (New York: Simon & Schuster, 2015); Charles Harvard Gibbs-Smith, The Wright Brothers: Aviation Pioneers and Their Work, 1899–1911, 2nd ed. (London: Science Museum, 2002).
43. Ignác Goldziher, Abhandlungen zur arabischen Philologie (Leiden: Buchhandlung und Druckerei vormals EJ Brill, 1896), II:li–lii, cited in B. Heller and N.A. Stillmann, "Luḳmān," in Encyclopaedia of Islam, 2nd ed..
44. Ibid.
45. Dimitri Gutas, "Classical Arabic Wisdom Literature: Nature and Scope," Journal of the American Oriental Society *101*, no. 1 (January 1981): 49, https://doi.org/10.2307/602164
46. Qur'an 31:12, trans. Marmaduke Pickthall, The Meaning of the Glorious Koran, NAL Mentor Books, MS. 94 (New York: New American Library, 1953).
47. Gutas, "Classical Arabic Wisdom Literature," 58.
48. Viré, "Nasr."
49. I would like to thank my collaborators in the "Medieval First in Flight" project, which took a creative interdisciplinary exploration of this design challenge. The team consisted of myself; Jan Chambers, a theater set and costume designer; Laura Miller, a biologist/mathematician; and Julie Kimbell, a biomedical engineer. The aim was to produce imaginative interpretation and visualizations of a medieval flight garment and device, inspired by the account of Ibn Firnās's career and his experiment, to evoke the and visual and material culture of the caliphal age. Jan Chambers brought her creative sensibilities as a costume and set designer to the team's exploration of the ninth-century social, visual, and material contexts. Her sketchbook illustrates her responses to the design challenge, with her visual interpretations evolving over time in response to the team's collaborative research. The project is documented online: http://glairedanderson.com/medievalflight/
50. I would also like to thank Julia Galliker, whose observations informed what I have written here.
51. For recent discussions of silk in al-Andalus see David Jacoby, "The Production and Diffusion of Andalusi Silk and Silk Textiles, Mid-Eighth to Mid-Thirteenth Century," in The Chasuble of Thomas Becket. A Biography, ed. Avinoam Shalem (Chicago: 2017), 142–51, cited in Ana Cabrera Lafuente, "Textiles from the Museum of San Isidoro (León): New Evidence for Re-Evaluating Their Chronology and Provenance," Medieval Encounters: Jewish, Christian, and Muslim Culture in Confluence and Dialogue *25*, nos. 1–2 (2019): 88, https://doi.org/10.1163/15700674-12340039
52. Y.K. Stillman, N.A. Stillmann, and T. Majda, "Libās," in *Encyclopaedia of Islam*, 2nd ed.; N. Steensgaard et al., eds., "Ḥarīr," in *Encyclopaedia of Islam*, 2nd ed.; Goitein, "Clothing and Jewelry, *A Mediterranean Society*, 150–99.

53. See Julia Galliker, "Middle Byzantine Silk in Context: Integrating the Textual and Material Evidence" (PhD thesis, University of Birmingham, Centre for Byzantine, Ottoman and Modern Greek Studies, 2014), Appendix 4.2, "Varieties of Silk Found in Cairo Genizah Documents."
54. I would like to thank Jan Chambers and dramaturge Jules Odendahl-James, whose insights into materials and factors that may have informed approaches to making a medieval flight device were key to what I have written here.
55. See Ḥasan and Hill, *Islamic Technology*, 214, where the authors note that windmills were used in areas with favorable winds, such as Sistan and Khurasan in Iran.
56. Miquel Forcada, "Calendar of Córdoba," in *Encyclopaedia of Islam, THREE*; *Le Calendrier de Cordoue*, Nouv. éd., accompagnée d'une traduction française annotée par Ch. Pellat., vol. 1, Medieval Iberian Peninsula. Texts and Studies, vol. 1 (Leiden: Brill, 1961).
57. Hallion, *Taking Flight*, 10–11.
58. Ibid., 11.
59. Harry J. Magoulias, trans., O City of Byzantium: Annals of Niketas Choniatēs (Detroit: Wayne State University Press, 1984), 68. Also discussed in White Jr., "Eilmer of Malmesbury," 98–99.
60. After J.A Giles, William of Malmesbury's Chronicle of the Kings of England (n.p.: Henry G. Bohn, 1847), cited in White Jr., "Eilmer of Malmesbury," 98.
61. Hallion, *Taking Flight*, 16–17.

Epilogue

1. George Saliba, *Islamic Science and the Making of the European Renaissance* (Cambridge, Mass.: MIT Press, 2007). Anna Contadini, "Sharing a Taste? Material Culture and Intellectual Curiosity around the Mediterranean from the 11th to the 16th Century," in *The Renaissance and the Ottoman World*, ed. Anna Contadini and Claire Norton (Farnham, U.K.: Ashgate, 2013), 23–62.
2. On these persistent historiographic issues, and recent scholarly attempts to "reorient" the Renaissance, see Flood and Necipoğlu, *"Frameworks of Islamic Art and Architectural History: Concepts, Approaches, and Historiographies,"* pp. 13–14.
3. George Saliba, "A Sixteenth-Century Drawing of an Astrolabe Made by Khafīf Ghulām ʿAlī b.ʿĪsā (c. 850 AD)," pp. 221–222.
4. Colin Rowe, *Italian Architecture of the 16th Century* (New York: Princeton Architectural Press, 2002); Ludwig H. (Ludwig Heinrich) Heydenreich, *Architecture in Italy, 1400–1500*, Yale University Press Pelican History of Art (New Haven, Conn.: Yale University Press, 1996); Christoph Luitpold Frommel and Nicholas Adams, *The Architectural Drawings of Antonio da Sangallo the Younger and His Circle* (New York: Architectural History Foundation; MIT Press, 1994).
5. Meredith J. Gill, "Review of *Review of The Architectural Drawings of Antonio da Sangallo the Younger and His Circle*, by Nicholas Adams," *Renaissance Quarterly 56*, no. 1 (2003): p. 176. https://doi.org/10.2307/1262273
6. On attempts to integrate early modern Islamic art into art history's Eurocentric paradigm, see Finbarr Barry Flood and Gulru Necipoglu, "Frameworks of Islamic Art and Architectural History: Concepts, Approaches, and Historiographies," in *A Companion to Islamic Art and Architecture: From the Prophet to the Mongols*, vol. 1 (Bognor Regis, U.K.: John Wiley & Sons, 2017), pp. 13–15.
7. See Saliba, *Islamic Science and the Making of the European Renaissance*, p. 222, in which he notes, "the scientifically oriented men of the Renaissance, especially during the sixteenth century, must have thought very highly of all scientific things coming to them from

the Islamic world, even instruments that were made centuries earlier." Anna Contadini mentions the fourteenth-century North African astrolabe with Arabic and Latin inscriptions (Florence, Museo di Storia della Scienza, inv. no. 1109) in "Sharing a Taste? Material Culture and Intellectual Curiosity around the Mediterranean from the 11th to the 16th Century," p. 25.

8. Saliba, *Islamic Science and the Making of the European Renaissance*, pp. 226–30; Sonja Brentjes, *Travellers from Europe in the Ottoman and Safavid Empires, 16th–17th Centuries: Seeking, Transforming, Discarding Knowledge*, Collected Studies; CS961 (Farnham, U.K.; Burlington, Vt.: Ashgate/Variorum, 2010).
9. Saliba, *Islamic Science and the Making of the European Renaissance*, p. 223; Sonja Brentjes and Jürgen Renn, *Globalization of Knowledge in the Post-Antique Mediterranean, 700–1500* (Burlington, Vt.: Ashgate Publishing Company, 2016); Contadini, "Sharing a Taste? Material Culture and Intellectual Curiosity around the Mediterranean from the 11th to the 16th Century," pp. 24–27.
10. My thanks to Genevieve Warwick for the observation.
11. For an analysis of the circulation of art and luxury objects between Europe and the Islamic lands see Lisa Jardine, *Global Interests: Renaissance Art between East and West, Picturing History* (Ithaca, N.Y.: Cornell University Press, 2000).
12. On the Florentine Academy see Zygmunt Waźbiński, *L'Accademia medicea del disegno a Firenze nel Cinquecento: idea e istituzione*, Studi (Accademia toscana di scienze e lettere La Colombaria) 84 (Firenze: LSOlschki, 1987); Karen-edis Barzman, *The Florentine Academy and the Early Modern State: The Discipline of Disegno* (Cambridge; New York: Cambridge University Press, 2000).
13. On the significance of mathematics to Florentine Renaissance design practices see Filippo Camerota, "The Medici Collections," in *Museo Galileo: Masterpieces of Science*, 1. ed. (Firenze: Giunti, 2010), p. 71.
14. Camerota, "The Medici Collections," pp. 72–73.
15. Filippo Camerota and Mara Miniati, *I Medici e le scienze: strumenti e macchine nelle collezioni granducali* (Firenze: Giunti: Firenze musei, 2008). Also see *European Collections of Scientific Instruments, 1550–1750*, ed. Stephen Johnston, Mara Miniati, and Alison D. Morrison-Low, History of Science and Medicine Library, vol. 10 (Leiden: Brill, 2009).
16. Mark Rosen, "A New Chronology of the Construction and Restoration of the Medici Guardaroba in the Palazzo Vecchio, Florence," *Mitteilungen Des Kunsthistorischen Institutes in Florenz* 53, nos. 2/3 (2009): 285–308, http://www.jstor.org/stable/41229903

    The project is described by Giorgio Vasari, *Le opere di Giorgio Vasari*, vol. VII (Firenze: Sansoni, 1973), 633–636), as discussed in Camerota, "The Medici Collections," pp. 73–74.
17. Ibid., 81n11.
18. Ibid., p. 74.
19. Strano, "The Instruments of Egnazio Danti," pp. 82–83.
20. On these figures and European Arabists and orientalists and their pursuit of science from Islamic lands see Saliba, *Islamic Science and the Making of the European Renaissance*, pp. 226–30.
21. See Robert Morrison, "A Scholarly Intermediary between the Ottoman Empire and Renaissance Europe," *Isis* 105, no. 1 (March 1, 2014): 32–57, https://doi.org/10.1086/675550; Robert Morrison, "Religion and Science in the Eastern Mediterranean," *Isis* 107, no. 3 (September 20, 2016): 579–82, https://doi.org/10.1086/688435
22. Nicola Courtright, *The Papacy and the Art of Reform in Sixteenth-Century Rome: Gregory XIII's Tower of the Winds in the Vatican*, Monuments of Papal Rome (Cambridge; New York: Cambridge University Press, 2003). My thanks to Carol Richardson for bringing this to my attention.

23. I would like to thank Mary Pardo for drawing my attention to these sculptures and the Florence connections. Mariella Carlotti and Giorgio Pref Vittadini, *Il lavoro e l'ideale: il ciclo delle formelle del Campanile di Giotto*, 2008; Emma Simi Varanelli, *Artisti e dottori nel Medioevo: il campanile di Firenze e la rivalutazione delle "arti belle,"* Pensiero italiano (Rome, Italy), vol. 3 (Roma: Istituto poligrafico e zecca dello stato, Libreria dello stato, 1995); Marvin Trachtenberg, *The Campanile of Florence Cathedral: "Giotto's Tower."* (New York: University Press, 1971).
24. On the proposal that Brunelleschi derived the technique of perspective from the principles of stereographic projection governing the use of the astrolabe see Marco Jaff, "From the Vault of the Heavens: A Hypothesis Regarding Filippo Brunelleschi's Invention of Linear Perspective and the Costruzione Legittima, *Nexus Network Journal* 5, no. 1 (2003): pp. 49–63.
25. Antonio Manetti, *The Life of Brunelleschi* (University Park: Pennsylvania State University Press, 1970); Howard Saalman, *Filippo Brunelleschi: The Buildings* (University Park: Pennsylvania State University Press, 1993).
26. Jaff, "From the Vault of the Heavens," pp. 51–55.
27. I would like to thank Andrew Janiak for his suggestions as I considered this question with respect to early modern European natural philosophers and instrumentation. For a modern case study, see Seb Falk, "The Scholar as Craftsman: Derek de Solla Price and the Reconstruction of a Medieval Instrument," *Notes and Records of the Royal Society of London* 68, no. 2 (2014): 111–34, https://doi.org/10.1098/rsnr.2013.0062
28. On the microscope see Catherine Wilson, *The Invisible World: Early Modern Philosophy and the Invention of the Microscope*, Studies in Intellectual History and the History of Philosophy (Princeton, N.J.: Princeton University Press, 1995). My thanks to Andrew Janiak for drawing my attention to this work.
29. R.G.W. Anderson et al., *Making Instruments Count: Essays on Historical Scientific Instruments Presented to Gerard L'Estrange Turner* (Aldershot, U.K.: Variorum, 1993).
30. Cited in Andrew Janiak, *Newton*. Chichester, U.K.; Malden, Mass.: Wiley Blackwell, 2015, p. 7.
31. For instance, Newton's Query 29. See Isaac Newton, *Philosophical Writings*, ed. Andrew Janiak, rev. ed. Cambridge; New York: Cambridge University Press, 2014, pp. 176–78.
32. As evident in the *Anonymous Compendium* discussed by Necipoğlu, "Ornamental Geometries," 11–78.

Bibliography

Abel, Armand. "La place des sciences occultes dans la décadence." In *Classicisme et déclin culturel dans l'histoire de l'Islam: actes du symposium international d'histoire de la civilisation musulmane, Bordeaux . . . 1956. Organisé par R. Brunschvig et G.E. von Grunebaum avec . . . [autres]*, edited by Robert Brunschvig, 291–318. Paris: Besson-Chantemerle, 1957.

Acedo del Olmo, Antonio R. *Abbas Ibn Firnas: El sabio de al-Andalus*. Granada: El Legado Andalusi, 2016.

Ackermann, Silke. "*Introduction Hic Sunt Dracones*—Astrolabe Research Revisited." *Medieval Encounters* 23, no. 1–5 (September 22, 2017): 3–7. https://doi.org/10.1163/15700674-12342241

Ackermann, Silke. "Gerard Turner Memorial Lecture: In the Service of Religion? 'Islamic Science' in the Museum." *Bulletin of the Scientific Instrument Society* 139 (2018): 2–6.

Aillet, Cyrille. "La 'Fitna,' Pierre de Touche du Califat de Cordoue (IIIe/IXe–IVe/Xe siècle)." *Médiévales* 60, no. 60 (2011): 67–83.

Alaoui, Brahim. *L'âge d'or des sciences arabes: exposition présentée à l'Institut du monde arabe, Paris, 25 octobre 2005–19 mars 2006*. 1er éd. Arles; Paris: Actes sud; Institut du Monde Arabe, 2005.

Al-Hassani, Salim, Rabah Saoud, and Elizabeth Woodcock, eds. *1001 Inventions: Muslim Heritage in Our World*. 2nd ed. Manchester, U.K.: Foundation for Science Technology and Civilisation, 2007.

Alvarez Millán, Cristina, and Claudia Heide. *Pascual de Gayangos: A Nineteenth-Century Spanish Arabist*. Edinburgh: Edinburgh University Press, 2008.

Andalusī, Ṣā'id. *Science in the Medieval World: Book of the Categories of Nations*. Translated by Alok Kumar and Sema'an I. Salem. 1st ed. Austin: University of Texas, 1991.

Andalusī, Ṣā'id ibn Aḥmad. *Kitāb Ṭabaqāt al-umam*. Edited by Louis Cheikho. Translated by Régis Blachère. Manshūrāt Mahad Tārīkh al-Ulūm al-Arabīyah wa-al-Islāmīyah. Falsafah al-Islāmīyah, vol. 1. Frankfurt am Main: Institute for the History of Arabic-Islamic Science at the Johann Wolfgang Goethe University, 1999.

Anderson, Benjamin. *Cosmos and Community in Early Medieval Art*. New Haven, Conn.: Yale University Press, 2017.

Anderson, Glaire. *A Medieval "First in Flight": Visualizing Ibn Firnas & the Art of Early Aviation*. Accessed November 22, 2021. https://glairedanderson.com/medievalflight/

Anderson, Glaire. "Remembering 'Abbas Ibn Firnas: How a Medieval Polymath's Career Suggests a More Diverse History of Science, Technology, and Visual Culture." *Spain-North Africa Project Bulletin* Summer (July 2, 2021). Accessed June 2, 2023.
http://www.spainnorthafricaproject.org/bulletin/2021/7/1/ibn-firnas-storymap.

Anderson, Glaire D. "A Mother's Gift? Astrology and the Pyxis of al-Mughīra." *Journal of Medieval History* 42, no. 1 (January 1, 2016): 107–30. https://doi.org/10.1080/03044181.2015.1103777

Anderson, Glaire. *The Islamic Villa in Early Medieval Iberia: Architecture and Court Culture in Umayyad Córdoba*. Farnham, U.K.: Ashgate, 2013.

Anderson, Glaire. "Concubines, Eunuchs, and Patronage in Early Islamic Córdoba." In *Reassessing the Roles of Women as "Makers" of Medieval Art and Architecture*, edited by Therese Martin, 633–69. Leiden: Brill, 2012.

Anderson, Glaire D. "Islamic Spaces and Diplomacy in Constantinople (Tenth to Thirteenth Centuries C.E.)." *Medieval Encounters: Jewish, Christian and Muslim Culture in Confluence and Dialogue* 15, no. 1 (2009): 86–113.

Anderson, Glaire D., Corisande Fenwick, and Mariam Rosser-Owen, eds. *The Aghlabids and Their Neighbours: Art and Material Culture in Ninth-Century North Africa*. Leiden: Brill, 2017.

Anderson, Glaire D., and Jennifer Pruitt. "The Three Caliphates, a Comparative Approach." In *A Companion to Islamic Art and Architecture*, edited by Finbarr Barry Flood and Gulru Necipoglu, 223–49. Malden, Mass.: Blackwell Pub., 2017.

Anderson, Glaire, and Mariam Rosser-Owen. "Great Ladies and Noble Daughters: Ivories and Women in the Umayyad Court at Córdoba." In *Pearls on a String: Art in the Age of Great Islamic Empires*, edited by Amy Landau, 28–51. University of Washington Press, 2015.

Anonymous. "The World of Islam Festival." *British Society for Middle Eastern Studies. Bulletin* 1, no. 1 (January 1, 1974): 33–34. https://doi.org/10.1080/13530197408705107

Anonymous. "A Prophet of Aviation." *The Literary Digest*, April 27, 1912, 879.

Aragón Huerta, M. "Ibn Firnas, Abbas." In *Biblioteca de al-Andalus*, edited by Jorge Lirola Delgado and José Miguel Puerta Vílchez, 168–72. Vol. 3: De Ibn al-Dabbag a Ibn Kurz (790). Almería, Spain: Fundación Ibn Tufayl de Estudios Árabes, 2004.

Arīb ibn Saʿd (-979 or 980), and Reinhart Pieter Anne Dozy (1820–1883), ed. *Le Calendrier de Cordoue*. Nouv. éd., Accompagnée d'une traduction française annotée par Ch. Pellat. Medieval Iberian Peninsula. Texts and Studies, vol. 1. Leiden: Brill, 1961.

Arnold, Felix. "Mathematics and the Islamic Architecture of Córdoba." *Arts* 7, no. 3 (2018): 35, -5. https://doi.org/10.3390/arts7030035.

Arnold, Felix. *Islamic Palace Architecture in the Western Mediterranean: A History*. New York: Oxford University Press, 2017.

Arnold, Felix, Alberto Canto García, and Antonio Vallejo Triano. "Das islamische Landgut ar-Rumanīya bei Córdoba. Vorbericht einer Bauaufnahme." *Madrider Mitteilungen* 50 (2009): 503–23, 569–70.

Arnold, Felix, Alberto Canto García, and Antonio Vallejo Triano. "La Almunia de al-Rummaniyya. Resultados de una Documentación Arquitectónica." *Cuadernos de Madinat Al-Zahra* 6 (2008): 181–204.

Arnold, Felix, Alberto Canto García, Antonio Vallejo Triano, and Glaire D. Anderson. *Munyat ar-Rummaniya: ein islamischer Landsitz bei Córdoba. Teil 1: Palastanlagen*. Reichert, 2015. https://search.proquest.com/indexislamicus/docview/1914467524/72614B67BF644693PQ/9

Ashtor, E. "Essai sur les Prix et les Salaires dans l'empire Califien." *Rivista Degli Studi Orientali* 36 (1961): 19–69. http://www.jstor.org/stable/41879365.

Baia, A. *Leonora di Toledo: Duchessa di Firenze e Siena*. Todi, Italy: 1907.

Barceló, Carmen, and Ana Labarta. "Ocho relojes de sol hispano-musulmanes." *Al-Qantara: Revista de Estudios Árabes; Madrid* 9, no. 2 (January 1, 1988): 231–47.

Barzman, Karen-edis. *The Florentine Academy and the Early Modern State: The Discipline of Disegno*. Cambridge; New York: Cambridge University Press, 2000.

Beckmann, Johann, William Francis, J.W. (John William) Griffith, and William Johnston. *A History of Inventions, Discoveries, and Origins*. 4th ed. Carefully revised and enlarged by William Francis and J.W. Griffith. London: H.G. Bohn, 1846.

Beer, Arthur. "The Astronomical Significance of the Zodiac of the Qusayr ʿAmra." In *Early Muslim Architecture*, 2nd ed., vol. 1, 289–303. Oxford: Clarendon Press, 1932.

Behrens-Abouseif, Doris. *Islamic Architecture in Cairo: An Introduction*. Cairo: The American University in Cairo Press, 1989.

Bennison, Amira. *The Great Caliphs: The Golden Age of the ʿAbbasidEmpire*. London: I. B. Tauris, 2009.

Berlekamp, Persis. "Visible Art, Invisible Knowledge." *International Journal of Middle East Studies* 45, no. 3 (August 2013): 563–65. https://doi.org/10.1017/S0020743813000482

Bisaha, Nancy. *Creating East and West: Renaissance Humanists and the Ottoman Turks*. Philadelphia: University of Pennsylvania Press, Inc., 2006.

Blachère, R., and Goldziher, I. "Āla." In *Encyclopaedia of Islam*, 2nd ed., edited by P. Bearman, Th. Bianquis, C.E. Bosworth, E. van Donzel, and W.P. Heinrichs. Leiden, Brill.

Blair, Sheila S. "What the Inscriptions Tell Us: Text and Message on the Ivories from al-Andalus." *Journal of the David Collection* 2, no. 1 (2005): 74–99.

Bongianino, Umberto. "Islamic Calligraphy at a Standstill." *Art History* 42, no. 1 (2019): 20–26.

Bongianino, Umberto. "Some Remarks on the Origin of Round Quranic Scripts in al-Andalus (5th/11th–6th/12th Centuries)." *Al-Qantara: Revista de Estudios Arabes* 38, no. 2 (2018): 153–187. https://doi.org/10.3989/alqantara.2017.006

Bongianino, Umberto. "The Origin and Development of Maghribī Round Scripts: Arabic Palaeography in the Islamic West (4th/10th–6th/12th Centuries)." University of Oxford, 2017.

Bongianino, Umberto. "Quelques Remarques sur l'origine des Écritures Coraniques Arrondies en al-Andalus (Ve/XIe–VIe/XIIe Siècles)." *Al-Qanṭara* 38, no. 2 (2017): 153. https://doi.org/10.3989/alqantara.2017.006

Borrás Gualis, Gonzalo M., and Bernabé Cabañero Subiza. *La Aljafería y el arte del Islam Occidental en el siglo XI. Actas del Seminario Internacional celebrado en Zaragoza los días 1, 2 y 3 de diciembre de 2004. Coords. Gonzalo M. Borrás Gualis, Bernabé Caballero Subiza.* Institución "Fernando el Católico," 2012.

Bos, C., Burnett, and Al-Kindi. *Scientific Weather Forecasting in the Middle Ages.* London: Kegan Paul International / Routledge, 2000.

Bouras-Vallianatos, Petros. "Cross-Cultural Transfer of Medical Knowledge in the Medieval Mediterranean: The Introduction and Dissemination of Sugar-Based Potions from the Islamic World to Byzantium." *Speculum* 96, no. 4 (October 1, 2021): 963–1008. https://doi.org/10.1086/715838.

Brann, Ross. "The Moors?" *Medieval Encounters: Jewish, Christian and Muslim Culture in Confluence and Dialogue* 15, nos. ii–iv (2009): 307–18.

Brentjes, Sonja. *Travellers from Europe in the Ottoman and Safavid Empires, 16th–17th Centuries: Seeking, Transforming, Discarding Knowledge.* Collected Studies Series CS961. Farnham, U.K.: Ashgate/Variorum, 2010.

Brentjes, Sonja. "What Could It Mean to Contextualize the Sciences in Islamic Societies of the Past?" In *Les Sciences dans les Sociétés Islamiques*, 15–42. Casablanca: Fondation du Roi Abdul-Aziz, 2007.

Brentjes, Sonja. "On the Location of the Ancient or 'rational' Sciences in Muslim Educational Landscapes (AH 500-1100)." *Bulletin of the Royal Institute for Inter-Faith Studies* 4, no. i (2002): 47–71.

Brentjes, Sonja, Taner Edis, and Lutz Richter-Bernburg. *1001 Distortions: How (Not) to Narrate History of Science, Medicine, and Technology in Non-Western Cultures.* Bibliotheca Academica. Reihe Orientalistik, Bd. 25. Würzburg, Germany: Ergon Verlag, 2016.

Brentjes, Sonja, and Robert G. Morrison. "The Sciences in Islamic Societies (750–1800)." In *Islamic Cultures and Societies to the End of the Eighteenth Century*, edited by Robert Irwin, 564–639, vol. 4. The New Cambridge History of Islam. Cambridge: Cambridge University Press.

Brentjes, Sonja, and Jürgen Renn. *Globalization of Knowledge in the Post-Antique Mediterranean, 700–1500.* Burlington, Vt.: Ashgate Publishing Company, 2016.

Brett, Gerard. "The Automata in the Byzantine 'Throne of Solomon.'" *Speculum* 29, no. 3 (1954): 477–87.

Brockelmann, C. "Ibn ʿAbd Rabbih." In *Encyclopaedia of Islam*, 2nd ed.

Brown, Judith C., Giovanna Benadusi, Monica Chojnacka, Natalie Tomas, and Ont. Centre for Reformation and Renaissance Studies Victoria University, Toronto. *Medici Women: The Making of a Dynasty in Grand Ducal Tuscany.* Essays and Studies (Victoria University, Toronto, Ont.). Centre for Reformation and Renaissance Studies) 36. Toronto: Centre for Reformation and Renaissance Studies, 2015.

Brunet, J-P., R. Nadal, and C. Vibert-Guigue. "The Fresco of the Cupola of Qusayr ʿAmra." *Centaurus* 40 (1998): 97–123.

Burnett, Charles. "Weather Forecasting in the Arabic World." In *Magic and Divination in Early Islam*, edited by Emilie Savage-Smith, 201–10. London; New York: Ashgate, 2004.

Bush, Olga. *Reframing the Alhambra: Architecture, Poetry, Textiles and Court Ceremonial.* Edinburgh Studies in Islamic Art. Edinburgh: Edinburgh University Press, 2018.

Bush, Olga. "Poetic Inscriptions and Gift Exchange in the Medieval Islamicate World." *Gesta* 56, no. 2 (2017): 179–97. https://doi.org/10.1086/692802

Bush, Olga. "Prosopopeia: Performing the Reciprocal Gaze." *Muqarnas Online* 32, no. 1 (2015): 13–19. https://doi.org/10.1163/22118993-00321P03

Cabañero Subiza, Bernabé. *El Salón Dorado de la Aljafería: ensayo de reconstitución formal e interpretación simbólica*. 1a ed. Conocer Alandalús, vol. 1. Zaragoza, Spain: Instituto de Estudios Islámicos y del Oriente Próximo, 2004.

Cabrera Lafuente, Ana. "Textiles from the Museum of San Isidoro (León): New Evidence for Re-Evaluating Their Chronology and Provenance." *Medieval Encounters: Jewish, Christian, and Muslim Culture in Confluence and Dialogue* 25, nos. 1–2 (2019): 59–95. https://doi.org/10.1163/15700674-12340039

Calvo Capilla, Susana. "The Visual Construction of the Umayyad Caliphate in al-Andalus through the Great Mosque of Cordoba." *Arts* 7, no. 3 (2018): 36. https://doi.org/10.3390/arts7030036

Calvo Capilla, Susana. "The Reuse of Classical Antiquity in the Palace of Madinat al-Zahra and Its Role in the Construction of Caliphal Legitimacy." *Muqarnas* 31 (2014): 1–33.

Calvo Capillo, Susana "Madinat al-Zahra" y la observación del tiempo: el renacer de la Antigüedad Clásica en la Córdoba del siglo X." *Anales de Historia del Arte* 22 (2012): 131–60.

Camerota, Filippo. "The Medici Collections." In *Museo Galileo: Masterpieces of Science*, 1st ed., 71–81. Firenze: Giunti, 2010.

Camerota, Filippo. *Museo Galileo: A Guide to the Treasures of the Collection*. Firenze: Giunti, 2010.

Camerota, Filippo, and Mara Miniati. *I Medici e le scienze: strumenti e macchine nelle collezioni granducali*. Firenze: Giunti, Firenze Musei, 2008.

Carandell, Joan. "Dos cuadrantes solares andalusíes de Medina Azara." *Al-Qantara; Madrid* 10, no. 2 (January 1, 1989): 329–42.

Cardoso, Elsa. "The Scenography of Power in al-Andalus and the ʿAbbasid and Byzantine Ceremonials: Christian Ambassadorial Receptions in the Court of Cordoba in a Comparative Perspective." *Medieval Encounters* 24, no. 4 (2018): 390–434. https://doi.org/10.1163/15700674-12340007

Carey, Moya. "Al-Sufi and Son: Ibn al-Sufi"s Poem on the Stars and Its Prose Parent." *Muqarnas* 26 (January 1, 2009): 181–204. http://www.jstor.org/stable/27811140

Carey, Moya. "The Gold and Silver Lining: Shams al-Din Muhammad b. Mu"ayyad al-ʿUrdi's Inlaid Celestial Globe (c. AD 1288) from the Ilkhanid Observatory at Maragha." *Iran* 47 (2009): 97–108. http://www.jstor.org/stable/25651466

Carey, Moya Catherine. "Painting the Stars in a Century of Change: A Thirteenth-Century Copy of al-Sụfi"s Treatise on the Fixed Stars: British Library Or. 5323." PhD thesis, School of Oriental and African Studies, University of London, 2001.

Carlotti, Mariella, and Giorgio Pref Vittadini. *Il lavoro e l'ideale: il ciclo delle formelle del Campanile di Giotto*, 2008.

Choniates, Nicetas, and Harry J. Magoulias. *O City of Byzantium: Annals of Niketas Choniatēs*. Detroit, Mich.: Wayne State University Press, 1984.

Contadini, Anna, "Wondrous Animals: Zoomorphic Metal Figures from al-Andalus." In *Löwe, Wölfin, Greif/ Object Studies in Art History*, vol. 4, edited by Joanna Olchawa, 213–36. 2020.

Contadini, Anna. "Sharing a Taste? Material Culture and Intellectual Curiosity around the Mediterranean from the 11th to the 16th Century." In *The Renaissance and the Ottoman World*, edited by Anna Contadini and Claire Norton, 23–62. Farnham, U.K.: Ashgate, 2013.

Contadini, Anna, and Claire Norton. *The Renaissance and the Ottoman World*. Farnham, Surrey, U.K.; Burlington, Vt.: Ashgate, 2013.

Contessa, Andreina. "A Geography of Learning: The World of the Presumed Map of Theodulphe of Orleans and Its Mid-Eleventh-Century Catalan Author." In *Miscellanea Bibliothecae Apostolicae Vaticanae*, 55–110, vol. XVIII. Città del Vaticano: Biblioteca Apostolica Vaticana, 2011.

Courtright, Nicola. *The Papacy and the Art of Reform in Sixteenth-Century Rome: Gregory XIII's Tower of the Winds in the Vatican*. Monuments of Papal Rome. Cambridge; New York: Cambridge University Press, 2003.

Creswell, K.A.C., and Marguerite Gautier-van Berchem. *Early Muslim Architecture*. 2nd ed. New York: Hacker Art Books, 1979.

Cutler, Anthony. "Significant Gifts: Patterns of Exchange in Late Antique, Byzantine, and Early Islamic Diplomacy." *Journal of Medieval & Early Modern Studies* 38, no. 1 (Winter 2008): 79–101. https://doi.org/10.1215/10829636-2007-020

Dallal, Ahmad S. *Islam, Science, and the Challenge of History*. Terry Lectures. New Haven, Conn.: Yale University Press, 2010.

Delgado Valero, Clara. *Regreso a Tulaytula: Guía del Toledo Islámico: Siglos VIII–XI*. Conocer Castilla-La Mancha, vol. 23. Toledo, Spain: Junta de Comunidades de Castilla-La Mancha, 1999.

Dika, Alexandra. "Mahmoud Mukhtar: 'The First Sculptor from the Land of Sculpture.'" *World Art* 4, no. 1 (2014): 27–46. https://doi.org/10.1080/21500894.2014.893811

Dodds, Jerrilynn Denise, Abigail Krasner Balbale, and Maria Rosa Menocal. *The Arts of Intimacy: Christians, Jews, and Muslims in the Making of Castilian Culture*. New Haven, Conn.: Yale University Press, 2008.

Drpić, Ivan. *Epigram, Art, and Devotion in Later Byzantium*. Cambridge: Cambridge University Press, 2016.

Duda, Dorothea, Gisela Kircher, and Christian Ewert. *Islamische Funde in Balaguer und die Aljafería in Zaragoza*. Madrider Forschungen Bd. 7. Berlin: De Gruyter, 1971.

Dunlop, D.M., "D̲h̲u "l-Nūnids." In *Encyclopaedia of Islam*, 2nd ed. Consulted online on November 5, 2018, at http://dx.doi.org.ezproxy.is.ed.ac.uk/10.1163/1573-3912_islam_SIM_1833

Edis, Taner, and Sonja Brentjes. "A Golden Age of Harmony? Misrepresenting Science and History in 1001 Inventions." *Skeptical Inquirer*, 2012.

Ikhwān al-Ṣafā', Carmela Baffioni, and Godefroid de Callataÿ. *Epistles of the Brethren of Purity: Sciences of the Soul and Intellect*. Oxford: Oxford University Press, in association with the Institute of Ismaili Studies, 2015.

Fahd, T. "Nīrand̲j̲." In Encyclopaedia of Islam, 2nd ed. Consultedonline on April 18, 2019, at http://dx.doi.org.ezproxy.is.ed.ac.uk/10.1163/1573-3912_islam_SIM_5922 (first published online: 2012).

Fahd, T. *Sources orientales*, vol. vii. Paris: Editions de Seuil, 1966.

Falk, Seb. "The Scholar as Craftsman: Derek de Solla Price and the Reconstruction of a Medieval Instrument." *Notes and Records of the Royal Society of London* 68, no. 2 (2014): 111–34. https://doi.org/10.1098/rsnr.2013.0062

Ibn al-Faraḍī, 'Abd Allāh ibn Muḥammad. *Tārīkh al-'ulamā' wa-al-ruwāh lil-'ilm bi-al-Andalus*. Min turāth al-Andalus vol. 3. Cairo: Maktabat al-Khānjī, 1373.

Farghānī, al-, and Richard Lorch. *On the Astrolabe*. Boethius (Series), Bd. 52. Stuttgart: Steiner, 2005.

Fernández Fernández, Laura. "Astrolabes on Parchment: The Astrolabes Depicted in Alfonso X's *Libro del Saber de Astrologia* and Their Relationship to Contemporary Instruments." *Medieval Encounters* 23, no. 1–5 (September 22, 2017): 287–310. https://doi.org/10.1163/15700674-12342249

Fernández Puertas, Antonio. *Clepsidras y Relojes Musulmanes = Muslim Water Clocks and Mechanical Time Pieces*. Granada, Spain: Fundación El Legado Andalusí, 2010.

Ferry, Kathryn. "Owen Jones and the Alhambra Court at the Crystal Palace." In *Revisiting al-Andalus: Perspectives on the Material Culture of Islamic Iberia and Beyond*, edited by G.D. Anderson and M. Rosser-Owen, 227–45, vol. 34. Medieval and Early Modern Iberian World. Leiden: Brill, 2007.

Fierro, Maribel. *'Abd Al-Rahman III: The First Cordoban Caliph*. Oxford: Oneworld, 2005.

Fierro, Maribel. "Batinism in al-Andalus. Maslama b. Qasim al-Qurtubi (d. 353–964), Author of the Rutbat al-Hakim and the Ghayat al-Hakim (Picatrix)." *Studia Islamica* 2 (1996): 87–112.

"First Flights." *Saudi Aramco World*. February 1964, 8–9.

Flood, Finbarr Barry. *The Great Mosque of Damascus: Studies on the Makings of an Umayyad Visual Culture*. Leiden: Brill, 2001.

Flood, Finbarr Barry, and Gulru Necipoglu. "Frameworks of Islamic Art and Architectural History: Concepts, Approaches, and Historiographies." In *A Companion to Islamic Art and Architecture: From the Prophet to the Mongols*, 2–56, vol. 1. Bognor Regis, U.K.: John Wiley & Sons, 2017.

Forcada, Miquel, "Calendar of Córdoba." In *Encyclopaedia of Islam*, THREE, edited by Kate Fleet, Gudrun Krämer, Denis Matringe, John Nawas, and Everett Rowson. 2009.

Foulon, Brigitte. "L'impact de la fitna chez les lettrés andalous." *Médiévales* 60, no. 60 (2011): 45–66.

Frommel, Christoph Luitpold, Nicholas Adams, and Nicholas Adams. *The Architectural Drawings of Antonio da Sangallo the Younger and His Circle*. New York; Cambridge, Mass.: Architectural History Foundation; MIT Press, 1994.

Galliker, Julia. "Middle Byzantine Silk in Context: Integrating the Textual and Material Evidence." Unpublished PhD diss., University of Birmingham, Centre for Byzantine, Ottoman and Modern Greek Studies, 2014.

García Franco, Salvador. *Catálogo Crítico de Astrolabios Existentes en España*. Instituto Histórico de Marina: Madrid, 1945.

Geoffroy, E. "Shaykh." In *Encyclopaedia of Islam*, 2nd ed.

George, Alain. "Calligraphy, Colour and Light in the Blue Qur'an." *Journal of Qur'anic Studies* XI, no. 1 (2009): 75–125.

Gibbs-Smith, Charles Harvard. *The Wright Brothers: Aviation Pioneers and Their Work, 1899–1911*. 2nd ed. London: Science Museum, 2002.

Giles, J. A. *William of Malmesbury's Chronicle of the Kings of England*. N.p.: Henry G. Bohn, 1847.

Gill, Meredith J. Review of *Review of the Architectural Drawings of Antonio da Sangallo the Younger and His Circle*, by Nicholas Adams. *Renaissance Quarterly* 56, no. 1 (2003): 175–77. https://doi.org/10.2307/1262273

Gillispie, Charles Coulston, Frederic Lawrence Holmes, Charles Coulston Gillispie, and American Council of Learned Societies. *Dictionary of Scientific Biography*. New York: Scribner, 1970.

Gneuss, Helmut. *Handlist of Anglo-Saxon Manuscripts: A List of Manuscripts and Manuscript Fragments Written or Owned in England up to 1100*. Medieval & Renaissance Texts & Studies (Series), vol. 241. Tempe: Arizona Center for Medieval and Renaissance Studies, 2001.

Goitein, Shelomo Dov et al. *A Mediterranean Society: The Jewish Communities of the Arab World as Portrayed in the Documents of the Cairo Geniza*. Berkeley: University of California Press, 1967.

Goldziher, Ignác. *Abhandlungen zur arabischen Philologie*. Leiden: Buchhandlung und Druckerei vormals EJBrill, 1896.

Gonzalez, Valérie. *Beauty and Islam: Aesthetics in Islamic Art and Architecture*. London: I.B. Tauris, 2001.

Goodyear, Anne, and Margaret A. Weitekamp. *Analyzing Art and Aesthetics*. Washington, D.C.: Smithsonian Institution Scholarly Press, 2013.

Gottschalk, H.L., "Ibn al-Mudabbir." In *Encyclopaedia of Islam*, 2nd ed.

Grabar, Oleg. *The Formation of Islamic Art*. Rev. and enl. ed. New Haven, Conn.: Yale University Press, 1987.

Graves, Margaret S. *Arts of Allusion: Object, Ornament, and Architecture in Medieval Islam*. New York: Oxford University Press, 2018.

Grego Gómez, María. *Toledo en la época Omeya (ss. VIII–X)*. Toledo, Spain: Diputación Provincial de Toledo, 2007.

Grinel, Klas. "Framing Islam at the World of Islam Festival, London, 1976." *Journal of Muslims in Europe* 7, no. 1 (February 28, 2018): 73–93. https://doi.org/10.1163/22117954-12341365

Günel, Gökçe. "A Flying Man, a Scuttled Ship, and a Timekeeping Device: Reflections on Ibn Battuta Mall." *Public Culture* 23, no. 3 (65) (September 21, 2011): 541–49. https://doi.org/10.1215/08992363-1336408

Gunther, R., and William H. (William Hook) Morley. *The Astrolabes of the World: Based upon the Series of Instruments in the Lewis Evans Collection in the Old Ashmolean Museum at Oxford: With Notes on Astrolabes in the Collections of the British Museum, Science Museum, Sir J. Findlay, Mr. S. V. Hoffman, the Mensing Collection, and in Other Public and Private Collections*. London: Holland Press, 1976.

Günther, Sebastian, and Dorothee Pielow. *Die Geheimnisse der Oberen und der Unteren Welt: Magie im Islam Zwischen Glaube und Wissenschaft*. Boston: BRILL, 2018.

Guo, Li. *The Performing Arts in Medieval Islam: Shadow Play and Popular Poetry in Ibn Dāniyāl's Mamluk Cairo*. Islamic History and Civilization, vol. 93. Leiden: Brill, 2012.

Gutas, Dimitri. *Greek Thought, Arabic Culture: The Graeco-Arabic Translation Movement in Baghdad and Early 'Abbāsid Society (2nd–4th/8th–10th Centuries)*. London; New York: Routledge, 1998.

Gutas, Dimitri. "Classical Arabic Wisdom Literature: Nature and Scope." *Journal of the American Oriental Society* 101, no. 1 (January 1981): 49–86. https://doi.org/10.2307/602164

Gutas, Dimitri, and Kevin van Bladel. "Bayt Al-Ḥikma." In *Encyclopaedia of Islam, THREE*. 2009.

Hallion, Richard. *Taking Flight: Inventing the Aerial Age from Antiquity through the First World War*. New York: Oxford University Press, 2003.

Hämeen-Anttila, Jaako. "Ṣāʿid al-Andalusī, His System of Nations and the Progress of Science - Brill Bibliographies." *Zeitschrift für Geschichte der Arabisch-Islamischen Wissenschaften / Majallat Tārīkh al-'Ulūm al-'Arabīyah Wa "l-Islāmīyah* 19 (2012): 1–34.

Harvey, L.P. *Ibn Battuta*. Makers of Islamic Civilization. London; New York: IBTauris/Oxford Centre for Islamic Studies; distributed in the USA by Palgrave Macmillan, 2007.

Ḥasan, Aḥmad, and Donald Routledge Hill. *Islamic Technology: An Illustrated History*. New York: Cambridge University Press, 1986.

Heller, B., and Stillmann, N.A., "Luḳmān." In *Encyclopaedia of Islam*, 2nd ed.

Hernández Pérez, Azucena. *Astrolabios en al-Andalus y los reinos medievales hispanos*. Colección Arte y contextos, vol. 3. Madrid: Ediciones de la Ergástula, 2018.

Hernández Pérez, Azucena. *Catálogo razonado de los astrolabios de la España medieval*. Madrid: La Ergástula, 2018. http://laergastula.com/producto/catalogo-razonado-de-los-astrolabios-de-la-espana-medieval/

Hernández Pérez, Azucena. "Arte y ciencia en al-Andalus: el astrolabio nazarí de Alcalá la Real." *Boletín del Instituto de Estudios Giennenses*, no. 215 (2017): 259–84.

Hernández Pérez, Azucena. "Astrolabios Andalusíes e Hispanos: De la Precisión a la Suntuosidad*/Andalusi and Hispanic Astrolabes: From Precision to Sumptuousness." Universidad Complutense de Madrid, 2017.

Hernández, Azucena. "Astrolabes for the King: The Astrolabe of Petrus Raimundi of Barcelona." *Medieval Encounters* 23, nos. 1–5 (September 22, 2017): 421–43. https://doi.org/10.1163/15700674-12342254

Hernández Pérez, Azucena. "El Dragón en el Astrolabio." *Revista Digital de Iconografía Medieval* 7, no. 13 (2015): 19–31.

Hernández Pérez, Azucena. "Astrolabios andalusíes e hispanos: de la precisión a la suntuosidad." Special issue, *Anales de historia del arte* 24 (2014).

Hernando Sánchez, Carlos José. *Castilla y Nápoles en el siglo XVI: el virrey Pedro de Toledo: linaje, estado y cultura (1532–1553)*. Colección de estudios de historia. Valladolid, Spain: Junta de Castilla y León, Consejería de Cultura y Turismo, 1994.

Hill, Donald. "Andalusian Technology." In *Studies in Medieval Islamic Technology: From Philo to al-Jazarī, from Alexandria to Diyār Bakr*, edited by David A. King, XVIII/1–16. Aldershot, U.K.: Ashgate, 1998.

Hill, Donald. "Arabic Mechanical Engineering." In *Studies in Medieval Islamic Technology: From Philo to al-Jazarī, from Alexandria to Diyār Bakr*, edited by David A. King, V:167–86. Aldershot, U.K.; Brookfield, Vt.: Ashgate, 1998.

Hill, Donald. "The Banu Musa and Their Book of Ingenious Devices." In *Studies in Medieval Islamic Technology: From Philo to al-Jazarī, from Alexandria to Diyār Bakr*, edited by David A. King, XII: 39–76. Aldershot, U.K.; Brookfield, Vt.: Ashgate, 1998.

Hill, Donald R. "Al-Bīrūnī's Mechanical Calendar." *Annals of Science* 42, no. 2 (March 1985): 139–63. https://doi.org/10.1080/00033798500200141

Hill, Donald R. *Arabic Water-Clocks*. Maṣādir Wa-Dirāsāt Fī Tārīkh al-'ulūm al-'Arabīyah al-Islāmīyah. Silsilat Tārīkh al-Tiknūlūjiyā, vol. 4. Syria: University of Aleppo, Institute for the History of Arabic Science, 1981.

Hillenbrand, Robert. "'The Ornament of the World': Medieval Córdoba as a Cultural Centre." In *The Legacy of Muslim Spain*, edited by Salma Khadra Jayyusi, 112–35. Leiden: Brill, 1992.

Hirth, Friedrich. *China and the Roman Orient: Researches into Their Ancient and Mediaeval Relations as Represented in Old Chinese Records*. Paragon Book Reprint Corp., 1966.

Hodgson, Marshall. *The Venture of Islam; Conscience and History in a World Civilization.* University of Chicago Press, 1974.

Holod, Renata. "Text, Plan and Building: On the Transmission of Architectural Knowledge." In *Theories and Principles of Design in the Architecture of Islamic Societies: A Symposium . . . Cambridge, Massachusetts . . . 1987*, 1–12. Aga Khan Program for Islamic Architecture, 1988.

Hourani, Albert, and Malise Ruthven. *A History of the Arab Peoples.* Cambridge, Mass.: Belknap Press of Harvard University Press, 2002.

Hourani, George F. "The Early Growth of the Secular Sciences in Andalusia." *Studia Islamica*, no. 32 (January 1, 1970): 143–56. https://doi.org/10.2307/1595215

Hoyland, Robert. "Making of Islamic Civilization." In *In God's Path: The Arab Conquests and the Creation of an Islamic Empire.* New York: Oxford University Press, 2015.

Iafrate, Allegra. *The Wandering Throne of Solomon: Objects and Tales of Kingship in the Medieval Mediterranean.* Leiden: Brill, 2016.

Ibn ʿAbd Rabbih, Aḥmad ibn Muḥammad, and Issa J. Boullata. *The Unique Necklace = Al-ʿIqd al-Farīd.* 1st ed. Great Books of Islamic Civilisation. Reading, U.K.: Garnet Pub., 2006.

Ibn Ḥayyān and Maḥmūd ʿAlī Makkī. *Al-Sifr al-Thānī Min Kitāb al-Muqtabas.* Al-Ṭabʿah 1. al-Riyāḍ: Markaz al-Malik Fayṣal lil-Buḥūth wa-al-Dirāsāt al-Islāmīyah, 2003.

Ibn Ḥayyān, Abū Marwān Ḥayyān ibn Khalaf (987– or 988–1076), Maḥmūd ʿAlī Makkī, and F. (Federico) Corriente (b. 1940). *Crónica de los Emires Alḥakam I y ʿAbdarraḥmān II entre los Años 796 y 847 (Almuqtabis II-1).* Serie Estudios Islámicos. Zaragoza, Spain: Instituto de Estudios Islámicos y del Oriente Próximo, 2001.

Ibn Ḥayyān, Abū Marwān Ḥayyān ibn Khalaf (987 or 988–1076), and Joaquín Vallvé Bermejo. *Al-Muqtabas II: Anales de los Emires de Córdoba Alhaquém I . . . y Abderramán II . . .* Madrid: Real Academia de la Historia (Spain), 1999.

Ibn Khallikān, *Wafayāt al-aʿyān wa-anbāʾ abnāʾ al-zamān* (Bayrūt: Dar Ṣādir, 1398).

Ibn Shākir, Muḥammad Ibn Mūsá, and Donald R. Hill. *The Book of Ingenious Devices (Kitāb Al-ḥiyal).* Dordrecht; Boston: D. Reidel Pub., 1979.

Ibn Shākir, Muḥammad ibn Mūsá, Siegfried Zielinski, Peter Weibel, Jeremy Gaines, Sylee Gore, and Zentrum für Kunst und Medientechnologie Karlsruhe. *Allah's Automata: Artifacts of the Arab-Islamic Renaissance (800–1200).* Ostfildern, Germany: Hatje Cantz, 2015.

İhsanoğlu, Ekmeleddin, Konstantinos Chatzis, and E. Nikolaidēs. *Multicultural Science in the Ottoman Empire.* De Diversis Artibus t. 69. Turnhout, Belgium: Brepols, 2003.

Iqbal, Muzaffar. "Ahmad Dallal. Islam, Science, and the Challenge of History." *Islam & Science* 10, no. 2 (2012): 139–.

Irving, Washington. *The Alhambra.* Author's rev. ed. The Works of Washington Irving, 1783–1859, vol. 15. New-York: G.P. Putnam, 1851.

Irwin, Robert. "Review, *Magic and Divination in Early Islam, Edited by Emilie Savage-Smith. Magic, Ritual, and Witchcraft* 3, no. 1 (Summer 2008): 105–106.

Jabbar Beg, Muhammad Abdul. "A Contribution to the Economic History of the Caliphate: A Study of the Cost of Living and the Economic Status of Artisans in Abbasid Iraq." *Islamic Quarterly; London* 16, no. 3 (July 1, 1972): 140–67.

Jacoby, David. "The Production and Diffusion of Andalusi Silk and Silk Textiles, Mid-Eighth to Mid-Thirteenth Century." In *The Chasuble of Thomas Becket. A Biography*, edited by Avinoam Shalem, 142–51. Chicago: University of Chicago Press, 2017.

Jaff, Marco. "From the Vault of the Heavens." [Authorabstract]. *Nexus Network Journal* 5, no. 1 (2003): 49–63.

Jāḥiẓ, –868 or 869. *Le livre des animaux: de l'étonnante sagesse divine dans sa création et autres anecdotes.* Bibliothèque Maktaba. Paris: Fayard, 2003.

Jāḥiẓ, *Rasāʾil al-Jāḥiẓ*, vol. 3 of 4. Edited by ʿAbd al-Salām Muḥammad Hārūn. Cairo: Maktabat al-Khanjī, 1964–1979.

Janiak, Andrew. *Newton.* Chichester, U.K.; Malden, Mass.: Wiley Blackwell, 2015.

Jardine, Lisa. *Global Interests: Renaissance Art between East and West.* Picturing History. Ithaca, N.Y.: Cornell University Press, 2000.

Jazarī, Ismāʿīl Ibn Al-Razzāz, and Donald R. Hill. *The Book of Knowledge of Ingenious Mechanical Devices*. Dordrecht, the Netherlands; Boston: Reidel, 1974.

Johnston, Stephen, Mara Miniati, and Alison D. Morrison-Low. *European Collections of Scientific Instruments, 1550–1750*. History of Science and Medicine Library, vol. 10. Leiden: Brill, 2009.

Jones, Alexander. *A Portable Cosmos: Revealing the Antikythera Mechanism, Scientific Wonder of the Ancient World*. New York: Oxford University Press, 2017.

Jones, Alexander, and James Evans. *Time and Cosmos in Greco-Roman Antiquity*. New Haven, Conn.; Princeton University Press, 2016.

Jones, Owen, and Antonio Fernández Puertas. *The Alhambra*. London: Saqi Books, 1997.

Kalin, Ibrahim. "Review of Dimitri Gutas, *Greek Thought, Arabic Culture: The Graeco-Arabic Translation Movement in Baghdad and Early Ábbasid Society (Second–Fourth/Eighth–Tenth Centuries)*." *Isis* 94, no.1 (March 2003), 138–40.

Kemp, Alan, Ian Newton, Alan Kemp, and Ian Newton. "Hawks, Eagles, and Old World Vultures." In *The New Encyclopedia of Birds*. Oxford: Oxford University Press, 2003.

Kennedy, Hugh. *Caliphate: The History of an Idea*. New York: Basic Books, 2016.

Kennedy, Hugh. *Muslim Spain and Portugal: A Political History of al-Andalus*. London: Longman, 1996.

Khalili, al-, Jim. *Pathfinders: The Golden Age of Arabic Science*. London: Allen Lane, 2010.

Khan, M.A.R. "A Note on Ibn Firnas's Successful Attempt at Soaring Flight." *Islamic Culture* 21 (1947): 404–5.

King, David A. *Islamic Astronomy and Geography*. Collected Studies. Farnham, U.K.: Ashgate Variorum, 2012.

King, David A. *Instruments of Mass Calculation (Studies X–XVIII)* [Electronic Resource]. Leiden: Brill, 2005.

King, David A. *In Synchrony with the Heavens: Studies in Astronomical Timekeeping and Instrumentation in Medieval Islamic Civilization*. Islamic Philosophy, Theology, and Science, vol. 55. Leiden: Brill, 2004.

King, David A. "Some Medieval Astronomical Instruments and their Secrets." In *Non-Verbal Communication in Science prior to 1900*, edited by R.G. Mazzolini, 29–52. Florence, 1993.

King, David. "Three Sundials from Andalusia." In *Islamic Astronomical Instruments*, XV: 358–392. London: Variorum Reprints, 1987.

Klein, Yaron. "Imagination and Music: Takhyīl and the Production of Music in al-Fārābī"s Kitāb al-Mūsīqī al-Kabīr." In *Takhyīl: The Imaginary in Classical Arabic Poetics*, edited by G.J.H. van Gelder and Marlé Hammond, 179–95. Cambridge: Gibb Memorial Trust, 2008.

Komaroff, Linda, John W. Hirx, Anke Scharrahs, Sandra Williams, Manal Alghannam, and Keelan Overton. *Beauty and Identity: Islamic Art from the Los Angeles County Museum of Art*. Los Angeles: Los Angeles County Museum Art, 2016.

Kuhn, Thomas. *The Structure of Scientific Revolutions*. Chicago: University of Chicago Press, 1962.

Kunitzsch, P. "Al-Tinnīn." In *Encyclopaedia of Islam*, 2nd ed.

Kunitzsch, Paul, Menso Folkerts, and Richard Lorch. *Sic Itur ad Astra: Studien zur Geschichte der Mathematik und Naturwissenschaften: Festschrift für den Arabisten Paul Kunitzsch zum 70. Geburtstag*. Wiesbaden, Germany: Harrassowitz, 2000.

Labarta, Ana, and Carmen Barceló. "Un nuevo fragmento de reloj de sol andalusí." *Al-Qantara; Madrid* 16, no. 1 (January 1, 1995): 147–50.

Landau, J.M. "Ibn Dāniyāl." In *Encyclopaedia of Islam*, 2nd ed.

Langdon, Gabrielle. *Medici Women: Portraits of Power, Love and Betrayal from the Court of Duke Cosimo I*. Toronto: University of Toronto Press, 2006.

Lee, Chae. "Ibn Battuta: Edutaining the World?" *Visible Language* 44, no. 1 (2010): 103–25.

Lenssen, Anneka. *Beautiful Agitation: Modern Painting and Politics in Syria*. Oakland: University of California Press, 2020.

Lenssen, Anneka, Sarah A. Rogers, and Nada M. Shabout. *Modern Art in the Arab World*. Primary Documents Publication Series, Museum of Modern Art, vol. 8. New York: The Museum of Modern Art, 2018.

León, Alberto, and Juan Fco. Murillo. "Advances in Research on Islamic Cordoba." *Journal of Islamic Archaeology* 1, no. 1 (August 18, 2014): 5–35. https://doi.org/10.1558/jia.v1i1.5

Leonardo, da Vinci. *Il codice sul volo degli uccelli nella Biblioteca reale di Torino*. Edizione nazionale dei manoscritti e dei disegni di Leonardo da Vinci. Firenze: Giunti-Barbera, 1976.

Leoni, Francesca. *Power and Protection: Islamic Art and the Supernatural*. Oxford: Ashmolean Museum, 2016.

Lévi-Provençal, Evariste. *Inscriptions Arabes d'Espagne: Avec Quarante-Quatre Planches en Phototypie*. Leyde: E.J. Brill, 1931.

Lintz, Yannick, et al. *Le Maroc médiéval: un empire de l'Afrique à l'Espagne: album de l"exposition*. Paris: Musée du Louvre: Hazan, 2014.

Long, Pamela O. *Openness, Secrecy, Authorship: Technical Arts and the Culture of Knowledge from Antiquity to the Renaissance*. Johns Hopkins paperbacks ed. Baltimore: Johns Hopkins University Press, 2004.

Lory, Pierre. "Divination & Religion in Islamic Medieval Culture." In *Power and Protection: Islamic Art and the Supernatural*, 13–32. Oxford: Ashmolean Museum, 2016.

MacDonald, Angus, A.D. Morrison-Low, Owen Gingerich, Edinburgh Royal Observatory, and National Museums of Scotland. *A Heavenly Library: Treasures from the Royal Observatory's Crawford Collection: An Exhibition Held at the National Museums of Scotland, Chambers Street, Edinburgh, 8 October–31 December 1994*. Edinburgh: Royal Observatory, Edinburgh, 1994.

Mackintosh-Smith, Tim. "Edutaining Dubai." *Saudi Aramco World*, 2008.

Maddison, Francis. "Al-Jazarī's Combination Lock: Two Contemporary Examples." In *The Art of Syria and the Jazīra, 1100–1250*, edited by Julian Raby, 141–57. Oxford Studies in Islamic Art 1. Oxford: Oxford University Press, 1985.

Maddison, Francis, and Anthony Turner. *Catalogue: Science and Technology in Islam: An International Loan Exhibition, held in the Science Museum, London 6 April—31 August 1976, as part of the World of Islam Festival* [corrected typescript]. National Museums Scotland, 1976.

Magdalino, Paul. "Pharmaceutical Diplomacy: A New Document on Fatimid-Byzantine Gift Exchange." In *Myriobiblos: Essays on Byzantine Literature and Culture*, 29: 245–52. Byzantinisches Archiv 29. Berlin: De Gruyter, 2015. https://doi.org/10.1515/9781501501562.245.

Makdisi, George. *The Rise of Colleges: Institutions of Learning in Islam and the West*. Edinburgh: University Press, 1981.

Manetti, Antonio. *The Life of Brunelleschi*. University Park: Pennsylvania State University Press, 1970.

Manzano Moreno, Eduardo. *La corte del califa: cuatro años en la Córdoba de los omeyas*. Primera edición. Serie mayor (Editorial Crítica). Barcelona: Crítica, 2019.

Manzano Moreno, Eduardo. "¿El fin de la historia? La historiografía árabe en torno al año 1000." In *Hommes et sociétés dans l'Europe de l'An Mil*, edited by Pierre Bonnassie and Pierre Toubert, 407–19. Toulouse, France: Presses Universitaires du Mirail, 2004.

Maqqarī, Aḥmad ibn Muḥammad. *Nafḥ al-ṭīb min ghuṣn al-Andalus al-raṭīb*. Bayrūt: Dār Ṣādir, 1968.

Maqqarī, Aḥmad ibn Muḥammad, and Reinhart Pieter Anne Dozy. *Analectes sur l'histoire et la Littérature des Arabes d'Espagne*. Amsterdam: Oriental Press, 1967.

Maqqarī, Aḥmad ibn Muḥammad, Pascual de Gayangos, and Ibn al-Khaṭīb (d. 1374). *The History of the Mohammedan Dynasties in Spain; Extracted from the Nafhu-t-Tíb Min Ghosni-l-Andalusi-r-Rattíb Wa Táríkh Lisánu-d-Dín Ibni-l-Khattíb*. London: Printed for the Oriental Translation Fund of Great Britain and Ireland, 1840–43; New York: Johnson Reprint Corp., 1964.

Marín, Manuela. "El «halcón Maltes» del Arabismo Español: El Volumen II/1 de al-Muqtabis de Ibn Hayyán." *Al-Qanṭara: Revista de Estudios Árabes* 20, no. 2 (1999): 543–49.

Marín, Manuela, Julio Samsó, Ma Isabel Fierro, and Manuela Marín. *The Formation of al-Andalus*. Formation of the Classical Islamic World, vols. 46–47. Aldershot, U.K.; Brookfield, Vt.: Ashgate, 1998.

Martin, Therese. "The Margin to Act: A Framework of Investigation for Women's (and Men's) Medieval Art-Making." *Journal of Medieval History* 42, no. 1 (January 2016): 1–25. https://doi.org/10.1080/03044181.2015.1107751

Martin, Therese. "Exceptions and Assumptions: Women in Medieval Art History." In *Reassessing the Roles of Women as "Makers" of Medieval Art and Architecture*, 1–36. Boston; Leiden: Brill, 2012.

Martin, Therese, ed. *Reassessing the Roles of Women as "Makers" of Medieval Art and Architecture*. Boston; Leiden: Brill, 2012.

Martínez Enamorado, Virgilio. "Ibn Hayyan, el Abanderado de la Historia de al Ándalus." *Jábega* 97 (2008): 30–34.

Martínez Núñez, María Antonia. "Epigrafía Árabe e Historia de al-Andalus: Nuevos Hallazgos y Datos." *Xelb: Revista de Arqueologia, Arte, Etnologia e História* 9 (2009): 39–53.

Martínez Núñez, María Antonia. "Sentido de la Epigrafía Omeya de al-Andalus." In *El Esplendor de los Omeyas Cordobeses: La Civilización Musulmana de Europa Occidental: Exposición en Madīnat al-Zahrā'... 2001. Estudios. Coord. Científica María Jesús Viguera Molins, Concepción Castillo*, 408–417. Granada, Spain: Fundación el Legado Andalusí, 2001.

Masterpieces from the Department of Islamic Art in the Metropolitan Museum of Art. New Haven, Conn.: Yale University Press, 2011.

Mayer, L.A. (Leo Ary). "Islamic Astrolabists: Some New Material." In *Aus der Welt der Islamischen Kunst: Festschrift für Ernst Kühnel zum 75. Geburtstag am 26.10.1957*, edited by Richard Ettinghausen, 293–96. Mann, Germany: 1959.

Mayer, L.A. (Leo Ary). *Islamic Metalworkers and Their Works*. Geneva: A. Kundig, 1959.

Mayer, L.A. (Leo Ary). *Islamic Astrolabists and Their Works*. Genève: A. Kundig, 1956.

McCullough, David G. *The Wright Brothers*. 1st Simon & Schuster hardcover ed. New York: Simon & Schuster, 2015.

A la Mémoire de Louis Pierre Mouillard: Hommage del'Institut égyptien. Institut égyptien. Le Caire: L'Institute, 1912.

Menocal, Maria. *The Ornament of the World: How Muslims, Jews, and Christians Created a Culture of Tolerance in Medieval Spain*. Boston: Little, Brown, 2002.

Milwright, Marcus. *Islamic Arts and Crafts: An Anthology*. Edinburgh: Edinburgh University Press Ltd, 2017.

Moffatt, Ann, Maxeme Tall, Ann Reiske, Reiske, Johann Jacob, Philotheus, Pseudo-Epiphanius, Constantine VII Porphyrogenitus, Philotheos, and Australian Association for Byzantine Studies. *The Book of Ceremonies: With the Greek Edition of the Corpus Scriptorum Historiae Byzantinae (Bonn, 1829)*. Byzantina Australiensia, vol. 18. Canberra: Australian Association for Byzantine Studies, 2012.

Moral y Pérez de Zayas, José María del. *El Virrey de Nápoles: don Pedro de Toledo y la guerra contra el turco*. Madrid: Consejo Superior de Investigaciones Científicas, 1966.

Morrison, Robert. "Religion and Science in the Eastern Mediterranean." *Isis* 107, no. 3 (September 20, 2016): 579–82. https://doi.org/10.1086/688435

Morrison, Robert. "A Scholarly Intermediary between the Ottoman Empire and Renaissance Europe." *Isis* 105, no. 1 (March 1, 2014): 32–57. https://doi.org/10.1086/675550

Morrison, Robert. *Islam and Science: The Intellectual Career of Nīẓām al-Dīn al-Nīsābūrī*. Culture and Civilisation in the Middle East. London: Routledge, 2007.

Morrison-Low, A.D., Sara Schechner, and Paolo Brenni. *How Scientific Instruments Have Changed Hands*. History of Science and Medicine Library, vol. 56. Leiden; Boston: Brill, 2017.

Mouillard, Louis-Pierre. *L'empire de l'air; essai d'ornithologie appliqu e l'aviation*. Paris, G. Masson, 1881.

Müller-Wiener, Martina. "Science as the Handmaiden of Power: Science, Art and Technology in Ayyubid Syria." In *Ayyubid Jerusalem: The Holy City in Context 1187–1250*, edited by Robert Hillenbrand and Sylvia Auld, 418–22. London: Altajir Trust, 2009.

Al-Murādī, Ibn Khalaf. *The Book of Secrets in the Results of Ideas: Incredible Machines from 1000 Years Ago = Kitāb Al-asrār Fī Natāyij Al-afkār*. 1st ed. Milano: Leonardo3, 2008.

Murillo, J.F., F. Castillo, E. Castro, M.T. Casal, and T. Dortez. "La almunia y el arrabal de al-Rusafa, en el Yanib al-Garbi de Madinat Qurtuba." In *El anfiteatro romano de Córdoba y su entorno urbano: análisis arqueológico (ss. I–XIII d.C.)*. 565–614. Arqueología cordobesa, vol. 19. Córdoba: Universidad de Córdoba, 2011.

Murillo Redondo, Juan F. "La Almunia de al-Rusafa en Córdoba." *Madrider Mitteilungen* 50 (2009): 449–568.

Navarro Palazón, Julio, and José Miguel Puerta Vílchez. *Almunias: Las fincas de la élite en el Occidente islámico: poder, solaz y producción*. Granada, Spain: Universidad de Granada, 2018.

Necipoğlu, Gülru. "Ornamental Geometries: A Persian Compendium at the Intersection of the Visual Arts and Mathematical Sciences." In *The Arts of Ornamental Geometry: A Persian Compendium on Similar and Complementary Interlocking Figures, Fī Tadākhul al-Ashkāl al-Mutashābiha Aw al-Mutāwafiqa (Bibliothèque Nationale de France, Ms. Persan 169, Fols. 180r-199r): A Volume Commemorating Alpay Özdural*, 11–78. Muqarnas, Supplements; Volume XIII. Leiden: Brill, 2016.

Necipoğlu, Gülru. *The Topkapı Scroll: Geometry and Ornament in Islamic Architecture: Topkapı Palace Museum Library MS H. 1956*. Sketchbooks & Albums. Santa Monica, CA: Getty Center for the History of Art and the Humanities, 1995.

Nees, Lawrence. "Blue behind Gold: The Inscription of the Dome of the Rock and Its Relatives." In *And Diverse Are Their Hues: Color in Islamic Art and Culture*, edited by Jonathan Bloom and Sheila Blair, 153–73. New Haven, Conn.:Yale University Press, 2011.

Newton, Isaac, and Andrew Janiak. *Philosophical Writings*. Rev. ed. Cambridge; New York: Cambridge University Press, 2014.

Nykl, A.R. *Hispano-Arabic Poetry and Its Relations with the Old Provençal Troubadours*. Baltimore, 1946.

Ocaña Jiménez, Manuel. "Arquitectos y mano de obra en la construcción de la Gran Mezquita de Occidente." *Cuadernos de la Alhambra*, no. 22 (1986): 55–86.

Ocaña Jiménez, Manuel. "Las Inscripciones en Mosaico del Mihrab de la Gran Mezquita de Córdoba y la Incógnita de Su Data." In *Les Mosaïques de la Grande Mosquée de Cordoue*, edited by Henri Stern, Dorothea Duda, and Manuel Ocaña Jiménez. Bd. 11:48–52. Madrider Forschungen. Berlin: de Gruyter, 1976.

Ovid. *Metamorphoses*. Translated by Frank Justus Miller. Cambridge, Mass.: 1951.

Özdural, Alpay. "Mathematics and Arts: Connections between Theory and Practice in the Medieval Islamic World." *Historia Mathematica* 27, no. 2 (May 2000): 171–201. https://doi.org/10.1006/hmat.1999.2274

Özdural, Alpay. "Omar Khayyam, Mathematicians, and Conversazioni with Artisans." *Journal of the Society of Architectural Historians* 54, no. 1 (1995): 54–71.

Özdural, Alpay, and ʿUmar Khayyām. "A Mathematical Sonata for Architecture: Omar Khayyam and the Friday Mosque of Isfahan." *Technology and Culture* 39, no. 4 (1998): 699–715.

Pakzad, Ashkan, Francesco Iacoviello, Andrew Ramsey, Robert Speller, Jennifer Griffiths, Tony Freeth, and Adam Gibson. "Improved X-Ray Computed Tomography Reconstruction of the Largest Fragment of the Antikythera Mechanism, an Ancient Greek Astronomical Calculator." *PLOS ONE* 13, no. 11 (November 9, 2018): e0207430. https://doi.org/10.1371/journal.pone.0207430

Parker, Rozsika, and Griselda Pollock. *Old Mistresses: Women, Art and Ideology*. London: Pandora, 1995.

Petersen, Leif Inge Ree. "Sultans of Science: An Opportunity Lost." *Technology and Culture* 55, no. 4 (December 3, 2014): 973–87.

Pickthall, Marmaduke. *The Meaning of the Glorious Koran*. NAL Mentor Books, Ms. 94. New York: New American Library, 1953.

Pines, Shlomo. "Philosophy, Mathematics and the Concepts of Space in the Middle Ages." In *Studies in Arabic Versions of Greek Texts and in Mediaeval Science*, edited by Shlomo Pines, 75–90, vol. 2. Leiden: Brill, 1986.

Popper, William. *The Cairo Nilometer; Studies in Ibn Taghrî Birdî's Chronicles of Egypt: I*. University of California Publications in Semitic Philology, vol. 12. Berkeley: University of California Press, 1951.

Porter, Yves. "Les Art et les Sciences: Ars Gratia Ars." In *L'âge d'or des Sciences Arabes: Exposition Présentée à l'Institut du Monde Arabe, Paris, 25 Octobre 2005–19 Mars 2006*. 1er éd. Arles, France: Actes sud, 2005.

Prado-Vilar, Francisco. "Enclosed in Ivory: The Miseducation of al-Mughira." *Journal of the David Collection* 2, no. 1 (2005): 138–63.

Price, Derek J. de Solla. "Mechanical Waterclocks of the 14th Century in Fez, Morocco." In *Proceedings of the Tenth International Congress of the History of Science*. 599–602. Ithaca, N.Y; Paris: Hermann, 1962.

Rabbat, Nasser. "Architects and Artists in Mamluk Society: The Perspective of the Sources." In *Mamluk History through Architecture: Monuments, Culture and Politics in Medieval Egypt and Syria*, 33–44. London: I. B. Tauris, 2010.

Raby, Julian. "Mosul Metalworkers after the Mongols." In *Court and Craft: A Masterpiece from Northern Iraq*, edited by Rachel Ward, 56–67. London: Courtauld Gallery, 2014.

Ramadan, Dina. "The Aesthetics of the Modern: Art, Education, and Taste in Egypt 1903–1952." PhD thesis, Columbia University, 2013.

Ramírez-Weaver, Eric. *A Saving Science: Capturing the Heavens in Carolingian Manuscripts*. University Park: The Pennsylvania State University Press, 2017.

Reiske, Johann Jacob, and Constantine VII Porphyrogenitus. *Constantini Porphyrogeniti Imperatoris de Cerimoniis Aulae Byzantinae Libri Duo*: Graece et Latine. Corpus Scriptorum Historiae Byzantinae. Bonnae: Impensis Ed. Weberi, 1829.

Rius Piniés, Mònica. "El sabio total: Ibn Firnás," *Jábega*, 2008, 9–13.

Robinson, Andrew. *Sudden Genius?: The Gradual Path to Creative Breakthroughs*. Oxford: Oxford University Press, 2010.

Robinson, Cynthia. *In Praise of Song: The Making of Courtly Culture in al-Andalus and Provence, 1005–1134 A.D.* Leiden: Brill, 2002.

Robinson, Cynthia. "Arts of the Taifa Kingdoms." In *Al-Andalus: The Art of Islamic Spain*, edited by Jerrilynn Denise Dodds, 49–61. New York: Metropolitan Museum of Art; Distributed by HNAbrams, 1992.

Rodríguez-Arribas, Josefina, Charles Burnett, and Silke Ackermann. "Astrolabes in Medieval Cultures." *Medieval Encounters* 23, nos. 1–5 (September 22, 2017): 1–2. https://doi.org/10.1163/15700674-12342240

Rosen, Mark. "A New Chronology of the Construction and Restoration of the Medici Guardaroba in the Palazzo Vecchio, Florence." *Mitteilungen des Kunsthistorischen Institutes in Florenz* 53, nos. 2/3 (2009): 285–308.

Rosser-Owen, Mariam. *Articulating the Ḥijāba: Cultural Patronage and Political Legitimacy in al-Andalus: The ʿĀmirid Regency c. 970–1010 AD*. Vol. 156. Handbook of Oriental Studies. Leiden: Brill, 2021.

Rothstein, Edward. "'1001 Inventions" at New York Hall of Science - Review." *The New York Times*, December 9, 2010, sec. Art & Design.

Rowe, Colin. *Italian Architecture of the 16th Century*. New York: Princeton Architectural Press, 2002.

Ruggles, D. *Islamic Gardens and Landscapes*. Philadelphia: University of Pennsylvania Press, 2008.

Ruggles, D. Fairchild. *Gardens, Landscape, and Vision in the Palaces of Islamic Spain*. University Park: Pennsylvania State University Press, 2000.

Saalman, Howard. *Filippo Brunelleschi: The Buildings*. University Park: Pennsylvania State University Press, 1993.

Sabra, A.I. "A Note on Codex Medicea Laurenziana Or. 152." *Journal for the History of Arabic Science* 1 (1977), 276–83.

Safran, Janina M. *Defining Boundaries in al-Andalus: Muslims, Christians, and Jews in Islamic Iberia*. Ithaca, N.Y.: Cornell University Press, 2013.

Saliba, George. *Islamic Science and the Making of the European Renaissance*. Cambridge, Mass.: MIT Press, 2007.

Saliba, George. "A Sixteenth-Century Drawing of an Astrolabe Made by Khafīf Ghulām ʿAlī b. ʿĪsā (c. 850 AD)." *Nuncius, Annali Di Storia Della Scienza* 6, no. 2 (1991): 109–19.

Samsó, Julio. *On Both Sides of the Strait of Gibraltar: Studies in the History of Medieval Astronomy in the Iberian Peninsula and the Maghrib*. Handbook of Oriental Studies. Section 1, Near and Middle East (2014), vol. 144. Leiden; Boston: Brill, 2020.

Samsó, Julio. *Las ciencias de los antiguos en al-Andalus*. Revised, 2nd ed. Almería, Spain: Fundación Ibn Tufayl de Estudios Árabes, 2011.

Samsó, Julio. "Reviews: Massimiliano Lisa, Mario Taddei & Edoardo Zanon, The Book of Secrets in the Results of Ideas. Incredible Machines from 1000 Years Ago, Ibn Khalaf Al-Muradi." *Suhayl. International Journal for the History of the Exact and Natural Sciences in Islamic Civilisation* 9 (2009): 234–38.

Samsó, Julio. *Astronomy and Astrology in al-Andalus and the Maghrib*. U.K.: Ashgate, 2007.

Samsó, Julio. "Is a Social History of Andalusī Exact Sciences Possible?" *Early Science and Medicine* 7, no. 3 (2002): 296–99.

Samsó, Julio. "Originalidad en la ciencia andalusí de la época taifa." In *Los reinos de taifas: un siglo de oro en la cultura hispanomusulmana. Ciclo de conferencias in memoriam de D. Emilio García Gómez*. 115–36. Madrid: Real Academia de la Historia & Fundación Ramón Areces, 1997.

Savage-Smith, Emilie. "The Most Authoritative Copy of ʿAbd al-Rahman al-Sufi's Tenth-Century Guide to the Constellations." In *God Is Beautiful and Loves Beauty: The Object in Islamic Art and Culture*, edited by Sheila Blair and Jonathan Bloom, 122–55. New Haven, Conn: Yale University Press, 2013.

Savage-Smith, Emilie. "Magic and Divination in Early Islam." In *Magic and Divination in Early Islam*, xiii–li. Oxford; New York: Ashgate, 2004.

Savage-Smith, Emilie. "Divination." In Francis Maddison and Emilie Savage-Smith, *Science, Tools and Magic. Part One. Body and Spirit, Mapping the Universe*, 148–59. London: Nour Foundation, in association with Azimuth Editions and Oxford University Press, 1997.

Savage-Smith, Emilie. "Magic and Islam." In Francis Maddison and Emilie Savage-Smith, *Science, Tools and Magic. Part One*. 1997, 58–71.

Savage-Smith, Emilie, and Andrea P.A. Belloli. *Islamicate Celestial Globes, Their History, Construction, and Use*. Washington, D.C.: Smithsonian Institution Press, 1985.

Savage-Smith, Emilie, and Marion B. Smith. "Islamic Geomancy and a Thirteenth-Century Divinatory Device: Another Look." In *Magic and Divination in Early Islam*, 211–76. London: Ashgate, 2004.

Savage-Smith, Emilie, and Marion B. (Marion Bush) Smith. *Islamic Geomancy and a Thirteenth-Century Divinatory Device*. Malibu, Calif.: Undena Publications, 1980.

Saxl, Fritz. *The Zodiac of Quṣayr ʿAmra*. Oxford: Clarendon Press, 1932.

Schechner Genuth, S. "Armillary Sphere." In *Instruments of Science: An Historical Encyclopedia*, edited by Robert Bud and Deborah Jean Warner. Garland Encyclopedias in the History of Science; Vol. 2. New York: Science Museum, London, and National Museum of American History, Smithsonian Institution, in association with Garland Pub, 1998.

Sellheim, R., "Al-Khalīl b. Aḥmad." In *Encyclopaedia of Islam*, 2nd ed. First published online: 2012. First print edition, 1960–2007.

Shafir, Nir. "Forging Islamic Science: Fake Miniatures Detract from the Real Work of Early-Modern Ottoman Scientists." *American Scientist* 107, no. 3 (2019): 156–161.

Shalem, Avinoam. "What Do We Mean When We Say 'Islamic Art'? A Plea for a Critical Rewriting of the History of the Arts of Islam." *Journal of Art Historiography*, no. 6 (June 1, 2012): 1–18.

Shalem, Avinoam. "If Objects Could Speak." In *The Aura of Alif: The Art of Writing in Islam*, edited by Jürgen Wasim Frembgen, 127–47. Munich: Prestel, 2010.

Seibold, Ingrid, and Andreas J. Helbig. "Evolutionary History of New and Old World Vultures Inferred from Nucleotide Sequences of the Mitochondrial Cytochrome *b* Gene." *Philosophical Transactions: Biological Sciences* 350, no. 1332 (November 29, 1995): 163–78.

Simi Varanelli, Emma. *Artisti e dottori nel Medioevo: il campanile di Firenze e la rivalutazione delle "arti belle."* Pensiero italiano (Rome, Italy), vol. 3. Roma: Istituto poligrafico e zecca dello stato, Libreria dello stato, 1995.

Smith, Pamela H. *The Body of the Artisan: Art and Experience in the Scientific Revolution*. Chicago; London: University of Chicago Press, 2004.

Snow, D.W., and C.M. Perrins. "Species account: Griffon Vulture *Gyps fulvus*." *The Birds of the Western Palearctic, Volume 1: Non-Passerines*. Oxford: Oxford University Press, 1998; Global Raptor Information Network. 2015.

Stern, S.M. "A Letter of the Byzantine Emperor to the Court of the Spanish Umayyad Caliph al-Hakam." *Al-Andalus; Madrid* 26, no. 1 (January 1, 1961): 37–42.

Stevenson, Joseph. *The Church Historians of England*. Pre-Reformation Series. London: Seeleys, 1853.

Strano, Giorgio. "The Instruments of Egnazio Danti." In *Museo Galileo: Masterpieces of Science*, edited by Filippo Camerota, 1. ed., 82–83. Firenze: Giunti, 2010.

Strano, Giorgio, ed. *European Collections of Scientific Instruments, 1550–1750*. History of Science and Medicine Library, vol. 10. Leiden: Brill, 2009.

Ṣūfī, ʿAbd al-Raḥmān ibn ʿUmar. *Kitāb Ṣuwar al-kawākib*. Manshūrat Maʿhad Tārīkh al-ʿUlūm al-ʿArabīyah wa-al-Islāmīyah. Silsilah J, ʿUyūn al-turath; mujallad 29. Frankfurt am Main, Jumhūrīyat Almāniyā al-Ittiḥādīyah: Maʿhad Tārīkh al-ʿUlūm al-ʿArabīyah wa-al-Islāmīyah fī iṭār Jāmiʿat Frānkfūrt, 1986.

Taragan, Hana. "The "Speaking" Inkwell from Khurasan: Object as "World" in Iranian Medieval Metalwork." *Muqarnas* 22, no. 1 (January 1, 2005): 29–44. https://doi.org/10.1163/22118993-90000082

Terés, Elías. "Sobre el vuelo de Abbas Ibn Firnas." *Al-Andalus* 29, no. 2 (1964): 365.

Terés, Elías. "Abbas Ibn Firnas." *Al-Andalus* 25, no. 1 (1960): 239.

Thomas, Joe A. "Fabric and Dress in Bronzino's Portrait of Eleanor of Toledo and Son Giovanni." *Zeitschrift für Kunstgeschichte* 57, no. 2 (1994): 262–67. https://doi.org/10.2307/1482735

Tixier du Mesnil, Emmanuelle. "La 'Fitna' Andalouse du XIe Siècle." *Médiévales*, no. 60 (2011): 17–28.

Trachtenberg, Marvin. *The Campanile of Florence Cathedral: "Giotto's Tower."* New York: University Press, 1971.

Truitt, Elly. *Medieval Robots: Mechanism, Magic, Nature, and Art*. Philadelphia: University of Pennsylvania Press, 2015.

Tschanz, David W. "Flights of Fancy on Manmade Wings." *Saudi Aramco World*, December 2008: 33–35.

Vaiou, M., and Ibn al-Farra. *Diplomacy in the Early Islamic World: A Tenth-Century Treatise on Arab-Byzantine Relations*. London: I. B. Tauris & Company, Limited, 2015.

Vallejo Triano, Antonio. "Piezas Metálicas Suntuarias del Periodo Califal de al-Andalus." In *The Pisa Griffin and the Mari-Cha Lion: Metalwork, Art, and Technology in the Medieval Islamicate Mediterranean*, edited by Anna Contadini, Damiano Anedda, and Rafael Azuar Ruiz, 257–80. Pisa, Italy: Pacini Editore, 2018.

Vallejo Triano, Antonio. *La Ciudad Califal de Madinat al-Zahrā': Arqueología de Su Excavación*. 1a ed. Colección Naturaleza y Medio Ambiente. Córdoba, Spain: Editorial Almuzara, 2010.

Vallejo Triano, Antonio, and Andalusia (Spain) Consejería de Cultura. *Madinat al-Zahra: Official Guide to the Archeological complex*. Andalusia, Spain: Junta de Andalucía, Consejería de Cultura, 2006.

Vasari, Giorgio. *Lives of the Most Eminent Painters, Sculptors & Architects*, London: Macmillan & The Medici society, 1912.

Vasari, Giorgio. *Le opere di Giorgio Vasari*. Firenze: Sansoni, 1973.

Vernet, Juan. " 'Abbas Ibn Firnas." In *Dictionary of Scientific Biography*, edited by Charles Coulston Gillispie, 5. New York: Scribner's, 1970.

Vernet Ginés, Juan, Julio. Samsó, *El legado científico andalusí*. Madrid: Ministerio de Cultura, Dirección General de Cooperación Cultural, 1992.

Vernet, Juan, R. Casals, and M.V. Villuendas. "El capítulo primer del Kitab asrar fi nata'iy al-afkar." *Awraq: Estudios sobre el mundo árabe e islámico contemporáneo*, no. 5 (1982): 7–18.

Viguera, M.J. "Saraḳusṭa." In *Encyclopaedia of Islam*, 2nd ed. Consulted online on November 5, 2018, at http://dx.doi.org.ezproxy.is.ed.ac.uk/10.1163/1573-3912_islam_SIM_6621

Viguera Molins, J. "El manuscrito del Muqtabis II-1." *Qurtuba: Revista de Estudios Andalusies* 2 (1997), 327–28.

Viladrich, Mercé. "Astrolabios andalusíes." In *El Legado científico andalusí: Museo Arqueológico Nacional, Madrid, Abril–Junio 1992*, edited by Juan Vernet Ginés and Julio Samsó, 53–65. Madrid: Centro Nacional de Exposiciones, Ministerio de Cultura, Dirección General de Bellas Artes y Archivos: Ministerio de Asuntos Exteriores, Agencia Española de Cooperación Internacional: Instituto de Cooperación con el Mundo Arabe, 1992.

Villuendas, M.V. "A Further Note on a Mechanical Treatise Contained in Codex Medicea Laurenziana Or. 152," Journal for the History of Arabic Science 2 (1978), 395–96.

Viré, F., "Nasr." In *Encyclopaedia of Islam*, 2nd ed. Consulted online on July 13, 2019, at http://dx.doi.org.ezproxy.is.ed.ac.uk/10.1163/1573-3912_islam_SIM_5834

Volait, Mercedes. *Architectes et architectures de l'Égypte moderne (1830–1950): genèse et essor d'une expertise locale*. Architectures modernes en Méditerranée: sources, identité, actualité. Paris: Maisonneuve et Larose, 2005.

Ward, Rachel. "The Inscription on the Astrolabe by "Abd al-Karim in the British Museum." *Muqarnas* 21, no. 1 (2004): 345–57.

Waźbiński, Zygmunt. *L'Accademia medicea del disegno a Firenze nel Cinquecento: idea e istituzione*. Studi (Accademia toscana di scienze e lettere La Colombaria), vol. 84. Firenze: L.S. Olschki, 1987.

Weather Forecasting for Soaring Flight. Geneva: World Meteorological Organization, 2009.

West, Ashley. *The Body of the Artisan: Art and Experience in the Scientific Revolution*. New York: College Art Association, Inc., 2004.

White, Lynn, Jr. "Eilmer of Malmesbury, an Eleventh Century Aviator: A Case Study of Technological Innovation, Its Context and Tradition." *Technology and Culture* 2, no. 2 (April 1, 1961): 97–111. https://doi.org/10.2307/3101411

Wilson, Catherine. *The Invisible World: Early Modern Philosophy and the Invention of the Microscope*. Studies in Intellectual History and the History of Philosophy. Princeton, N.J.: Princeton University Press, 1995.

Worthen, Shana. "The Influence of Lynn White, Jr.' s Medieval Technology and Social Change." *History Compass* 7, no. 4 (2009): 1201–17. https://doi.org/10.1111/j.1478-0542.2009.00615.x

Yaman, Hikmet. *Prophetic Niche in the Virtuous City: The Concept of Ḥikmah in Early Islamic Thought*. Islamic Philosophy, Theology, and Science, vol. 81. Leiden; Boston: Brill, 2011.

Yonan, Michael. "Toward a Fusion of Art History and Material Culture Studies." *West 86th* 18, no. 2 (2011): 232–48. https://doi.org/10.1086/662520

Zakī, Aḥmad. "L'aviation chez les Arabes / Ahmed Pacha Zéki." *Bulletin de l'Institut Égyptien* 5 (1911): 92–101.

Zanon, Edoardo. *Il libro del Codice del volo: Leonardo da Vinci: dallo studio del volo degli uccelli all'aeroplano = The Book of the Codex on Flight: Leonardo da Vinci: From the Study of Bird Flight to the Airplane*. 1. ed. Milano: Leonardo3, 2009.

Index

For the benefit of digital users, indexed terms that span two pages (e.g., 52–53) may, on occasion, appear on only one of those pages.

Figures are indicated by *f* following the page number

'Abd al-Jalil ibn 'Ali ibn Muhammad, 'Ali ibn, 123–25, 127*f*, 128*f*, 129*f*
'Abd al-Rahman, Mutarrif ibn, 111–12
'Abd al-Rahman I (emir), 131–32, 136
'Abd al-Rahman II (emir), 14–15, 25, 28, 32, 36, 37–38, 80–81, 131, 134–35
'Abd al-Rahman III, 87–90, 101, 102–6
al-'Abdari, al-Hasan b. Muhammad al-Iskandari al-Kūshi, 81–82
Abu l-Wafa', 170n.29
Ackermann, Silke, 97–98
Ahmad al-Hasib, 116–19, 161
Alfonso X (king), 93–94
Aljafería Palace, 44, 50*f*
Allan, James, 30
al-Andalus, 1–2, 7, 9–11, 161–62
  earliest engineering treatise from, 93–106
  earliest scientific instruments, 41–60
  science and visual culture in, 69, 71–72
Anderson, Benjamin, 107–8
Apollonius of Tyana, 90
Aratus manuscripts, 70, 73*f*, 74*f*, 87
Archytas, 149
armillary sphere, 35–36, 38–39, 41, 43, 80–81, 81*f*
Arnold, Felix, 46–49, 111–12
astrolabes, 36–37, 39–41, 40*f*, 43–44, 45*f*, 87–90, 147–48
  al-Muradi on, 94, 96*f*
  of Cosimo I de' Medici, 157–58
  families making, 68
  geared, 39, 41, 90, 91*f*, 92*f*
  of Ibn Abi Bakr, 91*f*
  Ibn Sa'id on makers of, 60–64
  by Khafif, 58–60, 63*f*, 154*f*, 155–56, 155*f*, 178n.63
  Kufic inscriptions on, 44, 50–54, 64–66
  metalwork box and, 67–68, 69*f*
  of al-Saffar, 50–59, 55*f*, 56*f*, 57*f*, 58*f*, 59*f*, 60*f*, 61*f*, 62, 62*f*, 64, 65
  of al-Sahli, 44–54, 45*f*, 46*f*, 47*f*, 48*f*, 49*f*, 52*f*, 53*f*, 54*f*, 58–59, 62–64, 66–67
  Sangallo's drawings of, 153, 154–58, 154*f*, 155*f*
  signature inscriptions on, 39, 41, 44, 48*f*, 54*f*, 57*f*, 58, 60–65, 61*f*, 66–67, 68–69, 72–78, 77*f*, 78*f*, 155–56, 178n.71
  of 'Umar Ibn Yusuf, 72–78, 77*f*, 78*f*
automata, 11, 30, 85–86, 93–109, 95*f*, 119

Banū Mūsa, 29–30, 31, 119, 135–36, 138, 161
  animal imagery and devices from manuscript, 102, 103*f*, 104*f*, 105*f*
  Nilometer of Cairo and, 113, 117–19
  on water in engineering, 114–16, 115*f*
Bongianino, Umberto, 64
boon companions, 20, 68–69, 131, 134–35, 138
Brahe, Tycho, 159–61
Brentjes, Sonja, 8, 170n.29
Brethren of Purity, 108, 109–10
Brunelleschi, 158–59
Bustan of Sa'di, 123, 124*f*
Byzantine courts, automata in, 106–8

Calvo Capilla, Susana, 101–2, 111–12, 135–36
Carey, Moya, 70, 81–82, 84–85
celestial globe, of al-Sahli, 65–78, 66*f*, 67*f*, 70*f*, 71*f*, 72*f*, 84–85, 85*f*, 87
Chambers, Jan, 143*f*, 144–46, 145*f*, 147–48, 148*f*, 149*f*
Choniates, Niketas, 150–51
clepsydra. *See* water clocks
"Clepsydra of the Gazelles, The," 97–98, 98*f*, 99*f*, 100*f*
Constantine Porphyrogenitus (emperor), 106–7
Constantine VII (emperor), 87–90
Contadini, Ana, 101–2, 153, 156

Córdoba, 1–2, 2*f*, 3–6, 5*f*, 12–13, 14
bronze deer from, 101–2, 102*f*
Great Mosque of, 51*f*, 68, 79–80, 110–12, 111*f*, 117–19, 118*f*
al-Rusafa archaeological remains in contemporary, 131–34, 132*f*, 133*f*, 134*f*
signature inscriptions on instruments in, 65
vultures in, 139–40
Cordoban court, 3–6, 7, 37–38
diplomacy and, 87–90
Ibn Firnās in, 3–6, 7, 9–10, 13, 22–23, 24–25, 28, 30, 33–34, 87–90, 120–21
Ibn Firnās poem on, 23–24, 138
at al-Rusafa, 131
villa culture of, 23–24
in visual culture of ninth-century, 110, 147–48, 161–62
Cordoban court chronicle
on Ibn Firnās, 8–10, 11, 14–15, 16*f*, 17*f*, 18*f*, 20–21, 22–28, 37–38, 41–43, 161
literary genres and, 21–22
manuscript, 14–15, 16*f*, 17*f*, 18*f*, 20, 24
sources for, 20–21
on Ziryab, 20
Cosimo I de' Medici, 153–54, 156–58
Coste, Pascal, 113*f*
Creswell, K.A.C., 113, 117

al-Ḍabbi, 15, 23
Daedalus (mythological figure), 123, 138–39, 151, 158, 159*f*, 160*f*
Dallal, Ahmad, 7–8
Danti, Egnazio, 157–58
al-Dawla, Abu Bakr Yahya Sharaf, 64
al-Dawla, Sayf, 68
Descartes, René, 29, 161
design and making, 6, 10, 64, 153, 161–62
Dhu'l-Nunid dynasty, 54–55
Dioscorides, 87–90
Draco, 83–85, 86*f*, 181n.11

Eilmer, 151–52
European Renaissance, 13, 153–62

al-Farabi, 37, 68
al-Faraj, Abu, 20–21
al-Farghani, 36–37, 161
Farré, Eduard, 97–98, 98*f*, 99*f*, 100*f*
Ferdinand de Medici, 157–58
Fierro, Maribel, 109–10
Flood, Finbarr Barry, 108–9, 153–54

Galileo, 159–61
García Gómez, Emilio, 14–15
Gayangos, 19–20, 125–29, 139, 144, 146
geomancy and geomantic tablet, 41, 42*f*, 90
al-Ghazal, 87–90
Gigante, Federica, 10–11
Giotto, 158
Grabar, Oleg, 106
Graves, Margaret, 3–5, 10–11, 72–73, 108, 109–10
Great Mosque of Córdoba, 51*f*, 68, 79–80, 110–12, 111*f*, 117–19, 118*f*
Gregory XIII (pope), 158
Grimsdale, Michael, 80–81, 81*f*
Gutas, Dmitri, 140–41

al-Hakam I (emir), 14–15
al-Hakam II (caliph), 20, 46–49, 79–80, 90, 110, 111*f*, 111–12, 117–19, 118*f*
Hallion, Richard, 148–51
Hämeen-Anttila, 20–21
Harun al-Rashid, 183n.63
al-Hasib, Ahmad, 117–19
Hernández, Azucena, 41–42, 44
Hill, Donald, 94, 98–101, 102, 116

Iafrate, Allegra, 101–2
Ibn ʿAbd Rabbih, 15–19, 23
Ibn Abi Bakr, Muhammad, 39–41, 40*f*, 91*f*, 92*f*
Ibn Abi Jamil, Mahmud, 23
Ibn Abi Usaybiʿa, 116
Ibn al-Nadim, 59, 65, 68
Ibn al-Shamir, 28
Ibn Basil, ʿAbdalhamid, 20–21, 24, 26, 30–31
Ibn Daniyal, 5
Ibn al-Day'a, 116
Ibn Firnās, ʿAbbas, 8
armillary sphere of, 35–36, 38–39, 41, 43, 80–81
arts and intellect, 7–13
contemporary reputation, 1, 2–3
in Córdoban court, 3–6, 7, 9–10, 13, 22–25, 28, 30, 33–34, 87–90, 120–21, 138
Córdoban court chronicle on, 8–10, 11, 14–15, 16*f*, 17*f*, 18*f*, 20–21, 22–28, 37–38, 41–43, 161
European Renaissance and, 153, 159–62
finances of, 25–26, 27–28
Gayangos on, 19–20
Ibn Hayyan on, 3, 9–10, 14, 20–22, 27, 30–32, 35–36, 37–38, 109, 119, 134–36, 138, 144, 161–62
Ibn Lubabah on, 20
Ibn Saʿid and, 64
intellectual world of, 28–32
as inventor, designer, and maker, 35–41

in Islamic Spain, 1–5, 6
Islamic visual culture and, 5–6, 71–72, 79–80, 161–62
Luqman and, 140–43
al-Maqqari, 15–19
Mu'min and, 26–28, 30–31
as musician, 23, 24–25
al-Nahwhi on, 20
occult knowledge and magic of, 109
as poet, 23–25, 28, 37–39, 83–84, 136–38
as polymath, 14–20, 22–23, 153
prosody of, 24
as "Renaissance Man," 153
scientific instruments of, 9, 12, 35–36, 37–38, 71–73
ʿUbada on, 22, 24, 28, 31, 37–38, 41
water clock of, 38–39, 41, 108, 146, 147
Ibn Firnās, ʿAbbas, aeronautics experiment of, 1, 3, 11, 12–13, 33, 121
Chambers's drawings imagining, 144–46, 145*f*, 147–48, 148*f*, 149*f*
conjectural model of glider, 4*f*, 147–48, 150*f*
Gayangos on, 125–29, 139, 144, 146
Hallion on, 148–51
Ibn Hayyan on, 18*f*, 122, 125, 129–31, 134–35, 144, 146–47, 150–52
Ibn Lubabah on, 130–31, 136, 138–39, 144, 146, 147, 150–52
al-Maqqari on, 122, 125–29, 139, 144
medieval flight, imagining, 144–52
al-Rusafa as possible location of, 122, 131–39, 152
silk and, 144–48, 145*f*, 149*f*
vultures and, 139–44, 147–48, 149*f*
White on, 127–29, 151
Ibn Firnās, ʿAbbas, celestial/meteorological chamber in home of
armillary spheres and, 80–81, 81*f*
astrolabes and, 90
as astronomical and astrological features of, 80–87, 107, 119
automata and, 93–94, 97–98, 107, 119
Grimsdale's rendering of, 80–81, 81*f*
Ibn Hayyan on, 79–81, 82–83, 107
Islamic visual culture, diplomacy and, 87–90
Islamic visual culture and, 79–80, 83–87
meteorological information and, 11, 79, 80, 107–8, 109, 119, 120
Mu'min on, 82–83
al-Muradi's *Kitab al-Asrar Fi Nata'ij al-Afkar* and, 93–94, 96, 101, 119
Nilometer of Cairo and, 79–80, 112
as planetarium, 79
poetry on, 83–84
as representation of the heavens, 80–83
visualizing, 83–87
water clocks and, 101, 108, 109
Ibn Firnās Bridge, 5*f*, 133*f*
Ibn Hayyan, 3, 9–10, 14, 35–36, 37–38, 122, 129–31. *See also* Córdoban court chronicle
on Ibn Firnās, 3, 9–10, 14, 20–22, 27, 30–32, 35–36, 37–38, 109, 119, 134–36, 138, 144, 161–62
on Ibn Firnās, aeronautics experiment of, 18*f*, 122, 125, 129–31, 134–35, 144, 146–47, 150–52
on Ibn Firnās, celestial vault in home of, 79–81, 82–83, 107
on Muhammad I, 135–36
al-Nahwi, 19
Ibn ʿId̲h̲ari, 23
Ibn Ishaq, Hunayn, 141–43
Ibn Isma'il, Muhammad, 32
Ibn Labbun, Abu 'ilsa, 68–69
Ibn Lubabah, Muhammad ibn 'Umar, 20, 130–31, 136, 138–39, 144, 146, 147, 150–52
Ibn Ma' al-Sama', 'Ubadah, 26
Ibn Saʿid al-Andalusi, 60–64, 68, 79–80, 110
Ibn Tamlih, Muhammad, 110–12
Ibn Yunus, 59
Icarus (mythological figure), 138–39
'ilm, 8
inscription program, on Nilometer of Cairo, 116*f*, 116–17
Islamic art, 10–11, 12
flight depicted in, 123–25, 124*f*, 126*f*
Islamic science and, 13, 69
Islamic civilization, European Renaissance and, 153–61
Islamic courts, Frankish courts and, 107–8
Islamic material culture, 12
Islamic science
architecture and, 112–19
European Renaissance and, 153–54
Islamic art and, 13, 69
Islamic philosophy and, 28–29
Islamic visual culture and, 41–42, 69, 71–72, 79–80, 157–58, 159
the occult, intellectual culture and, 109–12
Islamic scientific instruments. *See also* armillary sphere; astrolabes; automata; water clocks
Arabic texts and, 9–10
earliest Andalusi instruments, 41–60
in European Renaissance, 13, 153–58
Ibn Firnās designing and making, 9, 12, 35–36, 37–38, 71–73

Islamic scientific instruments (*cont.*)
Islamic art and, 10–11, 12
Islamic visual culture and, 43, 71–72
Nilometer of Cairo, architecture and, 112–19
poetic inscriptions on, 35, 37–41, 40*f*, 42*f*
signature inscriptions on, 39, 41, 44, 48*f*, 54*f*, 57*f*, 58, 60–65, 61*f*
Islamic Scientific Revolution, 3–5, 7–9
Islamic visual culture, 11–13
celestial globe of al-Sahli and, 69–71, 84–85
celestial/meteorological vault of Ibn Firnās and, 79–80, 83–90
of Córdoban court, 110, 147–48, 161–62
exact sciences and, 153–54, 157–58
flight imagined and depicted in, 122, 123–25, 124*f*, 126*f*, 127*f*, 128*f*, 129*f*
Ibn Firnās and, 5–6, 71–72, 79–80, 161–62
Islamic science and, 41–42, 69, 71–72, 79–80, 157–58, 159
Islamic scientific instruments and, 43, 71–72

Jacopo da Siena, Mariano di, 158–59
al-Jazari, Ibn al-Razzaz, 29–30, 67–68, 94
on automaton, 94, 95*f*
on Castle Water Clock, 85–87, 88*f*, 89*f*

Kairouan, 54–55
Khafif, 58–60, 63*f*, 65, 154*f*, 155–56, 155*f*, 178n.63
al-Khalili, Jim, 1
al-Khalil ibn Ahmad al-Farahidi, 15–19, 24
al-Khatib al-Baghdadi, 106
Khayyam, Omar, 111–12
al-Khazin, Abu Ja'far, 170n.29
al-Kindi, 29, 31, 138
King, David A., 59, 65
Kitab al-Asrar Fi Nata' ij al-Afkar (al-Muradi), 93–106, 93*f*, 96*f*, 97*f*, 119
Kufic inscriptions
on astrolabes, 44, 50–54, 64–66
on celestial globe, 65–67, 66*f*
on Great Mosque of Córdoba mihrab, 110–12, 111*f*, 118*f*
on Nilometer of Cairo, 117
Kuhn, Thomas, 8
Kunitschz, Paul, 43

Leo Africanus, 158
Leonardo da Vinci, 1, 10
Lévi-Provencal, Evariste, 14–15, 110
Liudprand of Cremona, 106–7
Luqman, 101–2, 140–44

Maddison, Francis, 67–68
magic, the occult and, 109–12
makers, 65, 73–78, 170n.29
al-Ma'mun, 68–69, 122
manuscript paintings and illustrated manuscripts, 70–71, 73*f*, 74*f*, 75*f*, 76*f*
al-Maqqari, Ahmad ibn Muhammad, 15–20, 101–2, 122, 125–29, 139, 144
Marín, Manuela, 14
Martin, Therese, 12, 65
material culture, 11
al-Mawsili, Muhammad ibn Khutlukh, 41, 42*f*
Mayer, Leo, 65, 178n.71
McCullough, David, 1
metalwork animal figures, 101–2, 102*f*
Michelangelo, 157
"Mi'raj or the Night Flight of Muhammad on his Steed Buraq, The," 123, 124*f*
Milwright, Marcus, 10–11, 30
Morrison, Robert, 8
Mouillard, Louis, 140, 142*f*, 151–52
Muhammad (prophet), 123
Muhammad I (emir), 27, 38, 134–36
Müller-Wiener, Martina, 3–5
Mu'min Ibn Sa'id, 26–28, 30–31, 82–83, 139, 146–47
al-Muradi, 93–106, 93*f*, 96*f*, 100*f*, 108, 119
Murillo, Juan, 131–32
al-Nahwi, Muhammad Ibn Isma'il, 19, 20
naḳa'iḍ, 27

NASA, 2–3
Necipoğlu, Gülru, 153–54
Nehemias, 158
Newton, Isaac, 161
Nilometer of Cairo, 79–80, 112–19, 113*f*, 116*f*, 188n.98
nirandj, 109–10
Nykl, A.R., 68–69
the occult, 109–12

Ocaña Jimenez, Manuel, 110, 111–12
Ovid, 122, 138–39
Özdural, Alpay, 111–12

Pisano, Andrea, 158, 159*f*, 160*f*
Pitti, Miniato, 157–58
poetic inscriptions, on Islamic scientific instruments, 35, 37–41, 40*f*, 42*f*
poetry, science and, 37–38

polylobed forms, 46–49, 50*f*, 51*f*
Ptolemy, 36, 38, 59, 66–67, 83–87

Qur'an, 116–17, 116*f*, 123, 138
al-Qurtubi, Maslama ibn Qasim, 109–10
Qusayr 'Amra, fresco of, 83–84, 84*f*, 119, 123, 126*f*

al-Razi, 'Isa ibn Ahmad, 20–21, 24–25, 28, 37–38
Romanos II (emperor), 87–90
al-Rusafa
  aeronautics experiment of Ibn Firnās and, 122, 131–39, 152
  archaeological remains, 131–34, 132*f*, 133*f*, 134*f*
  Ibn Firnās poem on, 136–38

al-Saffar, Muhammad ibn
  astrolabes of, 50–59, 55*f*, 56*f*, 57*f*, 58*f*, 59*f*, 60*f*, 61*f*, 62*f*, 62, 64, 65
  brother of, 68
al-Sahli, Ibrahim ibn Sa'īd
  astrolabes of, 44–54, 45*f*, 46*f*, 47*f*, 48*f*, 49*f*, 52*f*, 53*f*, 54*f*, 58–59, 62–64, 66–67
  celestial globe of, 65–78, 66*f*, 67*f*, 70*f*, 71*f*, 72*f*, 84–85, 85*f*, 87
Sakkara Bird, 149
Saliba, George, 8–9, 32, 153, 154–55, 156, 192–93n.7
Samsó, Julio, 41–42, 93–94, 97–98
Sangallo, Antonio da, 153, 154–58, 154*f*, 155*f*
al-Shaffaq, Muhammad Ibn 'Utbah, 26
signature inscriptions
  on astrolabes, 39, 41, 44, 48*f*, 54*f*, 57*f*, 58, 60–65, 61*f*, 66–67, 68–69, 72–78, 77*f*, 78*f*, 155–56, 178n.71
  on celestial globe, 65–67, 67*f*, 68–69
  on thirteenth-century metalwork box, 67–68, 69*f*
silk, 144–48, 145*f*, 149*f*
Smith, Pamela, 3–5
speaking objects, 39, 41
Stern, S.M., 90
Structure of Scientific Revolutions, The (Kuhn), 8
al-Ṣufi, 84–85, 86*f*, 123–25, 127*f*, 128*f*, 129*f*
Sultan Muhammad Nur, 123, 124*f*
takhyil, 37

al-Tawhidi, Abu-Hayyan, 28
al-T̲h̲a'alibi, 23
Theophilus (emperor), 87–90
Toledo, 54–55, 109
Treatise on the Fixed Stars (al-Ṣufi), 123–25, 127*f*, 128*f*, 129*f*

'Ubada, 22, 24, 26, 28, 31, 37–38, 41
'Umar Ibn Yusuf, 72–78, 77*f*, 78*f*
Umayyad dynasty, 1–2, 3, 5–6, 7–8, 9–10, 12–13, 14, 54–55. *See also* Córdoban court
  Ibn Hayyan on, 21–22
  al-Rusafa during, 131, 152

Vallejo Triano, Antonio, 101–2
Vasari, Giorgio, 157–58
Vernet, Juan, 127–29
visual culture, 11, 67–68, 161. *See also* Islamic visual culture
vultures, 139–44, 140*f*, 141*f*, 142*f*, 143*f*, 147–48, 149*f*

water clocks, 185nn.63–64
  al-Muradi on, 94, 96–101, 96*f*, 97*f*, 100*f*, 108
  automata and, 108–9
  "Clepsydra of the Gazelles, The," 97–98, 98*f*, 99*f*, 100*f*
  of Ibn Firnās, 38–39, 41, 108, 146, 147
  al-Jazari on Castle Water Clock, 85–87, 88*f*, 89*f*
White, Lynn, Jr., 127–29, 151
Widmanstadt, Jean-Albert, 158
William of Malmesbury, 151–52
Wright Brothers, the, 140, 151–52
Wright Brothers, The (McCullough), 1

Yonan, Michael, 10–11

Zaragoza, 54–55
Ziryab, 20, 23, 24–25
zodiac fresco, at Qusayr Amra bathhouse, 83–84, 84*f*
al-Zubaydi, 23

www.ingramcontent.com/pod-product-compliance
Lightning Source LLC
Chambersburg PA
CBHW081458300525
27491CB00006B/244
9780190913243